Wife Chooses Laughter Over Headaches

I was just thanking God for Patsy Rae this week! We took a trip, just my husband and I, for 5 days and it was fantastic! We are doing so very great! I can't quite put into words the peace we're living in. I started craving my husband, and loving sex, and hounding him for it, ha! Internal, vaginal orgasms that make me laugh uncontrollably.

— East Coast Reader and Client

This Book Dropped a Brick on Man's Head

I feel like Patsy Rae dropped a brick on my head, but in a good and glorious way.

I have struggled in an intimacy-anorexia marriage for over thirty years but didn't know what I was really up against or what the name for it was. So Patsy Rae's insight connected the dots and gave me the resolve to demand change, communication, and understanding come "hell or high water." Yes, I've self-analyzed, read books, and dragged my wife to counselling but without any real interest from her. The cold water quickly washes the various approaches away. So yes, when pushed, she did share something from her childhood and it seems as if we have made great strides forward.

— International Reader and Bible Class Teacher

Best Help Out of Eight Tries

Working with Patsy Rae was the most valuable coaching experience I've had so far, and I've worked with 4 other coaches plus 3 therapists in the last 3 years. Her approach is well structured. She uses a lot of great tools that helped me go deep in my work. I enjoyed the personality work as it helped me understand better who I am and how being in a sexless marriage and coming from a dysfunctional home of origin negatively impacted me. After only 2 months of working with Patsy Rae, I am proud to say that I learned what I can expect from a healthy relationship and also how to identify the red flags in the future. However, my best intake was the deep knowledge I received on how sexuality works. I wish every couple dealing with a sexless marriage would have a chance to work with Patsy Rae. She's wonderful!

— International Reader and Client

Men Are Searching for a Christian Woman Who "Gets" Sex

Patsy Rae will never know how much respect I have for her, in large part because of her willingness to thumb her nose at conventional wisdom. Remember the Greek mythological figure Diogenes who went out with a lantern in the dark, searching for the one honest man? I (and many of my male contemporaries) are searching for a prominent Christian (preferably female) who "gets" sex. Patsy Rae is that person. She puts out some unbelievably good stuff.

East Coast Reader and Client

Couples Are Suffering

I learned a lot on how sex really works, which is very different than what the techniques books teach us. These truths need to be shared widely as too many couples are suffering because they are not properly informed. I am really grateful for this as I know that I can also use it to help my daughter in the future.

—International Reader and Client

Patsy Rae's Heart Speaks to Your Heart

Patsy Rae's teaching on the Song of Solomon comes from her heart. It speaks to your heart and makes you think of ways to touch the hearts of those you love by first recognizing your own strengths...and weaknesses.

—Phyliss Miranda, NY Times & USA Today Bestselling Romance Author

Patsy Rae Instills Hope

Patsy Rae's ability to instill hope is well-known. She is a highly respected author, consultant, and adviser in the field of marriage and sex from a Biblical perspective. I keep extra copies of her books on hand for my clients in pre-marital, marital, and sex-addiction counseling. Additionally, Patsy Rae's consultation has given me and my clients the tools to prepare for, save, and improve their marriages. I highly recommend Patsy Rae as an author, speaker, and spiritual consultant.

—Oscar Miles, MA, NCC, DCC, Teaching & Counseling Minister

A Revolutionary Way of Thinking

The sexually abused women I work with who listen to Patsy Rae on my radio show and who listened to her at a breakout in Houston continually thank me for having her as a guest, because they feel empowered after hearing her. She has advanced women into the 21st Century by instilling in them the understanding of what they deserve in life. She presents a revolutionary way of thinking for many women. Patsy has had a profound effect on their outlook by giving them new hope and respect for themselves.

—Bonnie Kaye, M.Ed., Counselor and Author

Where Can Male Readers Go?

Patsy Rae writes so freely and easily about something so private, so enjoyable, so exhilarating. She names the word [vaginal orgasm] and she's not even a locker room peer. She helps men understand something that is very peculiar to us. Women!!! Patsy Rae is irreplaceable! Where are her male readers and I going to go? Who will tell us the things we really want to know about our women? Playboy? No!!! There's no insight there! Another Christian woman, who??? Where is she?

—Eric Widmer, *Embarrass the Alligator Newsletter* Subscriber

God's 11 Secrets of Sex for a Lifetime of Passion

Embrace
The Song of Solomon's
Soulmating and Lovemaking Guide

Bonus:
How to Overcome a Sexless Marriage

Patsy Rae Dawson

Two-toned ribbons reveal the theme of the Song of Solomon — soulmating before lovemaking. The Shepherd swirls up with a loving heart bonding with the Shulammite Maiden. Internal dilemmas about whom to marry in this love triangle with King Solomon curl the Maiden's thoughts inward as her vibrant core pledges to find true love.

MARRIAGE: A TASTE OF HEAVEN MEDIA
TRANSFORMING LIVES WITH THE POWER OF THE SCRIPTURES

Published by:
Marriage: A Taste of Heaven Media
an imprint of Patsy Rae Dawson LLC
101 N Kaufman Street, Suite 146
Seagoville, TX 75159 USA
PatsyRaeDawson.com

Trademarks of Patsy Rae Dawson LLC:
Butterfly Swoosh Logo
SPEAKING GOD'S BEAUTIFUL LANGUAGE OF LOVE
TRANSFORMING LIVES WITH THE POWER OF THE SCRIPTURES
God Wants You to Love and Enjoy Passionate Sex

Except where otherwise indicated, all scripture quotations are taken from The New American Standard Bible, Copyright © 1960, 1962, 1963, 1968, 1971, 1972, 1973, 1975, 1977, 1995 by The Lockman Foundation. All rights reserved. Used by permission.

Translation abbreviations: ASV (American Standard Version), CJB (Complete Jewish Bible), JB (Jewish Bible), KJV (King James Version), NASB (New American Standard Bible), NIV (New International Version), NKJV (New King James Version), and RSV (Revised Standard Version), YLT (Young's Literal Translation).

Library of Congress Cataloging in Publication Data
Dawson, Patsy Rae.
God's 11 secrets of sex for a lifetime of passion: embrace the song of solomon's soulmating and lovemaking guide, bonus: how to overcome a sexless marriage.
Includes appendices and works cited.
1. Marriage—United States—Religious aspects—Christianity. 2. Love. 3. Sex—Religious aspects—Christianity.

Cover Design: Phillip Gessert, visit gessertbooks.com to see his work.

ISBN-10: 0938855093; ISBN-13: 9780938855095

Table of Contents

THE SONG OF SOLOMON HOAX

God Loves Passionate Sex 11

GOD'S 11 SECRETS OF SEX FOR A LIFETIME OF PASSION

Secret 1: Awaken True Love with Your 5 Senses 33
Song of Solomon 1:1-8: The Shulammite's Dilemma Begins 34
Case Studies: How to Overcome a Sexless Marriage 55

Secret 2: Insist on Soulmating Before Lovemaking 61
Song of Solomon 1:9-2:7: The King's Aphrodisiac Backfires 62

Secret 3: Practice Your Sensuous-Love Mirror Lines 91
Song of Solomon 2:8-4:7: Solomon Proposes Sensuous Love 92

Secret 4: Grow the 4 Parts of Intimacy and Love 115
Song of Solomon 4:8-15: The Shepherd Proposes True Love 116

Secret 5: Sip the Divine Wine of Passion 139
Song of Solomon 4:16-5:1: "Eat and Drink Until Tipsy With Love!" 140

Secret 6: Surrender to Your Wet Dreams of Love 167
Song of Solomon 5:2-7: The Love Aphrodisiac Wakes Up the Maiden 168

Secret 7: Turn On Double-Dose #10 Orgasms 183
Song of Solomon 5:8-6:3: The Maiden Exclaims, "I'm Ready for Love!" 184

Secret 8: Avoid the 12 Love-Defying Traits of a Sexless Spouse ..203
Song of Solomon 6:4-7:5: Solomon Reigns Over Sexless Marriages 204

Secret 9: Layer Your Hormones to Intensify Emotional Ecstasy ...227
Song of Solomon 7:6-13: The Shulammite Jilts King Solomon 230

Secret 10: Face Your Past to Get Fired Up About Sexual Love 255
Song of Solomon 8:1-4: The Maiden Promises to Be Passionate 256

Secret 11: Pay Passionate Love Forward 277
Song of Solomon 8:5-14: The Maiden Answers the Wedding Riddle 278

SOLOMON'S MATH THEN AND NOW

Solomon Never Had Great Sex with 1000 Virgins 305

Take 7 Steps for Sexual Healing 319

APPENDICES

Wet Dreams, Laws of Cleanness, and Masturbation......................327

Orgasms of Love with Cervical Kisses..343

The 4 Parts of One Flesh, Love, and Intimacy 353

Sexual Words Used by Teenagers, College Students, and University Health Professionals 357

Works Cited...359

Patsy Rae Dawson 365

Dedication

To my daughter Amanda who, at age 11, was in the first class I taught on the Song of Solomon for preteens. Then twice more at ages 14 and 16 when I taught the Song of Solomon at two other congregations for teenagers, their mothers, and grandmothers. When advisers began telling me I needed to specialize in spouse abuse, she said, "Mom, you will always talk about sex. You need to go where your heart is."

I love you, Amanda, your spirit, and your strength. I'm proud of the way you have become your own person.

In loving memory to my son Westley Garrett and to my grandson Jacob Westley. I love and miss both of you, my sweet boys. May God wrap his arms around you and keep you until he brings us together again.

Acknowledgments

Liz Briscoe who read the revised *Song of Solomon* manuscript and said, "You need to pull the Song of Solomon out of your marriage book and make it be a standalone." Wow! Liz, what a two-year journey of research you started for me with an 80% rewrite.

Bill Briscoe who encouraged me to not shy away from other people's embarrassment saying, "Why wouldn't you keep the wet dreams in the account? It's in the Bible." Your words became my mantra.

Deryl Stephens who writes under the pen name Scaramouche and shared his knowledge of screenplays, fiction writing, and wines. You provided expert editing of this book and urged me to speak out boldly.

Cynthia Dillworth who recommended I read *Intimacy Anorexia* by Dr. Douglas Weiss. You changed everything! Thank you, Sweet Friend.

Stacey who gave permission for me to tell her story to help others step out of their misery into God's beautiful love.

My students and readers who've shared their pain, asked questions, and made comments over the years to motivate me to keep studying the beautiful Song of Solomon. I love you and value your transparency.

My family, friends, critique partners, and newsletter subscribers who prayed for my health and insights throughout this project. You kept me going when doubt tried to halt my progress.

I love you all. Patsy Rae

Instructions and Discounts for Classes

Chapters 1-12 of this book contain Study, Research, and Personal Exercises and are designed to be taught in quarterly Bible classes. For semester classes, split up the homework and allow more class participation. Chapters 13-14 and the appendices contain supplemental material for semester classes or study at home.

Obviously, you won't be able to discuss all the material in your classes. Your primary goal should be to help the students understand the story and the scriptures so they can apply the principles to their lives. Going over some of the homework at the beginning of the class is a great way to review the previous week's lesson and motivate students to learn the Song of Solomon. You may want to ask the students to turn in their homework (with the exception of Personal Exercises). This gives you a chance to offer individual encouragement and evaluate both your teaching and their progress.

I'm an independent Bible student and encourage others to do their own studying. Thus question 9 in the Study Exercises gives students and teachers a chance to disagree with anything taught.

Class discounts for paperbacks. The discounts apply only to the full price for USA orders. I'll send you a PayPal invoice for paperbacks plus the actual shipping cost. Smaller additional orders for new students will be discounted the same as the original order. Email me for information on discounts for International orders as they are figured individually.

1-9 books = full price
10-19 books = 10% discount
20-29 books = 20% discount
30+ books = 30% discount

Please email me at Patsy@PatsyRaeDawson.com to take advantage of these discounts. If I can help in any way as you teach *God's 11 Secrets of Sex for a Lifetime of Passion,* please contact me.

May God bless us all in our efforts to promote
love in our homes and the world,
Patsy Rae Dawson

Warning and Disclaimer

Warning and Disclaimer

The Song of Solomon is filled with aphrodisiacs that use essential oils and foods to appeal to all 5 senses, plus the intellect and the emotions. The discussions in this book are for informational purposes only to help us understand why the Israelites used these substances and how these servings of love promoted many health benefits for them.

If the Song of Solomon makes you interested in essential oils and aphrodisiacs, then let the verses prompt your own study of their proper use. This book is not intended to treat, diagnose, or prescribe. The information contained herein is in no way to be considered a substitute for working with a licensed health care profession. Consult a medical professional, essential oils books, or other professional reference sources for suggested uses.

Natural essential oils are highly concentrated and should be used with care. For example, some essential oils need to be diluted with a carrier as they can burn if applied directly to the skin or ingested. Essential oils should never be put in one's eyes or ears. Consult with a professional when using them for children or on sensitive body parts.

Not all essential oil products are the same. Some are made from pure products while others are manufactured from synthetics or poor quality ingredients. Always do your research and consult professionals.

Legal and Disclaimer

The contents of this book are for informational purposes only. It isn't the purpose of this material to provide all the information that is otherwise available. The information provided is on an as-is basis and without warranties of any kind, either expressed or implied. This book is not a replacement for professional services such as psychiatric or medical advice, diagnosis, or treatment. Always seek the advice of a qualified health provider with any questions regarding any psychological or medical condition. Never disregard professional medical advice or delay seeking treatment or diagnosis because of something you read in this book. This book does not provide legal services or legal advice.

Patsy Rae Dawson's study and faith are not a substitute for any person's own study and faith. Readers are responsible for their own well-being, choices, and decisions, including when using this material. Reliance on any information provided by this book is undertaken at your own risk.

2 Corinthians 13:5: "Test yourselves to see if you are in the faith; examine yourselves!"

Emergency

If you think you may have a medical or safety emergency, call 911 immediately. Most of the numbers below respond 24/7.

- National Domestic Violence Hotline: 1-800-799-SAFE (7233)
- National Teen Dating Abuse Helpline: 1-866-331-9474
- National Sexual Assault Hotline: 1-800-656-HOPE (4673)
- National Suicide Prevention Lifeline: 1-800-273-TALK (8255)
- Crisis Text Line: Text "LISTEN" to 741-741

Never Argue with Your Gut Instincts!

If your gut is telling you something is wrong, probably 95% of the time something is wrong. Don't take a chance on being in the other 5%. Many women who are murdered had a gut feeling they were in danger, but talked themselves out of it. Go to a women's shelter or other qualified health professional and let a counselor help you analyze what is going on in your life. They are trained. You and your religious leaders probably aren't.

THE SONG OF SOLOMON HOAX

God Loves Passionate Sex

Contrary to mankind's belief that God, sex, and the Bible don't go together, God loves sex more than we mortals do. He devotes more space in the Bible to teaching how to delight in a wonderful love life than to any other area of marriage. He openly boasts about lovemaking being his proudest, most brilliant accomplishment in the creation:

Proverbs 30:18-19:
There are three things which are too wonderful for me,
Four which I do not understand:
The way of an eagle in the sky,
The way of a serpent on a rock,
The way of a ship in the middle of the sea,
And the way of a man with a maid.

This is not God's empty locker-room brag. It's God's genius for husbands and wives to enjoy! Proverbs says the first three things are too wonderful to understand: an eagle soaring in the sky, a snake slithering across the mountain, or a ship sailing in the midst of the sea. But four amazing things are hidden from man's understanding.

Ancient man has always attempted to fly like the eagle. Finally, the Wright Brothers solved the puzzle. Man continues to improve on their initial genius from airplanes, to rocket ships, to drones.

To scale a mountain, man must strap on cleats and use safety lines. Even then, he can't go wherever he wants like the agile snake. Many men and women die trying to imitate the serpent.

Matthew Maury said, "If God said paths are in the sea, I'm going to find them" (Psalms 8:8). He spent eighteen years charting the ocean's currents. Today worldwide commerce and travel depend on them.

The eagle, the snake, and the paths in the sea testify to God's superior intelligence in creating the world. And mankind seeks to replicate his divine wisdom. But the fourth is the most profound and difficult for man to figure out—the way of a man with a maid.

It's more than a male hopping a female's bones. Animals do that.
It's more than a woman moaning and groaning. Prostitutes do that.
It's more than a vibrator shaking up an orgasm. Laboratory subjects do that.

None can compare to God's design for a man's gentle touch to stir up a maid's emotions and powerful sensations.

With machines to measure and watch men and women perform sexologists often assume they've figured out sex. Alfred Kinsey thought he discovered the secret with his prostitutes. Masters and Johnson claimed success with their bionic experiments. But they all neglected the role of the mind and intimacy for giving wonderful orgasms to men and women. Now using MRI and SPECT scans scientists are finally beginning to understand the role the brain plays in sex.

God declares, "Ecstatic lovemaking is my crowning act of creation!" He intends for husbands and wives to surrender their minds and hearts to each other to speak with their bodies his beautiful language of love. Clearly, God expects earthly marriages to be tastes of heaven.

The Hoax that Desexualized the Song of Solomon

After Jesus died, the Apostle Paul warned that a great religious hoax regarding marriage would come. He called it a doctrine of demons that would forbid marriage. Lying hypocrites, seared in their own conscience, would promote it (1 Timothy 4:1-3).

At this time, the Israelites viewed the Song of Solomon as a sacred book and had for hundreds of years before Jesus came. They sang selections from it at certain festivals in the temple at Jerusalem. Thus it was in the canon of scriptures from which Jesus and his apostles quoted (*International Standard Bible Encyclopedia* [ISBE] "Song of Songs").

Jewish Rabbis Started the Hoax

After Jesus's death and Titus's destruction of Jerusalem in 70 AD, the prophesy began to be fulfilled in the form of a religious hoax that exists today. With their temple gone along with their system of religion, surviving Jewish rabbis worked to protect the sacred scrolls. Some of them tried to leave the Song of Solomon out of the collection of inspired writings because of its sexual teaching. When their efforts failed, they fabricated the allegorical interpretation of the Song of Solomon as God's marital relationship with Israel (ISBE "Song of Songs").

The rabbis moved away from a literal view of the book and merged the two suitors, King Solomon and the Shepherd boyfriend, into one man. They ignored the typical Hebrew marriage rituals at the end of the true story. Then they transformed the dialogue into an exchange between a husband and wife whom they claimed was God and Israel.

Early Church Fathers Reworked the Hoax

The early Church Fathers of Christianity admired pagan virgins who served their cults of Achaean Juno, Delphi, and ministered to the African Ceres. The Song of Solomon celebrating a woman's sexuality horrified them. Some leaders began suppressing the book (LeSaint 18-9).

The most notable Church Father who attacked the Song of Solomon was the 3rd-century theologian Origen. He denounced married lovemaking in answering Celsus's attacks on Christianity. Origen wrote, "Christianity actually transformed a man's conduct...from the time they adopt it...certain among them...abstain even from the permitted indulgences of (lawful) love" (Harrell 205-6).

Origen tamed his own sexual desires by castrating himself (Instone-Brewer, *Jesus* 24). He successfully hid the sexual teaching of the Song of Solomon by reinventing the Jewish allegory to be about Christ and the church. Then he applied his mystic visions to create his own illusions. Origen castrated the Song of Solomon right along with his own body.

Origen's Hoax Is Fit Only for Old Women

After warning about a coming hoax against married love, the Apostle Paul concluded, "But have nothing to do with worldly fables fit only for old women" (1 Timothy 4:7a).

Origen, who gave up his manhood by castrating himself, audaciously commanded sexually healthy husbands and wives to give up voluntarily their lawful sex lives. Then he perverted the beautiful sexual teaching of the Song of Solomon. What irony! Origen's allegory is "a worldly fable fit only for man-made old women."

The Hoax Is Alive and Thriving

Within a few hundred years, the hoax had spread over the Christian world. For the next 2000 years, the swindle bubbled under the surface wielding its harm—unnoticed by many. But it sprang to new life at the turn of the 21st century when the Internet made the Song of Solomon more popular. The hoax thrives in blogs, tweets, and YouTube sermons.

One YouTube preacher said, "Do you know why preachers love the allegory position on the Song of Solomon? It's because we don't have to talk about the embarrassing subject called s-e-x." He admitted a similar prejudice against married lovemaking that motivated Origen to mutilate the Song of Solomon just as he deformed his own body.

The victims of the hoax aren't cheated out of their life savings as many Internet scammers try to do. Instead, their identity is stolen as they never rise to their full potential as a loving person. As the deceivers camouflage the beautiful sexual teaching of the Song of Solomon, they deprive their followers of passionate love for their mate that spills out to envelop their children.

Believing the hoax, the victims cheat their children out of a loving home. Then the children grow up to deny the grandchildren emotional stability. Thus the hoax self-propagates and proliferates.

The Hoax Supports Three Major Love Disorders

The sexual deceit of Origen and his followers continues to suck victims into three major love disorders:

The Purity Culture — on one extreme
The Hookup Culture — on the other extreme
The Sexless Marriages Culture — embracing both extremes

Unfortunately, we can't check out this urban legend on Snopes, MythBusters, or TruthOrFiction. But the Song of Solomon exposes the hoax that fuels all three cultures and destroys lives. It limbers us all up to begin *SPEAKING GOD'S BEAUTIFUL LANGUAGE OF LOVE.*

For the unmarried, it teaches how to be intellectually, emotionally, sexually, and spiritually healthy. It reveals the secrets for choosing a like-minded mate for a lifetime of wonderful lovemaking. It showcases the sensual delights of true love including adoring looks, melodious sounds, inviting fragrances, intoxicating tastes, and passionate touches.

For the married, it allows couples to analyze themselves and their marriage no matter their age or love history. If needed, they can begin to make lasting changes to bless their family and their own life. Finally, it teaches how to praise God in the arms of your mate.

The Purity Culture

"No! No! No!"
"Dirty! Dirty! Dirty!"
"Sex is just for the guy."
"Sex is not to be enjoyed."

These answers were given in response to the question, "What is the one line that comes to mind when it comes to sex?" The question was posed to young women in a 2013 premarital and new bride sex-education class taught by Dr. Mark McGinniss, a professor at Baptist Bible College and Seminary in Clarks Summit, Pennsylvania, and his wife. They routinely ask their students to text their answers to similar questions to maintain anonymity and openness.

Then in October 2013, McGinniss taught three sessions on "The Song of Solomon and Hot Topics." He said in his *Outside My Door Blog,* "I was asked to address sexual hot topics such as masturbation, pornography, homosexuality, and the like. I used the Song of Songs to help the students think biblically about these topics and draw conclusions that are in line with God's viewpoint" (11/10/2013).

In the first class McGinniss asked the young men and women, both single and married, to text their answer to the same question. He received over seventy replies. Here's a sample of their answers:

"Sex is sinful."

"Be fruitful and multiply."

"Sex is for marriage."

"Sex is designed by God."

"Sex ruins your life."

"Sex is forbidden, and it's a sin to talk about it."

"Actually, having sex terrifies me."

"How do I convince my spouse sex is to be enjoyed by her as well?"

McGinniss spent the first two sessions reviewing the Song of Solomon. In the final class, he asked a series of questions about conclusions the students could draw from the Song of Solomon on the hot topics. He explained, "You're attending a Bible college. That means the world is going to regard you as an expert. Teenagers are going to ask you all kinds of questions once they trust you. Their questions will leave you gasping for air" (10/29-31/2013).

Young people on our college campuses are immersed in sexual extremes—neither of which brings true happiness. Those in the Purity Culture often view sex as a necessary evil they must always fight against to be pleasing to God. Dianna E. Anderson in her blog "Taking the Lead in Developing New Sexual Ethics" shares their common attitude of a "God of sexual shame, a heavenly father who sits upon his throne and condemns" their sexual thoughts and desires (2/4/2015). This attitude doesn't magically disappear with marriage.

Virginity-Pledging Young Women

At age 10, Samantha Pugsley pledged to keep her virginity until she married. Her parents and her church applauded her righteousness for making the public pledge. She knew nothing about sex. She still "played with Barbie dolls and had tea parties with imaginary friends."

Now married, she recently stepped into the limelight to renounce her youthful pledge with her blog "I Waited Until My Wedding Night to

Lose My Virginity and I Wish I Hadn't." She hit a nerve, receiving nearly 5000 comments. Some wrote to describe similar experiences. Others criticized her lack of faith. Still others attacked religion in general.

Like other girls who comment and blog about taking a virginity pledge, it stole Samantha's identity by the time she became a teenager. She was taught, "Once I got married, it will be my duty to fulfill my husband's sexual needs. I was told over and over again, so many times I lost count, that if I remained pure, my marriage would be blessed by God, and if I didn't that it would fall apart and end in tragic divorce."

She was never told the Old and New Testaments portray the woman as the man's sexual equal in desire and ability to receive and give pleasure. Instead, she was told to keep herself pure and she'd enjoy a fairy-tale marriage. How is this different from teaching kids to believe in Santa Claus? "If you're nice, presents will appear under the tree."

You can read Samantha's story online. She experienced so much guilt from the one-sided teaching of her church, she was unable to enjoy sex with her husband. After two years of doing her duty, she broke down. She got counseling.

Samantha says, "I don't go to church anymore, nor am I religious. As I started to heal, I realized that I couldn't figure out how to be both religious and sexual at the same time. I chose sex. Every single day is a battle to remember that my body belongs to me and not to the church of my childhood. I have to constantly remind myself that a pledge I took when I was only 10 doesn't define who I am today" (8/11/2014).

Dianna Anderson made a similar pledge at a purity ball with her father at age 14. The week before, her parents gave her a small diamond ring from Walmart. Instead of a web article, Dianna wrote *Damaged Goods, New Perspectives on Christian Purity* to describe her experiences. After her pledge, she flaunted her holier-than-thou condemnation of others who had sex outside marriage.

She tells about watching the 2007 movie *Atonement* and viewing the sex scene in a library. The "intensely erotic scene managed to feature no nudity." This was her first exposure to the concept that she was a sexual being who might actually enjoy sex. She was 22 years old, 8 years older than when she took a virginity pledge before her congregation. She said, "Sex became something I wanted, rather than something I would cooperate with once I got married" (45).

Instead of rejecting God, Dianna redefines the Bible's teaching on sex in her chapter, "Let's Get Biblical: Sex in Scriptures." She views the Song of Solomon as singing the praises of premarital sex. She concludes: "From Genesis to Revelation, the Bible contains numerous instances of polygamous marriages, premarital and extramarital sexcapades, and complicated and complex gendered relationships." Then she urges her readers to study their Bibles for themselves and draw their own conclusions. She shares interviews with many young women who had similar experiences with the Purity Culture.

Samantha and Dianna, their parents, and their churches are victims of the hoax against the Song of Solomon and the love lives of Christians. The Shulammite and the Shepherd were both virgins when they married. The difference? Instead of scaring them about sex, their parents prepared them to celebrate the wonder of God's creation — the way of a man with a maid.

Nowhere does the Bible portray sex as something for men and women to "cooperate with once they get married." Instead, the Song of Solomon exults the Shulammite's femininity and her promise to initiate lovemaking in marriage — for both her husband's pleasure — and her own. In fact, the Shulammite talks more about looking forward to the sexual relationship in marriage than the Shepherd does.

Women Sexually Inhibited in Marriage

I get many emails from angry middle-aged husbands. They are frustrated from being married to a mental virgin proudly living in a Victorian time warp which perpetuates feelings of shame and guilt for God-given sexual desires. These husbands, full of passionate love for their wife, are rejected by antiquated virginal timidity. The ticking away of their own biological clocks causes these men to fight resentment and the temptation to commit adultery. They fear the loss of their potency to age and dying without ever realizing the ecstasy of world-shaking lovemaking with the wife they love and desire.

I get as many, if not more, emails from wives lamenting being married to a man who shows no sexual interest in them. Sometimes I wonder, "Are there any hot-blooded men and women out there... among Christians?" Few of them seem to marry a like-minded person. In these instances, the idea of opposites attract is a sexual train wreck.

Men and women who are married to someone who seldom engages in sex never experience the freedom to delight in the daily sexual twinges that occur in a healthy person. They know if they allow desire to build into looking forward to a romantic interlude at home, the awaiting answer is a definitive, "No," a lukewarm, "Yes," an impatient, "Wait a few days," or as one husband said, "Laughter." Constantly being forced to stifle normal sexual love dries up the emotional bond with the mate as the loneliness increases over the years.

As you follow along with *Stacey's Story*, interspersed between the Song of Solomon chapters, you'll meet such a wife. You'll read how hard she worked to save her marriage. Her story offers hope for miserable marriages that are victims of the great sexual hoax and swindle. She shows the power of God's word to transform lives and marriages.

Virginity-Pledging Young Men

In 2008, Sarah Diefendorf, a doctoral candidate in sociology at the University of Washington, studied a group of 15 young evangelical Christian men. She wanted to know how they manifested their sexuality after pledging sexual abstinence until marriage. Her main concern was how virginity-pledging, normally thought of as something women do, would affect their views of their masculinity.

When she started the study, the men were all single, and most of them had already attended a two or four-year college. They went to support groups through their church and held each other accountable for their conduct. "The men talked about sex as both 'sacred' — a gift from God meant for the marriage bed — and 'beastly' if it occurs outside marriage. Instead of talking about scoring, the Christian men talk about how hard it is to manage temptation." They believed "to maintain this gift from God, they must refrain from sex before marriage."

The men lamented to Diefendorf, "The church tells us sex is bad, but we are not told *why* sex is bad." In their support group, they discussed the "beastly" threats to their pledges of abstinence. Diefendorf said, "Specifically, topics relating to pornography, masturbation, lust, and same-sex desire were recurring themes in our conversations, and central to the ways in which these men understand their pledges of abstinence, sexuality, and gender."

These young men believe the use of pornography is prevalent in the Christian community. They opened up to Diefendorf about their own struggles with pornography. She wrote in her study "After the Wedding Night: Sexual Abstinence and Masculinities Over the Life Course":

> The men understand masturbation and pornography as heavily related. Pornography helps men, who Aidan [leader of the group] calls "visual animals," with masturbation. For Aidan, masturbation before marriage is fine, with certain boundaries in place: Simply pleasuring yourself without porn is fine, as long as you're not always relying on it or scheduling time around it.
>
> Chase worries masturbation could substitute [for] sex with his [future] wife, and as both marriage and the act of sex within marriage are sacred, anything that could hinder the act remains a sin that must be controlled.
>
> For Jason, masturbation is heavily related to lust, a feeling these young men consider very dangerous…. Jason believes one can masturbate not just because of lust — you can do it to deal

with stress, to help you fall asleep—to give you that high just before you go to bed (2014-2015).

To maintain their virginity pledges some of these young men are developing a habit of masturbation. For many married men, as Chase worried, self-pleasuring does become a substitute for lovemaking with one's wife. It also interferes with emotional intimacy in the marriage.

Men Sexually Inhibited in Marriage

A few years later in 2011 and 2012, Diefendorf reconnected with the young men, all but one was married. She wrote "Where is the Sacred?" and said:

> While sex is framed as "sacred", "wonderful" and a "gift from God" post-marriage, these married men still think of sex in its "beastly" terms. In focusing solely on the goal of abstinence until marriage, conversations on healthy sexuality *within* marriage were never part of the discussion for these young men....
>
> Aidan adds, "It's a myth that I think is kind of perpetuated by the lack of communication, is that once you get married, suddenly all those desires are fulfilled in your spouse. It's not true. Guys are so visually driven. The desire for porn, especially if you struggled with it in the past, is still there. It doesn't go away once the ring slips on!"

Diefendorf states in various sections of her paper:
- *These men have been promised a sacred, sexually active marriage.* Their wives, as Seth says, have a job of entertaining them "both visually and sexually."
- *These men have a very narrow understanding of female sexuality.* If Adrian thinks of Christian women as, he says, "prudish", he won't think of them as sitting around and talking about sex.
- *They understand sex as something that needs to be controlled, and masculinity as something dependent on their wives.* At the same time, they view their wives as simultaneously protected, non-sexual beings *and* their sexual partners. Women are given a fairly impossible and contradictory role as wives to these men, with seemingly few resources to navigate such assumed responsibilities.

Diefendorf observed the contradictions and concluded: "This highly-gendered, highly-contextualized understanding of sexuality as 'beastly', wonderful, promised and unfulfilled requires years of conversation pre-marriage, and, although not offered, seems to require the same after marriage" (2014-2015).

In the press release for Diefendorf's paper, Molly McElroy ended with this plea:

> She [Diefendorf] hopes her study leads to more positive discussions of sex and how it is healthy, especially within the context of abstinence-only sex education. "There's an obsession with virginity in this country," Diefendorf said. "And we forget to have informative, successful conversations on sex" (8/16/2014).

Many churches forget to discuss the benefits and wonderfulness of married lovemaking when teaching young people. But God did not forget. The way of a man with a maid is his proudest creation, and he did not leave us without instructions. He preserved the beautiful, sexually-explicit Song of Solomon to show us the way to enjoy a lifetime of passionate lovemaking.

1st Century Pagans

Before the hoax started, 1st century pagans exclaimed, "What women those Christians have!" (Lockyear 14).

But they're not saying it now. Instead, they're saying, "You're a Christian? Guess that means you never get a good lay job." And all because of the great hoax against the Song of Solomon and married love.

The Hookup Culture

"Hookups? What's that?" parents and older adults often ask when hearing the term for the first time.

Young people seldom tell their parents it refers to casual-dating sex without getting to know the person or having a relationship. However, it can lead to a steady hookup where the partner actually becomes a boyfriend or girlfriend. They might even fall in love. More often, they just stay "in like" as "friends with benefits." No strings attached.

Some youths boast of primary and casual sex partners. They openly pursue multiple hookups while courting a special "steady hookup." Girls usually don't enjoy these options. Yet realistically, many accept it as their only chance of snagging a boyfriend — pseudo boyfriend, that is.

To adapt to this peer-approved lifestyle of anything goes with sex, both boys and girls work at emotional survival. Laura Sessions Stepp shares such a story in *Unhooked: How Young Women Pursue Sex, Delay Love and Lose at Both.* Stepp interviewed several Duke University students over the course of a school year to learn the effect of the Hookup Culture on their lives. Her book is filled with candid conversations with these young women who were trying to figure out boy-girl relationships.

To protect their self-images the girls learned to react to sex by beating the boys at their own game of impersonalizing sex. Two of the girls bragged about being the first to jump out of bed after their tryst. This left their partners beyond surprised. One young woman said the look on the boys' face gave her a rush (240-1).

Throughout the book Stepp provides examples of girls saying variations of "I tell the boy, 'You can use my body, but don't expect anything from me.' Hookups are easy because I don't have to do anything."

Girls Drink to Numb Their Brains

Frequent sex without love is a major problem on college campuses, including Catholic and other religious institutions. Donna Freitas explains the hookup rules in her book *The End of Sex: How Hookup Culture Is Leaving a Generation Unhappy, Sexually Unfulfilled, and Confused About Intimacy.* She interviewed thousands of boys and girls over several years:

> Typically, students used three major criteria to characterize the hookup:
> 1. A hookup includes some form of sexual intimacy, anything from kissing to oral, vaginal, or anal sex and everything in between.
> 2. A hookup is brief—it can last as short as a few minutes to as long as several hours over a single night.
> 3. A hookup is intended to be purely physical in nature and involves both parties shutting down any communication or connection that might lead to emotional attachment.
>
> To sum up briefly, the three qualities that make up a hookup are its sexual content, its brevity, and its apparent lack of emotional involvement (25).

Freitas drew her conclusions from interviewing both male and female students on a multitude of college campuses. In her chapter "The All-Purpose Alcohol Solution," she explained that both boys and girls numb their emotions with alcohol. This allows them to survive the attack on their psyches that emotionally-bankrupt sex creates. Many young people use alcohol to loosen up for uninhibited fun. She summarized:

> Alcohol can transform the politest, nicest students into people who commit shocking, reckless, and dangerous behaviors. It also functions as that X factor of hookup culture, the ingredient that students turn to in order to overcome their

hesitation (40).

Although science has not discovered all the secrets about how the brain functions during sex, it recognizes the mind as the most important sexual organ. The students are zonking out with alcohol to disable their most important sexual organ. Consequently, they may have a difficult time establishing a healthy emotional bond with someone. A few years of being cool can translate into a lifetime of emotional loneliness.

Girls Perform at Theme Parties

In the chapter "Learning to Play the Part (of Porn Star): The Sexualization of College Girls" Freitas exposes theme parties. These take place at some high schools, but are expected on many college campuses. The girls must appear at the door almost naked to be admitted. The boys stand around ogling them, hoping the girls will get drunk enough for them to get lucky. The girls drink more and get drunk more often than the boys do in this emotional vacuum.

The parties cater to dressing up to some theme such as doctors and nurses, maids and millionaires, or housewives and handymen. The boys are always cast as GOD/MAN while the girls portray the lowly HUMAN/WOMAN. Without some adult help, the girls often don't realize the degradation they're being subjected to as a powerless second-class piece of meat to the boys playing god (75ff, 81, 84).

Most of these girls claim they want to go to these parties and relish the male attention. But they need alcohol to loosen up and perform. Consequently, both the girls and boys are programing their minds and bodies that sex is a rum-dumb comatose act. The girls deliberately zone out, anesthetizing themselves with alcohol. Since they are only providing a masturbation receptacle, the boys must close their eyes and fantasize to perform.

Both the boys and girls are setting themselves up for a lifetime of mediocre sex in any relationship—especially marriage. With this kind of emotionally-stifling sexual history, I expect these young women to be turned off of sex in marriage. They will have to work hard to reboot their bodies and minds, to slough off all their android rituals, to be a compassionate loving spouse.

Boys Are Bored with Sex

In the chapter, "Why We Get Boys Wrong: The Emotional Glass Ceiling," Freitas discusses how the Hookup Culture doesn't create a satisfying sexual relationship for many of the young men. About half of them talked about hookups like "eating a bowl of cereal every morning."

The main feeling they expressed was boredom with sex. They didn't view it as the wonderful, exhilarating expression of love that God designed it to be.

Many of the young men felt pressured by their peers to pursue hookups. Some pretended to work the hookup scene to avoid being ridiculed. They spoke of the disgust of waking up next to someone they didn't remember being with. They hoped she'd be gone by the time they got out of the bathroom. And horrors if she stayed for breakfast. A few recognized the emotional emptiness of the hookups and decided to wait for someone special (111).

What kind of husbands will these young men make? If they marry a woman with healthy sexual attitudes, will they be able or willing to satisfy her. They may well be ruining the future happiness of two people.

VIAGRA Demasculinizes Young Studs

Many young men complain of performance anxiety and failure. Pornographic email spam targets their vulnerability with ads for VIAGRA and other performance-enhancing products. The Internet hawks black-market who-knows-what's-in-it drugs. A young virile husband who understands the emotional aspect of sex only needs the aphrodisiac of love to perform with gusto.

Many young adults who were very sexually active as teens regularly use a dangerous drug that can kill. Long-term use of VIAGRA carries risks of blue-tinged vision, heart problems, and hearing loss. And that's just a few of the dangers (Pfizer 3/2015).

Tanith Carey exposed the addiction in her article "Addicted to Viagra: They should be at their most virile, but a growing number of young men can't cope without those little blue pills" for *Daily Mail Online* out of London. She interviewed 32-year-old Daniel who started taking VIAGRA when he was 20 and was out picking up girls with friends. Now he needs two of the blue pills to perform and takes up to six a week. Even if he likes the girl, the tablets don't always work for him. He says his ears ring and his heart beats so hard and fast, he breaks out into a cold sweat. Even though he fears having a heart attack he keeps taking the pills (10/3/2012).

The problem is not just with the men. Young adult women, not understanding the role their mind and heart play in earth-shaking vaginal orgasms, often require marathon male performance to climax. Thus they exert tremendous pressure on men to keep going so they can respond in spite of their attitudes toward men and their femininity.

Because young women don't know the dynamics of a vaginal orgasm, they assume no such erotic pleasure exists for women. Yet mothers of the Song-of-Solomon era enjoyed vaginal orgasms and taught their daughters the secret. Losing this wisdom of the ancients is one of the consequences of the hoax on the Song of Solomon. And it impacts society by demasculinizing men and defemininizing women.

Too Holy, too Drunk, or too Drugged for True Love

What we've just read from the lips of the young people themselves is that many of them today are too holy, too drunk, or too drugged to enjoy a wonderful love life in marriage. They have closed up their emotions of tenderness and delight in the opposite sex.

Some flaunt their virginity and deny their sexuality, not only while dating, but also in marriage. Others drink themselves into mindless stupors and numb their sensations so they don't care or remember what their bodies do. And young men in the prime of their sexual lives worry about having a heart attack because they must take two VIAGRA tablets to perform—even when they love their partner. And this is supposed to be fun? But that's not the worst of it.

Both Culture Extremes Often Result in Atheism

In 2012, I put 8,400 miles on my little Victory Red Chevy HHR traveling from Amarillo to Dallas, to Houston, to Las Vegas, to North Carolina, and back to Houston to attend seminars, boot camps, and conferences. Everywhere I went, when men and women learned during round-robin introductions that I taught about sex and the Bible, at breaks and lunch, they confided their personal pain to me.

At one conference a woman, whom I'll call Jean, invited me to lunch. After saying she'd looked at my website on her iPad she shared her story. Her eyes misted, "I'm a heathen. How can I believe in a God of love when he didn't even exist in the Christian home I grew up in? My dad was an elder and preached sometimes. He always put his arm around Mom in church and smiled at her.... But it all changed on the ride home.... The tension between them was unbearable. I couldn't wait to get home and get away from them.... The rest of the week was full of putdowns as they ridiculed each other and us kids."

She swallowed hard and continued, "I married the same kind of ol' boy. We always went to church. When he died, I swore I would never marry another Christian. Now I'm polyamorous with a man who has a wife and four kids. They all lived with me for a while, but his wife was abusive to me and their kids, so I asked them to leave."

Playing with her food Jean said, "Now he lives down the block, and I have sex twice a week with him.... It's the best sex I've ever had. He says an older woman taught him.... He keeps begging me to let them move back in. If I do, I'll pay all the bills as I did before. I figure I will commit suicide someday…. I have no children and no one cares…." Jean's story is only one of many similar scenarios I listened to that year.

The Children of Christians Are Turning to Atheism

Many churches lament that attendance by young people is decreasing by alarming rates. At the same time, the U.S. Census Bureau supports the claim that atheism is on the rise (2012). However, the Census Bureau doesn't attempt to discover the reason apathy and unbelief are growing in the United States.

That job falls to the Pew Research Center in Washington, D.C. that compares the statistics with their own surveys and current writings about the data. In "'Nones' on the Rise" the center evaluated the impact on politics of people who say, "None," when asked about their religious affiliation.

The Majority of Nones Are Raised with Religion

"The overwhelming majority [74%] of the 'nones' were brought up in a religious tradition." The nones expressed concern that "religious organizations are too concerned with money and power, too focused on rules, and too involved in politics." Too focused on rules was later explained as "judgmental, homophobic, and hypocritical" (10/9/2012).

In our hooked-to-a-handheld mobile society, few people invest time in lengthy books or articles. More than ever the world is observing Christians rather than reading the Bible to learn about God. And they are rejecting Christianity because of what they see.

What Goes On in Our Homes Doesn't Stay There

Young people have legitimate doubts and reject organized religion as too "judgmental and hypocritical" for a basic reason. Our children are denouncing God because of the hypocrisy of their parents and churches who preach love while failing to practice love in their own homes. Their skepticism and atheism stem from their parents and religious leaders believing the hoax perpetrated against married love. When religious leaders don't enjoy healthy love lives themselves, the hoax against the Song of Solomon affects everyone in the congregation and their families.

The Sexless Marriages Culture

Dr. Seth Stephens-Davidowitz is an economist and former quantitative analyst at Google. As a Harvard graduate student, he began writing about how Google searches can give "us fresh insights into socially sensitive topics." In response to numerous requests, he ran the numbers on sex. In his article "Searching for Sex," his statistics show that between a quarter and a third of a million people google each month for one of these key phrases in this order of frequency:

- Sexless marriage
- Sexless relationship
- Sex starved marriage
- No sex marriage
- Won't have sex with me

His figures reveal that a nearly equal number of husbands and wives suffer in dead-bedroom marriages. These sexless-marriage statistics are much higher than searches for "unhappy marriage," "loveless marriage," "abusive relationship," "unhappy relationship," and "bad relationship" (1/24/2015).

Looking back over nearly half a century of being the confidante of both husbands and wives trying to survive an unloving marriage, I've observed this: If the sexual relationship is defective, then the marriage is defective on all levels. Without a doubt, such a home environment is also defective for nurturing children. The family lives in an emotional vacuum in which the couple and their children are all starved for love.

The Song of Solomon and Sexless Marriages

As I began updating my Song of Solomon material, a friend recommended *Intimacy Anorexia: Healing the Hidden Addiction in Your Marriage* by Dr. Douglas Weiss, a licensed psychologist and the author of more than twenty books on addiction and relationships. I studied the intimacy-anorexia issue for months reading five of Weiss's books and looking up word definitions in the Song of Solomon.

I immediately realized Solomon was an intimacy anorexic. In contrast, both the Shulammite maiden and the Shepherd displayed many of the sexually-healthy attitudes Weiss highlighted in his books. A whole new dimension of the Song of Solomon opened up and put me down on my knees in admiration of God and this wonderful book he's preserved to bless our marriages and the lives of our children.

In 1995, Weiss and other leaders in the emerging field of sexual addiction met in Dallas, Texas to discuss the shocking behavior they were noticing in male clients who habitually had sex with themselves, looked at pornography, or engaged in extramarital affairs. At this time treatment was more focused on men than women.

The doctors observed that after the husbands were in recovery, many of the men continued to avoid sex with their wives. They might not have sex for weeks, months, or even years. These psychologists wanted to know what was causing this anomaly.

This meeting put Weiss on a professional journey to write *Intimacy Anorexia.* He defines intimacy anorexia as the hidden addiction of avoiding sex with the mate—not necessarily avoiding sex, but *avoiding sex with the mate.* Sexual anorexia is a *withholding addiction* manifested in marriage. When sex does occur, it is mechanical and emotionless. Society calls this a sexless marriage.

Certainly, the mate is well aware that he or she is not enjoying sexual intimacy with the spouse. What the husband or wife doesn't know is that the spouse's withholding of sex and affection is an addiction. And like any addict, intimacy anorexics employ many devices to keep their addiction a festering secret. They deliberately and compulsively starve their mate of sexual love and all forms of intimacy.

The Sexless Marriages Culture Is Passed on to Future Generations

Weiss discusses in his book *Beyond the Bedroom, Healing for Adult Children of Sex Addicts* how intimacy anorexia is passed on from generation to generation. Everyone in the family is affected when one mate withholds emotional and sexual love from the other. The children usually grow up to withhold love from their own mate or to marry an anorexic. It's all they've experienced, and they don't know how to choose a sexually-healthy partner.

Blaming the deprived mate is the most frequent gimmick intimacy anorexics use to avoid sexual love. For example, men who've talked to me about their extreme emotional pain in trying to survive a sexless marriage frequently say, "My wife avoids sex with me by accusing me of being a sexual addict."

I always know these men are not sexual addicts for two reasons:

1. *They understand the emotional aspect of lovemaking.* A lack of an emotional response from their wives is their major complaint and their greatest source of pain. Their wives are emotionally distant during sex and don't initiate lovemaking—classic characteristics of an intimacy anorexic. Sexual addicts know nothing about the emotional aspects of sex for both men and women.

2. *They want sex only with their wives.* These men are offended when their wives suggest they take care of themselves with masturbation. They adamantly insist they don't want to have an affair. Some of them view porn as a necessary evil because of their wives' coldness. Others install computer and television controls so they can't watch porn out of frustration. These husbands desire to share sexual intimacy with

their wives whom they are emotionally bonded with.

Sexless Marriages Defined

Here's the definition of sexless marriages, i.e. intimacy anorexia as portrayed in the Song of Solomon:

The Song of Solomon's Definition of Sexless Marriages: The inability to love the mate intellectually, emotionally, sexually, and spiritually.

In my earlier editions of the Song of Solomon, I defined sensuous love as "satisfaction of the 5 senses without an emotional attachment." Working on this book, I expanded sensuous love to the following:

The Song of Solomon's Definition of Sensuous Love: Satisfaction of the 5 senses without intellectual, emotional, sexual, and spiritual love.

Previously I defined true love as "satisfaction of the 5 senses along with an emotional and sexual commitment." After further study, I realized I had only 50% of the equation right:

The Song of Solomon's Definition of True Love: Satisfaction of the 5 senses with intellectual, emotional, sexual, and spiritual love.

Unloving, Without Natural Affection, and Sexless Marriages

When he was in prison, Paul wrote the young evangelist Timothy to come assist him. He encouraged Timothy to defend the faith in dangerous times. He warned that people would lose their natural love for family and become involved in all kinds of family-destroying sins:

2 Timothy 3:2-5: "But mark this: There will be terrible times in the last days. People will be lovers of themselves, lovers of money, boastful, proud, abusive, disobedient to their parents, ungrateful, unholy, **without love [unloving]***, unforgiving, slanderous, without self-control, brutal, not lovers of the good, treacherous, rash, conceited, lovers of pleasure rather than lovers of God — having a form of godliness but denying its power. Have nothing to do with such people" (NIV).*

"Unloving," a compound word, is used only two times in the New Testament (2 Timothy 3:3 and Romans 1:31). It comes from the Greek *a* (negative) plus *storge* (pronounced stor-JAY). The negative in these two passages means "without natural love for family" (Thayer 82).

A positive form of *storge*, also a compound word, is used one time:

Romans 12:10: "Be **devoted [philos plus storge]** *to one another in brotherly love [philos plus delphos--brother]; give preference to one another in honor."*

The compound word "devoted" comes from *philos* (affectionate love) plus *storge* (love of family). It refers to "the mutual love of parents and children; also of husbands and wives, loving affection, prone to love, loving tenderly; used chiefly of the reciprocal tenderness of parents and children; love of the brethren tenderly affectioned one to another, Romans 12:10" (Thayer 655).

The devotion we are to manifest toward other Christians should mirror *storge*—the natural love between parents and their children and between husbands and wives. In contrast, the list of 18 sins clustered around the negative of *storge,* the absence of parental and marital love, in 2 Timothy 3:1-5 reflects the usual 24/7 conduct of unloving spouses.

Do 19 sins common in sexless marriages sound extreme to you? Sadly, my *Sexless Marriages Self-Assessment Survey* verifies that these sins against the family abound in sexless marriages. The longer the marriage continues in a sexless state, the more pronounced the 19 love-defying sins become. Sin never stagnates, but always grows, often secretively.

Sexless marriages aren't simply about sexual dysfunction. They are about the participant's whole character, soul, and lack of intimacy with the mate. Intimacy anorexia is an addiction of deliberately withholding intellectual, emotional, sexual, and spiritual love from the spouse to create a sexless marriage.

God calls it the sin of being unloving—without natural affection for family. At the end of the verses, Paul told Timothy, "Have nothing to do with such people." God doesn't want us to tolerate the sin of being unloving in our homes or in our congregations.

Toward the end of Solomon's life, God condemned him as a sinner without natural affection. As The King of Sexless Marriages, he displayed many facets of intimacy anorexia including all 12 classic characteristics that Weiss identified. A later chapter, "Secret 8: Avoid the 12 Love-Defying Traits of a Sexless Spouse," exposes Solomon's love defects. You'll probably come away from this study with a different view of Solomon than you had before.

I hope you'll also grow in your love and admiration for God. This study has made my heart sing God's praises for the way he has preserved the secrets for a wonderful love life for us. He's just waiting for modern science and research to catch up with more of his wisdom and love to bless our marriages.

Overview of the Song of Solomon

For 3000 years, the Song of Solomon has taught the secrets of a lifetime of passionate lovemaking. God used real people to tell a true story of sexual pursuit that took place over 3 whirlwind days. King Solomon is the perfect example of the sensuous, rich, influential man who is obsessed with finding the perfect feminine body. He married 1000 virgins, averaging 25 a year for 40 years. And all that before VIAGRA!

Commentators often dispute Solomon's Herculean track record as being impossible for any man. In contrast to their speculation, such a feat is not that difficult. Several years ago when I attended a writers' conference, the instructor for one session asked us to share what we were working on. When my turn came I said, "I'm studying the Song of Solomon and how Solomon averaged deflowering 25 virgins every year of his 40-year reign."

Although most of the people at the table gasped, the older woman next to me said, "I'm the director of the local Planned Parenthood. I believe it. We are seeing these same numbers with teenage boys. And we now know it does lasting damage to their brains."

After the program, I asked for her documentation about the brain damage to these boys. She was retiring and wasn't able to find the reference. In recent years, a friend found the medical proof in the book *Hooked: New Science on How Casual Sex Is Affecting Our Children* by Doctors Joe S. McIlhaney, Jr. and Freda McKissic Bush.

The Song of Solomon reveals that while Solomon was inspecting his vineyard, he was instantly infatuated with a young virgin, the Shulammite (Song 6:11-12). However, the Maiden was promised to the Shepherd, and they were planning their wedding. The love triangle preserves the Maiden's internal turmoil as she compares the proposals of the two suitors and tries to decide whom to marry.

The Song of Solomon Captures Our Emotions

This marvelous drama combines four action-type performances to speak directly to our emotions about an emotionally-charged subject— love and sex. Each technique adds life to the story to create a powerful, unforgettable presentation.

A Dramatic Dialogue

The story contains only dialogue—no narration. The Maiden shares her inner struggles with us over whom to marry. She continually compares Solomon's lustful words in her mind with her Shepherd boyfriend's pledges of love. This creates a thrilling, fast-moving story.

A Play

The characters' dialogue is written in the format of a modern play, which could be produced as is. The acts and scenes end with cliff hangers just as we expect in plays and movies today. I assume the role of a movie director to set up the scenes to make them more obvious.

A Musical

The Hebrew language in the Song of Solomon contains all the elements for a musical play and even an opera. The Israelite women and girls put on plays and sang in the evenings (Réville 65). The story is written perfectly for a captivating performance.

A Poem

A favorite use of poetry is to convey the intense emotions surrounding romance to touch hearts. The story's skillful use of words makes it easier to remember the concepts. I highlight some of the plays on words and assonance inside the Hebrew language.

Embrace God's 11 Secrets to Partake of True Love

The events in the Song of Solomon create drama to pull us in and to help us remember the story. The true story illuminates God's secrets for understanding and implementing the finer points of passionate love. The secrets follow the order of the story from courtship through marriage and then passing the wisdom of lasting love on to the next generation.

Secrets 1-4 are courtship musts. They help you develop *intellectual and emotional love* as you choose a lifelong sexual partner. If you can't achieve these goals while dating, run away as the Shulammite did. But if you're already married, it's not too late to bond emotionally for ecstasy.

Secrets 5-10 take up the story when God speaks to tell you who he wants the Maiden to marry. Secret 5 taps into *spiritual love* as God shares his 3-part formula for passionate lovemaking. Secrets 6-10 highlight the keys for enjoying *sexual love* for a lifetime.

Secret 11 reveals the grand finale lesson of the Song of Solomon. God wants parents to model the 4 parts of true love—*intellectual, emotional, spiritual, and sexual love* to provide a nurturing home for the next generation. The Song of Solomon is all about creating true love—one couple, one family at a time—in a world desperate for love.

Solomon's Siren Song

Each secret begins with a snippet of the backstory a movie director might add to the production. You'll notice Solomon's obsession for chasing after bountiful bosoms—thus "siren song." I hope you enjoy these glimpses into the era in which the Shulammite lived and loved.

It's Time to Reject the Hoax

The true story of the Song of Solomon is more relevant today than ever before as society struggles between two extremes—the lingering prudish morals of the Purity Culture pitted against the anything-goes Hookup Culture. Both opposing views of sexuality often involve the Sexless Marriage Culture. All three cultures deny the theme of the Song of Solomon—that sex is not about the release of pent-up hormones. Rather, God designed the hormones of sex to bond the male and female minds and emotions together in a monogamous loving relationship.

In other words, proper soulmating during courtship along with healthy sexual examples and teaching at home leads to a lifetime of ravishing lovemaking—all to the glory of the God who loves passionate sex more than we mortals do.

Study Exercise

Answer all questions in your own words.
1. Do you know someone who was influenced by the Purity Culture? How did it affect his or her life?
2. Why do you think 1st century pagans said, "What women those Christians have"?
3. Do you know anyone who was involved in the Hookup Culture? How did it affect his or her life?
4. What advice would you give someone in the Hookup Culture knowing that many of them reject God?
5. What should a person's attitude be toward someone like Origen who changes the meaning of the scriptures for a personal agenda?
6. Give three reasons why you want to study the Song of Solomon?
7. If the Song of Solomon teaches something about sex that contradicts what your parents taught you, what should you do? Why?
8. If the Song of Solomon contradicts something you've always believed about soulmating and lovemaking, what should you do? Why?
9. Do you disagree with anything in the lesson? If so, explain giving scriptures for your reasons.

Personal Exercise

If you want to gain the most from this study, I invite you to read "Your Marriage and Your Love Life Will Never Be the Same If...You Do the Homework Exercises." The article contains the stories of previous students to encourage you. It explains why the exercises at the end of the chapters are important. You can find it at PatsyRaeDawson.com on the sidebar in the Book Shelf. Teachers may print the article for students.

GOD'S 11 SECRETS OF SEX
FOR A LIFETIME OF PASSION

Secret 1: Awaken True Love with Your 5 Senses

Solomon's Siren Song: Solomon Ruins Everything

The soldiers come to the vineyard in the afternoon bringing the Shulammite's mother. When the Maiden looks up, her mother is holding out her arms to her. The Maiden runs to her and falls into her mother's embrace.

Her mother stands back with her hands on her daughter's shoulders. Looking into her eyes she brushes a wisp of hair out of her eyes, then softly touches her cheek. "The King saw you working in the vineyard and wants to marry you. I told his men you're 13 now...you're of age...you can decide for yourself."

"But, Mama, what about my beloved Shepherd? You know we planned to get married this spring."

"Hush, dear, hush... You're only promised to him. You can change your mind."

"But, Mama! I don't want to change my mind!"

"Hush now and listen. Please listen." She takes her daughter's hands and brings them to her lips and kisses them. "Missy, my dear, if you decide to marry the King, we'll all go to Jerusalem and live with you. It will be wonderful for all of us. It will make life so much easier since your father died."

"But, Maaama...."

Her mother stares into her eyes and moves their clasped hands to the Maiden's lips for several seconds. Then she wraps her arms around her daughter for a parting hug and whispers, "Don't forget what I always told you about the gazelles and the hinds of the field. Take time to think about everything the King says to you. You'll know what to do."

With a parting kiss on her cheek, she moves back and speaks loud enough for the soldiers to hear, "I love you, Missy. Now go and make your family proud."

Song of Solomon 1:1-8:
The Shulammite's Dilemma Begins

ACT ONE, SCENE ONE
FIRST DAY – AFTERNOON

The curtains open to reveal a backdrop of vineyards dotting the countryside of the town of Shunem, the Shulammite's hometown. Solomon camps here while he inspects his vineyard that he leases to the Shulammite's family (Song 6:10-11; 8:11-12). Stage center are the tents of the King's camp. These multi-purpose tents contain many rooms. One chamber or inner room of the largest tent opens with the Shulammite and the King's virgins-in-waiting inside. The Virgins hover around the Maiden, preparing her to dine with the King (Song 1:12).

Longing for the Shepherd

Song of Solomon 1:1-4a:
"The Song of Songs, which is Solomon's.
'May he kiss me with the kisses of his mouth!
For your love is better than wine.
Your oils have a pleasing fragrance,
Your name is like purified oil;
Therefore the maidens love you.
Draw me after you and let us run together!
The king has brought me into his chambers.'"

When I took *New York Times* and *USA Today* bestselling romance author Phyliss Miranda's creative writing class, she taught us how to captivate our readers in the first scene, "You must begin with a jolt into action. Your opening can use a complication or conflict, a particular work place or historical setting. You can describe a kiss or a fight or the realization of being in love or a love scene."

The Song of Solomon, a true historical romance, was recorded over 3000 years before the first bestselling Texas romance used a kiss to hook readers. As I attend writing classes, I am constantly amazed at how modern the Shulammite's story is even into the 21st century. Truly, the Song of Solomon is a timeless literary masterpiece.

For example, notice how the first 4 verses begin with all 4 techniques Phyliss taught us:

1. The kiss
2. The realization of being in love with the Shepherd
3. The conflict of wanting to run away with the Shepherd
4. The historical setting of being brought to Solomon's tent for his inspection

Thus the first scene of this exciting true romance called the Song of Solomon captures our attention as the Shulammite maiden's thoughts race as she realizes her dilemma. She surveys Solomon's magnificent tent. Even the richest man in the village doesn't begin to have a luxurious tent like this.

In the midst of amazing splendor, the Maiden's words reflect extreme emotional loneliness bordering on panic. Several wide-eyed Virgins from Jerusalem that she's never met before flit about her. Some pull at her clothes with obvious disgust. Others fill a golden tub with warm water and milk to soften and silken her skin. They add essential oils and dried flower petals to put her in the mood for love (Song 1:12).

Although enticed by curiosity about Solomon and the chance for financial rewards for her family, the Maiden's predicament alarms her. Overwhelmed, she yearns, then pleads for the Shepherd to come rescue her. All of her 5 senses are on high alert adding to her increasing anxiety.

The expensive furnishings, unusual fragrances, and private chatter and snickers make her head spin. The disapproving touches and offers of rich pastries nauseate her. Perhaps the bath will soothe her nerves.

Professor of Old Testament at Denver Seminary, Dr. Richard Hess, in his excellent study of the Hebrew words in his book *Song of Songs*, points out how these first four verses are unique in the Song of Solomon:

> The sense created is the (paratactic [a literary technique, in writing or speaking, that favors short, simple sentences, with the use of coordinating rather than subordinating conjunctions]) piling on of one descriptive phrase after another. Indeed, the one theme that does run through vv. 2-4 is the appeal to every one of the senses in describing the love envisioned by the female and shared by the couple. There are examples of wordplay, moving from sound-centered assonance in the opening verses to repetitions, paronomasia [literary word for puns], and connections of content in vv. 5-7. The opening speech of the female lover flashes from one sensuous image to another, thereby expressing a height of emotion and delight that ignores rules of parallelism or other poetic structure. Instead, the perception of the reader is a breathtaking adventure of love that will be difficult to keep up with (47-48).

Secret 1: Awaken True Love With Your 5 Senses

The Song of Solomon's "jolt into action" begins by appealing to the Shulammite's 5 senses to add intense memories to the drama. She desperately longs for the Shepherd to come to her aid. As you follow along, you'll notice the role her 5 senses play in validating her love for the Shepherd.

Then when you explore Secret 4, you'll see the impact of the Shepherd's 5 senses on his love for the Maiden. Both the Shulammite and the Shepherd experience love for each other through satisfaction of their 5 senses. For now, notice how the Maiden's 5 senses define her love:

Touch: "The Kisses of His Mouth!"

Song of Solomon 1:2a:
"May he kiss me with the kisses of his mouth!"

Phyliss advised us, "Draw out the first kiss as long as possible to create sexual tension…but then something happens to get in the way."

The Song of Solomon does not disappoint us. The play begins with a dramatic opening—longing for an extraordinary kiss. Many commentators don't know what to make of "May he kiss me with the kisses of his mouth." It sounds like double talk to them—"Don't all kisses come from your mouth? Maybe the kiss contrasts with nose rubbing like some cultures did."

Although the word kiss is used many times in the Old Testament with a few romantic implications, this is a special kind of kiss. The Shulammite just says it differently from what modern romance authors write: "He wants to taste her."

Skipping ahead, we recognize the "taste" or the Oriental Frenchy *un baiser amoureux* ("a lover's kiss") part of "the kisses of his mouth" when Solomon makes his most outrageous sensuous proposal to the Maiden:

Song of Solomon 7:7-9a:
"Your stature is like a palm tree,
And your breasts are like its clusters.
I said, 'I will climb the palm tree,
I will take hold of its fruit stalks.'
Oh, may your breasts be like clusters of the vine,
And the fragrance of your breath like apples,
And your mouth like the best wine!"

"Mouth" means "the sense of tasting; properly, the palate or inside of the mouth; hence, the mouth itself (as the organ of speech, taste, and kissing):--(roof of the) mouth, taste" (Strong 39).

We'll save the raunchy sexual implications of Solomon's speech until we come to it in the story. For now, notice that Solomon craves open-mouth kissing with the Maiden. The experience will yield the exhilarating taste sensations of sweet apple cider coupled with the best wine to be swirled and sipped slowly in prolonged deep tongue play.

In her crowded isolation and insecurity of not knowing what is about to happen in Solomon's tent, the Maiden wishes for the comfort of her beloved Shepherd's kisses. His kisses have moved beyond friendship and beginning courtship to a sample of the marital passion to come. He is her soulmate, and she longs for his soothing lips to still her fears.

Jack Schafer, Ph.D., in his online *Psychology Today* column wrote an article titled "Odd Facts About Kissing." He sheds light on the Shulammite's craving for the Shepherd's kisses of love. It seems that the moist mucus membranes inside the mouth are perfect for absorbing the man's hormones. "Through open-mouth kissing, men introduce testosterone into a woman's mouth." Testosterone increases a woman's libido and arouses her for sex. Schafer says, "Men prefer open-mouth kissing with tongue contact when kissing short-term partners to increase the probability of mating" (12/2012).

Since mouth to mouth kissing releases hormones which stir up sexual feelings and desires, it's not a safe practice for beginning a relationship. Kissing can fool a woman into thinking she loves a man when she's just reacting to the dose of testosterone he injects into her system. The moist mucus membranes may make it even more effective than if he used a hypodermic needle to inject his drug of choice.

Upon learning this, one woman said, "When I started dating my husband, I didn't even like him. I only went out with him to have someone to hang out with. We dated for three months before I let him kiss me. That night I lay awake for a long time thinking over and over, *I love him. I know I love him.* I never, ever thought I might love him until I let him kiss me."

She paused, "We dated for three years, and it never occurred to me I might not really love him or he might not really love me.... Our marriage was a disaster. I learned the hard way I should never have dated a boy I wasn't attracted to, and I certainly should never have let him kiss me. Everything changed after our first night of kissing, and not for the best. From then on I was blind to his faults and character."

Both men and women can manipulate kissing when trying to initiate sex for just the physical release instead of for soulmating or bonding through lovemaking. Dr. Schafer says prostitutes usually refuse to kiss clients on the mouth (12/2012).

"Sorry, buster, it's all about the money. I don't want to get romantically attached — so no kisses to stir up my emotions or hormones. Do your thing and go, but leave a big tip on the nightstand."

Men may innately know kissing turns a woman on or perhaps they've observed the power of their kisses over women. With the release of their testosterone into the woman's mouth, kissing can quickly make her ready for action. Loving wives enjoy the flood of hormones from both kissing and intercourse. They may want to bolster the experience with more kissing afterward to bond more closely with their husband.

However, kissing can lead to forming unhealthy emotional relationships, especially for women. Perhaps dating couples need to reconsider self-made kissing rules such as, "I never kiss on the first date, but it's okay on the third date." The safest course is to fall in love before you kiss and not think you're in love because you kissed too soon.

Taste: "Your Love Is Better than Wine"

Song of Solomon 1:2b:
"For your love is better than wine."

The reason the Shulammite aches for the Shepherd's deep kisses is because his love is better than wine. All the way through the Song of Solomon, the speakers compare the various aspects of love, kisses, and sex to wine.

As a vineyard keeper, the Maiden knows all about making the different varieties of wines. She harvests the very sweet wine which is released from the weight of the ripe grapes pressing together before the treading begins. She works with her mother boiling the grape juice down into a sugary syrup to be mixed with water later. She also helps her brothers bury the large jugs of fermented wine in the ground to preserve them. And we'll see later that she knows all about the differences in decanting (pouring and mixing) older and newer wines for enhancing their most robust, pleasing flavors.

These words appear to be spoken out loud before the Virgins who are getting her ready to dine with the King that evening. She lets them know she is emotionally involved with the Shepherd saying, "His love is better than wine." Surely, they understand she has a special boyfriend.

Society uses wine to mellow out. True love does the same thing. It pacifies a person. Both wine and love are euphoric and soothing. Thus in her dilemma of being brought before the King the Shulammite yearns for the comfort of the one whose love is sweeter than wine.

Smell: "Your Oils Have a Pleasing Fragrance"

Song of Solomon 1:3a:
"Your oils [ointments – KJV] have a pleasing fragrance."

"Oils" *(shemen)* is the general word for liquid oil "as from the olive, often perfumed." It was used as an ointment and for anointing (Strong 118).

"Fragrance" means "odor (as if blown):--savour, scent, smell." It comes from a primary root that means "properly to blow, i.e. breathe; only (literally) to smell or (by implication) perceive (figuratively to anticipate, enjoy)" (Strong 107, 108).

As the Shulammite desires the taste of the Shepherd's kisses of love, she remembers the way he smells when he wraps his arms around her. The two memories blend and come forth in rapid fire. Although the Israelites of this time didn't take daily baths, they added essential oils to olive oil to protect their skin and stay fragrant.

A good shepherd knew how to use oils to protect his sheep from nose flies in the summer. These flies buzz around a sheep's head looking for a chance to lay their eggs in the moist mucous membranes of the sheep's nose. Without treatment, in a few days, the slender worm-like larvae will hatch out and begin working their way up the nasal passages into the sheep's head.

From then on, the sheep is tormented relentlessly. Its thrashing about, rubbing its head in the dirt, on trees, and bushes will disturb the whole herd. The mothers' milk can dry up and their babies cease to thrive. The infected sheep sometimes kills itself trying to find relief. So at the first sign of the pesky flies, the shepherd smears oil over the sheep's nose and head (Keller 114-6).

Her Shepherd knows all about oils for both his sheep and himself. She closes her eyes as the memory of his fragrance soothes her nerves. His name echoes in her ears.

Hear: "Your Name Is Like Purified Oil"

Song of Solomon 1:3b:
"Your name is like purified [poured out — NIV] oil;
Therefore the maidens love you."

"Purified" is more commonly translated "poured out" and means "literally which is emptied (from one vessel to another)" (New American Standard Bible footnote).

If we can't read Hebrew, we can miss the Shulammite's inferences unless a knowledgeable person shares the subtle differences of her words. David Hubbard gives us a small hint in his commentary about her wordplay. *Shemen* for "oil" and *shēm* for "name" have a definite assonance (278).

The Maiden also makes a play on ideas. She starts the stanza by saying the Shepherd's pleasing body oils are "blown" into her nostrils for olfactory pleasure. Then she metaphorically equates the sound of his name as an essential oil that is "poured out" from him to envelop her.

Everything about the Shepherd appeals to the Maiden from the perfumed oils he wears to his name. She finds comfort in calling out his name over and over with a "Mrs." in front of it. She will be proud to wear his name—no "Ms." for her!

When my mother was in high school in California, one of her teachers married a man by the name of Snodgrass. My mother and her schoolmates talked about what a horrible name Snodgrass was. They didn't see how anyone could ever love a man with such a name.

The next summer my mother and her brother rode the bus to Oklahoma to help their grandparents harvest wheat. MawMaw, as she was called, taught my mother how to cook beans for the work crew. Her grandfather, PawPaw, employed a young harvest hand by the name of Snodgrass who always wore clean white coveralls. My mother fell in love with him, and he rode the bus with her and her brother back to California. Soon she became Mrs. Ray Snodgrass.

And through the years until her death at age 89, she was proud to be a Snodgrass. True love makes a man's name as appealing as "purified oil" to the woman who loves him, even if his name happens to be Snodgrass. After all, Scottish "smooth" grass is beautiful to behold waving in the breeze.

And what about all those maidens loving the Shepherd? To dispel her anxiety in being brought to Solomon's tent for his inspection, the Shulammite wishes for the reassurance of her girlfriends. They know and love the Shepherd, too. They understand her anguish. This scene is similar to slumber parties where girls talk and giggle about boys. The Maiden remembers her peers exclaiming over her boyfriend.

"What did you two do last weekend?"

"He's so hot! His curly locks are to die for!"

"When you get tired of him, I'm next in line."

See: "Let Us Run Away Together!"

Song of Solomon 1:4a:
"Draw me after you and let us run together!
The king has brought me into his chambers.'"

With the Shulammite's 5 senses screaming at her and begging for the familiar, she cries out, "Let me see you! Right now! I'm in trouble! I'm in the King's tent because he wants to marry me. But I love you. Come get me this instant so we can run away together. I need you now!"

Even though she has won the lottery for her herself and her family, she's still emotionally attached to the Shepherd. They were planning a fall wedding. Now she's offered the opportunity of a lifetime…. So why can't she relax and enjoy the attentions of the King?

Sensory Overload: "The King Brought Me to His Chambers"

Many commentators read "chambers" and think "marriage bedroom." They assume the Song of Solomon portrays a married couple consummating their vows. However, Solomon later explains what's going on when he introduces the Maiden to the Queens and Concubines. He says, "I was in the country inspecting my vineyard when I saw this beautiful vineyard keeper. Before I knew it, it was lust at first sight. I said to myself, 'I must possess her body.' I had her brought to my tent so I could inspect her more closely and propose marriage" (Song 6:11-12).

Obviously, Solomon was living in a tent while he toured his farmlands. But the Israelites' tents were much different from the ones we camp in today. At the time of the Song of Solomon, most of the common people in the country still lived in tents. They lived mostly outdoors and used their tents for sleeping and shelter. The tents had at least three rooms. A central sitting room divided the men's sleeping quarters from the women's rooms. As their children married, often a new room was added for the young couple. The wealthier a person became, the more rooms he added to his tent (Wight 13-9).

Even when he camps out during his inspection trips, Solomon always surrounds himself with great wealth (2 Chronicles 9:13-27). We get a small idea of how opulent his tent is from the description of his sedan chair in Song 3:9-10. Its posts were made of silver and its back was fashioned from gold. The daughters of Jerusalem fitted it with luxurious purple fabric. The Maiden has never even imagined anything so obscenely luxurious.

The extravagant sights and textures in the King's tent along with the exotic smells Solomon traveled with overwhelm her (Song 3:6). And outside servants prepare a scrumptious gourmet dinner. The open sides of the tent let in the strange aromas of new flavors. Her stomach jumps in anticipation.

In her state of bewilderment, awe, and nervousness, she pines for the Shepherd. He is more than just her comfort zone — he's her beloved. The Virgins interrupt her fervent speech to mock her.

The Virgins' Mockery

Song of Solomon 1:4b:
"We will rejoice in you [masculine singular] and be glad;
We will extol your [masculine singular] love more than wine.
Rightly do they love you [masculine singular]."

The Shulammite identifies the speakers in verse 5 when she

addresses them as "O daughters of Jerusalem." These are probably the same Virgins in Song 6:8. At this time Solomon's harem consisted of 60 queens (free women he married), 80 concubines (slaves he married), and maidens or virgins without number who serve Solomon and his wives while they wait for the King to take them as one of his wives.

Some authors think the Virgins are exclaiming over the Shulammite as the perfect bride for Solomon. However, Gary Martin, a Hebrew scholar, explains in *The Song of Songs* that the original language shows "you" and "your" are masculine singular and refer to a man, not a woman (35, 39-40).

The Virgins do not know the Shepherd like the local maidens do, so they cannot rejoice in him or extol his love more than wine. They know and love the King. But the Maiden pleads for the Shepherd to rescue her. Her dilemma? She loves the Shepherd; everybody else loves the King. This produces tremendous peer pressure for a girl to marry someone she doesn't know or love.

With derision barely concealed in their voices, the Virgins tell her, "You think you love the Shepherd, but we rejoice in the King." Then they lapse into sing-song mockery, "This silly girl thinks a shepherd's love is better than wine, but we will extol your love, Solomon, more than wine. Rightly do all the maidens without number love you." They giggle and blush at the thought of the King choosing one of them for his next bride. Everyone knows Solomon's love is better than wine even though he shares it with so many women.

Throughout the Song of Solomon, the characters banter with each other with plays on the previous speaker's words. The Virgins taunt the Maiden as they assert, "The wine of the King's love is so much sweeter than the wine of your common shepherd boyfriend!"

The Shulammite's Persona

Black but Lovely and Swarthy

> *Song of Solomon 1:5-6a:*
> *"I am black but lovely,*
> *O daughters of Jerusalem,*
> *Like the tents of Kedar,*
> *Like the curtains of Solomon.*
> *Do not stare at me because I am swarthy,*
> *For the sun has burned me."*

"Lovely" means "beautiful:--becometh, comely, seemly" (Strong 75).

In other words, although the Shulammite's skin is black from the sun, she's comfortable in her skin. She accepts the new beauty her blackness creates for her persona. Thus she tells the Virgins, "I'm black, but beautiful."

Then she makes a play on the words "black" and "swarthy." "Black" identifies a color, not a race, i.e., her hair color in Song 5:11. The scholar Richard Hess says she coined the word "swarthy":

> Instead of using the term for "black" (*sahor*) found in the preceding verse, she coins a reduplication stem of the same root (*seharhoret*), found only here. The effect of such reduplication is to intensify the adjective [swarthy]. In this case, it makes what is black too black (57).

The Maiden's dark tan contrasts sharply from the Virgins. Solomon married women from all over the world who brought the latest beautifying tools and ingredients with them:

> Women and men alike had been doing their best to improve on nature throughout most of recorded history. As far back as Sumerian times, they had painted kohl around their eyes to enlarge them and tinted their cheeks with red dyes. Athenian women, said Aristophanes, used grease paint, antimony ore (mascara), red paint, white lead (as face powder), seaweed paint (possibly as an eye shadow), and beauty plasters (face packs). Many of these preparations were unfortunately not waterproof. "When you go out in the summer," said Eubulus nastily, "two black rivulets flow from your eyes, the sweat from your cheeks carries trickles of rouge right down to your neck, and your hair turns gray from the powder on your forehead."… For gray hair, Mesopotamian experts recommended a mixture of opium with a dash each of the gall of a black ox, a scorpion, and a pig, brewed up with the head of a black raven and the head of a stork. The Egyptians preferred a blend of laudanum, oil, cat's womb, and raven's egg. For baldness, they said, it was best to rub into the scalp a salve made from the fat of a lion, a hippopotamus, a crocodile, a cat, a serpent, and an ibex (Tannahill 113, 115).

In the company of these made-up Virgins, she asserts that her blackness only adds to her charm—and she has the self-confidence to know it. Even though she feels conspicuous and out of place in this lavish tent, she makes a play on her surroundings. She compares herself to the beautiful tents of Kedar which were made of black goat's hair (Wight 14). Surely, they know about Solomon's beautiful black curtains.

The Maiden recognizes and accepts her own unique brand of beauty without placing all her hopes in her attractiveness. She continues to play with words all through this section:

> ["Stare"] occurs only here and in Job (20:9; 28:7), where it describes the sharp eye of a bird of prey. It forms a poetic variant on the common verb "to see" in the first line. Therefore, it intensifies the process of seeing. If the daughters of Jerusalem stared at the female lover, the sun (the second word mentioned above) had already "stared" that much harder at her; effecting a darkening of the skin's pigments (Hess 57).

Myrrh and Her Gorgeous Brown Body

The Shulammite's language throughout the Song of Solomon indicates she and the Shepherd use myrrh (Song 1:13, 4:6, 14; 5:1, 5, 13). In fact, the Maiden's longings for the Shepherd frequently revolve around the many herbs and essential oils of the country folks revealing a working knowledge of their benefits. Her numerous references to myrrh suggest she kept it in her medicine cabinet and with her beauty supplies.

Dr. David Stewart, a retired minister and former university science professor, reveals some of the benefits of myrrh in *Healing Oils of the Bible*. He states that the Egyptians used myrrh as both a sunscreen and an insect repellent:

> Perhaps you have seen pictures of ancient Egyptians with cones on their heads. You may have mistaken these as knots of hair, but they are not. They were lumps of fat from ox, duck, goose, or hippopotamus saturated with myrrh.... The idea was to place the unguent cone on the top of their heads in the morning and then as the heat rose during the day the fat would melt slowly, running down their half-naked bodies, keeping their skin moist and repelling insects (151-2).

Tiffany Rowan blogged about how she uses myrrh in "Myrrh—The Egyptians Choice for Sunscreen and Insect Repellent." Her results with myrrh shed some light on the Shulammite's beautiful brown skin. Tiffany put a very high number of drops of myrrh into half a cup of extra virgin olive oil for a sunscreen. She said, "Because the mixture is pulled into the skin, and not sitting on top of the skin like most sunscreens, I only have to apply it once for the four-hour period my family is usually at the lake or pool."

It didn't seem to make any difference if she put the mixture on before she went out into the sun or afterward to soothe a sunburn. She said, "I get a gorgeous tan. That could explain why Egyptians had such gorgeous brown bodies." She concluded, "Myrrh is so nourishing to the skin that after long-term use, I have enjoyed soft, supple skin"

(3/18/2010).

We read about myrrh's special benefits to the skin in the account of Esther. For one year, she went through a special beautification program before being presented to King Ahasuerus. It was as follows: "six months with oil of myrrh and six months with spices and the cosmetics for women" (Esther 2:12).

As a vineyard keeper, the Shulammite didn't have the luxury of avoiding the hot midday sun. Her knowledge of myrrh and the loveliness of her deeply tanned body imply she uses the essential oil to protect and beautify her skin. This adds a new dimension to her coining the word swarthy to describe her exquisiteness to the staring Virgins.

Solomon's many descriptions of the Maiden's body provide a glimpse of her physical attributes. He portrays her as a tall, well-developed, slender beauty with curly hair. She has beautiful even teeth and her eyes radiate inner peace. Her perfect complexion frames her luscious mouth (Song 4:1-6; 7:6-8). The Queens describe her as perfectly built for entertaining them with sensuous belly dancing. They tell her, "The King is captivated by your long, flowing black hair" (Song 7:1-5).

The Shulammite's comfortableness with her appearance contrasts with girls today who let rock and porn stars set the standards for outward beauty. Even some grade-school girls expose their crotches by refusing to wear panties. They degrade themselves to lure male attention their way. Yet the Shulammite respects herself with her makeup-free tanned skin. And the world's greatest judge of horse and female flesh, King Solomon, sees and admires her genuine inner glow.

Although physical loveliness attracts a boy's attention, appearance will not ensure his devotion if beauty of character is lacking. Solomon's 1000 wives prove the fallacy of exposing one's genitals to gain a boyfriend. Lust lasts for a season, then moves on to the next lovely body.

Indeed, the Proverbs writer agrees in the description of the woman of great price:

Proverbs 31:30:
"Charm is deceitful and beauty is vain,
But a woman who fears the LORD, she shall be praised."

Yes, charm is deceitful as every young woman easily praises the man of her dreams. Unfortunately, as the marriage wears on, too many times her innocent admiration turns to nagging and complaining. And beauty? It fades for everyone who doesn't invest in expensive face lifts and collagen injections. A woman's heart grows more charming and beautiful over the years when she strives to fill her life with love for her family and others.

Her Brothers' Anger

Song of Solomon 1:6b:
"My mother's sons were angry with me;
They made me caretaker of the vineyards,
But I have not taken care of my own vineyard."

The Shulammite shares why the sun blackened her skin—she is a working girl who oversees her family's vineyards. But she is not finished with making plays on words as she confronts the lily-white Virgins:

> The word picture of the burning rays of the sun also ties together the following line, where the female's brothers act in hostility toward her. She uses a form of the verb meaning "to burn, be angry" to describe how they became angry. This is the idiom of burning in rage. Thus, the wordplay of verbs connects the fire of her brothers with the heat of the sun to produce her dark skin. And the sun's stare couples with the critical gaze of her companions [the Virgins] to tie together the whole picture (Hess 57).

Later the Maiden tells the Shepherd she wishes he were like a loving brother to her who nursed at her mother's breasts (Song 8:1). Although her brothers are extremely angry with her now, she knows they normally treat her with love and delight. By studying the historical background of Solomon's reign, we learn the brothers had plenty of reasons to be angry—not with her, but with the King. Solomon had taken over their lives. And like many people, they allowed their anger to destroy their patience. They took their frustration out on their sister when she didn't immediately agree to do what they wanted.

Her Brothers Help Feed the King and His Harem

Some commentators find it hard to believe Solomon actually married 1000 women, saying they don't see how he could have kept so many women happy or even fed them. However, he set up a system of government to provide for his growing family. The first thing he did as king was to establish a residual-income program better than any Internet get-rich-quick scheme.

He divided the country into twelve regions without respect for the twelve tribes except for the Levites who took care of the temple. He set deputies over the twelve sections. The tribes immediately lost influence and political power (1 Kings 4:1-7, 27).

Then he installed tax collectors. Each of the twelve sections provided food for one month each year for Solomon's harem, their relatives, and children along with his employees. The Israelites also furnished hay and barley for his horses. The amount of food Solomon required for just one day was staggering (*Great* 187-8).

Thus Solomon designed an ingenious organization for a young king who indulged himself in deflowering virgins, horticulture and botany, and building projects. With his government installed soon after he was crowned king, he enjoyed plenty of time to pursue his obsessions in grandiose style. As his harem grew and his government became more bloated, his taxation program became more burdensome each year.

The magnitude of the tax burden fell on the farmers and shepherds. It's easy to imagine the anger and resentment burning in the brothers' chests toward the playboy king who requires them to pay for his excesses. But food was not the only taxation.

Her Brothers Work on the King's Building Projects

Solomon also needed workers for his huge building projects—the temple, his palace, a home for his favorite wife, Pharaoh's daughter, and strategically placed cities for storing the collected foods. He began building the temple in the fourth year of his reign and it took seven years. Now into the sixth year of his reign, the temple is well underway. Solomon was known for his great building projects which consumed most of his early years.

Over 150,000 of the old Canaanite slaves serve on the roads in the quarries. Then 30,000 drafted Israelites work as forced laborers. He sends them in relays of 10,000 to Lebanon to harvest trees. The men spend one month in the forests and then two months at home (1 Kings 5:13-18).

Including the food taxes, the Maiden's brothers would have been drafted for Solomon's building endeavors. This means they slave for Solomon four months out of every year. Thus they are double taxed in providing both food and labor.

No doubt, this causes the brothers' anger to burn as they transfer their bitterness toward the King onto their sister. They need her to take charge of the vineyards while they are gone. The story doesn't mention her father which many scholars believe indicates he was dead.

Her Brothers Made the Shulammite the Caretaker

Many think a woman's place is always in the home, and only in the home, while the man works in the fields. Our view is tainted by our remembrance of an unusual time in history. Immediately after World War II husbands came home to take over supporting their families while their wives left the war factories to become stay-at-home moms during the golden age of the United States. Throughout much of history women worked alongside their men to survive harsh economies.

During Solomon's reign, the country people lived on family compounds. The grandmothers provided loving daycare for the children including serving as wet nurses. The mothers often worked alongside the men.

Two other places in the Song of Solomon expand on the Shulammite's responsibilities as caretaker of the vineyards. They show she was not a common field laborer, but was the overseer when Solomon spied her. We will let the Maiden share those details when she's ready.

We also learn later that she planned to get married in the spring and move to the Shepherd's home. This implies she was self-conscious about her dark skin before the Virgins started staring at her like a hawk stalking a field mouse. More than anything, she wants to be a beautiful bride for the Shepherd.

Virgins spent a whole year preparing their trousseau and beautifying their skin. They worked hard to make their complexions "glossy and shining with a luster like marble." David said, "That our daughters may be as corner stones, polished after the similitude of a palace" (Psalms 144:12) (Wight 130).

Then when her brothers asked, then demanded, she change her wedding plans to oversee the care of the vineyards, she balked. We can imagine the family dynamics of the boys being sent off for forced labor on Solomon's building project while the little sister had other plans than working in the hot sun every day.

As she took charge of the vineyards she probably talked to herself in self-effacing puns about her predicament. So when the pale palace Virgins from Jerusalem with their made-up eyes looked at her with disdain, her words burst forth. "How dare you stare at me like the sun stares unmercifully at me!" Not only is her skin burnt black she coins a swarthy reduplication to make fun of their ridicule. Does her voice betray her own anger at her brothers as she rants at the Virgins?

Her voice softens momentarily to inject some comic relief as she humorously calls her brothers, "my mother's sons." Then she continues her animated lecture. She changes the form of the blackened verb to ignite the raging fire in her brothers' anger as they forced her to give up her plans and expose herself to the skin-darkening rays of the sun.

Understanding her brothers' anger helps us appreciate the Maiden's dilemma. If she accepts Solomon's proposal of marriage it will give her family a huge financial boost. She, her mother, brothers, and little sister will take their place at Solomon's table alongside the other wives and their relatives. They will wear beautiful clothes. Her brothers can become gentleman farmers or even government employees. Wow! What a life Solomon offers the young Maiden toiling under the broiling sun.

"O You Whom My Soul Loves"

Song of Solomon 1:7a:
"Tell me, O you whom my soul loves…"

"Soul" (*nephesh*) refers to "a breathing creature, i.e. animal or (abstract) vitality; used very widely in a literal, accommodated or figurative sense (bodily or mental):--any, appetite, beast, body, breath, creature, desire, heart, lust, man, mind, mortally, person, pleasure, will" (Strong 80). This same word is used in Leviticus 17:11 where it says the soul of a person "is in the blood." In other words, *nephesh* conveys the idea of life itself (Hess 103).

"Loves" (*'âhab*) is a primary root that means "to have affection for (sexually or otherwise)" and is used frequently in the book (Strong 9).

Today instead of saying him "whom my soul loves" we say, "My boyfriend is the love of my life." In the first four verses revealing the Shulammite's dilemma we see her sensory overload as she describes the love of her life.

True Love Versus Sensuous Love

Your dilemma in courtship of whom to marry and in marriage of how to keep true love alive is the same as the Shulammite's problem. Do you pursue true love or do you succumb to sensuous love's bidding?

True Love Revolves Around Satisfying the 5 Senses

In the Maiden's expression of her deep longing through her 5 senses, we experience her emotional involvement with the Shepherd as she turns to him for comfort. In summary, true love in courtship and marriage is a satiation of the 5 senses with deep intellectual, emotional, and spiritual commitment to the object of one's sexual desire.

Sensuous Love Also Satisfies the 5 Senses

Sensuous love lacks the intellectual, emotional, and spiritual commitment to act in the other person's best interest. Sensuous love seeks physical comfort for the self-absorbed person while ignoring one's own and the target's emotional needs.

The Shulammite wrestles with comparing true love with sensuous love throughout the story. She must sort out the differences between the way she and the Shepherd love each other in the context of how she and the King interact. This is the essence of the Song of Solomon. God preserved this story to help you sort out your own love life and the role of your 5 senses in finding a lifelong sexual partner. Your understanding of Secret 1 will grow as you follow the story and learn the other secrets.

"Where Do You Pasture Your Flock?"

Song of Solomon 1:7b:
"Where do you pasture your flock,
Where do you make it lie down at noon?
For why should I be like one who veils herself
Beside the flocks of your companions?"

The Maiden's energy spent on her outburst, her eyes and voice become syrupy. If the one she loves won't come to her then perhaps she should go to him. And she moans, "Where do you pasture your flock?"

Although she realizes the opportunity the King's infatuation offers her, she loves the Shepherd. She still wants to run away, only now as she's calmer, she proposes to run to the Shepherd instead of begging him to come get her. What a dilemma! Can her love for the Shepherd begin to compare with a life with the King—and the benefits for her family?

She asks, "Should I be like one who veils herself beside the flocks of your companions?" Hebrew women enjoyed more liberty concerning when and where they wore veils than Arab women do today. With the exception of peasant women, maidservants, and prostitutes, all women wore veils. However, the women had great freedom regarding how and if they wore a veil in public. A man could not lift a woman's veil, but she could if she chose to (Wight 98-9). The Shulammite suggests that as a working vineyard keeper she was not accustomed to wearing a veil.

Thus she asks, "Should I do what all the girls do? Wander accidentally on purpose to where you and the other boys are?" Like girls from generation to generation, the Maiden asks if she should act coy and play hard to get. Should she just happen to walk by the place where he pastures his flocks with her veil innocently in place? Maybe he would notice her and rescue her from her dilemma. Or perhaps she should openly declare she is ready to forget the vineyards and marry him now, putting an end to their courtship and the intentions of the King? Before Solomon came along she knew what she wanted—now she isn't so sure.

Her Beloved Is a Successful Shepherd

The expression "make it [his flock] lie down at noon" shows how well the Shepherd takes care of his sheep. For example, sheep refuse to lie down at noon to rest (1) if they feel the least bit hungry, (2) if disease or insects bother them, (3) if any kind of danger presents itself, or (4) if friction exists between their own social orders (Keller 35).

A shepherd who makes his flock lie down at noon must prevent all four problems from happening. The Maiden describes the Shepherd as a hard, dependable worker. Besides, what better time to visit him than when his flocks are lying down, and he can give her some attention?

Solomon and the Shepherd Are Two Distinct Individuals

The Shulammite asks, "Where are you? Where is the one whom my soul loves?" Solomon tells where he is at this time. He is inspecting his vineyard in the orchard of nut trees (Song 6:11). The vineyard is where he found her and where the two of them are right now. Later she says Solomon had a vineyard at Baal-hamon which he entrusted to caretakers (Song 8:11). Both Solomon and the Shulammite are at the vineyard at Baal-hamon; the Shepherd or the beloved is the only one missing.

Yet the Maiden knows where the Shepherd is—he is pasturing his flocks. Later in the story when the Virgins ask where her beloved is, she doesn't tell them where Solomon is because they all know he's in the palace with her. In fact, the King soon shows up at his tent to continue trying to persuade her to marry him. Instead, she tells the Virgins her beloved is pasturing his flock among the lilies (Song 6:2). Unless Solomon can be in two places at the same time, the King and the Shepherd must be two different men, both in love with the Shulammite.

The Shepherd Is the "Beloved"

In the two verses that tell where her boyfriend is, the Maiden also introduces the Shepherd as "you whom my soul loves" and "my beloved." This is noteworthy because these two expressions appear thirty-four times in the Song of Solomon. Since she says the Shepherd is also the one her soul loves and her beloved, all of the beloved passages logically refer to the Shepherd—not to King Solomon.

Additionally, she says her beloved is watching over his flocks like his shepherd friends. Solomon isn't hanging out with shepherds. He's too busy pursuing women to worry about finding lost sheep.

Therefore, we don't need to decide arbitrarily if a speaker is Solomon or the Shepherd. All the beloved passages establish a clear pattern of the Maiden referring to the Shepherd. Some commentators switch back and forth between the beloved being either the Maiden or the Shepherd. But the beloved passages consistently refer to the Shepherd. The Maiden identifies herself as a vineyard keeper.

If you'd like to study additional internal evidences in the Song of Solomon that the Shepherd and Solomon are two different individuals read my article "King Solomon Wasn't the Shepherd." You'll find it at my website SongOfSolomonLoveTriangle.com.

"Go Pasture Your Goats by the Tents of the Shepherds"

Song of Solomon 1:8:
"If you yourself do not know,
Most beautiful among women,

Go forth on the trail of the flock,
And pasture your young goats
By the tents of the shepherds."

"Most beautiful" is the same Hebrew word throughout the Song of Solomon. The Virgins and Solomon frequently use this word. It comes from a primary root that means "properly to be bright, i.e. (by implication) beautiful (literally or figuratively)" (Strong 51).

After the Maiden's reprimand about her darkened skin and how her brothers forced her to work in the vineyards, the Virgins stop staring and begin praising her unique beauty. They use a stronger word for "most beautiful" than the Maiden used for "lovely" (Song 1:5). They praise her excessively by calling her "most beautiful *among women.*"

Many people think Israelite parents forced their daughters to marry whomever they chose. Not true. For example, Rebekah's mother and brother gave her a choice about marrying Isaac (Genesis 24:57-58). After the age of 12, each girl made her own choice to either accept or reject the arrangements her parents made. But she still required her parents' approval of her choice until she turned 21.

For this reason, the Virgins assure the Shulammite she is free to go to the Shepherd. If she wants to leave that badly, the King won't force himself on her. But since the King already showers his attentions on her, wouldn't it be better to find out what he wants before she makes her decision? Besides, she has smelled a fabulous meal cooking all afternoon, and it'll soon be time to dine with the King. She lingers.

Just as modern screenplays break for a commercial after a cliff hanger, the scene ends with the Shulammite pondering whom to choose. Will she go find the Shepherd or stay in Solomon's camp? The tent flap closes on the Maiden's bedroom and her indecision.

Study Exercise

Answer all questions in your own words.
1. What advice would you give young girls about being self-conscious about their appearance?
2. What advice would you give young boys about being self-conscious about their appearance?
3. How would most girls feel if a rich playboy asked them to marry him?
4. Should girls or women feel obligated to give sex to pay for an expensive meal and nice date?
5. How would you define the Shulammite's dilemma?
6. Can you think of situations other than at single bars where boys or men might act like lusty horses, or sex fiends, around beautiful girls?

7. How did the peer pressure of the daughters of Jerusalem affect the Shulammite when she wanted to leave Solomon's tent? How does peer pressure affect courting couples today?
8. In what ways was the Shepherd successful at taking care of his sheep?
9. Do you disagree with anything in the lesson? If so, explain giving scriptures for your reasons.

Research Exercise

True Love Versus Sensuous Love Charts: To help you analyze the differences between true love and sensuous love start six charts, one for each of the following relationships:

1. The Shepherd Rates the Shulammite
2. The Shulammite Rates the Shepherd
3. Solomon Rates the Shulammite
4. The Shulammite Rates Solomon
5. You if you're married: a chart for you and one for your mate
6. You if you're single: a chart for you and one for your dating friend or your ideal future mate

On each chart, make nine columns. Label the columns:

1. Hear
2. See
3. Smell
4. Taste
5. Touch
6. Intellectual Love
7. Emotional Love
8. Sexual Love
9. Spiritual Love

As you go through the Song of Solomon, analyze each of the four relationships by listing each example of satisfying the 5 senses plus intellectual, emotional, and spiritual love. Record examples of looking forward to the sexual relationship. Include the verses.

Start with the Shulammite's 5 senses screaming at her as she longs for the Shepherd. Continue this exercise through the end of the Song of Solomon. Be prepared at the end of the class to write a 1-2 page summary of the advantages and disadvantages of true love versus sensuous love.

Remember, the 5 senses plus intellectual, emotional, sexual, and spiritual love equal true love. The 5 senses plus only sexual attraction equal sensuous love.

If you put in the time to complete this exercise, you will be a different person by the time you complete this study. Keep in mind that you are the only person you can change. However, by changing ourselves, we create an environment that makes it easier for the other person to make changes. The primary goal for doing the charts is to open your eyes to ways you can help love grow in your marriage.

Personal Exercise

Claim the Song of Solomon for yourself and make it a natural aspect of your thinking. Each week read the Song of Solomon beginning with chapter one and read up to your last class. Reading the verses many times during this study makes the story become more familiar. It also helps you better understand the overall storyline. If you'll put in time reading the Song of Solomon, the events of your life will remind you of the Shulammite, the Shepherd, or King Solomon.

If the words in your Bible make it hard to understand the Song of Solomon, go to BibleGateway.com and read the book in other translations. Find a version that makes it easy for you to follow along in this beautiful book of poetry. You may want to print several versions to compare.

Dating Female. You'll begin to compare your boyfriends with the Shepherd and Solomon. You'll compare yourself to the Shulammite. You'll ask, "What would the Shulammite do? What would she say?" You'll also ask yourself, "Do I have the healthy attitudes toward love that the Shulammite did?"

Dating Male. You'll start to compare your dates to the Shulammite, the Virgins, and Solomon's 140 wives. You'll ask yourself if you're treating your date like the Shepherd or Solomon. We saw in the first chapter that teenage boys have the ability to go through as many women as Solomon did. Reading through the Song of Solomon every week will enable you to use it to protect yourself from Solomon's emotional loneliness in the midst of 1000 wives.

Married Couple. You'll examine your attitudes toward your mate and the kind of love residing in your home. You'll wonder if you're teaching your children as well as the Shulammite's mother did. You'll become skillful at teaching your children how to lay a foundation for a happy marriage and a fulfilling love life by your example and your words.

Case Studies:
How to Overcome a Sexless Marriage

Dry eyed, without emotion, Donna, a woman in her late sixties, said, "It's all I can do to sit through your classes. I don't know if I can hang on until you finish the Song of Solomon and start teaching the classes on spouse abuse...."

She took a sip of water and continued, "This is my second marriage.... My present husband physically abused me until my grown son took him out in the front yard and beat him up. My son told him, 'If you ever lay another hand on my mother, I will give you more of the same.' My husband no longer hits me. But the daily verbal abuse has destroyed my spirit. I'm a shadow of the woman I was when we married."

It was 1990 and I was teaching *The Song of Solomon: God's Sex Education for Ages 11 Through 99*. I shared with Donna my reasoning on the order of the classes. I was teaching the Song of Solomon first to allow people in miserable marriages to see what a healthy relationship looks and feels like. This would give them goals to work toward. And then I would teach *Challenges in Marriage: What to Do When Sin Inhibits Love*. The second scriptural study of how to stand up to abuse would give the women insights for changing their marriage.

I encouraged Donna to keep coming to the Song of Solomon lessons. I told her I would help her apply the principles in the *Challenges* classes. She required lots of private reinforcement to stay the course and to do the homework. But she did. Other women, dealing with similar issues, dropped out of the classes rather than talking to me about their pain.

After the classes ended, one of the men in the congregation and I met with Donna and her husband in their home each week for several months. We didn't hint at the husband's verbal abuse, dance around it, or accept excuses for it. It was out in the open.

Donna finally experienced validation of her suffering and she spoke freely. Whether her husband was sincere in his comments and desires to change, I don't know. But in the *Challenges in Marriage* classes, Donna developed skills for holding him accountable for his words and actions. She had more strength than she realized and she never walked on eggshells around him again. And she transformed into a woman with happy eyes and laughter in her voice.

As people contacted me wanting to use the MP3s of the two series for classes around their dining room tables and in their congregations, I told them about this experience. I advised them to start with *Challenges in*

Marriage first, then teach God's ideal from the Song of Solomon.

The Song of Solomon Classes Upset Men

Years later, two men told me how listening to the Song of Solomon MP3s made them cry. Both men had suffered for decades married to wives who barely tolerated sex and rebuffed daytime touching and affection. The descriptions of how a loving wife enjoys her husband's touch of her breasts and initiates lovemaking caused them to sob at the reminder of how far removed their marriages were from God's plan.

Another husband confided how he couldn't stop crying for weeks after he committed adultery to get out of a so-called Christian marriage with an unloving woman. He tried everything he knew from romancing her to blowing up in anger at his frustrations. No matter what he did, she remained untouchable emotionally and sexually.

Men and Women React Differently to Sexual Neglect

I have observed a different effect on men than women who have suffered for years, and even decades, in a loveless marriage. Over time, a woman loses her ability to cry over her husband's rejection. A man reacts entirely different and cries easily when his wife makes him feel like a hopeless sexual beggar. However, his wife may never see his tears of devastating emotional pain. These are survival techniques of loving men and women who feel trapped in an emotionally devastating marriage.

"My Spouse Is Perfect Except for Sex."

In nearly every desperate marriage the person has said to me, "My spouse is perfect except for sex." Then the person lists all the good qualities of the spouse. But the emotional devastation the person suffers from being in a sexless marriage is heart wrenching. Yet the "perfect spouse" doesn't seem to notice the mate's overwhelming loneliness and emotional pain.

I reject this notion that the unloving spouse is perfect except for sex. It's a lie loving husbands and wives tell themselves to survive an emotionally and sexually bankrupt marriage. It's a fantasy emotionally deprived mates believe because they falsely think nearly everyone is a good person at heart—just like they are. It's a fictional story that hurting husbands and wives invent to motivate themselves to keep working harder and harder to turn their marriage around.

The truth? Weiss explains that many unloving spouses deliberately inflict emotional and sexual pain on their mates. They are experts at making comments and picking fights to ruin special moments of intimacy. He cites numerous examples of how anorexics are devious and punish their unsuspecting mate. They do this to distance themselves emotionally from their mates. Such a spouse is far from being perfect. As the marriage ages their self-delusional blame and mistreatment of their spouse increases. It never gets better until the problem is addressed. However, Weiss offers hope if the unloving spouse is willing to work at learning how to love from the heart.

"My Spouse Is a Wonderful Parent."

This is a close second to the first lie. In fact, it often supports the first untruth. Again, "No, your spouse is not a wonderful mother or father." People who don't know how to love their mate are clueless about how to love their children. It's impossible for a person to close up his or her heart toward the spouse and have it overflowing with emotional love for the children. If you think otherwise, you deceive yourself.

The adult children of these unloving parents talk to me all the time. Many of them have rejected their parents' faith because of the emotional suffering they endured from a mother or father who pretended to be perfect except for sex. My experience is that the #1 reason adult children turn their back on God is because they grew up living with their parents' hypocrisy. They watched their parents claiming to love God, all the while failing to practice love for each other or them.

Solomon Was Perfect Except for Sex

What does all this have to do with studying the Song of Solomon? Solomon's wives could have said, "Solomon is perfect except for sex."

I was fortunate during the rewriting of my previous chapters on the Song of Solomon to read Dr. Douglas Weiss's books and workbooks on intimacy anorexia. I recognized Solomon as the perfect embodiment of a spouse who doesn't know how to love the mate intellectually, emotionally, sexually, or spiritually. In contrast, both the Shulammite and the Shepherd demonstrate the qualities of a loving mate.

Weiss's books were eye opening as I revised my Song of Solomon material and looked back on 44 years of being the confidante of both husbands and wives. In his first book, *Intimacy Anorexia*, Weiss quotes both the anorexics and their spouses. He addresses *Married & Alone* primarily to neglected spouses to show that although they endure a roommate relationship instead of a marriage, they're not alone in their suffering. He also helps readers work through options for their marriage.

A Case Study of Failure:
Harold Refused to Change His Sexless Ways

A husband, whom I'll call Harold, confided in me about why his wife divorced him after a decades-long sexless marriage. He said, "I never learned how to love a woman emotionally and sexually." He didn't say "my wife." He said "a woman." He didn't know how to love any woman.

Harold continued, "If my wife had had sexual experiences before we married, she would have known what a sick puppy I am...how incapable I am of loving a woman. I never put in the effort to learn how to do better.... And I'm not interested in learning now."

As I read the true stories in *Intimacy Anorexia,* I recognized many of Harold's characteristics through details both he and his wife shared with me. His wife thought he was adultery proof since he wasn't interested in sex with her. How wrong she was as she discovered in their later years that he had been an adulterer most of their marriage—perhaps even unfaithful during courtship. Weiss shares in his book many similar stories about how men and women have suffered being unloved, untouched, and often betrayed.

Intimacy Anorexics Don't Withhold Sex from Themselves

Male anorexics experience stronger temptations for covert sexual sins than emotionally healthy husbands do. Sexual addictions along with mental and physical adulterous acts provide opportunities for secret sexual release with little intimate attachment to the object of their lust. Weiss says after years of working with both male and female anorexics:

> Very few men and only some women avoid sex. However, both the men and the women actively avoided intimacy [sex with their mate] (8).

We now know why when a man is caught in an affair, he often tells his wife, "She didn't mean anything to me, so it shouldn't be such a big deal to you." The anorexic tells the truth. She didn't mean anything to him. But his wife doesn't mean anything to him either. He avoids emotional intimacy with both the other woman and his wife.

The same is true for female anorexics who can be either dry flirts or active adulteresses. The Bible preserves the portrait of such a cougar stalking a young man in Proverbs 7:6-23. (I devote two chapters in *God's People Make the Best Lovers* to this adulterous wife and her lover.) A lack of sexual love in the marriage makes the spouse more susceptible to sexual deviations, rather than adultery-proofing the mate.

Harold Figured Out Only 50% of Why His Marriage Failed

As I went through the Song of Solomon, Harold's account of why his marriage failed provided a real-life concise way of comparing what the Shepherd pledges to the Shulammite with what Solomon can't deliver—emotional and sexual love. Harold's intimacy inhibitions were so severe, he couldn't give his wife even 10% of the love and affection the Shepherd promises the Shulammite.

Harold figured out only 50% of why his marriage failed. Not only did he not know how to love a woman emotionally and sexually, he also didn't know how to love a woman intellectually and spiritually. He didn't respect, value, or honor his wife as a woman. God refuses to hear the prayers of such men as Harold:

> *1 Peter 3:7: "You husbands in the same way, live with your wives in an understanding way, as with someone weaker, since she is a woman; and show her honor as a fellow heir of the grace of life, so that your prayers will not be hindered."*

His wife said, "He grew up hearing his father make fun of his mother every day at the dinner table. His dad disguised his ill-feelings toward his mother with humor. Harold and his siblings laughed at their dad's jokes...even his mother laughed." Through deceptive, abusive humor, Harold was programmed to believe women are inferior to men and objects of ridicule.

> *Proverbs 26:18-19:*
> *"Like a madman who throws*
> *Firebrands, arrows and death,*
> *So is the man who deceives his neighbor,*
> *And says, "Was I not joking?"*

Harold neglected to unlearn his upbringing. When he tried to ridicule his wife the same way his dad made fun of his mother, his wife didn't laugh. She insisted he stop making her the brunt of his jokes. He stopped the public putdowns, but he continued to harbor them in his heart. This allowed him to justify withholding sexual and emotional love from her. He got away with this abuse until his wife found evidence of his unfaithfulness and discovered he was not adultery proof after all.

5 Reasons I Now Recommend the Song of Solomon for Desperate and Sexless Marriages

1. It will open your eyes if you're trying to survive a loveless marriage. You'll gain insights into the scriptures for convicting your spouse of the gross sin of being unloving (1 Timothy 3:1-5—ASV).

2. It will increase your love for God as you see his bountiful love for you and his desire for you to love and enjoy passionate sex. As you observe the spiritual side of lovemaking, you'll begin to understand that God doesn't trap anyone in a harmful marriage. Instead, he provides the Song of Solomon as only one of a multiple of tools for correcting the situation.

3. It will help you analyze yourself and your marriage to determine your weaknesses and how you can strengthen your marriage. God has patiently exposed the sin of not being able to love one's mate intellectually, emotionally, sexually, and spiritually in all its depravity and cruelty for over 3000 years through Solomon's warped view of sex.

4. It will make you much more effective in helping others as you won't be so naive when couples complain to you about sexual issues. You'll increase your understanding of the good, the bad, and the ugly of marriages, and especially the powerful teaching of the Song of Solomon.

5. It's past time for God's people to learn what true love is all about. Then we can say with the Apostle Paul, "If I do not have love, I am nothing" (1 Corinthians 13:1-2). And "When I was a child, I used to speak as a child, think as a child, reason as a child; when I became a man, I did away with childish things" (verse 11).

An Exciting Case Study of Success: Stacey's Story: How I Overcame My Sexless Marriage

To help readers who are struggling in an unloving marriage, Stacey (not her real name) gave permission to share her story. She emailed me in 2007 for help with her husband Joe (not his real name) who didn't show interest in having sex with her. I'll let her describe her anguish in the next account of her story. You can follow her struggles in short sections at the end of each of the Song of Solomon chapters.

Her problem was the #1 complaint I get from both husbands and wives—trying to survive a sexless marriage. In some marriages, it's just a matter of ignorance about God's teaching about sex. Those marriages usually turn around quickly when the couple studies God's scriptures such as the Song of Solomon.

Other marriages suffer from more deep-seated problems as Stacey's did. Her husband fought from his heart to keep their marriage from changing. Then when she finally taught him how to fight fair so they could work on the real problems, when he changed, he changed from his heart. Eight years later when I contacted Stacey for an update, she said their love life just keeps getting better.

Unfortunately, not all spouses have a good heart like Joe. Many are intimacy anorexics like Harold. They specialize in manipulating and degrading their mate sexually. Yet some of these marriages can be saved.

I often ask clients to read all of Stacey's Story in one setting for ideas on how to help their marriage.

Secret 2: Insist on Soulmating
Before Lovemaking

Solomon's Siren Song: Solomon Tries to Buy Love

"Never have I endured such…such…such…. Oh! What's the word? These Virgins from Jerusalem! You'd think they'd never been to the country before. If I hadn't told them the black wouldn't wash off, they'd scrubbed me raw!" the Maiden fumes.

"Oh, Mother! What have you gotten me into? I thought life was complicated enough when my brothers got angry with me. The Shepherd and I were going to get married this spring. Now everything's ruined!"

"Helloooo? Are you in therrre?" One of the Virgins softly pats the Shulammite's cheek. "You keep lapsing into daydreams and muttering garbled gibberish. The King will be here soon to eat dinner with you. You need to pick out the jewelry you want to wear."

"But I don't wear jewelry. It snags on the grapevines, especially now when they're just twigs starting to bud."

"Silly girl. When you marry the King, you won't have to worry about silly grapevines. The King is so much fun. He brings in musicians and singers to entertain us. And some of us enjoy playing instruments. That's why he always brings Sarah and Abby on these trips. You'll love listening to them. They'll sing songs the King wrote during dinner. Now pick out the jewelry you want to wear" (1 Kings 4:32; Ecclesiastes 2:8; Isaiah 5:12).

The Maiden picks up a gold rope chain and is surprised when two shorter chains come with it. "Oh! They're hooked together…. But it's still not heavy or gaudy."

"The King always takes lots of jewelry on his trips. Sometimes he brings several new girls home with him. You're the first one he's found this time so you get first pick."

She takes the chains from the Maiden and slips them over her head. "Lovely." The Virgin steps back, tilts her head with her fingers cupping her chin, and slowly looks the Maiden up and down.

"When will you stop staring at me?"

"I'm sorry…. Your dark skin is so unusual…. You need something dramatic. I'll be right back."

The Virgin soon returns with a single strand of white iridescent opals with silver beads strung between them. "These aren't as expensive as the gold chains, but the King imported them from Egypt. Look at how the light frolics on them." She sways the necklace close to the oil lamp and a kaleidoscope sparkles on the tent wall. She slips the necklace over the Maiden's head and positions it over the gold chains between her breasts.

"I've never seen anything like it." The Maiden fondles the jewels. "They are so beautiful and unique."

"Look! I have a surprise for you. Matching earrings and combs for your hair. Now sit down and let me finish getting you ready to dine with the King."

Song of Solomon 1:9-2:7:
The King's Aphrodisiac Backfires

ACT ONE, SCENE TWO
FIRST DAY - EVENING

A tent flap rises to reveal Solomon and the Maiden reclining on upholstered lounges. The Virgins serve dinner on trays. The virgins Sarah and Abby stand behind them softly strumming a small harp and lyre and singing love songs. Solomon sits down a golden goblet and begins courting the Maiden. He takes her hand and gazes into her eyes.

Solomon's First Proposal

During Solomon's three-day courtship, he proposes four times to the Shulammite. All of his proposals show he cares about only one thing—having sex with her. His first proposal is very daring. Without hesitation, he tells her, "You are no ordinary beauty."

Solomon Says, "You Are Like My Mare in Heat"

Song of Solomon 1:9:
"To me, my darling, you are like
My mare among the chariots of Pharaoh."

The first words out of Solomon's mouth leap into the middle of lewdness as he tells the Maiden how strongly he's aroused by her. As a king and owner of many horses and chariots, Solomon knows the power of a mare in heat running among the stallions of Pharaoh. Marcia Falk, a

Hebrew scholar, explains:

> This image is puzzling when one realizes that only stallions, never mares, drew chariots in ancient Egypt. The meaning becomes clear only when we understand the function of mares in ancient warfare; a passage from Egyptian literature suggests that they were set loose in battle by the enemy to allure and distract the chariot-harnessed stallions of the Pharaoh.... To stampede the stallions of the Egyptian chariotry.
>
> Thus, the point of the image is not simply that the beloved is as beautiful as a regal horse, as most translations suggest, but that she is as tempting, as distracting, even as dangerous as the presence of a single mare among many stallions (170).

Solomon's relationship to horses makes this interpretation reasonable. He is not the owner of a single little mare, or even just a few mares. Rather, in 1 Kings 4:26 he required 40,000 horse stalls for his chariots and for his 12,000 horsemen. He acquired chariots and horses on a national scale and built cities to keep them in (1 Kings 9:19). He also imported droves of horses from Egypt (1 Kings 10:29; 2 Chronicles 9:28). The horses of the Bible are almost exclusively warhorses and the property of kings and not of the common people (ISBE "Chariot").

Every time Solomon speaks to the Maiden, he praises her sexual charms. He never sees her as a person with a brain or a personality. She is only the most ravishing body he's ever seen and she drives him wild. Comparing her to a mare in heat and himself to the warhorses pulling the chariots of Pharaoh is fitting. No doubt, Solomon has observed the actions of horses. His choice of simile amplifies the truth of God's description of a sex-crazed nation: "They committed adultery and trooped to the harlot's house. They were well-fed lusty horses, each one neighing after his neighbor's wife" (Jeremiah 5:7-8).

The King's flattery is akin to a sexy babe walking through a singles bar with all the male heads turning to appraise the exquisite creature in their midst. "Hey, Beautiful! You must be a model with all those curves! You're hot!" With whistles and husky descriptions of her body, they jockey for position to buy her drinks while hoping to score before the night is over.

Solomon Promises a Large Dowry

Song of Solomon 1:10:
"Your cheeks are lovely with ornaments,
Your neck with strings of beads."

She's such a captivating creature, Solomon makes sure he praises all of her physical assets. "Ah, I see you're wearing the Egyptian opals, the gems of love. Perfectly lovely on you, my dear. My virgins always know how to adorn someone as ravishing as you." He fully appreciates her mind-boggling charms to set his loins aflame.

Solomon admiring his collection of jewels on the Maiden indicates he's ready to pay her family the customary large dowry. It also lets her know he'll give her a generous personal dowry as was the custom (Wight 127-8).

The dowry presents intense financial pressure for the Maiden to say, "Yes," to Solomon's sensuous proposal of marriage! She fingers the beautiful string of precious stones around her neck. "Say, 'Yes,' my darling, and it's yours plus much more," he assures her.

The Virgins Promise a Large Dowry

Song of Solomon 1:11:
"We will make for you ornaments of gold
With beads of silver."

Right on cue since Solomon already has 140 other wives, the proficient Virgins sweeten Solomon's offer. "If you like the King's costume jewelry, we'll make even more expensive pieces for you. We have a whole vault of gold and silver to make anything you want."

The common vineyard keeper realizes a life of luxury, ease, and splendor awaits her. She'll own so many exquisite baubles she'll have a difficult time choosing what to wear. She'll never worry about dishpan hands or the ironing piling up. She can spend her days primping, reading, or swaying to music. What a life of luxury awaits her!

The King's Aphrodisiac

Song of Solomon 1:12:
"While the king was at his table,
My perfume [spikenard – KJV, ASV] gave forth its fragrance."

This is no ordinary meal with the King. All his drinking vessels are gold since silver is too common for him (1 Kings 10:21). The chef's entrees make modern gourmet food look like a peasant's rations (Proverbs 23:1-3).

In the midst of Solomon's splendor the Maiden inhales the expensive imported spikenard the Virgins messaged into her skin after her bath. The semi-sweet musky fragrance enhances romantic moments, and as a skin tonic it relieves anxiety and insomnia. An expert botanist, Solomon knows well the properties of the various essential oils and fragrances. He's witnessed its power over 140 wives.

But this time Solomon's aphrodisiac misfires. A key characteristic of all aphrodisiacs is that the recipient must be a willing participant. The Maiden's mind flashes back to the familiar smells of her beloved—the Shepherd. We saw in verse 3 how his fragrance comforts her. Now she elaborates on his personal aroma.

The Shepherd Is a Pouch of Myrrh

Song of Solomon 1:13:
"My beloved is to me a pouch of myrrh
Which lies all night between my breasts."

"Breasts" (*shôd*) is a biological term used eight times in Song of Solomon 1:13; 4:5; 7:3, 7, 8; 8:1, 8, 10. It means "the breast of a woman or animal (as bulging):--breast, pap, teat" (Strong 112).

When Solomon told the Maiden she was *like* his mare he used a simile. In talking about her beloved, she uses a metaphor, "My beloved *is* a pouch of myrrh." He is not "like," but the embodiment of a pouch of myrrh lying all night between her breasts.

Some commentators interpret this as a sexual scene because of the word breast. However, as the definition shows "breasts" identifies a body part and illustrates maturity. Instead of sex, the verse refers to a common Israelite practice. They often tied a small sack of flower petals, herbs, or resins around their necks. This provided a pleasant smell during the night to replace the unpleasant odors of their hot sweaty land. Myrrh has a faint agreeable smell conducive to sleep.

Many Bible dictionaries state myrrh is probably the "cistus or 'rock rose' that is exceedingly common all over the mountains of Palestine." Later the Shulammite goes to the mountain of myrrh to think (Song 4:6). It is a species of balsam (Balsamodendron myrrha). The brown resin comes from the bark of small bushes. The gum of various species of cistus is still collected from the beards of goats and the wool of sheep who feed on the shrubs. It is rolled into small black balls which the Maiden could easily place in a pouch to wear around her neck at night. Or she may wear a sachet of dried pink or white flower petals (ISBE and BibleHub "Myrrh").

The Israelites used the aromatic resin and natural gum as a perfume, incense, and medicine. Besides enhancing sleep, wearing a pouch of myrrh repelled sand fleas and mosquitos, nuisances of the night. The scented pouch was a forerunner of our modern diffusers for releasing essential oil vapors into the air for aromatherapy.

The Shepherd probably uses myrrh to protect his sheep from nose flies and himself from the sun. The Maiden shared her longing for the Shepherd when she was taken to Solomon's tent saying, "Your oils have a pleasing fragrance" (Song 1:2). She associates myrrh with the Shepherd's natural fragrance and his loving care of his sheep.

Thus Solomon's use of the calming smell of spikenard to help the Maiden relax and make her more receptive to his passionate words is of no avail. Instead, the strange spikenard stirs up thoughts of a common countryside aphrodisiac and of her beloved. Rather than swooning over the handsome King, she reminisces about the Shepherd. The memory of his scent comforts her during this time of extreme stress and uncertainty.

The Shepherd Is a Cluster of Henna Blossoms

Song of Solomon 1:14:
"My beloved is to me a cluster of henna blossoms
In the vineyards of En-gedi."

The heady spikenard reminds the Maiden of another metaphor: the Shepherd is a cluster of yellow henna blossoms in the vineyards of En-gedi. The popular plant, a native of Palestine, was readily available to the Israelites. They planted flower gardens outside their towns to stroll through in the evenings while they meditated. Then they picked bouquets to carry home. When they passed something putrid, instead of pinching their noses and saying, "Pew!" they smelled the flowers.

Like myrrh, henna provided many benefits to the Israelities. We all know about its use in hair dyes. They also wore the leaves in their clothing as a deodorant to freshen their clothes and bodies. They used it as a hair and body wash. It was reputed to help with many ailments. The Maiden also associates this beneficial scent with the Shepherd.

We see the Shulammite's love of word play and sense of humor when she says her beloved is as a cluster of the country folks' deodorant and shampoo in Solomon's exotic vineyards of En-gedi. This is a classic technique for creating humor—to lead one's audience down a logical path only to end with a surprise out-of-character zinger.

The Maiden spoofs Solomon's kingly presence by daring to elevate the Shepherd to his equal as a suitor. Beginning by speaking of the King's expensive perfume, she describes the Shepherd's country fragrances as a pouch of myrrh between her breasts adorned with the common air-freshener henna. Then she delivers a great punch line by claiming for the Shepherd one of Solomon's pride and joys—En-gedi, the King's Garden for displaying his expertise in botany (1 Kings 4:29-34; Ecclesiastes 2:4-5).

The En-gedi natural oasis of vineyards and gardens was allotted to Solomon's tribe of Judah. It was situated on the western bank of the Dead Sea south of Jerusalem. Four freshwater springs cascading down from the mountains and two freshwater creeks tumbling down from the hills watered it.

Aryeh Naftaly, one of Israel's leading Hebrew/English translators, says in *The Song of Songs, A Messiah's Confession, An Explanation, English Translation and Dramatic Adaptation of the World's Most Ancient Opera* that this created a "paradisiacal habitat for flora and fauna…. Although Jerusalem is about 3,800 feet higher in altitude than Ein Gédi, it is only about 20 miles away as the crow flies" (101).

But Solomon had another interest in En-gedi. Naftaly enlightens us:

> King Sh'lomó, builder of the Holy Temple, was also responsible for instating the Temple services, which included two Incense offerings each day [morning and evening]. Once again, a primary ingredient of the Incense and the first one mentioned in God's recipe was balsam. The King had to have had access to this plant long before the Queen of Sheba showed up. The turn-of-the-millennium Greek historian and geographer Strabo…describes the cultivation of balsam trees in the Jericho Valley area in two gardens: "The Garden of Balsam" and "the King's Garden" (156).

Avraham Sand, a professional aromatherapist and natural perfumer, says in *Mystical Aromatherapy, The Divine Gift of Fragrance:*

> It is possible that at one time this plant [balsam used in the Temple services] grew wild in the Ein Gedi area, and then was brought under cultivation. The balsam trees were only cultivated and the perfume extracted in three regions of the world, all of them within ancient Israel: at Jericho [north of Jerusalem], at Zoar on the southeastern coast of the Dead Sea, and especially at Ein Gedi on the western shore. Ein Gedi became the most famous area for the production of the rare fragrant oil, identified in the Talmud as being the world famous "Balm of Gilead," referred to in Jeremiah 8:22 (54).

No doubt, the Shulammite's brothers who were drafted to labor on Solomon's projects were involved in landscaping and planting trees, herbs, and shrubs in his gardens, parks, and vineyards. En-gedi still displays an ancient system of man-made terraces from the King's botany experiments. Development of the King's Garden would have gone on simultaneously with building the Temple in Jerusalem in preparation for burning incense twice daily. Thus the Maiden would be familiar with the henna plants in En-gedi and could play word games with the location. Solomon may stroll through his beautiful park-like gardens, but her Shepherd makes her head swirl more than any fragrance does.

Her Shepherd cannot give her a rich dowry of either gold

ornaments or the more common silver beads. But he bestows something better on her. He offers her mental safety, pleasure, and comfort. Should she give up the emotional delight she enjoys with him for the security of the King's palace? She can't keep them both. She can choose either true love or sensuous luxury. Such a dilemma!

Although Solomon began the evening with a simile of lusty horses neighing after a mare, the Shulammite uses two metaphors of pleasant smells that protect and give comfort to both her body and mind. They are sniffs of the country people and her beloved. Since the common folks didn't own horses, she probably doesn't know about the mating habits of the king's warhorses. Her naivety prevents her from fully understanding the coarseness of Solomon's first greeting.

Later in the drama, the King gives a watered-down version of a mare in heat when he introduces her to his wives. At that time, her eyes open to the fact that all he cares about is sex. She responds much differently than just remembering how the Shepherd brings such joy to her (Song 6:11-12).

The Shulammite's Beauty

Song of Solomon 1:15:
"How beautiful you are, my darling,
How beautiful you are!
Your eyes are like doves."

"Darling" means "a female associate:--fellow, love" (Strong 109).

"Beautiful" is the same word that Solomon and the Virgins use throughout the story. It refers to outward appearance (Strong 51).

Solomon interrupts the Maiden's thoughts to remind her how beautiful she is. Twice now Solomon calls her "my darling." Before the evening is over, he'll address her as his darling again. Then he'll use my darling three more times over the next two days in his efforts to woo her. He never uses a more personal or endearing name for the Maiden showing his shallow pursuit of her as the perfect feminine body.

While the Shepherd calls her my darling several times, he also uses more intimate terms, as we'll see later. My darling can be compared to a courting fellow calling his date "babe." Babe serves as both a casual name and as an expression of emotional attachment for a steady girlfriend or a wife. The circumstances surrounding the way a man uses babe tells a woman if he is hitting on her or if he genuinely cares for her.

Every girl likes compliments on her attractiveness, and when a man notices her, his praise makes her eager to please him. The Shulammite isn't immune to the King's charm and flattery because he appeals to her femininity. Yet she doesn't linger long on his words.

Memories of the Shepherd

Song of Solomon 1:16-17:
"How handsome you are, my beloved,
And so pleasant!
Indeed, our couch is luxuriant!
The beams of our houses are cedars,
Our rafters, cypresses."

"Handsome" is the masculine form of "beautiful" that Solomon uses twice in the preceding verse.

"Beloved" means "properly to boil, i.e., (figuratively) to love; by implication, a love-token, lover, friend" (Strong 30).

The Maiden politely listens to Solomon's words, and then goes back to dreaming of the Shepherd. She makes a play on Solomon's words by turning his praise of her beauty into remembering her handsome Shepherd. She faces a big decision. She must choose between two completely different kinds of love, lives, and husbands. Before Solomon came to inspect his vineyard, she was sure of her love for the Shepherd. Now the King offers her a luxurious life she never could have imagined.

But she can't get the Shepherd out of her mind. Even in the presence of Solomon's grand offer, she still calls the Shepherd "my beloved" showing her deep emotional intimacy with him. She remembers how handsome and pleasant he is. She feels safe with him.

Every bride dreams about decorating her future home. The Maiden compares the home she and the Shepherd will share with the King's extravagant abode being built in Jerusalem. Since her brothers are forced to work on the King's projects one month out of every three, surely they keep her informed about how much cedar Solomon uses in his buildings:

> 1 Kings 7:1-3: "Now Solomon was building his own house thirteen years, and he finished all his house. He built the house of the forest of Lebanon; its length was 100 cubits and its width 50 cubits and its height 30 cubits, on four rows of cedar pillars with cedar beams on the pillars. It was paneled with cedar above the side chambers which were on the 45 pillars, 15 in each row."

Since Solomon used so much magnificent cedar wood to build his palace, they called it the "House of the Forest of Lebanon." Walking in the paneled halls of the palace was like walking in a forest. When it was finished the Queen of Sheba, astounded at the beauty of it, said, "In fact, the half of it wasn't even told to me!" (1 Kings 10:1-10, 27).

In contrast to Solomon's amazing cedar palace where everything was made of gold (1 Kings 10:21) the Maiden mentally brags to the Shepherd about the canopy of the live evergreens over their outdoor living quarters. And awe...the cypresses will change with the seasons to delight them as they search the bare branches for signs of spring buds.

Thus the Shulammite compares living in a tent in the midst of the wondrous outdoors with the Shepherd to dwelling in the outrageous structure her brothers help build for Solomon. While some authors claim forests didn't grow in the vicinity, note these Biblical facts:

> With regard to Bible evidence, it is clear from very many references in the historical books of the OT that "forest" or "woodland" was very plentiful in those days.... It would certainly appear probable that at the time of the arrival of the Hebrews there were considerable forests of trees—oaks, terebinths, pines, etc.—over a great part of the higher mountains. In Joshua 17:14-18 we have reference to Joshua's twice-repeated command to the people to cut down the "forest," as the inhabited areas were too narrow for them.... But the land then with its millions of olive trees and countless vineyards in the mountains and its great palm groves at Jericho and the coast, not to mention all kinds of imported fruit trees, must have presented a very different appearance from its present comparative barrenness (ISBE "Botany").

Solomon wooed the young vineyard keeper during the early years of his reign when cedar trees were still plentiful. By the time of his death he had ravaged the land with his obsessive building. Dr. David Steward laments the destruction:

> Unfortunately, Solomon's wisdom did not extend to a sense of responsibility to the environment nor an awareness of the irreversible destruction his insatiable desire for cedar timber would have on the Lebanese landscape. Singlehandedly, he practically brought to extinction a hallowed species of one of God's most sacred creations.
>
> The scale of his exploitation was staggering.... The total workforce [slaves and Israelites] came to 183,000 men, working day in and day out for years, methodically stripping the lush forestlands of Lebanon of their centuried treasures, destroying them forever (1 Kings 5:13-15) (136-7).

Dr. Steward says goats were allowed to graze on the deforested land preventing any regrowth. Eventually, the wind and rain eroded away the rich top soil. "What had been a good land of bubbling brooks and copious springs flowing out of the valleys and hills was left to become one of the most desolate and impoverished in all the world."

Wherever grazing the sheep takes them, the Maiden knows their love will transform the outdoors into a glorious showplace in which to live, love, and work. True love converts even the most humble tent into a palace while sensuous love gives a castle the warmth of a drafty shack.

The Shulammite's Self-Image

Song of Solomon 2:1:
"I am the rose of Sharon,
The lily of the valleys."

The Maiden stops in her inner longing for the Shepherd to address the King directly for the first time. Just as she commanded the Virgins to stop staring at her because she accepted her own brand of black beauty, she gives Solomon a similar speech. Earlier she probably kept her eyes down as he sensuously compared her to his mare among the stallions. Now she lifts her head to look him in the eye. She pauses. With a clear voice she dares to demand respect from the King himself. She assures him she doesn't have to accept just any fellow's proposal—even if he's the king. After all, she is the rose of Sharon, the lily of the valleys.

She Is the Rose of Sharon

Modern scholars agree on this verse more than any other in the Song of Solomon. Most say in one way or another, "We don't know what kind of flowers the Shulammite refers to. We know where the Plain of Sharon is—about 30 miles southwest of the Maiden's home in Shunem. We suspect both plants are bulbous." Dr. David Stewart identifies the most likely candidate for the rose of Sharon in *Healing Oils of the Bible:*

A bright red tulip-like flower (*Tulpa montana*) or the sweet fragrant gum-bearing rock rose (*Cistus ladanifer*)—both of which flourished in the Plains of Sharon. The myrrh mentioned in Genesis 37:25 and 45:11 may also have been cistus or rock rose, and not true myrrh (*Commiphora myrrha*). Scholars conclude this because the Midianites carrying "myrrh" in Genesis had passed through the regions of Gilead and Sharon going south toward Egypt, which would have been the wrong direction for myrrh to be transported. Myrrh does not come from north of Jacob's location, but from the south next to Egypt. *Rock rose was a similar gum-bearing plant whose oil may have been confused for myrrh and, perhaps, substituted for it* [emphasis added] (128).

Earlier in the book he said, "Rock rose produced a medicinal resin and oil with *some of the same properties as true myrrh*" (8). In other words, the rose of Sharon may have been a less expensive local knock-off for imported myrrh. Since the Maiden refers to myrrh many times, it's reasonable to think she sometimes uses a local substitute, or at least knows about it. It's like when we buy Walmart's Equate brand.

Dr. Stewart's connection of rock rose or cistus to a type of myrrh is supported by *Dr. Smith's Bible Dictionary, Easton's Bible Dictionary,* and the *International Standard Bible Encyclopedia* (ISBE "Myrrh").

The shepherds pastured their sheep in the drought-resistant rock rose shrubs. They collected the sticky resin and lanceolate evergreen leaves embedded in the sheep's wool with a special comb. After combing the sheep they noticed their sticky hands were healed because the herb is a natural salve. The shepherds both used and sold the rock rose combings to traveling merchants. Rock rose is still a highly valued plant in Mediterranean areas.

Certainly the Shulammite is familiar with the rock rose of Sharon as is her beloved shepherd. Her skillful use of word play, puns, and coined words regarding her black beauty, calling herself the rock rose of Sharon, a knock-off of myrrh, fits her personality. Indeed, substituting the local rock rose of Sharon for imported myrrh as she stands up for herself with Solomon sounds like a pun that appeals to my quirky sense of humor.

Comparing herself to similar herbs reflects a healthy self-image. She doesn't say, "I'm the myrrh of Egypt," a grandiose narcissistic statement. Or in modern terms, "I'm the best you can find in the w…h…o…l…e world…period!" But saying, "I'm the rock rose of Sharon—a high-quality myrrh knock-off" shows humbleness while recognizing her unique talents and character and perhaps her sense of humor.

She Is the Lily of the Valleys

"Lily" comes from a primary root that means "to be bright, i.e., cheerful:--be glad, greatly, joy, make mirth, rejoice" (Strong 114).

The word for lily is used eight times in the Song of Solomon. Three times refer to the Shulammite (Song 2:1, 2; 7:2) and five times refer to the Shepherd (Song 2:16; 4:5; 5:13; 6:2, 3). The Israelites gathered lilies as a medicinal herb, to make an essential oil, and for food. They used every part of the plant including the bulb, flower, stem, root, and juice.

The plant's health benefits for the heart are well known. Since the herb affects the heartbeat, it is considered "UNSAFE when used for self-medication." As the meaning of the primary root for lily suggests, the herb is used in perfumes and for aromatherapy for depression to create a sense of happiness and security (WebMD, Home "Lily").

Having said all this, it doesn't matter exactly what kind of flowers the rose of Sharon or the lily of the valleys are. The Shulammite makes it clear she's no wilting wall-flower. Solomon gets the point.

She Is Like a Lily Among Thorns

Song of Solomon 2:2:
"Like a lily among the thorns,
So is my darling among the maidens."

Solomon answers with similes. The first line compares plants while the second one compares women. He assures the Shulammite, "All the other maidens are like thorns or thistles compared to you. They have no redeeming worth to me. They are weeds to be cast aside."

These words reflect Solomon's negative view of all women. In Song of Solomon 6:8-9, he says he has 140 wives, BUT in comparison to them, the Shulammite is unique — the best of the lot. None of his 140 wives count compared to her. Thus he promises the Maiden the #1 wife position if she'll marry him. Looking ahead to his acquiring 860 more wives, he casts them all off as thorns when he's done with them. He's always on the lookout for the next beautiful lily.

Solomon's statement about all the other maidens being thorns compared to the Shulammite is consistent with him saying he hasn't found one good woman in 1000 (Ecclesiastes 7:29). His view of femininity and love are defective. He is a shallow, empty man.

In contrast to Solomon, the Proverbs writer compares women very differently to the older woman of great price:

Proverbs 31:29:
"Many daughters have done nobly,
But you excel them all."

In other words, "There's lots of good young women, but you're the best because you've faced the many challenges in life." The implication? The good young women will grow over the years; they just haven't arrived to the status of the excellent older wife of great price.

We're starting to get a glimpse of Solomon's narcissism and intimacy anorexia. One of the first classic signs of the mental defect is withholding compliments. As narcissists and anorexics progress in their sins, they complain and criticize their spouse. While they become experts at both obvious and subtle put-downs, they secretly indulge in outrageously disrespectful views of their mate which have no foundation in truth. They are the fantasies of sinful attitudes.

Both male and female narcissists and anorexics turn their negative unrealistic views of their spouse into justification to punish their mate by withholding compliments and sex. Many use their disapproval to rationalize pursuing porn and affairs. Others use their condemnation of the one who loves them to excuse self-masturbation, sexual addictions, and actual affairs. These sundry sexual outlets enable them to engage in sex without the inconvenience of establishing emotional intimacy with their new targets.

Narcissists and anorexics don't have a clue about how to appreciate their mate for their personal qualities. In fact, they don't even recognize much inherent value in their spouse. Consequently, the open and secret attacks on their mate's habits, character, and value grows progressively worse over the years (*Intimacy* 105ff).

The King assures the Maiden he made a wise choice when he had her brought to his tent. She is so beautiful, none of the other Virgins or his wives deserve his attention. He leaves her deep in thought while the daughters of Jerusalem busy themselves. We won't hear from Solomon again until later the next day.

Her self-respect protects the Shulammite from hastily accepting the proposal of any man who desires her—even the King. She can afford to wait for the right husband. And so she tells Solomon to his face, "I'm the rose of Sharon, the lily of the valleys."

Protect Yourself With a Healthy Self-Image

Several young women who nearly fell away from Christ as teenagers only to come back with strength and dedication in their twenties, manifested several similarities. For example, they all came from homes where their mothers and fathers loved each other. They had several brothers and sisters whom they loved. Their parents actively participated in the work of their local congregations as class teachers and serious Bible students. Yet these young women all went through a rebellious stage where they nearly rejected serving God.

I asked these young women, "Did you like yourself during your rebellious years?"

Each replied, "No. I had a very low self-image."

One young woman who came from an exceptionally loving home said, "My parents drummed it into our heads, 'Don't get to thinking too highly of yourself, lest you fall.' My parents constantly emphasized something was wrong with us if we liked ourselves."

The Bible contains balances—it teaches us how to balance our lives without going to one extreme or another. It's easy to go to extremes in the area of self-respect. Many parents refuse to pay their children compliments for fear their children will develop "big heads."

God wants us to look at ourselves realistically as people with both strengths and weaknesses. We must accept our talents before we can use them in service to God. When we think less of ourselves than we really are, we inhibit our ability to serve God with all our heart, soul, and might. After all, God created us in his own image. He wants us to have a balanced view of ourselves—not better or worse than we are—healthy self-images.

One father said his teenage daughter struggled with a low self-image. She was going through a rebellious stage where life at home had gotten so bad that her parents sent her to live with another family. His daughter confided in the lady about wanting to marry a young man who everyone thought would not make a good husband. The lady asked her, "Why do you want to marry him?" This was a legitimate question the Shulammite answers later when the Virgins ask her the same question.

The teenager replied, "Because he proposed to me, and I'm afraid it will be the only proposal I'll ever get. I don't want to end up an old maid." Yet this young woman was the kind of girl everyone thought could have her pick of young men and could say, "I'm the rose of Sharon, the lily of the valleys." Unfortunately, her poor self-image made her vulnerable to the marriage proposal of any boy who came along. She didn't view herself realistically and didn't recognize her qualities that gave her the right to be particular about the man she married.

Another young woman maintained a proper self-image. Even though everyone thought she'd make an excellent wife, she kept turning down marriage proposals. No one understood why until she finally told them, "Serving God is very important to me. And I'm not going to marry anyone who doesn't want to become a gospel preacher."

Many girls who share this same ideal of marrying a preacher don't know what they're wishing for. They see only the love and fruitfulness in a preacher's life. They don't know about the heartaches inherent in working with people who don't share their zeal for serving God. Many preachers and their wives yearn for a normal life with only their own problems to solve without trying to remedy their congregation's as well.

However, this young woman kept turning down proposals. She kept getting older making her family and friends worry about her. When she was twenty-six, the right man proposed and she became a preacher's wife. Throughout this time she thought, "I'm the rose of Sharon, the lily of the valleys. I'm going to be particular about the man I marry."

Tranquility, peace, and serenity surround a woman who respects herself and enjoys her femininity. Although her features may be imperfect, her character and inner happiness give her radiant beauty prettier girls with rebellious hearts can't duplicate with makeup. Such a girl can choose whom she wants to marry; she doesn't need to accept the first proposal she receives.

Men who open doors for some women don't even think of being considerate of others. Boys who would never pet with some girls are determined to go all the way with others. Men generally treat women as the women anticipate being treated. When a woman expects men to treat her as a lady, then generally even the harshest of men do. On the other hand, when she fails to conduct herself with self-respect and dignity, even gentlemen sometimes fail to treat her as a lady.

The Shepherd Is the Best of the Best

After Solomon left, the Shulammite can't stop thinking about the Shepherd. The weight of her decision presses on her as she realizes the choice she makes will affect the rest of her life. She never expected to be in this situation. "If I could just make these chattering girls understand, I wouldn't feel so alone. But all they've known is the King. They keep talking about when he'll bring them into his chambers. They think I'm so lucky," she broods.

She motions for the Virgins to come to her and pats the couch. A couple sit beside her and the others sit on the floor in a semicircle in front. She begins, "Solomon is so different from my Shepherd."

The Shepherd Is Like an Apple Tree

Song of Solomon 2:3a:
"Like an apple tree among the trees of the forest,
So is my beloved among the young men."

The Virgins probably heard Solomon's simile comparing the Maiden first to thorns and then to other maidens. The Shulammite follows the King's form and applies it to the Shepherd. Only she flips his negative into a double-positive comparison. Her simile says her beloved is like something good — the trees of the forest. Indeed, as she speaks, her brothers are in the forest harvesting the cedars.

Her second line continues with a metaphor of praise in comparing the Shepherd to worthy young men. We can easily see this in a parallel passage when she declares, "My beloved is outstanding among ten thousand" (Song 5:10). Her point? "Line up the best of the best and my beloved stands out just like a fruit-bearing apple tree catches your attention in a forest of cedars."

The Shepherd's Fruit Is Sweet to Her Taste

Song of Solomon 2:3b:
"In his shade I took great delight and sat down,
And his fruit was sweet to my taste."

"Great delight" (*châmad*) is a primary root that means "to delight in:--beauty, greatly beloved, covet, delectable thing" (Strong 40).

"Fruit" means "(*per-eê*) fruit (literally or figuratively):--bough (first-)

fruit (-ful), reward" (Strong 96).

"Sweet" means "sweet:--sweet (er, ness)." It comes from a primary root that means "to suck; by implication to relish, or be sweet" (Strong 75). This word is often used for comparison. For example, in both Ezekiel and Revelation a man of God was told to eat God's word and it became "sweet as honey" (Ezekiel 3:3; Revelation 10:10). Proverbs 16:24 says, "Pleasant words are a honeycomb, Sweet to the soul and healing to the bones" (*Theological* 537).

"Taste" means "in the sense of tasting; properly the palate or inside of the mouth; hence, the mouth itself (as the organ of speech, taste and kissing):--(roof of the) mouth, taste" (Strong 39).

These second two lines continue the Shulammite's celebration of the Shepherd as being the best of the best. An apple tree spreads out its branches to provide a shield from the hot sun. In a similar manner, the Shepherd shows genuine concern for her welfare rather than looking out only for himself. He protects her and encourages her in her endeavors. As a result, he gives her such emotional comfort and delight she can relax in his shade and call him "sweet to her taste."

In other words, she trusts him in every realm. She feels emotionally and physically safe with him. She doesn't walk on eggshells worrying about saying or doing something to offend him. She feels comfortable around him in every way.

"Fruit" could be translated "first fruits." The first fruits were the best of the crops. God told the Israelites to give the best to him in their offerings—the best fresh oil, the best of the fresh wine and the best grain. Then he told the priests to use those offerings for their own living (Numbers 18:12-13).

Interestingly, the word for taste involving the roof of the mouth implies more than basic flavors. The taste buds can distinguish only four sensations—sweet, salty, sour, and bitter. The rest of a person's ability to recognize flavors that are more delicate comes through the roof of the mouth and the olfactory bulb (Sand 135-6).

Once again the Shulammite makes a comparison of the best of the best. The Shepherd's sweeter first fruits fill her mouth with sweetness on her tongue while the aroma permeates the roof of her mouth for an indescribable honeyed and fragrant experience. He gives her sweet, nourishing first fruit in the form of strength, pleasure, and genuine affection. All of his ways exhibit kindness and consideration of her.

The Shepherd's Banner Over Her Is Love

Song of Solomon 2:4:
"He has brought me to his banquet hall,

And his banner over me is love."

"Love" is a form of the primary root for love used earlier in Song 1:7 and means "to have affection for (sexually or otherwise)" (Strong 9).

As she dined at the King's table the Maiden enjoyed an elegant feast. Such banquets usually included music, dancers, and merriment. The King follows the pattern of the rich and royalty by decorating the dining room in his tent with banners. These flags and streamers proclaimed political offices and the ensigns of their fathers' houses much like the speaker's stand of the president displays the seal of the United States of America. When Solomon travels, servants carry his banners so everyone will recognize his importance (ISBE "Banner").

As the Maiden gazes at Solomon's banners, she points to them and tells the Virgins, "My beloved's banner over me is love." Too poor for cloth banners, let alone entertainment, the Shepherd serves his humble meal with only an emotional banner of love over her. What a banner! Love turns the Shepherd's simple food into a source of great pleasure.

Proverbs 15:17:
"Better is a dish of vegetables where love is,
Than a fattened ox and hatred with it."

"Love" is the same word used earlier in Song 1:7 and 2:4. It refers to both romantic love and love of family.

Even if a person is too poor to afford meat to go with his garden vegetables, when love reigns, the meal is better than the choicest cut of prime rib without love. Love changes everything. As a result, the Maiden delights in the Shepherd's humble meal more than in the King's elegant one. She basks under her Shepherd's banner of love—the best of the best.

Protect Yourself From Rotten Fruit

Matthew 7:16-20: "You will know them by their fruits. Grapes are not gathered from thorn bushes nor figs from thistles, are they? So every good tree bears good fruit, but the bad tree bears bad fruit.... So then, you will know them by their fruits."

Jesus tells us to make judgments according to the fruit a person bears—judgments based on the way the person acts. That's what the Shulammite did. She examined the way the Shepherd talks to her and treats her. She looked at how he makes her feel—protected and loved. She recognized his great capacity for emotional intimacy with her.

Likewise, Weiss advises in his book *Intimacy Anorexia* to look at how your date or mate treats you. Emotional anorexics are skilled at withholding affection and sex. If you complain, they're masters at manipulating, changing the subject, and blaming you. Weiss says,

"Believe anorexics' behavior—not what they say." In other words, you know if they're truly working the program to become more loving by the way their actions improve, not by what they say (*Intimacy* 161ff).

The Rotten Fruit of Physical Abuse Crosses Gender Lines

Not every courting woman or wife can say like the Shulammite, "My beloved is like an apple tree loaded with sweet fruit." Likewise, not every courting man or husband can say, "My beloved is like the rose of Sharon." Too many dates and spouses are verbally, physically, sexually, or financially abusive—bearers of rotten fruit that needs to be thrown out. Sometimes the abuse is a surprise in marriage. More often, it starts during courtship as the following classic story of growing abuse shows:

> I have been married for eight months. These have been the worst eight months of my life. To look at us, you would bet we are the happiest couple in town. "Ed" and I are attractive, outgoing professionals with excellent incomes. We have a lovely home and two new cars. In public, Ed treats me like a queen.
>
> At home, he is both physically and mentally abusive. I have no one to blame but myself. The abuse started well before we married. If I went into detail about the beatings, you'd think I was making it up. If you met Ed, you would not believe my story. He is totally charming. I can't count the number of women who have told me how lucky I am.
>
> I'm telling my story to warn other women. Men who are abusive will not change after marriage, no matter what they say. It only gets worse. I don't know what is going to happen, but I hope I live to start my live over (Landers 7/13/1988).

Violence in High School

The Centers for Disease Control and Prevention published statistics titled "Youth Risk Behavior Surveillance—United States, 2013." They surveyed 73.9% of students nationwide who dated or went out with someone in the previous 12 months. Of that group "10.3% had been hit, slammed into something, or injured with an object or weapon on purpose by their date."

They presented the percentages for violence against teenagers by their boyfriend or girlfriend according to sex and grade beginning with the 9th grade. The statistics show that both boys and girls perpetuate violence against their dates with boys being slightly more abusive than girls. The percentages also reveal that violence increases year by year with seniors experiencing more violence than 9th graders (CDC 2013).

The CDC's numbers support what abuse shelters say about abuse often starting during courtship. The facts also indicate that the abuse gets worse with each additional school year. But they also demonstrate that many girlfriends physically abuse their boyfriends—teenage abusers cross gender lines.

Violence in College

The numbers regarding young people abusing each other continue to get worse in college. Jordan Lite in his *New York Daily News* article, "Gals Gone Whack-y. Many Abuse Males: Survey," quoted two surveys that give startling results. The first survey of 13,600 college students revealed that girls were the sole perpetrator 21% of the time compared to the boys being the sole attacker 10% of the time. In the second survey of 12,000 university students 41% of the women had been hit compared to 31% of the men being hit (5/24/2006).

Violence in Marriage

Dr. Edward Rhymes in "Woman as Aggressor: The Unspoken Truth of Domestic Violence" balances his article with statistics of how in most global instances women are the victim of various forms of abuse such as trafficking for sexual exploitation, sexual assaults, and rape. However, in the United States boys make up about half of the victims of commercial sexual exploitation. (See his article online for in-depth information.)

He says that in the United States every 15 seconds a woman is a victim of domestic violence. That compares to every 38.7 seconds when the man is the victim (9/19/2014). The main difference between male and female abuse is that men usually have more brute strength to inflict damage to a woman than she can to him without a weapon.

A boyfriend who slaps and pushes during courtship will punch and choke in marriage. As the marriage continues, he will break bones and send the woman to the hospital. He will call her such filthy names her children will not respect her, and she will lose control over them.

Professor in the Women's Studies Program at the University of Hawaii, Meda Chesney-Lind, addresses the issue of girls as violent perpetrators in "Are Girls Closing the Gender Gap in Violence?" for *Criminal Justice Magazine.* She says it used to be rare for girls to be in the juvenile justice system. However, "the number of girls arrested has dramatically outstripped that of boys for most of the last decade." The majority of the arrests of girls are for violent offenses (2001).

Certainly, it's as important for us to talk with our sons about the importance of avoiding abusive relationships as it is with our daughters. Our children need to know what kind of behavior should raise red flags and be encouraged to trust their gut instincts. In this way, we can help our children escape disastrous marriages and relationships.

The Cycle of Violence

In all abusive relationships, a cycle of violence always exists whether the abuser is female or male or is a teenager or an adult. This cycle consists of a period where tension builds. The tension may not have anything to do with the targeted person. It can build because of the abuser's frustrations at school or work. The tension continues to build until the second stage happens—an acute episode of some type of abuse—verbal, physical, and/or sexual abuse.

After the abusive episode, the third stage is loving respite where the abuser is so sorry for what he or she did. The abuser promises never to do it again and may shower the target with affection and gifts. The abuser is so affectionate during this stage that the target may even think the abuse is worth it just to have all the attention.

The loving consideration lasts for a while, then the tension begins to build as the cycle repeats itself. As the cycles continue, the time between acute episodes grows shorter. At the same time, the abuse becomes more severe and may even result in the target's death. Sweetheart murders aren't unusual for dating couples. At the same time, the loving respite stage will grow shorter and may even disappear.

Every young woman should look to the Shulammite for guidance as she tells herself, "I'm the rose of Sharon, the lily of the valleys. I don't deserve to be treated this way, and I won't be treated this way!" Likewise, she should determine if her boyfriend bears sweet apples or if he tries to feed her putrid spoiled fruit. If he isn't an apple tree, then it'll be impossible for her to enjoy a loving relationship with him although she may try very hard to make it one.

Before marriage, a woman should see true concern and care for her welfare. If these qualities are lacking in courtship, they'll be missing after marriage as well. Then it will be harder to deal with them.

When his friends asked about the scratches on his face, one young man said, "My girlfriend jumped on my back and clawed me." When he broke off the relationship, his ex-girlfriend frequently ran a key down the side of his car when he was at work. Boys need to search for the same caring and consideration in their dates that girls do.

The Rotten Fruit of Verbal Abuse Crosses Gender Lines

Three of the first instances of spouse abuse I worked with nearly half a century ago involved husband abuse. Women can easily excel in spewing out sarcasm or screaming verbal abuse. Many a female abuser uses sexual putdowns so vicious her husband loses his ability to perform. Or perhaps she withholds her favors until he does what she wants.

But as we saw in the CDC's statistics, some women also resort to violence. One wife chased her husband down the stairs with a skillet of hot gravy. She regularly threw glasses at him.

I attended a class in East Texas to be tested for a professional license to become certified as a process server. The legal instructions were interspersed with stories about protecting our safety. One veteran of the business said, "I barely made it back inside my car after the guy sicced his dogs on me. They were so mean—they bit and tore at my tires."

As I listened to these stories about the dangerous hill country, I soon realized this wasn't the safest job in the big city of Amarillo either. But I stayed the course and passed the exam with one mistake making a better grade than many of the long-time officers of the court.

We started the morning session with introductions where I said I wrote books on marriage and the Bible. During a break, one of the men who had spoken frequently about his narrow escapes approached me. He wore the traditional working garb of the group—jeans and vest accented with cowboy boots and hat. He said, "I was married for a while, but my wife had the most evil mouth. She totally tore me down."

He turned his head away for a couple of seconds, then looked me in the eye, "I will never marry again. I prefer my horses and dogs to the company of a Christian woman."

Boys and men need to determine if their date is like the Maiden, a rose of Sharon, able to love them with emotional intimacy. If not—they better run like someone sicced their dogs on them—more than their tires will get bitten. Some women's shelters now work with abused husbands.

The Shulammite Is Lovesick

Song of Solomon 2:5:
"Sustain me with raisin cakes,
Refresh me with apples,
Because I am lovesick."

"Love" is a form of the primary root for love used earlier in Song 1:7 for "you whom my soul loves" and for the Shepherd's "banner of love" over the Maiden in Song 2:4. It means "to have affection for (sexually or otherwise)" (Strong 9).

"Sick" means "properly to be rubbed or worn; hence (figuratively) to be weak, sick, afflicted; or (causatively) to grieve, make sick" (Strong 39).

Talking about the Shepherd makes the Maiden lovesick. One of the

Virgins quickly offers her a platter of rich pastries. She spurns them and pleads, "Sustain me with raisin cakes, refresh me with apples." Gary Martin has fun with this verse in his book *The Song of Songs*:

> Lovesick is a psychosomatic condition hindering the eyes from focusing properly, causing the heart to beat faster or irregularly, and otherwise characterized by a general state of disorientation coupled with a weakening of intellectual capacity, especially in regard to coherent speech and sound reasoning. The disease is regarded to be as old as man himself, affecting people of all races, creeds and cultures, and is one of the few health disorders upon which modern medical science has had little or no influence (69).

Lovers have always associated sweets with being lovesick. Since the vineyard keeper is emotionally involved with the Shepherd, she can hardly bear the thought of leaving him—even for the King. She begs the Virgins to bring her some dried grapes and apples to sustain her with natural sugars... and it won't hurt if the grapes have fermented a little.

She Looks Forward to Marriage

Song of Solomon 2:6:
"Let his left hand be under my head
And his right hand embrace me."

The Shulammite shares her most private longings with the Virgins. Women of her era were more comfortable with their sexuality than are women of our time. The Maiden's transparent speech shows the healthy attitudes the Israelite women had toward sex.

Due to her emotional attachment to the Shepherd, she eagerly anticipates sexual love with him in marriage. Her sexuality is maturing properly. Ironically, although the King started this dinner with a very sensuous proposal of sex with her, the Maiden ends it desiring her Shepherd—the one she is emotionally involved with—her apple tree.

If a young woman doesn't look forward to lovemaking in marriage, something is wrong. Either she fails to make a proper emotional bond with her fiancé or she clings to some unhealthy attitudes toward sexual love. God created a woman's sexuality so that, ideally, it should be awakened in courtship before marriage.

During her girl talk with the Virgins, the Shulammite's body aches for her Shepherd. They had planned a spring wedding. Now everything has changed because of Solomon. What a dilemma! Can she enjoy real love with the King? She pleads with the Virgins not to force Solomon on her before they learn to love each other.

Secret 2: Insist on Soulmating Before Lovemaking

Song of Solomon 2:7:
"I adjure you, O daughters of Jerusalem,
By the gazelles [male] or by the hinds [female] of the field,
That you will not arouse or awaken my love,
Until she [it — NASB footnote] pleases."

"Arouse" and "awaken" come from the same root word which means "(through the idea of opening the eyes), to wake (literally or figuratively" (Strong 86).

"Love" is the same word used for the Shepherd's banner of love. It means "to have affection for (sexually or otherwise)" (Strong 9).

"Pleases" means "to incline to; to bend; to be pleased with, desire:-any at all, (have, take) delight, favour, like, move, be (well) pleased, have pleasure, will, would" (Strong 42).

Gary Martin explains the Shulammite's play on words by using two similar ones of different intensities. "Arouse" carries the idea of waking from sleep either mentally or physically. "Awaken" also indicates to "stir up," but is probably more intense than the first word. He cites examples of "stirring up the dead in Sheol (Is. 14:9), to raise up a mourning (Job 3:8), stir up strength (Ps. 80:2), a cry of distress (Is. 15:5)." He concludes:

> Both words carry the idea of "arouse" in the sense of inciting to (some kind of) action. Thus, to "arouse" or "stir up" love would mean to incite it to action, to "wake it up" from its sleeping, resting state and set it into motion (72-3).

The expression "by the gazelles or by the hinds of the field" refers to the male and female deer or antelope and exemplifies intelligent mating. While Solomon compares himself to a lusty horse chasing after a mare in heat, the Shulammite uses gentle animals to teach the Virgins about love — the gazelles and hinds of the field.

Most animals instinctively understand enough about mating and love not to force themselves on each other. They go through a courting period of getting acquainted before they breed. Males perform elaborate rituals of showing off their beautiful colors, dancing, fighting, or snuggling to impress the chosen female. Sex takes place only after the male sufficiently arouses the female's emotions to accept him.

As a country girl, the Shulammite understands the way of animals and the importance of courtship for "waking up" and then "stirring up" a woman's affections. She begs the Virgins, "By the example of nature, don't force me to marry the King before love has a chance to develop between us." She continues, "I know what it's like to be emotionally intimate with a man for I love the Shepherd. I don't want to settle for a loveless marriage — even if the man is King Solomon."

The Shulammite repeats this plea each day of her 3-day whirlwind romance with Solomon. These verses comprise the theme or overriding secret of the Song of Solomon. Where and how did she learn this important lesson about love and marriage? As a country girl, she's observed the courting rituals of the male and female antelope. Nonetheless, how did she come to such a logical conclusion about love at such a tender age from just watching the animals?

Later she says her mother "used to instruct me." Her mother talked to her about boys and sex and love and marriage. Because she listened and observed, she has more insight about sex than many of her peers.

This secret of the Song of Solomon is that a couple should take time to intimately soulmate before making love. Love must be allowed to develop naturally of its own accord. It's better to never marry than to marry someone you don't love and risk not being able to learn to love the mate later. The Shulammite believes we ought to use as much common sense as the gazelles and the hinds by building an emotional bond before marriage if we want to succeed at loving and being loved.

She wonders aloud, "Will you, Virgins, ever understand? Will you help me find true love instead of pushing me toward a quick marriage to the King?" She takes a raisin cake and an apple and stands up, "I'm ready for bed." Sighing, she slowly takes a bite.

Study Exercise

Answer all questions in your own words.
1. What were the important parts of Solomon's first proposal?
2. What should a girl do when a boy makes a sensuous proposal to her?
3. How did the Shulammite know she could be particular about who she married?
4. How did Solomon react to the Shulammite's view of herself?
5. What does it mean for a man to be like an apple tree to a woman?
6. How can parents protect their children from getting involved with abusive boyfriends and girlfriends?
7. Why was the Shulammite lovesick? What did she want to do?
8. How does the secret or theme of the Song of Solomon apply to you?
9. Do you disagree with anything in the lesson? If so, explain giving scriptures for your reasons.

Research Exercise

Young men and women make unwise dating and marriage choices because of poor self-images. They often stay in bad relationships because they believe the putdowns and think they need to earn the other person's love. The Shulammite gives two opinions of herself:

"I am black but lovely" (Song 1:5).
"I am the rose of Sharon, the lily of the valleys" (Song 2:1).

Write a one to two page report on these two verses answering these questions:

1. What kind of self-image did the Shulammite have? Explain.
2. How can men and women apply these verses to themselves?
3. How can you incorporate these attitudes into your life?
4. How can you help your children develop a good self-image?

Personal Exercise

I give this assignment to my clients to help them discover hidden talents. Analyzing compliments is especially helpful if you've ever lived with abuse and are masking your true personality. To get started, write down six compliments—three you believe and three you don't believe. The three you don't believe must come from non-relatives and not your boyfriend or girlfriend or spouse.

The reason for choosing compliments from non-family members is because one cause of loss of self-esteem comes from manipulation by others. Manipulators don't always attack our weak points. They often criticize our assets. If we're pretty, they slyly make supposedly innocent comments. For example, while looking at family albums, they point to an unflattering picture and say, "You really favor your grandmother in this picture." They're brilliant at underhanded putdowns.

Eventually, we start questioning our strengths. As we become vulnerable, we begin to lose our identity. Although friends, people at work, and acquaintances can manipulate us, the most skillful at this are usually our own family members—parents, siblings, spouses, children, parents-in-law, and people we're dating.

After you write down the compliments start doing some soul searching about why you don't believe the accolades. If you can't work your way through this yourself, ask the people who praised you why they said that about you. Tell them you're trying to develop your hidden talents which you are. Keep searching to discover missing pieces of yourself to bless your life. Now answer these questions:

1. List three compliments you believe.
2. List three compliments you don't believe from non-relatives.
3. Why do you not believe these three compliments? Be specific. What negative things do you believe about yourself that keep you from accepting these compliments?

4. List people who can help you make an honest evaluation of the compliments you don't believe?
5. What are some things you can do to enhance these qualities in you? Perhaps you can take some classes, join a club, or seek friends who have mastered these same areas.
6. Analyze what you've learned from this project. Be prepared to discuss your conclusion in class.

Stacey's Story:
"Help! We Fight About Our Sexless Marriage!"

Dear Patsy Rae,

My husband, Joe, and I have been married for eighteen years. We have five beautiful children. By all accounts, everyone considers him a nice guy. He is a hard worker, a good provider, a family man, spends time with the children, prefers to be at home with us in his free time, etc.

I am a Christian. My husband is a professing Christian. He has taken us to church through the years but has never shown an interest in personal Bible study and prayer. I love my husband deeply and have many reasons to respect him. We are a family that does everything together, from meals to recreation, working to relaxing.... But our intimate relationship has been an ongoing struggle, particularly for me.

First, let me say, when we are together, we love it, probably more so now than when we were younger. My struggle is that our love life has always been sporadic. I realize now that I was a young, naive child in the early years of our marriage. Our first child came along a little more than a year after we were married. Time would go by and Joe showed no interest in sexual relations with me. But after the baby came, months would pass with no interest on Joe's part. When I brought it up, he always had an excuse or something.

More often than not, I am the initiator in relations, not always, but most of the time. Through the years, our marriage has had some very volatile times. I've learned many areas where the Lord has had to work on me to make me a godly wife. And of course, it is an ongoing work. :) But I have always been here for my husband and loved him deeply.

I never could figure out why Joe wasn't interested in me sexually. I've kept myself in good shape even after five babies. I'm not tooting my own horn, but I knew in my heart my husband could do a lot worse, and that many men would probably be pleased to have me for a wife.

I've struggled with insecurity, etc. because of Joe's lack of interest. Don't get me wrong, I've always gotten a good-bye kiss in the morning, the hello embrace when he came home from work, the goodnight kiss, etc. We even take walks and hold hands.

I have always shown an interest in Joe and made myself available to him. I flirt with him and show that I enjoy being with him. But many, many times to no avail.

I realize now that I was a naive child in the early, if not most of the years, of our marriage. In the past three or four years, my frustration and anger grew to a point where I had to grow up. I started looking for answers as to why this has been a regular pattern in our marriage.

We will be intimate for a few days, maybe several weeks in a row, and then it wanes off and Joe shows no interest. I express my frustration to him but to no avail.

Anyway, I remembered reading a book in the first years of our marriage that if a husband doesn't show interest, and another woman is not in the picture, the husband probably masturbates. I didn't think much of it then but I think it has always been in the back of my head all these years. Let me clarify, I have never had any reason to suspect Joe has or is committing actual adultery with a real woman. He spends all his time with the children and I. We always know where the other is. He comes right home at night, his work schedule and setting are not conducive to cheating, etc., etc.

But after doing research and growing up as to how a man is affected by the sight of a woman, and seeing the culture we live in, I started to see the whole picture. I expressed my frustration at commercials that would come on with scantily clad women. I asked him how he thought it made me feel as his wife to sit there in our own living room having these women right in front of my husband.

I started talking about my concern with things on TV that showed skin. Of course, I'm not talking about hardcore bad shows. At first, he said I was being prudish. But he eventually started changing the channel when the skin appeared. Our, and his, more particularly, television viewing became less and less. This would be great; but in my heart, I wish I could believe Joe would, or does change the channel when I'm not in the room, or not at home.

One night, I went to bed before Joe. I had suspicions and listened intently to hear what he was watching on TV. He had the volume low, but it seemed like he was changing channels regularly, going to the same channels, up then down. Eventually, he went to the bathroom.

I quietly went into the room and checked the remote. When I went up a few channels, sure enough, there was a naked woman on a video channel. When he came back, I confronted him on it. I was so upset I was shaking. Of course, he denied it profusely. I slept on the couch for several nights, crying myself to sleep.

The next day, roses appeared. Joe has always been generous with gifts on birthdays and anniversaries, but this was new. It was the nicest flower bouquet I had ever seen.

I cancelled our cable television and then called my husband at work to inform him of this. It met with no resistance. Another unusual thing. Normally, doing something without his consent wouldn't have gone over so easy. I felt his guilty conscience was weighing on him. 'Til this day, he has never admitted viewing that porn program, but his actions afterwards convinced me he had been.

Soon afterward Joe came to me one night when I was on the couch and said he missed me and wanted me back in our bed. The next time we were intimate, I cried and expressed my concern over whether or not it was me he was really seeing when we were together. He assured me he was, but I had grown up by this time.

We stayed in status quo for a while. Then in the heat of an argument, I confronted Joe with my suspicion that he was masturbating regularly. He has always taken very long showers every work morning. He gets up well in advance of leaving for work. He has always said he relaxes in there. I realized my husband always seemed to be more interested in intimacy in the mornings than in the evenings. I suspected the long showers were where he had been cheating on me all these years. When I brought it up, he denied it vehemently, almost violently. But then I noticed during the following week he was taking ten-minute showers, if that. Of course, the same old patterns fell in place and the long showers returned.

When we've had disagreements and I confronted him with this issue, he turned it around and said I have a dirty mind. I told him I suspected the "gentleman doth protest too much." He now just brushes me off when I bring it up.

I should clarify, I have no reason to suspect Joe of being into pornography. He does not use our home computer and his work situation absolutely prohibits it. They have filters, etc. that even prevent emails with any word even closely associated with sex from ever coming through. Employee computers are monitored and he would never risk his job. I know he is a good worker. We watch minimal TV at home.

Yet I am not so naive anymore. I realize pornography is everywhere you go in our society. The grocery store checkout counters hit you right in the face with it. And guess who makes the frequent runs to the store for milk or bread? Joe. I know everywhere a man goes in our culture he is confronted with skin. So I do know the temptations are all around and I realize that if a pattern or habit has taken hold since probably before we were even married, it's most likely still a pattern in Joe's life. But this sin habit is cheating us out of a glorious marriage.

I have always deeply desired that Joe would just be honest with me about this. He does not know what it is doing to me or to our marriage relationship. I know it's not a subject he even wants to discuss.

This month the same old pattern has taken hold. It has been weeks since we've been intimate. A week ago, I was flirting with Joe one evening but to no avail. When we got in bed, I confronted him and asked him how I was supposed to believe a normal, red-blooded American man wasn't interested in sexual relations. He brushed me off, and I cried myself to sleep. Avoidance is his answer. Ignore it and it will go away.

My urgent question is, "What do I do?" I know I can't be his conscience. Frankly, I'm tired of keeping track of what he watches on the TV. I see what confronts his eyes at the checkout counters and I'm angry and bitter inside over it. I want to deal with this openly and frankly.

I can't prove anything if he's in the shower away from prying eyes. I've even imagined getting some kind of hidden device to record him in the act so I could confront him with the evidence. But I don't know how to approach this whole issue in a Christ-like manner. I am of course concerned for my husband and his soul. I also want honesty and believe I have been cheated on. It hurts as much as if the woman were real. It's almost harder, because any woman of his imagination is perfect.

I also feel that Joe has cheated himself even more. He has a real woman who loves and respects him and has stayed by him all these years. I feel like this issue has to be dealt with once and for all so we can go on and have the glorious marriage everyone thinks we already have. I want to honor God and my husband. What do I do? Where do I start? What do I say?

I don't know of a strong church where we can get help. I have been faithful to Joe in that I have not discussed this with others. I want to deal with this uprightly. Please, could you give me some direction, a starting point, anything? I don't want this to be a pattern for another eighteen years of our marriage. This is *the sore spot* in our marriage.

Honestly, to the outside world, I should be the happiest woman in the world. The life the Lord has given me with Joe is much to be thankful for. But I know this area of intimacy is crucial and the Lord wants better for us, too. What do I do on my part? How do I show Joe I'm serious about this? How do I make him see we cannot, I cannot, continue on like this? Please, I need some good counsel.

Thank you so much for your time. I eagerly look forward to hearing from you.

By His Grace,
Stacey

Secret 3: Practice Your Sensuous-Love Mirror Lines

Solomon's Siren Song: Urgent Change of Plans

"Sarah, tell me how it's going with the Shulammite. Is she about ready to agree to the marriage?"

"No, my Lord. She keeps talking about some shepherd she says she's in love with. She's also convinced he loves her. They were planning on getting married this spring. But she has to take care of the family's vineyards because her brothers are obligated to work in your forests. She's very lovesick. Her brothers insisted she put the wedding on hold until after grape harvest."

"Didn't she like the jewelry you gave her to wear? They always love the jewelry."

"Yes, my Lord. But she won't quit talking about her shepherd. She's lovesick."

"You mean some little snot-nosed shepherd is standing in my way of marrying the Shulammite?"

"Yes. I'm sorry, my Lord."

"What can that shepherd offer her that I haven't already given her?"

"My Lord, can I speak freely? I don't want to upset you."

"Yes, Sarah!" The King holds his head. "Why do you think we're having this conversation? I've never had so much trouble with a virgin before! Out with it, woman!"

"I'm sorry, my Lord..."

"Sarah! Stop being sorry! Spit it out!"

"Okay.... She told us twice she doesn't want us to force her to marry you before she learns to love you and before you love her in return. She keeps mumbling about the gazelles and the hinds of the field. According to her, the shepherd is her childhood sweetheart."

The King paces back and forth. Then he speaks. "If she weren't so beautiful I'd just forget about her. But I can't.... Ever since my mother brought Abishag to keep my father warm, and then my brother tried to take the throne away from me by asking to marry her...I've dreamed of a more beautiful Shulammite of my very own."

"I understand, my Lord. Her skin is so unusual and beautiful. I doubt there's another maiden around like her."

"My plans are to camp here another week and go out during the day to inspect some vineyards a little further north. That's why I brought my sporty new chariot.... I can't wait to take that baby for a spin and see how it handles. It's perfect for the day trips." The King resumes pacing.

"I'll leave right after breakfast for the next vineyard. I'll cut the trip short—we'll head for home in three days. I'll take half the soldiers with me and leave the other half with you and the Virgins."

"My Lord, may I suggest something?"

"Sarah, you're annoying me. Get on with it!"

"Why don't you head back to Jerusalem as soon as possible? Get her away from her shepherd. When she sees the palace...she'll forget him."

Song of Solomon 2:8-4:7: Solomon Proposes Sensuous Love

ACT ONE, SCENE THREE
FIRST DAY - EVENING

The tent flap opens on the Shulammite's bedroom. The Virgins busy themselves getting her bed ready. The Maiden sits on a stool slowly eating a raisin cake. She appears melancholy and unresponsive to the Virgins trying to help her undress for bed. She motions for the Virgins to stop what they're doing and to come sit at her feet.

The Shepherd's First Proposal

After begging the Virgins not to force the King on her, the Shulammite knows they don't understand. *I don't intend to pass up true love on their account. Maybe if I tell them about the love the Shepherd and I share, they'll be more sympathetic. They've lived in the palace all these years waiting for Solomon to select them. They don't have a clue about what true love feels like to a woman.*

He Is Like a Gazelle or a Young Stag

Song of Solomon 2:8-9:
"Listen, my beloved!
Behold, he is coming,
Climbing on the mountains,
Leaping on the hills!
My beloved is like a gazelle or a young stag.

Behold, he is standing behind our wall,
He is looking through the windows,
He is peering through the lattice."

"Gazelle" means "in the sense of prominence; splendor (as conspicuous), also a gazelle (as beautiful)" (Strong 98).

"Stag" means "strength, hence anything strong, specifically a chief (politically), also a ram (from his strength), a pilaster (as a strong support), an oak or other strong tree:--mighty (man), lintel, oak, post, ram, tree" (Strong 11).

No doubt, the news of Solomon taking the young Shulammite to his camp has spread over the countryside. The peasants wonder what will happen. They haven't been so excited since soldiers came many years ago and took the virgin, Abishag, to Jerusalem to nurse his father David (1 Kings 1:1-4). And now they've taken another beautiful virgin to Solomon's camp.

"Certainly," the Shulammite thinks, "My Shepherd has heard by now that Solomon brought me to his tent. He must know my dilemma." She subconsciously listens for his voice as he comes like a gazelle or a stag climbing and leaping over the hills. He's her gentle "gazelle," the male antelope, and the "young stag," the male mountain goat.

Both of these animals lead and protect their females. Nothing sissy or questionable characterizes her beloved, for he is a man's man—a man whom a woman can trust and rely on. And so the Maiden continues to use gentle, loving animals to describe him. She never refers to her beloved as a lusty horse neighing after females in heat.

Then as if she catches a glimpse of him looking for her, she declares to the Virgins, "Behold, my beloved is standing behind our wall, he is looking through the windows, he is peering through the lattice." Their heads whip around to where she points. They see nothing. She continues, "He will come.... I know he will come to await my decision. I can choose either the Shepherd or King Solomon."

She motions for the Virgins to sit at her feet again. As they take their places, she puts the raisin cake down. She scans their faces to look each of the Virgins in the eye before continuing.

He Wants to Get Married in the Spring

Song of Solomon 2:10-13:
"My beloved responded and said to me,
'Arise, my darling, my beautiful one,
And come along.
For behold, the winter is past,
The rain is over and gone.

The flowers have already appeared in the land;
The time has arrived for pruning the vines,
And the voice of the turtledove has been heard in our land.
The fig tree has ripened its figs,
And the vines in blossom have given forth their fragrance.
Arise, my darling, my beautiful one,
And come along!'"

"Fragrance" is the same word we saw in Song 1:3 and 12.

"Darling" is the same word Solomon uses and is similar to calling a woman "babe." The context shows the depth of feeling.

"Beautiful" is the same word the Virgins and Solomon use. It refers to outward beauty.

The Shulammite recounts the last time she saw the Shepherd—her beloved. A stanza of seven lines tells us it's spring—May. The rainy winter season of Palestine has ended. Wild flowers dot the landscape and it's time for pruning the grapevines. Birds sing as the fragrances of spring fill the air. The fig trees have ripened their spring crop of old-wood green figs (May in Israel), with a second crop due in the fall on the new growth (August and September).

The spring is both a practical and common time for Israelite weddings. Couples either marry in the spring—before beginning the hard work of planting and caring for their crops, or in the fall—after the harvest. Rather than a lengthy romance where the girl carries a crush on a boy who doesn't know she exists, the Shepherd asked the Maiden to marry him immediately and end their wait.

The Shepherd mentioned figs, a health-building aphrodisiac. Since the time of Adam and Eve, figs have provided potassium and antioxidants for healthy sexuality. And we remember how Adam and Eve tried to be modest by using fig leaves to cover their bodies after they ate from the tree of knowledge of good and evil (Jung n.d.).

The Shepherd frequently refers to aphrodisiacs. It's spring time and his thoughts naturally turn to marriage and lovemaking. Enjoying a vibrant sexual relationship with the Shulammite is important to him. He appeals to the foods and smells of love because he doesn't plan to leave their love life up to chance. He'll do everything possible to keep it robust including taking care of their health.

The Shepherd asked the Maiden to work alongside him pruning the vines and enjoying the great outdoors, for successful shepherds both care for their sheep and plant and harvest crops. They feed their sheep and themselves with the grain during the winter (Henderson and Gould 6-7). Working together as loving companions, the Shepherd and the Maiden planned to reap the fruitful blessings of hard work.

He Begs Her to Become His Source of Comfort

Song of Solomon 2:14:
"O my dove, in the clefts of the rock,
In the secret place of the steep pathway,
Let me see your form,
Let me hear your voice;
For your voice is sweet,
And your form is lovely."

"Lovely" is the same word the Shulammite uses to describe her black beauty to the Virgins and means "beautiful."

The Virgins listen as the Maiden reminisces about the Shepherd's proposal, pleading with her to end their separation and come down from her inaccessible places in the clefts of the rock and the secret places in the steep pathway. He begged, "O my dove," — my peace and my comfort, "Please, let's get married now."

This verse provides another play on words that English translations fail to capture. Marcia Falk explains how the last four lines of the poem ring with a musical quality:

For example, the repetition of Hebrew vowel patterns in the closing four lines of this poem (*har'ini 'et-mar'ayikh | hašmi'ini 'et-qolekh | ki-qolekh 'arev | umar'ekn na'weh*) adds to the effect created by the chiastic parallelism.... This assonance could not be easily preserved in translation (177-8).

The Maiden puts a sparkle in the Shepherd's life and he wants to see her and be near her every day. Her sweet voice soothes him. Her lovely form pleases him. Her soft, tender, loving nature makes him want to rush home from work to her — his dove — his haven of peace — his refuge from the world — his sanctuary for renewing his strength.

The Shulammite's Answer

The Shepherd brings out and enhances the Maiden's femininity. And she enjoys his masculinity. She displays important and healthy attitudes for a successful marriage. But to the Shepherd's passionate proposal of a spring wedding, the Maiden tells him, "We must wait."

Her Brothers Forbid Her to Marry in the Spring

Song of Solomon 2:15:
"Catch the foxes for us [plural male],
The little foxes that are ruining the vineyards,
While our [plural male] vineyards are in blossom."

For the most part, Hebrew scholars say "us" and "our" refer to a plurality of male voices determined to keep the young couple apart. They also agree the Shulammite is speaking and relates this problem to her beloved. However, they disagree on who the men are, mainly because they take the position Solomon and the Shepherd are the same man. The majority of authors claim the men are the Jerusalem guards whom we meet through the Maiden's two dreams which haven't occurred yet. At the time of this flashback, Solomon has not taken the Maiden to his tent. Neither the King nor his guards have anything to do with the Shulammite postponing her wedding.

She explained when she met the Virgins, "My brothers were angry with me. They made me work in the vineyards! That's why my skin is black from the sun." (Song 1:6) Her brothers insisted she take care of the family's physical vineyards—the same vineyards the little foxes are wreaking havoc in.

The historical setting of the story implies Solomon drafted her brothers to work in the cedar forests with the other young Israelite men. Their rotation cycle of one month in the forests, with two months at home, then another month in the forest, fits the time frame of the Shulammite's dilemma. Although the account covers 3 whirlwind days in the spring, it concludes 4 months later after the grape harvest (Song 8:11-12). This allows for her brothers chopping down cedar trees for 2 months during the critical 4-month grape growing and harvesting seasons.

The male voices in this verse echo the brothers' anger. It's spring and the grapevines are just starting to blossom. The tiny, green flowers are easy to overlook. The blossoms are "perfect flowers," meaning each flower has both male parts (stamens) and female parts (pistils and ovaries). Although they don't require bees to pollinate them, they are fragile. Wind, rain, and animals can upset their fertilization process (Ciolino 12/15/2011).

The baby foxes are coming out of their dens to leap and play among the vines. As they run up and down the rows, they're jostling the tiny green blossoms. The foxes will grow into a greater menace by eating the maturing grapes. The brothers insist she postpone her spring wedding to protect the vineyards—their livelihood.

The brothers have no choice about working on Solomon's building projects. Their anger flares when she argues, "My wedding is more important!"

"Catch the foxes!" they insist.

As a result, she had to tell the Shepherd they must put off their wedding. Not only that, she can't keep up with her beautification program or work on her hope chest. Taking care of vineyards requires hard work from spring through the harvest:

> The cultivation of the vine requires constant care or the fruit
> will very soon degenerate. After the rains the loosely made walls
> require to have breaches repaired; the ground must be plowed
> or harrowed and cleared of weeds--contrast with this the
> vineyard of the sluggard (Pr 24:30-31); in the early spring the
> plants must be pruned by cutting off dead and fruitless branches
> (Le 25:3-4; Isa 5:6) which are gathered and burned (Joh 15:6). As
> the grapes ripen they must be watched to keep off jackals and
> foxes (Song 2:15), and in some districts even wild boars (Ps
> 80:13). The watchman is stationed in one of the towers and
> overlooks a considerable area. When the grape season comes, the
> whole family of the owner frequently take their residence in a
> booth constructed upon one of the larger towers and remain
> there until the grapes are practically finished. It is a time of
> special happiness (compare Isa 16:10). The gleanings are left to
> the poor of the village or town (Le 19:10; De 24:21; Jg 8:2; Isa 17:6;
> 24:13; Jer 49:9; Mic 7:1). In the late summer the vineyards are a
> beautiful mass of green, as contrasted with the dried-up parched
> land around, but in the autumn the leaves are sere and yellow
> Isa 34:4), and the place desolate (ISBE "Vine").

She's Responsible for the Vineyards

The harvest scenario at the end of the story shows her brothers left the Shulammite in charge of the vineyards. She isn't a common laborer, but the overseer of the laborers. People work under her and she is in charge of paying them (Song 8:11-12).

Because she's about 13 years old, we might assume such a young girl wouldn't be able to take charge like that. But farm kids know she will rise to the challenge. When I was 14 and my brother Tom Snodgrass was 12, our dad was working with his harvest crew cutting wheat in the middle of June. One of the hired hands happened to see Dad fall to the ground in uncut wheat stalks which hid his body.

They rushed him to the hospital with severe adnominal pain. The doctor diagnosed appendicitis and they wheeled him to the operating room. Once he opened Dad up, the doctor discovered his appendix was fine, but took it out anyway. Then he followed the line of inflammation to Dad's stomach where an ulcer had blown a hole through the wall. The leaking digestive juices were eating him alive. The doctor patched up the hole with some fatty tissue.

Dad stayed in the hospital for ten days, drinking cream on the hour to coat his stomach so the patch could heal. This was before anti-acid medications. Mom spent every day and evening with him, coming home only long enough to nurse my fourth brother who was about one-month old and to sleep. I managed the house and meals while caring for my two middle brothers who were 10 and 8, plus the baby. Tom supervised the harvest crew. He was well prepared for this job.

When he was 4 and I was 6, Dad took our family on a custom-cutting trip from the Oklahoma Panhandle all the way into Canada. Tomie, as we called him then, was very interested in machinery and paid attention to everything.

One morning he watched as the hired hand greased the zerks on the combine, a very important maintenance job to prevent breakdowns in the field. Tomie said, "You missed some," and pointed them out. He continued to point to missed zerks that needed to be filled with grease.

The hired hand didn't like a little 4-year-old boy telling him how to do his job, and he began to sass Tomie. My brother didn't take much of it before he told him, "You're fired."

The hired hand was incensed and complained to Dad. Dad said, "If he fired you, you probably deserved to be fired. You're fired."

When I shared this with my brother Tom to check the details, he emailed back, "Yes, that's the way it happened. There were over 100 grease zerks on those old combines. Not only did I know where every zerk was, but I also knew how much grease each one should get. I also knew the part number of every belt and part that might have to be replaced on them. Dad would take me with him when we needed parts and would tell me to tell the parts man what we wanted. The parts man could hardly believe it when I would start rattling off the part numbers and not have anything written down. I knew if they brought out the wrong part."

Tom continued, "Too bad I don't still have that ability. Now I have a hard time remembering what day of the week it is sometimes. Ha."

When the Shulammite's brothers demanded she take charge of the vineyards, they knew she could do it. So the Maiden told the Shepherd, "I can't marry you this spring." She repeats her brothers' instructions to pay particular attention to the foxes. If she doesn't do this, the family will lose a valuable crop and won't be able to pay the lease on the land.

She Pledges Her Love to the Shepherd

Song of Solomon 2:16:
"My beloved is mine, and I am his;
He pastures his flock among the lilies."

After lamenting to the Virgins about her brothers not letting her marry her beloved in the spring, the Maiden declares their love for each other. Then she makes sure the Virgins know she's not talking about Solomon—the one they love. "My beloved," she says, "is the one who pastures his flock among the lilies—my Shepherd. Later she reverses this statement to the Virgins. Instead of saying, "My beloved is mine" she says, "I am my beloved's" (Song 6:3).

She doesn't use similes or metaphors to refer to her beloved as a shepherd. She tells what he does—pastures his flock. He can be found working among the lilies.

In contrast to these statements, the scriptures don't contain any examples of Solomon engaging in physical labor of any kind. On this excursion to the country, he is a gentleman farmer. He's not there to work, but to inspect the vineyards he leases to true farmers (Song 8:11-12). Oh! I almost forgot—and to look for beautiful bodies.

The Shulammite is a hard worker. She's in love with a blue-collar worker. Although Solomon offers her a life of ease, she brags to the Virgins about her working boyfriend. Even though the Shepherd's job seems common, he is a giant of a man when it came to hard work. His attitude toward labor, not his college degrees, position in a company, or family name, makes him dependable.

George Gilder says in *Men and Marriage* that marriage and a man's attitude toward work help him succeed far more than a college degree does. He cites statistics showing how men with large families and only a high-school education or less out-earn female college graduates. Rather than sex discrimination, the men are motivated to work overtime and at several jobs to support their families. Their attitudes toward work rather than their education credentials generate income and productivity. However, single men earn about the same as single women with the same education. Gilder concludes parents might be ahead to encourage their sons to marry rather than send them to college (94).

A husband who refuses to work makes it impossible for his wife to place total confidence in him. Without trust, a wife cannot let her guard down to allow her love to flourish. Sometimes a woman makes the mistake of believing in her husband's job rather than in his willingness to work. Jobs are only as secure as the economy and the goodwill of the employer. A wise wife values her husband's determination to work rather than the size of his paycheck.

She Sends the Shepherd Away

Song of Solomon 2:17:
"Until the cool of the day when the shadows flee away,
Turn [turn away – Hess], my beloved, and be like a gazelle
Or a young stag on the mountains of Bether."

"Turn" uses "a root that by itself cannot mean 'turn toward me' but must mean 'turn away'" (Hess 99).

The Maiden continues to recount to the Virgins the last time she saw the Shepherd. After explaining her brothers won't let her marry him until after the grape harvest she says, "I had no choice. I had to tell him, 'Turn away from me, my beloved. Go back to your home.' It broke my heart, but I had no choice...."

She told him she has work to do to protect the vines from the foxes. Now she reminds him he has work to do as well. She says, "Until the cool of the day when the shadows flee away," which refers to the early morning hours. The winter-time rains have ceased so she knows the Shepherd must rise each morning when it's still dark. He'll let his sheep graze on the dew-saturated grass in the cool of the day to both feed and water them. When the hot sun evaporates the dew, his sheep will lie down in the shadows and ruminate (Keller 51ff).

The Virgins heard the Maiden compare herself to the beneficial rose of Sharon and the lily of the valleys to the King. Now they listen as she compares the Shepherd to the powerful, loving gazelles and stags. She contrasts their natures and roles in life. Together, they will make a marvelous team loving and supporting each other. But Solomon interferes with their plans—the Shepherd's and hers for a spring wedding by not allowing her brothers' to be at home to bring in the crop of grapes.

The young Maiden is emotionally spent. She sighs, takes another bite of her raisin cake, and announces, "I'm ready to go to sleep." The Virgins show her the bed they've prepared. The lamp burns low flickering on the tent wall as she retires for the night.

The Shulammite's First Dream

Surrounded by the King's flattery and glamour the Maiden's love for the Shepherd refuses to be stilled. Even when she tries to sleep, a dream about the Shepherd haunts and disturbs her.

She Searches for the Shepherd

Song of Solomon 3:1-2:
"On my bed night after night I sought him
Whom my soul loves;
I sought him but did not find him.
'I must arise now and go about the city;
In the streets and in the squares
I must seek him whom my soul loves.'
I sought him but did not find him."

"Night after night" is one Hebrew word (*laylâ*) which is plural. The New International Version translates it as "all night long." Richard Hess says it "defines an extraordinary intensity to her yearning and desire. It is only because she is driven in such a way that she would venture out into the dangerous world of night in a city (v. 2)" (102).

The Shulammite uses "whom my soul loves" four times in describing her longing for the Shepherd in her dream. She first used this expression when Solomon brought her to his tent (Song 1:7). Now her dream intensifies her longing for the love of her soul.

"Soul" (*nephesh*) is sometimes used for the sexual drive and is translated as passion, craving, and lust. For example:

Jeremiah 2:24:
"A wild donkey accustomed to the wilderness,
That sniffs the wind in her [nephesh] passion [craving – NIV; lust--CJB].
In the time of her heat who can turn her away?"

Nephesh is often used with "love" as in "him whom my soul loves" (*Theological* 588-589). See Song 1:7 for Strong's definition.

"Loves" is the same word the Maiden uses when she begs the Virgins not to arouse or awaken her "love" until it pleases. A primary root, it means "to have affection for (sexually or otherwise)" (Strong 9).

Now more than ever the Maiden recognizes the Shepherd as the love of her life—she can't exist without him. In this dream, instead of her body anticipating sexual union with Solomon, sadness overcomes her. She visualizes night after lonely night in the palace. Rather than glowing with newlywed radiance, she sees herself tossing and turning—tormented by visions of her true love. Unfulfilled sexual desires for the Shepherd will prevent her from sleeping peacefully.

Dreams of marriage comprise a natural part of a young girl's transition into womanhood. After she starts dating her dreams center on her boyfriend as she visualizes life with him. Dreams of the night help her sort out her feelings and prepare her for marriage. Every emotionally healthy woman enjoys these feminine dreams as the awakening of her sexual love as she bonds, or soulmates, with a man. Thus the Maiden begs the Virgins not to force Solomon on her until they fall in love.

As a result of childhood trauma, exposure to Victorian hang-ups, or lack of proper sex education in our schools, churches, and homes, some girls fear their developing sexuality. They ignore these God-given urges pushing them toward sexual bonding and delight. However, the Song of Solomon reveals the Shulammite's mother taught her about courtship, marriage, and lovemaking. As a result, she displays healthy attitudes and responses to the King and the Shepherd. This allows her to analyze the implications of her dreams.

She Finds the Shepherd

Song of Solomon 3:3-4:
"The watchmen who make the rounds in the city found me,
And I said, 'Have you seen him whom my soul loves?'
Scarcely had I left them
When I found him whom my soul loves;
I held on to him and would not let him go,
Until I had brought him to my mother's house,
And into the room of her who conceived me."

The Shulammite dreams about what her life will be like in Jerusalem. She sees herself running around the city during the night searching everywhere for the Shepherd. When the guards find her, they let her pass because she's not married to the King. She still has a choice in who she'll marry.

When she finds her beloved in her dream, she refuses to let him go until she brings him home into her mother's room. The Israelites handed down their tents from generation to generation, repairing and replacing walls and adding rooms as needed. Family after family conceived their children in the same room. We see this with Isaac and Rebekah:

Genesis 24:67: "Then Isaac brought her into his mother Sarah's tent, and he took Rebekah, and she became his wife; and he loved her; thus Isaac was comforted after his mother's death."

In a night of restless sleep the Shulammite's emotional attachment to the Shepherd drives her to search for him until she finds him. The dream ends with marriage and her experiencing sexual love in her mother's bedroom. Later in the story she tells the Shepherd her mother taught her how to enjoy lovemaking and how to pleasure her husband. Imagine mother and daughter sitting in this room talking and giggling about sex and love. Overcome with lovesickness, this generational room of love beckons to the Maiden as the perfect place to share with her beloved what her mother taught her.

The Shulammite's dream wakes her up with her body aching for her Shepherd. When the Virgins come to prepare her for the day, she begs them a second time not to force her to marry Solomon before they've fallen in love. She can't bear the thought of being married to a man without them feeling true passion for each other.

She Repeats "Secret 2: Insist on Soulmating Before Lovemaking"

Song of Solomon 3:5:
"I adjure you, O daughter of Jerusalem,

By the gazelles [male] or by the hinds [female] of the field,
That you will not arouse or awaken my love,
Until she [it – NASB footnote] pleases."

"Adjure" means "properly to be complete; to seven oneself, i.e., swear (as if by repeating a declaration seven times):--adjure, charge (by an oath, with an oath)" (Strong 112).

True love and marrying the right person is so important, the Shulammite starts the day by asking the Virgins for the second time to swear they will not force marriage on her. Their peer pressure weighs heavily upon her. They love the King and think he is a wonderful catch. But if Solomon and the Shulammite learn to love each other the same way as she and the Shepherd love each other, it will take time to build an emotional attraction. She knows now if she marries Solomon before true love develops between them, she'll continue to dream about the Shepherd and be miserable. She might never find true love again. So she tells the Virgins, "Please, don't force Solomon and me together until we truly love each other with all our hearts!"

This is what all parents tell their teenagers when they start to notice the opposite sex:

"Go slow."

"Relax. Your date isn't the only fish in the sea."

"You have time to be particular about who you marry."

"Your first heart throb doesn't have to be your last."

"Get to know your boyfriend or girlfriend first."

Like modern parents who try to prevent their children from rushing into a disastrous relationship, the Maiden's mother pointed to the courting and mating animals. She said repeatedly, "By the gazelles or by the hinds of the field, do not arouse or awaken your love until it pleases.... You have plenty of time to fall in love.... Take your time and let your affections grow naturally."

Couples force love in many ways. For example, one woman who divorced her husband said, "When I married him, I didn't love him. He just loved me so much, I thought I'd learn to love him after marriage. I never did." She found out the hard way it's much easier to fall in love before marriage than to learn to love afterward.

Another wife with a horrible attitude toward her husband referred to him as "a big fat slob." She dealt with her marriage frustrations by abusing her daughter. When I asked if she loved him when she married him, she replied, "No, I married him because I was pregnant with his child." She never learned to love him.

Marrying a man because a woman is going to bear his child is one of the poorest reasons imaginable for marriage. The greatest gift parents can bestow on their children is to give them a mother and father who love each other. Trying to correct the sin of fornication with an unloving marriage can damage the child.

Although the right choice for the Shulammite might seem obvious to us, even a shallow man often possesses a disarming charm that captivates naive girls and women. Because flattery often influences a person to make an unwise marriage choice, a woman should spend as much time as possible getting to know the man before she marries him.

One woman said, "When I was a teenager and just starting to date, my grandmother told me to never date a boy I wouldn't want to be the father of my children. She knew once I started dating and spending time with a boy, I could easily fall in love and marry him. She warned me not to take a chance on falling in love with someone who wouldn't make a good husband and father."

Many wives started dating their husbands when they didn't even like them at first. They regarded their dates as a way to keep from staying home. One such wife admonished girls, "Never let a boy kiss you if you don't want to fall in love with him." She explained, "I was going to college when I starting dating my husband. I didn't want to drop out and get married. I let him kiss me good night to be polite and because I liked him. I didn't want to get emotionally involved with him. But soon afterward, we were making marriage plans."

It's almost impossible for males and females to kiss without arousing passions for each other that are easy to mistake for love. It's better to love before kissing than to kiss and be fooled into thinking it's love. Love is too precious a gift to gamble away through careless kissing.

As the Maiden contemplates marriage to the King, she realizes true love is more important than his money or prestige. After finding true affection with the Shepherd, she is unwilling to settle for Solomon's flattery. And so her dilemma and search for true love continues.

The curtain closes for an intermission for a scenery change.

ACT TWO, SCENE ONE
SECOND DAY - AFTERNOON

The curtains open to a backdrop of painted houses stage left suggesting a town. Center stage there's a forest near a meadow where shepherds tend their resting sheep. Stage right is the outskirts of Jerusalem. Stage left peasants line the street. Citizens of Jerusalem line the street. Solomon and his royal entourage make their way toward Jerusalem. The parade watchers speak as they exclaim over the sight of Solomon and the Maiden.

Solomon Takes the Shulammite to Jerusalem

Song of Solomon 3:6-8:
"What [Literally Who – NASB] is this coming up from the wilderness
Like columns of smoke,
Perfumed with myrrh and frankincense,
With all scented powders of the merchant?
Behold, it is the traveling couch of Solomon;
Sixty mighty men around it,
Of the mighty men of Israel.
All of them are wielders of the sword,
Expert in war;
Each man has his sword at his side,
Guarding against the terrors of the night."

This scene represents a typical Israelite wedding procession of the groom taking the bride from her home to his. Only Solomon's royal caravan is more elaborate than a couple walking from her house to his. If Solomon has his way, he'll soon marry the beautiful Shulammite and fulfill her wedding week. Then he can go on tour again and search for another beautiful virgin.

The description of the King's entourage presents a realistic picture of the traveling style of royalty. The Israelites went to great lengths to mask the offensive odors of their hot climate. When nobility rode in litters, attendants tossed up "columns of smoke" or handfuls of spices to perfume the path like a prototype of modern car fresheners. In fact, the country people see the smoke of the herbs long before they realize it is Solomon's caravan approaching.

A stanza of six lines emphasizes the expertise of the sixty mighty men with their swords ready—an elite group of well-trained soldiers guard the couple. Just the sight of them would discourage marauding bands. Solomon rides in grand style with a royal escort.

The Daughters of Jerusalem Fitted Out Solomon's Chariot

Song of Solomon 3:9-10:
"King Solomon has made for himself
a sedan chair [literally chariot – KJV, RSV]
From the timber of Lebanon.
He made its posts of silver,
Its back of gold and its seat of purple fabric,
With its interior lovingly fitted out
By the daughters of Jerusalem."

The Hebrew words for "traveling couch" in verse 7 and for "sedan chair" in verse 9 are different. *Strong's Complete Dictionary of Bible Words* says the first word refers to a "bed" for reclining and the second word means "chariot." Many scholars believe the Maiden rode on the couch while Solomon traveled in the chair. Perhaps Solomon slept on the couch when he camped.

As the owner of 1,400 chariots which he stationed in "the chariot cities," Solomon knows all about these amazing vehicles (2 Chronicles 1:14-17; 1 Kings 9:19). He imported chariots from Egypt where 400 years earlier King Tut was known for his high-performance chariots. Solomon could purchase chariots that ranged from large ceremonial models to smaller, lighter ones for daily use.

In the *Discovery News* article "King Tut's Chariots Marvels of Engineering" Rossella Lorenzi interviewed Alberto Rovetta, professor in robotics engineering at the Polytechnic of Milan. Professor Rovetta explained how these ancient vehicles provided an amazingly soft, comfortable ride. He called Tut's chariots "the Ferrari of antiquity." They incorporated modern technology that used mechanical systems "which combine the use of kinematics, dynamics and lubrication principles." The chariots used suspension techniques that rival "the intelligent suspensions in modern cars" (8/3/2010). You can read the article online for more details about these remarkable riding machines.

That Solomon's raging testosterone would take hold of the reins of some of his big-boy toys is characteristic of him not denying himself any pleasure (Ecclesiastes 2:9-10). However, Song of Solomon 3:9 indicates he made the chariot he drove from Shunem to Jerusalem with timber from Lebanon. With his obsessions with knowledge and building, it seems probable that he would try to improve upon King Tut's designs. Or he may have commissioned the Egyptians to custom build his favorite traveling Ferrari and embellished it with silver and gold. Then the Virgins lovingly decorated his chariot with expensive purple cloth.

The gold on the Shulammite's traveling bed and Solomon's chariot glisten in the sun from afar adding to the spectacle for the country people. Whatever vehicles Solomon and the Maiden rode in to Jerusalem, they traveled in jaw-dropping elegant, modern style.

Bathsheba Crowned Solomon King

Song of Solomon: 3:11:
"Go forth, O daughters of Zion,
And gaze on King Solomon with the crown
With which his mother crowned him
On the day of his wedding,
And on the day of his gladness of heart."

Solomon, wearing the wreath of a bridegroom (Isaiah 61:10), triumphantly takes the beautiful Shulammite through the countryside to his palace. The country folks lining the road excitedly ask, "Who is this coming up from the wilderness?" Once they recognize Solomon, they call to their daughters, "Hurry! Come see the Maiden who has stolen the King's heart! Maybe you'll be next!"

In actuality, Solomon's mother, Bathsheba, did crown him. When his father King David grew old, his family brought in Abishag, a beautiful Shunammite, to keep him warm by snuggling with him in bed. During this time, David's son, Adonijah, decided to anoint himself king. When the prophet Nathan heard of it, he went to Bathsheba and made a plan for her to remind David of his promise to make her son Solomon king after him. While she was still before the king, Nathan came in and told David about Adonijah. David reacted as they expected and gave orders for Solomon to be anointed king that very day. Solomon began co-reigning with David (1 Kings 1).

Bible scholars calculate that 4 years passed between 1 Kings 1 when the co-reign began and 1 Kings 2 when David died and Solomon was anointed king a second time (1 Chronicles 29:22-23). Some historians think Solomon was 12 years old when he began his co-reign, others say he was 14. Nathan going to Bathsheba indicates Solomon was too young to deal with Adonijah's attempt to take the throne.

I take the younger age of 12 and allow 4 years for the co-reign. Solomon married an average of 25 virgins a year after he began his solo reign. With 140 wives at the time of the Song of Solomon, that makes him about 5 1/2 years into his reign and about 21 or 22 years old. He is a young virile man.

The curtain closes as the entourage moves off stage to the right with the country folks gossiping about Solomon's gladness of heart.

ACT TWO, SCENE TWO
SECOND DAY - EVENING

The curtains open onto an ornate room in the palace. Since the King uses only gold, this room is very luxurious. Solomon and the Maiden are center stage. The virgin Abby plucks a lyre in the background with a group of other musicians softly accompanying her.

Solomon's Second Proposal

Solomon has the Maiden in Jerusalem away from her home, family, and the Shepherd. He thinks it'll be easier to charm her now that she's surrounded by the luxuries of his palace. Ecclesiastes 2:4-9 gives an idea of his extravagance. His numerous houses beckon visitors with beautiful gardens and parks filled with all kinds of fruit trees and ponds to irrigate a forest of transplanted evergreens. Slaves wait on him. Gold sparkles everywhere. Ah, the male and female singers and musicians provide the original surround-sound atmosphere.

"How Beautiful You Are"

Song of Solomon 4:1a:
"How beautiful you are, my darling,
How beautiful you are!

The King begins wooing the Shulammite in earnest. His shallow words flow smoothly from practice, charming the inexperienced young vineyard keeper. He focuses again on her outward appearance as he tells her, "How beautiful you are, my darling, how beautiful you are!"

"Your Head Is Lovely"

Song of Solomon 4:1b-3:
"Your eyes are like doves behind your veils;
Your hair is like a flock of goats
That have descended from Mount Gilead.
Your teeth are like a flock of newly shorn ewes
Which have come up from their washing,
All of which bear twins,
And not one among them has lost her young.
Your lips are like a scarlet thread,
And your mouth is lovely.
Your temples are like a slice of pomegranate
Behind your veil.

Now that the Shulammite is in the palace, the Virgins dressed her with a veil befitting a woman who will soon become one of Solomon's queens. The King's glowing admiration of her face and hair behind her veil reveals that she wears the typical long, sheer veil. The veil would have hung down from the top of her head and covered her upper body. It went over a high cap that kept the fabric away from her face.

Espoused and married women sewed their dowry coins to the high cap. This way, if their husband divorced them, they were allowed to take their clothing with them, and they would have a means of support (Wight 99, 127-8). Their portion of the dowry served like our modern prenuptial agreements do, which specify how much money the woman is allowed if the couple should divorce. Not yet espoused, the Shulammite didn't have any coins on her high cap to block Solomon's view of her temples.

Although the King praised her beauty before, now he expands his description. His proposal reveals only a sensuous infatuation with her. Her exquisite physique will turn her into a magnificent trophy wife to parade before others.

Solomon's words bring the Shulammite's beauty to life: Her eyes, like "doves" radiate peace and happiness. Her long black curly hair, like "a flock of goats [which were usually black] that have descended Mount Gilead" flows with beautiful curls down her back. Her white, even teeth, like a flock of sheep "which have come up from their washing, all of which bear twins" enhance her smile. Her red lips, like a "scarlet thread" innocently invite his kisses. Her temples and flawless complexion, like "a slice of pomegranate" present a picture of health and youth.

"Your Breasts Are Luscious"

> Song of Solomon 4:4-5:
> Your neck is like the tower of David
> Built with rows of stones,
> On which are hung a thousand shields,
> All the round shields of the mighty men.
> Your two breasts are like two fawns,
> Twins of a gazelle,
> Which feed among the lilies."

Solomon admires her long slender neck, like a beautiful, ornate corner column in "the tower of David" that adds grace to her posture (Psalms 144:12). The chains of her necklace "on which are hung a thousand shields, all the round shields of the mighty men" fall between her breasts.

And so the King's eyes follow the line of the radiant discs from her face to her ample bosom. Like "two fawns, twins of a gazelle, which feed among the lilies" they reveal a girl who has become a woman. He stops at her bosom—a habit he continues throughout the story revealing Solomon's breast fetish. She possesses everything necessary to make a good wife—an enchanting face and the perfect proportions. She replies with what every girl should say after such a sensuous proposal.

The Shulammite Pleads, "Give Me Time to Think"

> Song of Solomon 4:6:
> "Until the cool of the day
> When the shadows flee away,
> I will go my way to the mountain of myrrh
> And to the hill of frankincense."

The Maiden needs time to think about the King's proposal, so she asks him for time alone that evening "until the cool of the day when the shadows flee away." "The mountain of myrrh and the hill of frankincense" refer to the numerous gardens in and around Jerusalem. The vineyard keeper wants to walk among the sweet-smelling herbs and plants to clear her head as she tries to decide what to do.

Most of the towns had suburban gardens with a pavilion or summer-house where residents could sit to meditate and refresh their souls. The Hebrews used these communal grounds to grow medicinal herbs (*Popular* 689).

No doubt, the Shulammite chooses to go to one of Solomon's exotic gardens on the palace compound. She doesn't want to rush into marriage and refuses to allow Solomon to pressure her into making a quick decision that will affect the rest of her life. Likewise, a thoughtful boy gives a girl time to think his proposal through because her decision also affects the rest of his life. A whirlwind romance often precedes an unhappy marriage.

All the way through the story, each time Solomon makes a sensuous proposal to her, the Maiden asks for time to think. Then she leaves Solomon's presence and finds a garden where she can gather her thoughts. This simple act saves the Shulammite from making a bad decision. Following her example will protect us, too.

Secret 3: Practice Your Sensuous-Love Mirror Lines

As the Shulammite repeats Secret 2 and the theme of the Song of Solomon — soulmating before lovemaking — she appeals to the wisdom of the gazelles and hinds of the field by not making snap judgments about marriage. Each time Solomon praises her body and tries to get her to commit to him, she asks for time to think about his offer.

Practicing your mirror lines helps you follow the Maiden's example even when you're in the midst of a romantic moment. You can use mirror lines throughout courtship and marriage.

Use Mirror Lines to Help Resolve Arguments

I introduced mirror lines in the fighting fair classes in *Challenges in Marriage, What to Do When Sin Inhibits Love*. Just as in the heat of romance, often in the heat of an argument, it's hard to think of exactly the right words to defuse the situation. I instructed my students to remember past arguments and analyze what they could have said differently to have made the fight more productive.

For example, one rule of fighting fair is to stay on topic. Many people jump around from subject to subject that have nothing to do with the argument. This is called throwing out red herrings, which confuses the problem and forces the other person to abandon their logic to deal with side issues. Before long, the disagreement has gone so far afield that nothing gets settled, which can further enrage both participants.

I advised, "Stand in front of a mirror and say over and over what you've determined is the best phrase to keep the discussion on topic. And whatever you do, don't answer any red-herring arguments."

You might say, "You're missing the point."

The other person might counter, "But you always do such and such."

You calmly repeat, "You're missing the point."

"But you never do such and such."

"I'm not going to answer your accusation because you are missing the point. We are discussing a different issue. You need to stay on topic."

This back and forth goes on until the other person deals with the right problem. Only when it's settled does the couple move to a new topic. Amazingly, just one person enforcing the rules for fighting fair can teach the other how to have a constructive discussion.

In an emotional exchange, it's easy to forget what you planned to say the next time the subject gets switched. Practicing in front of the mirror helps turn what you need to say into an automatic response. Even with lots of forethought, you can still get caught up in the moment and forget.

If you can't remember what you planned to say, forgive yourself and practice your mirror lines some more. You're bound to have another argument…and another chance to use your mirror lines."

You can read in *Stacey's Story* how she used mirror lines to teach her husband Joe how to fight fair so they could have intelligent conversations about their sexless marriage. He resisted learning the fighting-fair rules until he had a major melt-down and destroyed some of her property. Even then, Stacey continued to use her mirror lines and fighting-fair techniques to eventually touch his heart. That's when they began to turn their sexless marriage into a loving one. See *Stacey's Story* at the end of this chapter and the end of chapters 5 and 7 for ideas.

Practice "I Need Time to Think" When It Comes to Romance

Throughout the Shulammite's dilemma of whom to marry, saying "I need time to think" is an automatic response for her. She doesn't think later, "I wish I'd thought of that at the time." No doubt, this is something her mother taught her to do.

By practicing your mirror line, "I need time to think," you don't need to know all the answers on the fly. You give yourself a chance to analyze the situation. Sometimes you may need to talk to someone else to get a different perspective before you make a decision.

When your date tries to jumpstart the relationship with a sensuous proposal, imitate the Shulammite and practice her mirror line, "I need time to think. I'll get back with you later." Waiting until passions are raging out of control to try to think logically courts disaster. The best time to make the decision to practice saying, "I need time to think," is right now. It's a great mirror line for courtship...and marriage.

Use Mirror Lines to Listen to Your Gut Instincts

Here's what I suggest my single clients do: Start a notebook about what you're looking for in a mate. Then list the positive characteristics you find in each person you date. Write down everything that seems odd, off, or strange. These may prove to be red flags that you don't have enough experience at the time to recognize as warning signs.

Too often, red flags fly right by us when they occur. It's only after something bad happens that we look back and realize we were seeing signs. But if you record several actions that seem weird, together they can indicate a pattern that you might not identify when considering them as single items.

Use the Shulammite's mirror line, "I need time to think" to buy time to investigate. Please tell your friends and family about your concerns. If your gut feels uncomfortable, listen to the people who love you and are further away from the situation. They possibly have noticed other characteristics that make them uncomfortable or even afraid for you.

When I went through training at two women's shelters, the counselors said that nearly every woman who is murdered by her boyfriend or husband has a feeling about impending danger, but talks herself out of it. You do not want to dismiss red flags no matter how minor. You can call the abuse hotline at the front of this book to discuss the questionable behavior with a counselor. Boys and men need to practice the mirror line, too. Women can be stalkers and murderers, too.

Solomon Replies, "You're Flawlessly Beautiful"

Song of Solomon 4:7:
"You are altogether beautiful, my darling,
And there is no blemish in you."

Solomon tells the Shulammite, "You can think about it all you want, but I won't change my mind." Why? "Because you have a beautiful body. You don't have even one blemish." With Solomon's sensuous flattery ringing in her ears, she goes to the garden to think.

Study Exercise

Answer all questions in your own words.

1. Why did the Shepherd want to get married in the spring?
2. Why did the Shulammite's brothers forbid her to marry in the spring? Did the Shulammite do the right thing in sending the Shepherd away? Why?
3. What did the Shulammite's dream tell her about marrying Solomon?
4. What is the difference between arousing and awakening love? Why did the Shulammite caution the Virgins not to arouse or awaken love?
5. What is the significance of the gazelles and hinds of the field? How do they compare to Solomon's simile of a mare in heat?
6. How can you apply the secret of the Song of Solomon to your life?
7. Why did the Shulammite go to Jerusalem with Solomon?
8. What is missing from Solomon's two proposals of marriage?
9. Do you disagree with anything in the lesson? If so, explain giving scriptures for your reasons.

Goal-Achieving Exercise

Change the following points to fit your needs. Review this exercise as you study future chapters and make additions as necessary.

Purpose
To increase romance in your marriage by helping love grow naturally and fully.

Goals
1. To be able to express your love and appreciation more freely.
2. To see the look of love and admiration shining in your mate's eyes.
3. To make sure your marriage is firmly built upon a foundation of soulmating love rather than sensuous love.

Priorities
1. Keep your appearance neat, clean, and sweet-smelling.
2. Set aside time to spend with your mate without the children.
3. Set aside time to pray and read the Song of Solomon together.

Plans
1. Make a list of things you can do to please your mate's 5 senses.
2. Start the day with sweet words and physical demonstrations of affection such as pats, hugs, and kisses for your mate and children.
3. Greet your mate with the look of love radiating from your eyes.
4. Write a love note to your mate.
5. Turn off your cell phone and the TV to spend quality time together.
6. Consider giving a card or little gift just to say, "I love you."

Stacey's Story:
Fighting Fair Begins

Dear Patsy Rae,

I took your advice and ordered the *Challenges in Marriage* material to help me learn how to communicate with Joe. It is really opening my eyes to the sin in my home. I'm working on the "How to Fight Fair" class now. I see lots of mistakes I've been making throughout our marriage.

One of the assignments is to analyze the normal course of arguments and to plan how to deal with them. I've been practicing my mirror lines so I can respond automatically. They still aren't natural to me, but I'm growing. You were right when you said to forgive yourself if you mess up in an argument because you get another chance to do it better.

This morning I attempted to talk to Joe. I told him this was no way to live. He said it would continue as long as I keep accusing him of awful things [sin on his part]. He turned it into a huge fight. I did my best to stay calm and in control. I stayed on topic. I realize now this is his way of controlling the situation and attempting to keep me silent on the issue.

He accused me of everything you could possibly think of, calling me names and telling me I was looney and needed a psychologist. I told him an innocent man would not respond in that way. If I was totally wrong and off the mark, a loving husband would want to know what led me to think that way and would want to discuss it. He wouldn't immediately resort to defending himself by calling his wife all kinds of terrible dirty names and making her the problem.

Joe interrupted me constantly, and I just continued to remind him I don't interrupt him, that he couldn't possibly know what I was going to say if he continually interrupted me. He kept calling me terrible names to which I responded by walking away and letting him know I would not listen to his verbal abuse.

I told Joe over and over again he was getting off topic and I would gladly discuss things with him if he would stick to the issue and discuss it with me in an adult manner. I told him if he wanted to fight about it, he would have to fight fair. No name calling, etc.

I know my refusing to get drawn into a "knockdown, drag it out" battle frustrated him greatly. I think he was a bit confused about how to respond to it. I did raise my voice more than I should have, and I know I'll have to work on that.

We settled nothing. But I'm not giving up. I'll keep you informed.

Thanks for your help,
Stacey

Secret 4: Grow the 4 Parts of Intimacy and Love

Solomon's Siren Song: Her Brothers Stand Firm

"No marriage this spring. We need you in the vineyards. You must wait 'til fall...after the grape harvest."

"But why?" the Shulammite challenges her brother's authority.

"Because the tax man was here while you were off visiting the Shepherd. He drafted Mark. I told him one brother needs to stay home to work the vineyards. He laughed and said, 'That's women's work.' Solomon is obsessed with cutting down trees. But his tax man is worse. He doesn't care if anyone is left behind to take care of our vineyards. You know that!"

"But if I wait 'til fall to get married, I need to be working inside to protect my skin. The sun will burn me up! You—know that!"

Anger flashes in her oldest brother's eyes. "Sister! Hush! Hush up now!... You know we had a wetter, colder winter than usual. The stone walls are in bad shape. Have you seen them?"

"No. I've been in the house helping Mom and getting ready for my wedding."

"More stones than usual have fallen out of place. The baby foxes are squeezing in and out of the crevices. They're scampering all over the place and jostling the tender blossoms. You know as well as we do, if they keep it up, they'll mess up the fertilization process and we won't have much of a crop. I wish we could make the repairs before we leave, but the tax man just laughed when I told him we need to wait another month before we leave for the forests."

"He said, 'You'll mess up my schedule. The growing season is your problem. Filling my quota is my concern,'" her middle brother scorns.

She opens her mouth to speak and her older brother lays his hand on her arm. "Someone has to oversee the repair of the wall and start weeding and pruning the dead branches. With all the rain, the weeds will take over if we let them. You know that."

"But I'm of age. I can make my own decisions about getting married! You know that!"

Her brother's anger flares. "Sister! You can choose your husband, but 'til you're 21 you can't marry without our okay!"

"Please…. Can't Michael do it? He's worked for you for years?"

"His father is dying and he's already left to go bury him and bring his mother back."

Her middle brother breaks in, "Quit arguing, Sis! If no one takes care of the vines while they're in bloom, we won't have any grapes to harvest and sell. We won't have any grapes to pay the King's food taxes. He'll kick us off his place! He'll say we're not dependable."

Her oldest brother's face softens as he pats her arm. "Sweet, Missy…we don't have any choice about what we must do this spring…and neither do you. The Shepherd will understand you have to stay home and take care of the vineyards. Our livelihood depends on it."

"Besides," her middle brother chimes in, "next year, Michael will be here and our baby sister will be mature enough to help. You can start training Raizel now. But this year…the responsibility falls on you. Your Shepherd should know when he's older they'll draft him for tree-cutting duty. And they won't care who takes care of his sheep."

Her youngest brother Mark puts his arm around her shoulders and pulls her against his side. "I'm sorry, Missy, I can't be here so you can get married this spring. I'd rather be here, you know that."

"What did Mother say?"

Her older brother looks her in the eye. "Everyone agrees. It's a done deal. There will be no wedding 'til after grape harvest."

Song of Solomon 4:8-15:
The Shepherd Proposes True Love

ACT TWO, SCENE THREE
SECOND DAY – NIGHT

The curtains open on a garden beside the palace. The Shulammite walks among the herbs, fruit trees, and evergreens deep in thought. The Virgin Abby plucks the strings of a small lyre.

Secret 4: Grow the 4 Parts of Intimacy and Love

Strolling through the garden on her first night in Jerusalem the Shulammite misses her country home in spite of all the exotic plants. Abby sits nearby softly plucking a sweet-sounding lyre (1 Kings 10:12; Psalms 81:1-2). The simple melody adds to the Maiden's loneliness as her lovesick thoughts turn to her Shepherd. She compares his second proposal to the one Solomon just made. Every girl should think seriously about the possible ramifications of a man's proposal before she accepts.

Does it contain all the parts of love that the Shepherd included in his proposal?

1. The Shepherd Proposes Intellectual Intimacy and Love

Song of Solomon 4:8:
"Come with me from Lebanon, my bride,
May you come with me from Lebanon.
Journey down from the summit of Amana,
From the summit of Senir and Hermon,
From the dens of lions,
From the mountains of leopards."

"Bride" means "a bride (as if perfect), hence a son's wife:--bride, daughter-in-law, spouse." It comes from a primary root that means "to complete:--make perfect" (Strong 55).

The Shulammite and the Shepherd are promised to each other. The custom of being promised is similar to our engagements, which can be broken. An espousal is different and begins with a formal ceremony and requires a divorce to break it. Although men could divorce an espoused bride, women couldn't easily divorce the man. Yet a woman had rights. She needed only to plead her case before a court of rabbis who would pressure her husband to divorce her (Instone-Brewer, *Divorce* 85ff).

Because of Solomon's hot pursuit of the Maiden, it seems unlikely she and the Shepherd were espoused, rather than promised. The speedy trip to Jerusalem suggests the King doesn't need to facilitate a divorce to free the Shulammite to marry him. Nor does the account imply the King's men visited the Shepherd to persuade him to divorce Solomon's latest love interest.

However, the King's marriage proposal trumps the brothers' edict declaring their sister must work in the vineyards now and wait until fall to marry. The anxious Maiden struggles over whether to wed the King now or marry the Shepherd after harvest. Thus she remembers her beloved's words of love and devotion as he asked her to marry him.

The Shepherd proposes to the Maiden as "my bride." Previously, he called her "my darling," or the affectionate greeting of a boyfriend or lover, i.e. "babe" (Song 2:10, 13). Now in his proposal of marriage, he gets serious. He calls her "my bride" five times; one in each section of his proposal. He keeps his intellectual attraction to her in the forefront.

The Shepherd wants to share love with the Shulammite for the rest of his life. As a helper designed by God for him, she will complete him and make him perfect. She is the answer to his problem of loneliness. His masculinity needs her femininity (Genesis 2:18). He values and cherishes her for the person she is and what she will bring to the marriage.

Wherever life leads, he wants her to accompany him.

He begs, "Come down from the summit of Amana, Senir, and Hermon and the dens of lions and leopards." These inaccessible places symbolize the obstacles separating the two lovers. She isn't an easy mark and he respects her purity. Now he wants to remove all hindrances and unite with her in marriage. Rather than a hookup or friends-with-benefits relationship, he desires loving companionship for a lifetime with his "bride."

2. The Shepherd Proposes Emotional Intimacy and Love

Song of Solomon 4:9a:
"You have made my heart beat faster, my sister, my bride."

"Made my heart beat faster" is a primary root that means "(in a good sense) transport (with love)." Its derivatives refer to "the heart; also used (figuratively) very widely for the feelings, the will and even the intellect; likewise for the center of anything" (Strong 58).

"Sister" is the feminine form of "brother" and is "used in the widest sense of literal relationship and metaphoric affinity or resemblance" (Strong 10).

Proverbs uses the sibling relationship to convey intimate friendship:

Proverbs 7:4:
"Say to wisdom, 'You are my sister,'
And call understanding your intimate friend."

This verse capitalizes on the special bond brothers and sisters share when raised in loving homes. Although brothers enjoy comradeship just as sisters delight in each other, the brother-sister relationship has its own special bond. If the sister is older, often she is the little mother to her brothers. If she's the baby, then she's the darling of her brothers. Above all, siblings who grow up in loving homes are intimate friends sharing their deepest and most private feelings.

The Shepherd confessing how his heart beats faster as he thinks of the Shulammite as "my sister, my bride" tells the Maiden he's consumed with intellectual and emotional love for her. He wants to experience the affectionate bond of siblings with her—but on the deeper level of married lovers. When this kind of love and confidence exists between brothers and sisters, there is no sibling rivalry. They share secrets and feelings with each other. True concern for the welfare of each other governs their actions. They make sacrifices for each other.

Later the Maiden cites the Shepherd's upbringing of love as an indication they'll enjoy a fulfilling marriage. She also credits her own loving home for teaching her how to love a man (Song 8:1-2, 5b). I often tell people in my classes to look at how their dates get along with their brothers and sisters. We tend to think siblings fussing and fighting is normal. Yes, it's normal in unloving families. It's abnormal when love reigns in the home.

In contrast to the Shulammite and the Shepherd, a later chapter explores Solomon's inability to engage in true intimacy with any woman on any level. His home of origin included rape and murder. If sibling intimacy is lacking, then a person lacks family experience in intellectual and emotional bonding. Until such an individual learns how to connect intimately, the marriage will experience problems.

As you study the Shepherd's proposal notice how his words shatter two hallmark characteristics of intimacy anorexia and narcissism. First, he is comfortable sharing his deepest feelings and vulnerabilities. Inhibited individuals live in leftover-childhood emotional-survival mode. Consequently, they don't feel safe to be real with their spouse—no matter how supportive their mate is. Second, the Shepherd's language is filled with genuine compliments of the Maiden as a person—for who she is—not for what she can do for him. Withholding praise, which later turns into active criticism, is a universal trait of love-defective spouses and parents.

3. The Shepherd Proposes Sexual Intimacy and Love

Song of Solomon 4:9b:
"You have made my heart beat faster with a single glance of your eyes,
With a single strand of your necklace."

In the first line, we see how the Shepherd's heart flutters with longing to share the emotional intimacy of siblings with her. And he reminds her of his intellectual attraction and desire for her. Now he gives two examples of his desire for sexual intimacy with her. A single glance of her eyes and a single strand of her necklace capture his heart.

He expresses his physical desire for the Shulammite differently than Solomon does. Solomon admires the individual features of her body in detail—she is a perfect specimen of femininity from the top of her head to her breasts. Although Solomon's wives go lower in their description, his eyes always stop at her well-developed bosom (Song 8:10).

The Shepherd, on the other hand, notices her femininity in a single glance of her eyes and a single strand of her necklace. He praises the expression of her eyes. A single strand of her necklace—insignificant compared to the jewelry Solomon gave her—showcases her loveliness, not her well-developed bosom. Although the Shepherd notices her physical attractiveness, he also sees her as a complete package—not body parts stacked on top of each other as Solomon does.

In two similar declarations of his love, the Shepherd accents different characteristics. In his first speech, he drew attention to her sweet voice; now he speaks of a single glance of her eyes. First, he praised her lovely form; now he notices a single strand of her necklace. He always describes her whole being instead of an assemblage of perfect individual pieces as Solomon did.

The Shepherd confessing how his heart beats faster tells the Maiden he's consumed with love for her. Her eyes reflect her emotional intimacy with him while her necklace summarizes her appearance. She captivates him on every level.

The Shepherd Is Aroused by "Secret 1: Awaken True Love with Your 5 Senses"

True love includes satisfaction of the 5 senses. We've already seen the Shepherd's commitments to the Maiden as he called her "my sister, my bride." Now he lavishes compliments upon her in regard to how she satisfies each of his 5 senses. His sensory delights far exceed the Shulammite's own sensory overload when she pined for her Shepherd after Solomon took her to his tent (Song 1:2-4).

See: The Shulammite's Eyes

Each time the Shepherd sees love and approval shining in the Shulammite's eyes, his heart beats faster. She excites him! She captivates him! He hopelessly loves her! The butterflies stirring within the Shepherd testify to his emotional intimacy with her.

The Shulammite's eyes play an important role all the way through the romance. The way she looks at the Shepherd and Solomon affects both men. Earlier, Solomon described her eyes as peaceful doves. Now the Shepherd says her eyes make his heart beat faster. Both want to see love shining from the Shulammite's eyes.

More important than the color of a woman's eyes is the way she looks at a man. A woman reveals many thoughts with her eyes that may never cross her lips. For example, a woman's eyes can sparkle with love, admiration, or contentment. A woman can flirt with smiling, twinkling eyes. Her eyes may appear dull with boredom, contempt, or disgust. Some women's eyes shine black with hatred, jealousy, or revenge. Or a woman's eyes may be dull and lifeless. The way a woman looks at a man tells him about her feelings toward him. Or her eyes may look downward hiding shame from unjust criticism or something in her past.

It's a red flag of danger if the person a man or woman dates has cold, black, or dead eyes. Emotional love softens the eyes and radiates from them as they caress the lover. If a date's eyes make a person feel uncomfortable, something is wrong. Maybe terribly wrong.

Many a boyfriend and husband likes to see affection shining in a woman's eyes. Proverbs 15:30 says, "Bright eyes gladden the heart." If a woman stands in front of a mirror and thinks loving thoughts of her boyfriend or husband, she sees firsthand how pleasant emotions bring liveliness to her eyes. She can radiate love to her beloved and caress him with her eyes without saying a word.

See: The Shulammite's Necklace

In addition to the glance of her eyes, a single strand of the Shulammite's necklace captivates the Shepherd. Although she isn't one of the ten best-dressed women in the land, she takes time to add feminine touches to her appearance. The Shepherd notices and appreciates her efforts. They make his heart beat faster.

When courting most women pay attention to their dress, hair, cleanliness, and the extra grooming touches that tell their date, "You're special." For some reason, many of these same women feel free to neglect their appearance after marriage and expect their husbands to remain hopelessly attracted to them. Even when couples build their marriages upon a foundation of true love, husbands still want their wives to attract them physically.

Several months after marriage a young wife was busy putting on makeup to go out. Watching her for a little bit her new husband asked, "I wonder who you're trying to impress?" Obviously, the way she dressed around the house let him know it was no longer him.

Because women place more emphasis on emotional rather than physical attraction, many fail to keep themselves appealing to their husbands. Yet even if wives fail to understand the importance of physical appeal to their husbands, the noble Shepherd testifies in the pages of inspired scripture how a loving man notices and reacts to his wife's appearance.

True love revolves around both an intellectual and an emotional commitment to always act in the best interest of the beloved plus satisfaction of the 5 senses. Rarely will a man take time to become involved with a woman who doesn't satisfy his 5 senses — taste, smell, sight, hearing, and touch. Fortunately, men find different clothing, hair styles, makeup, and physical characteristics attractive.

When a woman discovers her own style, it will appeal to a man who likes her as a person. He won't try to make her over into his own concept of the ideal woman. Instead, he'll treasure her for who she is — the rose of Sharon, the lily of the valleys. But a wife who doesn't attempt to satisfy her husband's 5 senses by being a fragrant, well-groomed companion places a strain on her marriage. Her beloved may long for the woman he courted, not the lack luster wife she has become.

Taste: The Shulammite's Love

Song of Solomon 4:10a:
"How beautiful is your love, my sister, my bride!
How much better is your love than wine."

"Beautiful" is the same word Solomon uses to describe the Maiden's body.

"Love" (dôd) is a different word than we've seen before. It means "properly to boil, i.e. (figuratively) to love; by implication a love-token, lover, friend; specifically an uncle:--(well-) beloved, father's brother, love, uncle" (Strong 30).

Throughout the story, the Shulammite and the Shepherd compare love to the soothing, mellowing attribute of wine. The Maiden's love intoxicates him more than the best wine. As long as she freely shares her love with him, he can face whatever life throws his way. He won't need to stop at the bar on the way home to drown his feelings in a bottle.

Smell: The Shulammite's Fragrances

Song of Solomon 4:10b:
"And the fragrance of your oils
Than all kinds of spices [balsam odors – NASB footnote]!"

Although defining the words in this short verse may seem tedious, it helps us grasp the magnitude of the compliment the Shepherd pays the Shulammite. Later the Maiden makes a play on his sentiments. Then the Shepherd turns his feelings of love in this verse into a grand finale. Thus the couple expands upon these thoughts when the climax happens in the next chapter of both the Song of Solomon and this book.

The Shepherd begins by using the same words for fragrance and oil that the Shulammite used when she said, "Your oils have a pleasing fragrance" when Solomon took her to his camp for inspection (Song 1:3).

"All" means "properly the whole; hence all, any or every:--(in) all (manner), altogether, any (manner), enough, every (one, place, thing)" (Strong 55). The word "kinds," which was added in the NASB, is left out of many of the translations. The Shepherd uses the same Hebrew word for "all" and language, "*all* kinds of spices," as he does in verse 14, "*all* the trees of frankincense."

"Spices" (bôsem) means "fragrance; by implication spicery; also the balsam plant:--smell, spice, sweet, (odour)" (Strong 24).

In "spices" versus "balsam," the only places the lexicons don't identify *bôsem* as the balsam shrub are the verses in this scene (Song 4:10, 14, 16; 5:1). Yet the New American Standard Bible's footnotes add "balsam odors" for all four verses. Thus throughout the Song of Solomon, *bôsem* is either translated as balsam or the footnote references it as balsam. The story refers only to a generic oil, never to a generic spice. So to translate these verses with a non-descript spice is out of character with the Shulammite's and the Shepherd's language.

Indeed, the Shepherd is well acquainted with the balsam shrub, not to be confused with balsam fir trees. The two-foot-tall balsam bushes often grow on the banks of creeks and rivers at both low and high elevations. Their three-to-five-inch bright yellow flowers resemble our sunflowers and are one of the first signs of spring. The shepherds graze their sheep on the tender petals beginning in mid-April. Different parts of the plant are edible all summer long.

The United States Department of Agriculture appreciates how valuable the balsam shrub is for sustaining a variety of animals including elk, antelope, mule deer, and small mammals including sage grouse. Growing quickly in the spring, the plant provides nourishment through the leaves, buds, and flower heads that bloom all summer. Other animals thrive on its nutritious seeds. The Department of Agriculture warns that domestic sheep can damage stands and reduce productivity through heavy spring grazing ("Arrowleaf" 9/26/2006).

Oils probably refer to the Shulammite's use of olive oil as a carrier or base oil for adding drops of pleasant-smelling essential oils of various herbs. Diluting the more expensive essential oils lets a person reap the benefit of their fragrances and healing properties while cutting the cost. Olive oil adds additional health benefits. As a country maiden, she is proficient in using all kinds of mixtures of oils for promoting health and staying fragrant.

Earlier we saw how she associates the smells of myrrh and henna with the Shepherd (Song 1:13-14). Now he praises her masterful blending of essential oils to create her own private label—somewhat like Elizabeth Taylor's warm and resonant designer fragrance of White Diamonds. Taylor's delicate, flowery scent includes essential oils of oakmoss, lily, rose, sandalwood, and amber.

The Shepherd compliments the Maiden, "Your unique, personal fragrance is better than the whole balsam shrub—the shrub that provides food for my sheep all spring and summer long along with essential oils for them and me." In other words, he says, "My sister, my bride, you are the best. Even the beautiful, fragrant, golden balsam shrub that inhabits the banks and hillsides can't compare to you. You are the embodiment of romantic perfumes blended into your own aroma."

Touch: The Shulammite's Lips

Song of Solomon 4:11a:
"Your lips, my bride, drip honey."

This is the Shepherd's version of saying he likes to taste her. For the Shulammite to long for him to kiss her with the kisses of his mouth suggests they've engaged in passionate kissing. It's easy to imagine the Shepherd's hands tenderly cradling her face while he experiences the sweet honey of her lips. In his longing to be fully united with her, he again calls her my bride. He is looking forward to the time when kissing will be their foreplay before sharing all their love for each other.

Intimacy anorexics typically withhold kisses and hugs after marriage. Over time, their touching continues to decrease. Because kissing releases bonding hormones, a person can be fooled during courtship about the other's true affection. Both husbands and wives are devastated when this avenue of daytime touching disappears. They often fight depression and feelings of being unloved and betrayed.

Hear: The Shulammite's Honey and Milk

Song of Solomon 4:11b:
"Honey and milk are under your tongue."

Earlier the Shepherd told the Maiden he longs to hear her sweet voice every day (Song 2:14). He thrills to the sound of her sweet voice and tidings, for honey and milk are under her tongue.

The Shepherd uses three aphrodisiacs to compliment the Maiden. The first two aphrodisiacs are food—honey and milk. The third comes from her persona—the sound of her voice.

Honey is a common element of love. Remember the birds and the bees? Is that something our parents made up to deal with their timidity in talking to us about sex? It turns out that the word "honeymoon" comes from the aphrodisiac effect of honey. In ancient times, when a couple married they were given an alcoholic drink made from honey to promote their marital happiness. Not only does honey give a natural energy boost, but it also contains boron which helps regulate the couples estrogen and testosterone levels. Certainly, honey is a perfect treat for a honeymoon to remember (Jung n.d.).

Milk readily boosts romance no matter what form it is consumed in—yogurt, milk, or cheese. All are high in zinc which helps increase a woman's libido (Curtis n.d.).

The most powerful of the aphrodisiacs is the Shulammite's tender words. Although many recipes for love combine warm milk with honey and spices to promote good sexual health the Shepherd thrives on the

Maiden's loving expressions. From her lips come honey—sweet comforting support and admiration; and milk—rich, creamy, life-sustaining encouragement and confidence in his abilities. Honey and milk under a person's tongue helps promote love.

The Shulammite and the Shepherd communicate. They make good use of this free aphrodisiac in courtship. And it increases their emotional bond.

Many married couples are starved for intimate communication with their significant other. Instead of sharing their own feelings, emotionally-challenged people often excel at *only* asking questions and listening. Because they show interest in your feelings, it may seem like they're also sharing. However, the anorexic and the narcissist are *only* gathering data to find your vulnerable spots for criticizing and manipulating you later.

Stop talking. Ask questions about *their* feelings. Listen. Do they answer with a question of their own...or share private thoughts?

See and Smell: The Shulammite's Appearance

Song of Solomon 4:11c:
"And the fragrance of your garments
Is like the fragrance of Lebanon."

Wow! The Shepherd mentioned how she takes care of her appearance twice. Can it be that daily appearance is important to a man?

The Shulammite's garments give forth the soft, sweet aroma of an appealing woman. Again, the Shepherd compliments her appearance and her delight in her femininity. The scent of her garments reminds him of Lebanon—refreshing and soothing. The Shepherd's words sound almost like a fabric softener commercial. The Maiden may not spend hours grooming each day and her skin is dark from the sun, but she keeps herself and her clothing clean and generously uses essential oils. She proudly enjoys and emphasizes her femininity.

Keeping clean and sweet-smelling requires little time or expense and offers great rewards as Solomon wrote in Proverbs 27:9: "Oil and perfume make the heart glad, so a man's counsel is sweet to his friend." Cleanliness and perfume perk up a person as much as visiting with a kind and helpful friend. The Shepherd praises the Maiden for exhibiting both of these traits. Her clean fragrance increases his enjoyment of associating with her and makes it easy for him to love her.

4. The Shepherd Proposes Spiritual Intimacy and Love

Song of Solomon 4:12:
"A garden locked is my sister, my bride,
A rock-garden locked, a spring sealed up."

The Shepherd respects God's plan for the way of a man with a maid by saving sex for lovemaking in marriage. And so he compliments the Shulammite for her sexual purity. Then in the following verses he highlights the marital benefits of keeping her garden locked.

Throughout the story, the Maiden uses a simile of masculinity for the Shepherd to be "like a gazelle or a young stag on the mountains" (Song 2:8-9, 17; 8:14). Now the Shepherd describes the Maiden with the metaphor of a garden — a special feminine garden. The Shulammite also uses this same metaphor for herself as a garden (Song 4:16).

The Jews understood the metaphor of "a spring sealed up" to be talking about the Shulammite's sexual favors. For example, Proverbs 5:15-18 refers to the older wife's sexual charms as a cistern and a well and the husband's sexual energies as springs and streams of water.

Genesis 29:3 gives an illustration of a water well sealed up with a rock which was rolled away to water the flocks, then rolled back to keep the well pure. Thus the self-respecting rose of Sharon locks her beautiful sexual garden to save her refreshing waters for her husband.

Although she looks forward to sexual love, she controls her desires and saves herself for marriage. Because of his esteem for God's design of the sexual relationship and his deep admiration for the Maiden as a person, the Shepherd doesn't try to force her into allowing him to drink from her spring before marriage. He assures her that he values her purity and pledges to help her keep it. The Shulammite and the Shepherd look forward to decades of expressing love in each other's arms.

Solomon admired only the Maiden's exquisite body — the outward signs of her feminine hormones. He never looked at her inner qualities — her character, life goals, and capacity to love. With his 140 wives, he showed no respect for the spiritual side of marriage — one woman joined to one man for life through the 4 parts of love — intellectual, emotional, sexual, and spiritual.

The Shulammite Will Make an Exciting Lover

Song of Solomon 4:13a:
"Your shoots are an orchard [park or paradise — NASB footnote] of
pomegranates."

The Shepherd continues his metaphor of the Shulammite being a garden. He starts with her as a protected, locked garden with its own water source. Now he describes her as an orchard of pomegranate trees, a beautiful park, or paradise.

Researchers at Queen Margaret University in Edinburgh, Scotland, found that as an aphrodisiac, pomegranate juice increases the testosterone level in both men and women. This helps preserve the health of their sexual organs and increases their libido. The fruit offers many other health-building benefits, especially for the heart (Sabharwal 2/18/2014).

Gary Martin says, "The pomegranate played an important role in Hebrew culture." He continues:

> Pomegranate figures were used to decorate priestly clothing (Ex. 28:33f.; 39:24ff.) and the temple (1 Ki. 7:18 and often). Pomegranates were among the products of the land brought back by the spies in Num. 13:23. A land without grain, figs, vines or pomegranates is a wretched place (Num. 20:5). The drying up of the pomegranate tree is one aspect of punishment for sin (Joel 1:12, cp. Hag. 2:19) (102-3).

By describing the Shulammite as an orchard of pomegranates trees that increases the libido of both men and women, the Shepherd views her as becoming a sexually active marriage partner. He looks forward to when they can combine her femininity with his masculinity in each other's arms. All the way through the Song of Solomon, the Shepherd and the Maiden view each other as sexual equals (1 Corinthians 7:2-5).

The Shulammite Will Make a Loving Mother

Song of Solomon 4:13b-14:
"With choice [first] fruits, henna with nard [spikenard – KJV, ASV] plants,
Nard [Spikenard – KJV, ASV] and saffron, calaimus and cinnamon,
With all the trees of frankincense,
Myrrh and aloes,
Along with all the finest spices [balsam odors – NASB footnote]."

"Choice" (*meged*) means "to be eminent; properly a distinguished thing; hence something valuable, as a product or fruit:--pleasant, precious fruit (thing)" (Strong 61).

The *Theological Wordbook* connects *meged* in verses 13 and 16 with Deuteronomy 33:13-16 where *meged* describes multiple "choice" blessings that the tribe of Joseph received from God through nature. In other words, *meged* designates certain distinguished, valuable, precious things as gifts from God to lovers (Song of Solomon) and the tribe of Joseph (Deuteronomy) (489).

"Fruits" is the same word in Song 2:3 which could be translated "first fruits" (Strong 96).

The Shepherd's compliments glow with admiration of the Maiden and appreciation for God's choice gifts of love and family. He recognizes her as a fertile love orchard. The Israelites used a metaphor of "plants" or "shoots" to describe their children. For example, Psalms 128:3 says,

"Your wife shall be like a fruited vine, within your house, your children like olive plants [shoots—NIV] around your table." Psalms 127:3-5 says, "Behold, children are a gift of the Lord, the fruit of the womb is a reward…. How blessed is the man whose quiver is full of them."

Thus the Shepherd says the children he and the Shulammite will bear together will be first fruits as loving gifts from God. The Maiden possesses excellent qualities for becoming a loving mother, and he asks her to become the mother of his children. He metaphorizes their children as henna, nard plants, saffron, calainus, cinnamon, and trees of frankincense, myrrh, aloes, along with the finest balsam.

The Shepherd's words are similar to the husband's compliment of the wife of great price in Proverbs 31:28-31. At the end of their lives, the Proverb writer says, "Her children rise up and bless her; her husband also, and he praises her, saying: 'Many daughters have done nobly, but you excel them all.'" Instead of looking back over a life well-lived, the Shepherd looks into the future to praise the Shulammite.

One student remarked, "It sounds like the Shepherd wants to have a lot of children!"

Yes, it does and that brings up an important premarital question. In our modern age it's not a given either the man or the woman will want children. Many divorces take place because the husband or the wife discovered after marriage that the partner didn't want children. Don't assume anything. Ask.

Another important premarital question involving children: Is having children the main reason the person wants to get married? For example, many husbands learn to their sorrow that the only reason their wife married them and engaged in sex was to have children. After the right number of children was born, their wife began refusing to make love with her husband. These men thought they were getting a life companion. Instead, they were used to fertilize the woman's eggs and provide for her offspring.

This is somewhat like the female praying mantis that bites off the head of the male after mating. If you think this simile is overdramatic, talk to a couple of these husbands. The ones who talk to me are very bitter at being tricked into marrying their wife just to give her children.

One young wife freely admitted, "I had a high libido until we had all the children we wanted. Now I prefer to masturbate rather than have sex with my husband. I often fantasize about my husband dying or having an affair so I can be rid of him." Ah, a human praying mantis….

Women get fooled the same way by suitors who are looking for a trophy wife and children. After the men father some children, their sexual interest in their wife dries up. Some of these husbands and wives subscribe to the ungodly doctrine that sex is only for procreation.

Courtship is the time to ask questions. Lots of questions. Questions from different perspectives to get at the truth.

The Shepherd and the Shulammite look forward to filling an orchard with baby shoots. By describing their children as different plants, the Shepherd acknowledges the uniqueness of each child and the individual care required. Each plant he names denotes a valuable service. Some provide nourishing food. Others supply dyes and perfumed ointments. The rest furnish essential oils that promote health and treat diseases. He's confident that his Maiden will be able to give loving guidance and care to each child.

Not only will their children become valuable citizens, the Shepherd also knows the Maiden will transform their home into an "orchard" or "a park or paradise." What a woman! The Shepherd expects to live in a well-run, organized orchard—not some run-down garden patch taken over by weeds. What a challenge to a woman!

We might be tempted to say, "This is very idealistic and sounds like young people who've never had children. They boldly assert they know all about it and try to tell us how to raise our kids." Although there may be a lot of truth in this statement, the young couple grew up in a very different family situation than most of us do today. We will see later that they both come from loving homes where their parents enjoyed lovemaking and provided an emotionally rich environment for their children—the kind of home the couple dearly wants to replicate.

The Shulammite Is the Love of His Life

Song of Solomon 4:15:
"You are a garden spring,
A well of fresh water,
And streams flowing from Lebanon."

The Shepherd returns to the metaphor of a garden to describe the Shulammite. This time he emphasizes 3 different water sources. Besides using springs and wells as metaphors for sexual favors, the Jews also use water to symbolize a life-sustaining quality. For example, God refers to himself as a "fountain of living waters" (Jeremiah 2:13). Jesus calls himself "living water" (John 7:37-38).

The Shepherd sums up his proposal by declaring the Maiden is a garden spring, a well of fresh water, and streams flowing from Lebanon. All 3 water metaphors emphasize freshness—a bubbling, vibrant woman—not a muddy pond. That's what every man wants for a lifelong sexual partner. Nothing provides nourishment and quenches a man's thirst like a loving woman. The Shulammite will be the opposite of a woman who just lays there and lets her husband try to find refreshment in her stagnant waters of indifference and sexual ignorance.

The Shulammite calls the Shepherd, "You whom my soul loves" (Song 1:7). She says, "You are the love of my life."

Now the Shepherd says his own words, "My sister, my bride, you are the love of my life." The couple displays the emotionally intimate characteristic of paying the highest possible compliments to each other.

George Gilder shares statistics in his book *Men and Marriage* that prove marriage to a loving woman increases a man's life span. He notes that single men have nearly double the death rate as married men. And they are 3 times more likely to die than single women. This is true from all kinds of accidents and diseases. Most of the diseases don't show up until after age 45.

Many sociologists assume a single man doesn't take as good care of himself as a wife would. However, research shows that it's more than a lack of knowing how to cook or eat properly. The wide range of afflictions that kill single men indicates "a failure of the will to live."

Gilder sums up his discussion of how badly men need wives by mentioning that many men give credit to their wife when accepting public recognition. He asserts that these husbands are stating an obvious fact. Without a wife to care, more than likely, the man would not have succeeded. He may not have even lived long enough to receive the honor if he'd been single or divorced (65-6).

The Maiden's purity, feminine ways, mothering qualities, and industry combine to transform her into the Shepherd's own private garden with crystal clear springs. After marriage, the Shepherd will drink from her life-giving waters and be satisfied. His beautiful proposal speaks to the deepest longings of every feminine woman—her desire to be loved and honored.

The Science Behind Why the Best Lovers Are Married

Current research proves sex continues to get better with age in a monogamous relationship. Joe E. McIlhaney Jr., MD and Freda McKissic Bush, MD validate what God has patiently taught for over 3000 years in Proverbs 5:15-20—the best lovers are the older husband and wife—not the hot-hormonal young lovers.

And what a wonderful lifelong sexual journey it is of growth and bonding from newlyweds to senior lovers. The passionate wonder of youth only gets better over time. Truly, God is great in providing his people with a lifetime of ecstasy in each other's arms!

Doctors McIlhaney and Bush explain in *Hooked: New Science on How Casual Sex Is Affecting Our Children* in the chapter "Meet the Brain" how this bonding phenomenon occurs over decades in each other's arms.

Indeed, MRI and SPECT brain scans and new developments in neuroscience are providing greater understanding of the role of three major hormones released during sex.

Dopamine Hooks People on Sex

The brain chemical *dopamine* affects a person's enjoyment of many activities. We sometimes call it the "feel-good hormone." We get a physical and emotional high of intense energy, excitement, and hyper-focusing when we do something we thoroughly enjoy. It makes us want to keep doing the pleasurable activity over and over—perhaps even to the point of blissful exhaustion.

Dopamine doesn't have a conscience or a sense of right or wrong. Dopamine doesn't care if the activity is good or bad for us or if it's harmful to other people. Dopamine rewards us for both healthy and destructive activities.

It doesn't care if we're getting our thrills from using illegal drugs, drinking until we throw up, or racing our car down the highway weaving in and out of traffic. The feel-good hormone can cause both adolescents and adults to become addicted to the activity that gives them a blast of pleasure.

Sex is one of the most powerful activities that gives a dopamine rush. As might be expected sexual activity releases dopamine into a person's system to give them a rush regardless of the circumstances or with whom the tryst occurs. We all probably already know sex is one of the most powerful generators of the feel-good reward of dopamine.

Teenagers and young adults can easily get hooked on indiscriminate sex. Teenagers and young adults are especially susceptible to the addictive effects of this hormone of pleasure for unhealthy sexual activity—sex only for the sake of sex. An emotional bond is not necessary for dopamine to flood a person's brain.

Sex plus dopamine makes married couples addicted to each other. Contrary to the negative affect of dopamine on unmarried people, the hormonal rush benefits married couples. Frequent lovemaking over a lifetime addicts married couples to sex with each other. It greatly strengthens their emotional attachment and delight in each other.

Oxytocin Is the Primary Hormone of Love for Women

Both men and women have the hormone *oxytocin*, but it's primarily a female hormone necessary for healthy sexual activity and bonding. It's released into the woman's brain by warm, intimate touch. Oxytocin has two roles:

1. It increases the woman's desire for more touching.
2. It bonds the woman to the man who is doing the touching.

Oxytocin and touching often lead to sexual contact and bonding. Intimate touching and orgasm bathe the woman's brain with oxytocin. This creates a cycle of desiring more touching and lovemaking which leads to more desire for touching and sex. At the same time the woman is becoming more and more bonded to the man.

Older couples get the most benefits from oxytocin, touching, and sex. Frequent lovemaking and oxytocin create a special long-term connectedness and happiness. A wife in such a relationship rarely seeks sexual activity outside her marriage. She is firmly bonded to her husband who gives her so much pleasure.

Oxytocin bonding is more than an emotional connection for older wives. The bonding takes place in the brain. Doctors McIlhaney and Bush state, "It is almost like the adhesive-effect of glue—a powerful connection that cannot be undone without great emotional pain" (37). Reacting with brain cells, oxytocin physically binds the wife to her husband.

God glued Adam and Eve together with the hormones of love. Interestingly, the doctors' description of oxytocin bonding like glue sounds similar to God's declaration after he created Adam and Eve that a man would leave his parents and *cleave* to his wife (Genesis 2:22-24). "Cleave" means "glue together, cement, join or fasten firmly together, join oneself to, cleave to, give oneself steadfastly to, labor for" (Thayer 353). Now science has shown us that God doesn't use superglue on a husband and wife—he uses oxytocin, which holds better than even The Original Super Glue.

Vasopressin Is the Man's Hormone of Love

God didn't overlook men when he passed out hormones for gluing a couple together during lovemaking. Men also bond to the woman during sex. *Vasopressin* controls the man's soulmating. This masculine hormone has two major roles in relationships:

1. It glues or bonds the man to the woman.
2. It also bonds the man to his children.

Vasopressin is the "monogamy molecule" or the "commitment chemical." Oxytocin and vasopressin affect the female and male brains in a very similar way to bond the husband and wife to each other. This bond becomes stronger over the years with frequent lovemaking. If a woman wants her husband to love her more, she needs to respond to his sexual desires with gusto. Even better, she should initiate lovemaking.

Touching releases the hormones of love when illness gets in the way. Diabetes and other medical issues can hamper a man's ability to express physical love to his wife. Certain drugs play havoc with a man's desires. Yet even in these instances, a couple can share love through passionate kissing, hugging, cuddling, and fondling each other. Even though it isn't as intense a form of lovemaking as sexual intercourse, the doctors say intimate touching still releases hormones of pleasure and bonding.

Multiple Partners Affect the Hormones of Love

In *Hooked* Doctors McIlhaney and Bush note many similarities between the male and female hormones when couples engage in sexual activity with multiple partners. Here is a summary:

The hormones of love are values-neutral. Dopamine (the pleasure hormone), oxytocin (primarily female hormone), and vasopressin (primarily male hormone) are all values-neutral. None of the hormones care if the people are married to each other, cheating on a mate, or partying in the Hookup Culture. They don't care if the people love each other or are abusive. They don't care if the couple has just met or is celebrating their fiftieth anniversary. The hormones do their job by bonding the couple together.

The hormones of love can lead to long-term bad relationships. The hormones don't care if one of the partners is a self-centered narcissist or a verbal abuser. The hormonal bonding caused by sexual activity can trap the more gentle and loving partner in a relationship with a person without natural affection and harmful behavior. Even men who are being abused by a woman frequently have a hard time mustering the emotional strength to end the relationship.

Men and women may try to figure out what's wrong with them. All three hormones greatly affect behavior. Women may wonder why they love someone who treats them so disrespectfully. Men may question why they keep dating a woman who verbally abuses them. Both men and women may ask what is wrong with them that they can't develop a deep permanent relationship with anyone after having many sexual partners.

Having multiple sexual partners bonds men and women to every partner they have. These cycles of casual sex with one partner and then another limits their cranial response to only one kind of sexual experience. They get hooked or addicted to the immature dopamine rush of sex. They never allow their brains to experience the full benefits of the hormones of a long-term relationship.

Thus, both men and women jeopardize developing a lasting satisfying sexual relationship when they engage in casual sex. Doctors

McIlhaney and Bush state, "They risk damaging a vital, innate ability to develop the long-term emotional attachment that results from sex with the same person over and over" (43). The effect of the hormones can be seen in brain MRI and SPECT scans of couples who have been engaging in sex for a few months.

Having multiple sexual partners damages the bonding mechanism. Concluding the section on the bonding similarities between oxytocin and vasopressin the doctors state that men and women lose their ability to bond after numerous sexual partners. They compare it to "tape that loses its stickiness after being applied and removed multiple times" (43).

The Hormones of Love Benefit Monogamous Couples

If a couple regularly expresses sexual love to each other, their emotional bond grows stronger over the years. As they age, the affection their bodies speak to each other deepens. The hot impatient hormones of youth give way to the mellow sweetness of a lifetime of sexual love.

God has wonderfully designed the hormones of love to bless husbands and wives. It's part of the way of a man with a maid and enjoying passionate love for a lifetime. Not only do the man and the woman give each other great mental and physical pleasure; but in doing so they also bind themselves together in greater love and commitment for facing the normal problems of life. Such a God deserves to be served with all our might—yes, even in bed!

The Shepherd and the Shulammite Protect Their Hormones

The Shepherd demonstrates his love for the Shulammite by helping her save herself for him until marriage. Sexual love provides one of the most happy and enjoyable experiences on earth when protected in marriage. When sex turns into a sensuous affair, it often deteriorates into a frustrating relationship.

A teenager wrote to Ann Landers over twenty years before scientists began scanning brains in love. Yet she articulates a scenario dominated by sexual hormones. She also shares what dating was like before the hormones of sex were aroused. Sadly, many young people today haven't much experience with sexless dating. They dive right into having sex. Consequently, they don't have a clue about what they're missing. This young woman tells us how great sexless dating is:

Dear Ann:
I am a 17-year-old girl, and I want to send a message to other teenage girls. I have fallen victim to my own stupidity twice now. A lot of girls use sex to try to keep a boy interested.

Why do we do this when all our lives we are told by our parents, church and school that it is wrong? I guess virginity seems old-fashioned in the '90s. But I have learned that some things never go out of style.

In both my relationships, I can look back and see that before sex entered the picture, we laughed more, talked more and went to a lot more places. Once you cross that line, it's all the guys want to do. Boys don't respect girls who put out. If a guy decides to break up, it won't make any difference whether you've had sex or not. If you use sex to try to hold on to him, that will be the only part of you he's interested in. Learn to say, "This is as far as we're going," and stick to it before you go too far.
—Feeling Used Again in Oregon (Landers 10/1/93).

The Shepherd reveals the secret for finding sexual satisfaction with a woman—honest respect for her. Minds and bodies cannot blend into harmony and sexual bliss unless respect reigns. The Shulammite's feminine qualities make her dear to the Shepherd. She chases away all his loneliness as they unite in emotional intimacy.

Additionally, God provides for the release of the Shepherd's buildup of semen while he waits to marry the Shulammite in the fall. He didn't have to face the temptation of Internet porn that plagues young men today. But his healthy hormones of youth made him beg the Maiden to marry him in the spring. He was a real, live, warm-blooded young man—he wasn't a super hero. For more information, read the appendix chapter "Wet Dreams, Laws of Cleanness, and Masturbation." God's blessing of wet dreams for both males and females differs from self-masturbation and helps prepare them for a wonderful marriage.

MayoClinic.org reports that some doctors believe that one cause of premature ejaculation comes from "early sexual experiences" ("Premature" n.d.). The boy often feels guilty about what he does in the backseat of a car. Instead of relaxing and enjoying himself, he worries about getting caught and tries to hurry up the act. As a result hormones teach his body to respond unnaturally. Overcoming this bad habit that was reinforced with hormone imprinting can be difficult. Just a few years of stolen pleasure during the courting years often rob couples of many years of delight in married lovemaking.

On the other hand, a man and woman who keep themselves pure during courtship protect their bonding hormones. This frees their minds and bodies to start sexual love off on a high level in marriage. Then they can build upon their purity and love through the years to continually increase the joy they experience in each other's arms.

The Shepherd's Universal Proposal

The Shepherd's proposal provides a universal example of mature love. He knows how to love a woman. Rather than a passing fancy, he wants a permanent relationship. Her whole person arouses his sexual desires—not just her measurements.

Every man who searches for a lifelong companion and lover should look for the same characteristics of the 4 parts of love that attracted the Shepherd to the Shulammite. If his desires center on sensuous lust as Solomon's did, he should be wary. When physical attractions diminish (and they will), strong intellectual, emotional, sexual, and spiritual bonds keep the marriage happy and passionate.

Additionally, the Shepherd's proposal reflects the 4 parts of one-flesh love that God ordained in the Garden of Eden when he created Adam and Eve. The appendix chapter "The 4 Parts of Love Parallel the 4 Parts of One-Flesh" develops this concept. You may want to take a break and read the short appendix chapter before continuing to increase your understanding of secrets 4 and 5.

The Shulammite may not know whom she should marry, but God and we do. In the next chapter, God shares his design for married lovemaking by interjecting himself into their love story to share his secret formula for a lifetime of passionate sex. With the Shepherd's words of affection stirring in her heart, the Maiden makes an important promise to herself....

Study Exercise

Answer all questions in your own words.
1. Why did the Shepherd refer to the Shulammite as "my sister, my bride"?
2. How do the Shepherd's and Solomon's marriage proposals differ?
3. What did the Shepherd mean when he told the Shulammite, "You have made my heart beat faster"?
4. Why should a girl guard her purity?
5. Is purity important for a boy? Why?
6. What is the most important fact you learned about sexual hormones as they apply to your life?
7. If husbands or wives frequently tell their mates, "No," when they want to make love, how are they harming themselves, their mates, and their marriages?
8. What do the sexual hormones teach us about lovemaking for older couples?
9. Do you disagree with anything in the lesson? If so, explain giving scriptures for your reasons.

Research Exercise

Using the Internet or an essential oils book look up each of the plants the Shepherd refers to as children (Song 4:13-14). Write two paragraphs on each plant. First describe what the plant looks and smells like and what kind of growing conditions it requires. In the second paragraph explain the special benefits of each plant for food and healing.

Conclude with three paragraphs. First, discuss how the Shepherd and the Shulammite could turn their home into an orchard of many different children in their day-to-day life. In the second paragraph, list ways they could help each child reach their full potentials. In the final paragraph, share what you can do differently in your home.

Personal Exercise

The esteem the Shepherd shows for the Shulammite is of universal application in selecting a mate or for turning a lack-luster marriage into an emotionally satisfying one. Narcissists and intimacy anorexics avoid giving compliments and specialize in criticism. Below are eight emotionally healthy compliments the Shepherd gave the Shulammite:

1. Enjoys her company
2. Treasures the glance of her eyes
3. Notices her appearance
4. Values her love
5. Likes the taste of her lips
6. Respects her purity
7. Thinks she will make a good mother
8. Considers her his source of life

Later we'll examine the Shulammite's reverence for the Shepherd and Solomon's admiration for the Maiden. The goal is to look into your own heart so you can rise to a higher standard of love. This activity will teach you about true emotional intimacy.

This exercise isn't to criticize your partner. It's to provoke self-awareness—to take care of the beam in your own eye so you can see clearly how to deal with legitimate problems with your mate or date. Whether male or female, single or married, the activity is the same:

1. For each of the Shepherd's compliments, list specific compliments you've given your partner in that area within the last three months.
2. For each of the Shepherd's compliments, list specific put-downs you've given your partner in that area within the last three months.
3. If you can't remember the compliments or put-downs you've given your partner, ask your companion to list them for you. No doubt, he

or she will remember.

4. Compare the lists of compliments and putdowns. Write a paper about how you can improve your ability to love on an emotionally intimate level. If you operate primarily in criticism mode, you have a serious problem. Your behavior is harmful to your family. Both you and your spouse need to read *Intimacy Anorexia* by Douglas Weiss and do the workbook. You may need professional counseling.

Stacey's Story:
My Children Know Something Is Going On

Dear Patsy Rae,

The other day my teenage daughter said, "Mom, you've changed so much in such a short time that there's no way Dad can't have noticed. He's probably stunned and confused by it. I'm amazed myself."

I told her when we get serious about obeying God, He works changes in us beyond what we can even imagine. I knew the Lord was working in me through all this, but I was also beginning to see that much work had to be done in my own heart before some things within our marriage could be addressed.

I gathered my children around and shared with them, on an age appropriate level without going into details, that Daddy and Mommy had some problems to work on. I assured them that they were in no way the cause, or to be blamed in any way. I could sense that it did them a world of good. I encouraged them to pray for both Daddy and Mommy, not to be fearful about the situation, and that they could trust God to work it all out to His glory and our good. We all prayed together.

I also took the opportunity, because I know how detrimental my husband's verbal abuse of me could be to their respect for me, to explain to them that I would not tolerate disrespect from them. I shared with them that Daddy's sin of disrespect towards me doesn't mean that it makes it okay for them to do the same. That's his sin, and it's wrong. Also, if I show their Dad disrespect in any way, it's my sin. It's wrong, and God will deal with me regarding it. If they are disrespectful to me or their Dad, God will hold them accountable for their sin.

I told them that I was going to begin teaching them to fight fair! I still have a long ways to go with Joe, but I'm excited about what is happening with our kids.

Thank you for encouraging me to keep on keeping on,
Stacey

Secret 5: Sip the Divine Wine of Passion

Solomon's Siren Song: Frolicking with the Shepherd

After giving the Shepherd the bad news about having to postpone their wedding until fall, it's two weeks before the Shulammite can search for him. His mother says, "He's with the other shepherds. They're still pasturing the sheep on the balsam blossoms along the stream two miles away."

The Shepherd sees her coming and waves his staff in the air. They both start running toward each other. Some of the mother sheep panic and begin bleating as they run after him on their short legs. Their babies' shrill voices add to the alarm as they scamper to keep up.

Finally he throws his staff down and grabs her, lifts her into the air, and twirls her around. He lowers her and stands back with his hands on her shoulders. "Let me look at you." He touches her face. "You're starting to tan. I like it." He pulls her to him, kisses her forehead and her nose. Then, he gently caresses her face while he tastes her longingly.

Suddenly, the fussing sheep, vying for attention around their feet, make them stop. The couple laughs. The Shepherd pats the heads of his babies. "It's okay, Flek and Glik. This is just my sweetheart. You need to get used to her. You'll grow to love her like I do."

The Shepherd picks up his staff and takes the Shulammite's hand. "Come on. Let's go over to the creek so the sheep can finish eating. The sun will soon be hot, and I'll need to move them to the shade to digest these beautiful yellow flowers. They'll be happy until it's time to head home."

His eyes mist, "The fragrance of these balsam flowers makes me think of you."

The couple sits on a large rock and the Shepherd puts his arm around his maiden's waist. She lays her head on his shoulder. He asks, "Have I told you lately how much I love you?"

"No," she coos as a smile spreads across her face.

"I can't live without you. I didn't think I could wait until spring to get married. Now the only way I can survive until fall is to keep busy — really busy."

The Shepherd rubs the nose of one of his ewes trying to push her way between him and the Shulammite. "Okay, Prissy," he laughs. "I know you need attention, but so does my gal. I don't get to see her very often." He turns Prissy around and pats her rear. "Get your little *tuckis* back to the flock."

"As you can see, it'll be time to shear the sheep in a few weeks."

"Tell your mother I'll help her cook for the shearers. We should have the walls around the vineyards in good enough shape so I can be gone for a couple of days.... It'll be great to get to see you.... Although you'll be sweaty from all that work...." She laughs, then teases, "Maybe I'll still kiss you when no one's looking."

The Shepherd cups her chin and turns her face up toward him. He looks into her eyes, then says, "All these babies suckling their mamas make me long for the day you and I will have our own babies. You'll be a wonderful mother."

"And the way you take care of your animals...I know you'll be a loving father.... I love your parents the way they tease and laugh with each other.... I miss my dad. Mom and he were like that. I miss laughing at them when they were flirting and acting silly."

"I know, my sweet sister. That's the kind of home I want, too. I'll always love you. And flirting with each other all day will be so much fun!"

"The sun will soon turn my skin black...maybe you'll want to wait until next spring to get married so I can be lily white for our wedding?" She tries to keep a straight face, but ducks her head as giggles escape.

"I love the way you laugh. And NO! I don't want to wait until next spring." He tilts her face up again. "The sun's kisses make you glow with beauty. This fall you'll be a radiant bride and my heart will beat faster than ever when you're finally in my arms."

His mouth covers hers.

Song of Solomon 4:16-5:1:
"Eat and Drink Until Tipsy With Love!"

ACT TWO, SCENE THREE CONTINUES
SECOND DAY - NIGHT

Still in the garden, the Shulammite walks along the path deep in thought comparing Solomon's sensuous proposal to the Shepherd's declaration of love. The virgin Abby sits on a cedar bench plucking a small lyre.

The Shulammite Prays to God—
The Author of Spiritual Love

The Shepherd's beautiful proposal asking her to become his wife cycles over and over in the Shulammite's mind. He pledged to love her intellectually, emotionally, sexually, and spiritually. Now she stops and takes her dilemma directly to God. She knows that whomever she marries, they must honor God's design for love for their marriage to rise to its full potential. With her arms stretched toward the heavens, she beseeches God, the author of spiritual love, to come to her aid.

She Asks for God's Protection and Guidance

Song of Solomon 4:16a:
"Awake, O north wind,
And come, wind of the south."

The definitions of the words in these next 4 lines reveal that the Maiden addresses God with ancient Hebrew symbols for appealing to him for help.

"Awake" is the same word the Shulammite uses for both "arouse" and "awaken" in the theme of the book when she begs the Virgins not to *"arouse* or *awaken* my love, until it pleases" (Song 2:7, 3:5, 8:4). As we saw earlier, Martin explains that both arouse and awaken "carry the idea of 'arouse' in the sense of inciting to (some kind of) action. Thus, to 'arouse' or 'stir up' love would mean to incite it to action, to 'wake it up' from its sleeping, resting state and set it into motion" (72-3).

"North wind" is used to refer to God's power. For example, Elihu introduced God to Job who was suffering from boils and grieving over the death of his children: "And now men do not see the light which is bright in the skies; But the wind has passed and cleared them. Out of the north comes golden splendor; Around God is awesome majesty" (Job 37:21-22). Then God answered Job out of a whirlwind (Job 38:1). Likewise, Ezekiel received a message from "a storm wind coming from the north" (Ezekiel 1:4ff) (*Theological* 774).

"South wind" refers to God's protection of his people. Zechariah declared, "Then the Lord will appear over them, And His arrow will go forth like lightning; And the Lord God will blow the trumpet, And will march in the storm winds of the south. The Lord of hosts will defend them" (Zechariah 9:14-15). Asaph, one of the leaders of David's choir, sang about how God used the east wind and directed the south wind to rain manna and quail on the Israelites as they traveled toward the promised land (Psalms 78:24-29) (*Theological* 383).

Hess cites Zechariah 9:14 and Psalms 78:26 and recognizes a

reference to God in the south wind. He says, "This suggests more than warmth; it implies a powerful wind that effects change. The female calls for this as she commands the winds to blow upon her garden" (153).

Thus the two winds the Shulammite summons refer to God. As an Israelite, she knows how her people call to the north wind to describe God's glory. She has heard the stories of God directing the south wind to provide manna and quail for her ancestors as they wandered around in the wilderness for 40 years. She understands that when the Hebrews moved into the Promised Land that the vineyards she now oversees were already there provided by that same God (Nehemiah 9:24-25).

The Maiden stands in Solomon's garden, separated from the Shepherd, her mother and brothers, and the vineyards—everything she has ever known and holds dear. She has just relived the Shepherd's beautiful, intimate proposal showering her with compliments and validation of her personal worth to him.

But she lives in a concealed virginal garden (Song 4:12). She patiently waits for marriage to open the gate to reveal her bountiful fruits of marital love. Rather, impatiently waits....

Using word plays, she praises God as the commander of the universe. She begs him to bring together the north and south winds in a powerful clash of emotional whirlwinds and intellectual thunderstorms to swirl his protection around her as he reveals her in all her feminine glory to her husband-to-be. She shivers in anticipation of his answer.

She Asks for God's Help to Be a Loving Wife and Mother

Song of Solomon 4:16b:
Make [Blow on – NIV,] my garden breathe out fragrance,
Let its spices [balsam odors – NASB footnote] be wafted [streams] abroad.

"Make breathe out" or "blow on," a primary root means "to puff, i.e. blow with the breath or air; hence to fan (as a breeze)" (Strong 93).

"Wafted abroad" is translated "streams" in verse 15—"streams flowing from Lebanon." The verb occurs 16 times in the Old Testament and figuratively refers to something coming from God. For example, in Psalms 147, verse 18 concludes a list of blessings from God for Israel with, "He causes His wind to blow and the waters to flow." Isaiah 44:3 refers to God "pouring out water" with his divine blessings. Additionally, "flowing waters" are used to describe the sexual blessings of the older wife in Proverbs 5:15 and the Maiden in Song 4:15 (*Theological* 567). The implication? These sexual blessings come from God in his design of the way of a man with a maid.

Emotionally alone in Solomon's garden, the Shulammite bares her soul to God. She continues the Shepherd's metaphor of her sexual favors as a spiritual garden with a life-giving stream flowing with love for him and their children (Song 4:12-15). As the word definitions show, all four lines of her prayer invoke God's favor to bless her as she seeks to be a ravishing wife and a loving mother.

She beseeches God to blow on her garden of love to scatter the fragrance of her multi-faceted sexual favors. Now, in the fourth line, she continues her previous thought. She asks God to open up her love in marriage by appealing to the metaphor of the multi-useful balsam bushes that thrive in her sexual garden to bless both her future husband and children (Song 4:14 — see discussion). As God-given hormones released during lovemaking join her stream of love, her soul will overflow with life-giving tenderness for her family that knows no boundaries.

We can easily see this escalading effect of emotional love through frequent lovemaking in Charla Muller's book *365 Nights, A Memoir of Intimacy*. She writes with humor and candor as she tells about wanting to give her husband Brad something extra special for his fortieth birthday. Like many couples they argued from time to time about her lack of interest in lovemaking. Brad tried to adjust by telling himself "quality was more important than quantity." They both knew that was a lie.

She explains, "The year our daughter was born, I think my husband could count on his fingers and toes (or perhaps just his fingers) the number of times we even had sex at all…. It was good when we had it; we just didn't have it all that much."

So for his fortieth birthday Charla offered him a "knock-your-socks-off, the-stuff-that-dreams-are-made-of-fantastic" gift that no one else could give him. The idea of "The Gift" of intimacy for 365 nights was born — no strings attached.

Because of their "fairly abysmal" sex life, Brad was reluctant to accept her birthday present. He didn't want to be set up for disappointment. When she assured him she would keep her pledge, The Gift began (8-14).

After a month, she wrote, "I don't know if anyone noticed a change in me…. But *I* noticed something. Brad and I flowed better as a couple. We were happier (yes, I was happier having sex every day, but it was only July). Our house ran better because we were both more agreeable, more helpful, more solicitous to each other" (33).

Seven months into her gift, she titled three sections "Our Gift Was Making Me Healthier," "Sex Was Making Me Happier," and "Our Intimate Moments Were Making Me Feel Younger" (142-6). But soon Charla did a major backslide in attitude. She struggled for months to gift herself emotionally while she continued to give her body to Brad. Overcoming her lack of enthusiasm, when their year was up she declared, "There is no denying that this might be the best year of our marriage...yet" (256).

I was fortunate to watch Oprah interview Charla and Brad soon after the book came out. Oprah asked about the effect on their children. Charla said that once she and Brad started having sex every day, the whole family became more loving and touching. The children responded to living with happier, more affectionate parents by being more loving to each other and their parents. The children developed the sibling intimacy we explored previously when the Shepherd calls the Shulammite "my sister."

Charla Muller's book is a good read for both husbands and wives who are dealing with a sexless marriage. Her candid approach will help open their eyes to faulty excuses and produce some weighty topics for honest conversation and self-examination. Hopefully reading *365 Nights* alongside the study of the Song of Solomon will assist in bringing more love into their homes.

She Asks for God's Help for the Shepherd to Be a Loving Husband and Father

Song of Solomon 4:16c:
May my beloved come into his garden
And eat its [his] choice [first] fruits!"

"Come" (*bô*) is a primary root and means "to go or come (in a wide variety of applications)" (Strong 19). It is used 2570 times in the Old Testament. It can be used idiomatically for dying or going to the fathers or for sexual relations as "come in to her" (*Theological* 93).

"Eat" (*'âkal*) is a primary root that means "to eat (literally or figuratively):--burn up, consume, devour, feed" (Strong 12).

"Choice" (*meged*) is the same word in Song 4:13 that designates certain distinguished, valuable, precious things as gifts from God (*Theological* 489).

"Fruits" is the same word in Song 2:3 and 4:13 that could be translated "first fruits" (Strong 96).

Are you noticing how many of the word definitions in the Shulammite's prayer include a reference to God—like "choice"? Do you see how involved God is in a couple's sexual relationship? How much he cares about our happiness? Do you see why spiritual love is important?

The Shulammite begins her prayer by talking about "my" garden, "make *my* garden breathe out fragrance." Now she prays for the Shepherd to come into "*his* garden and eat *his* choice first fruits." Gary Martin explains:

What a skillful mixing of the pronouns to emphasize that the sexual relationship in marriage belongs to each partner *equally!* How well this corresponds to God's design that man and woman are to become "one flesh."... Yet until the marriage is legally consummated, the garden must remain locked, the spring sealed. Thus we have perhaps the clearest picture of virginity presented in the Song (102).

In recognizing their joint ownership of her sexual garden, the Shulammite places the responsibility for "coming" and "eating" upon the Shepherd. She prays to God, "Let the Shepherd be a man who knows how to truly love a woman." *She defines masculinity as the qualities of a man who comes in to his wife and consumes her excellent first fruits — her intellectual, emotional, sexual, and spiritual charms.*

She Addresses the #1 Marriage Complaint

After nearly half a century of being the confidante of husbands and wives, this verse (Song 4:16) addresses the #1 complaint I get from both — trying to survive a sexless marriage with an intimacy anorexic. In other words, it speaks to a husband who doesn't come, nor consume his wife's sexual fruits. Instead, he prefers to self-masturbate, lust after porn (or other women or men), or pursue multiple adulteries.

Anorexic wives keep their sexual garden locked except when they want more children or to manipulate their husbands. Such a wife knows how to insult her husband to make him lose his erection, give up begging her for sex, and to stop flirting with her. Instead of offering the first fruits to her husband, she serves him spoiled and rotten produce.

The spouses of sexual deprivers live in a constant state of depression as they are prevented from drinking from the mate's life-giving fountains of love. According to Weiss, defective husbands and wives deliberately withhold intimacy to manipulate, punish, and inflict pain on their spouses. At the same time, anorexics are experts at blaming the mate for everything that's wrong in the marriage.

She Refuses to Accept an Anorexic's Blame

The Shulammite's prayer indicates she won't accept a sexless marriage or the blame for her husband refusing to consume her sexual favors. She prays, "May he come and eat." She recognizes the Shepherd's responsibility to bring an intellectually, emotionally, sexually, and spiritually healthy person to their bed. Likewise, Colossians 3:19 commands, "Husbands, love your wives, and do not be embittered against them." Thus God holds husbands responsible for cherishing and nurturing their wives so they function as true lovers (Ephesians 5:28-33).

Weiss says it's impossible for any woman or man to love an intimacy anorexic out of emotional coldness. The makeover must flow from the person's heart. We'll see later that Solomon wants the young woman to transform his life. Once she recognizes his emotional bankruptcy, she refuses to have anything to do with him. We need to teach our children how to recognize flawed dates to help them escape entering into a disastrous sexless marriage.

The movie, *Alexander and the Terrible, Horrible, No Good, Very Bad Day,* a family comedy, provides an interesting study of a loving family and an emotional anorexic. Big brother, Anthony, told his parents and two siblings, "I'm dating Cecilia, the hottest girl in the whole school. And tomorrow I'm taking her to the prom." In the first scene with Cecilia, we realize that the rich snot has major intimacy problems. But all Anthony can see is her beautiful body; and so, he cooperates with her attempts to turn him into someone worthy of her.

Many times the way we handle problems shows what we're made of—our true character and ability to empathize with others. As the terrible, horrible, no good, very bad day wears on into the evening and constantly changes Anthony's plans on the fly, he begins to see Cecilia's flaws. Finally she asks him, "You mean you'd rather spend this evening with your weird family than go to the prom with me?"

Fortunately, Anthony has learned something about love from his parents so he understands the significance of her question. We need to pray the Shulammite's prayer for our own sons and daughters and for ourselves and our spouses, that we might have the same good common sense. Likewise, we need to beseech God that our spouse and children will accept their personal responsibility to bring a responsible and healthy person to their marriage bed.

She Praises God

The Shulammite pleads with God, "Let me get married, and let the man I marry be glad he married me! Let him eat the choice fruits I grow and create through loving him, caring for our children, and overseeing our home. Let him be beside himself with happiness!" The Maiden makes this pledge to herself even though she doesn't know whom she will choose—Solomon or the Shepherd. She only knows she will not settle for less than true love in the arms of an adoring husband.

She holds the power to satisfy all of a sexually-healthy man's desires for a wife and lover. In her mind, she visualizes marriage with the Shepherd. He knows how to love a woman and she hears him tell her how satisfied he is. Indeed, more than satisfied! Happy beyond measure!

The Maiden concludes her prayer by praising and thanking God for the promise of a successful marriage if she chooses the Shepherd. Her words change as she foresees the Shepherd coming into her garden to bestow his love upon her as he experiences the first fruits she's saved for him. The Maiden expresses confidence that both she and the Shepherd will enter marriage as two sexually mature individuals.

A girl with feminine abilities need not hide her head in shame. Instead, she should boldly call to God to stir up his north and south winds to advertise her purity of body and mind and her desire to become a complete, loving wife. She should promise herself that she will gladly satisfy all of her future husband's needs for companionship.

As the Shulammite does, let every married or single woman turn her face toward the heavens and lift her arms in prayer, "May my beloved come into his garden and eat its choice first fruits! To God be the glory forever and ever. Amen."

The Maiden and the Shepherd
Praise the 4 Parts of Love

Song of Solomon 5:1a:
My sister, my bride, I have entered my garden;
I am gathering my myrrh and my spices [balsam – NASB];
I am eating my honeycomb along with my honey;
I am drinking my wine as well as my milk.
(Complete Jewish Bible)

Two scholars note how important the verbs are in this verse. Dr. G. Lloyd Carr and Dr. Richard Hess agree that the verbs can be translated as either present or present perfect tenses. Since Dr. Carr says the verbs indicate "action in progress," I used the Complete Jewish Bible translation which shows this action (Carr 128; Hess 154).

After praying to God to help her and the Shepherd become a loving husband and wife, the Maiden hears in her thoughts the satisfaction the Shepherd will find with her. The Shepherd says, "I have come into my garden." When he proposed, he described her as a locked sexual garden (Song 4:12-15). Now he speaks as if he has already tasted the first fruits from her park-like paradise. Essentially, the Shepherd says, "I'm getting ready to talk about making love with you."

The Shepherd sends beautiful, erotic, poetic words flowing over the Shulammite. The first 4 lines recognize the 4 parts of true love. Two names for her point to their soulmating or intellectual love. Four actions describe the intertwining of their sexual love. Two aphrodisiacs reflect spiritual love between God and husbands and wives. Finally, four aphrodisiacs cement their emotional love for each other.

2 Names of Intellectual Love

Intellectual love is joining the minds, or soulmating, on the deepest level. It contains no superiority or inferiority, and revolves around genuine appreciation for the similarities and differences of each person. It recognizes how the individuals balance and complement each other with heart-felt, touchable love. Different personalities. Different needs. Different talents. But together as soulmates.

Name 1: "My sister." The Shepherd calls the Maiden, "my sister," 5 times in the Song of Solomon. He acknowledges that they share the special intimacy of siblings. They are soulmates who share secrets and problems while supporting and loving each other.

Name 2: "My bride." The Shepherd calls the Shulammite "my bride" 6 times. They've talked about marriage and are promised to each other. He views her as someone with whom to raise a family. Then in their twilight years, she'll become a wife to enjoy the mellow sweetness of older companionship.

4 Actions of Sexual Love

This section uses 4 amazing verbs to describe what kind of husband the Shepherd will be. He says: "I come," "I gather," "I eat," and "I drink." In every instance, he initiates sexual love. The Maiden's response is implied because the Shepherd couldn't "come," "gather," "eat," and "drink," if she weren't an eager supplier of intimacy.

In a later passage, the Shulammite promises to initiate sexual love (Song 7:12). Both this verse and 7:12 portray the Shepherd as a willing recipient of her seductions. The Song of Solomon portrays the couple's equality as they each take responsibility for initiating and responding in the 4 acts of soulmating and lovemaking.

Action 1: "My sister, my bride, I have entered my garden." Earlier the Shulammite prays, "May my beloved come into his garden" (Song 4:16). Now she gives thanks as she visualizes what marriage will be like after he has come in to her when her garden is no longer locked. In marriage, she'll give him full and free access to her sexual charms as he claims her as his soulmate and bride.

Action 2: "I am gathering my myrrh and my spices [balsam — NASB]." Psalms 80:12 translates "gather" in a similar context with "pick its fruit." The first two lines of this verse are parallel thoughts while the last two are parallel. Thus the Shepherd uses two verbs that to the Jews illustrate the consummation of a marriage. He says, "I *came in* [went in] to my bride," and "I *took* her myrrh and balsam" (Genesis 24:67; 29:23, 30). Not only does the Shepherd look forward to claiming the Maiden as his soulmate and bride, but she will also stimulate and please him as the two most precious essential oils and perfumes deliver pleasure and healing.

Action 3: "I am eating my honeycomb along with my honey." The Shulammite in the previous verse prayed that the Shepherd might eat her excellent first fruits. The Israelites tithed with honey, milk, and wine (2 Chronicles 31:5). The Shepherd visualizes totally consuming the Maiden's sweet, rich gifts that portray both her emotional and sexual love for him. He lacks for nothing in finding total satisfaction with her.

Action 4: "I am drinking my wine as well as my milk." The last two lines complete the picture of eating and drinking—a complete meal. And what a meal it is with the sweet spiced wine of love and the rich creamy goat's milk for substance and endurance.

2 Aphrodisiacs of Spiritual Love

The first two aphrodisiacs in this group, myrrh and balsam, are unusual in that God commanded the priests to use them in Temple worship (Exodus 30:6-9). He declared the recipes "holy" and forbid them to be used for personal use.

Avraham Sand explains that 11 of the spices used for the Temple Incense are listed in the Talmud (Talmud *Keritot 6a*). This list includes 5 of the aphrodisiacs found in the Song of Solomon (balsam, myrrh, spikenard, saffron, and cinnamon) (Sand 52).

Thus, the history of the first two aphrodisiacs connects them with God and his covenant with the Israelites. In the context of the 4 parts of love reflected in becoming one flesh, they represent spiritual love.

It makes sense for God to command the use of aphrodisiac essential oils in worship of him—the mingling of the fragrances of both divine and human love. Aphrodisiacs provide a constant reminder that serving God is all about loving him and loving our neighbor; and especially our families, as ourselves (Matthew 22:36-40).

Aphrodisiacs 1 and 2: "Myrrh and balsam." The relationship of these aphrodisiacs to worship of God takes sexual love that originated within the mind of God to a whole new level. And the Shepherd knows it. He compares marriage to the Shulammite to a special combination of his-and-her love-enhancing aphrodisiacs—myrrh and balsam.

Japanese researchers discovered that the warm, musky scent of myrrh is for ladies only. It turns women on by increasing their level of testosterone as they associate the fragrance with their husband's own earthy sweat. However, it decreases a man's testosterone level ("Chanel" 8/15/2008).

What about balsam? Avraham Sand shares that the ancient sages said, "Balsam can make a man dizzy with lust!" (55). The Shepherd frequently says the Shulammite is like balsam to him. As a hot-bloodied lover—she's all the balsam he needs to enjoy everything about her.

The Shepherd views the Shulammite as his sexual equal in both desire and ability to give and receive pleasure. This is the message of God's compatibility law in 1 Corinthians 7:3-4. A woman can't satisfy her own sexual needs, nor can a man satisfy his own desires. It takes a wife radiating the smell of love, or myrrh, and a husband high on her balsam love to truly ravish each other.

4 Aphrodisiacs of Emotional Love

The aphrodisiacs in the Song of Solomon are a gift from God through nature. They contain mega-nutrients that keep us well and offer healing from many physical diseases. They affect our emotions. Some are calming and reduce stress. Others balance our hormones and help increase both estrogen and testosterone.

Aphrodisiacs 3 and 4: "Honeycomb and honey." A piece of the hexagonal wax in a jar of honey acts as a natural preservative. The honeycomb keeps the honey from turning to sugar for a very long time. And honey chewed out of a piece of honeycomb is the freshest and most delicious of all the sweet nectars.

Honeycombs and honey have been recognized as powerful aphrodisiacs from ancient times. Raw honey is rich in B vitamins and increases the libido of both men and women (Snyder 10/3/2011).

The Shepherd says, "I am eating my honeycomb and honey." Their lovemaking will never grow stale, even as the events of life change their circumstances. When a couple builds their marriage on intimate love, they bond even closer as they face the challenges of life together.

Aphrodisiacs 5 and 6: "Wine and milk." Both wine and milk are soothing aphrodisiacs. Wine increases blood flow, mellows a person out, and reduces inhibitions. Consequently, a person needs to use care when using wine as an aphrodisiac (Snyder 10/3/2011).

Milk is celebrated as an aphrodisiac by itself or warmed with honey and spices. Hmmm, or perhaps add milk to a luxurious bath for two with floating flower petals and essential oils. Milk softens and silkens the skin—perfect for skin to skin contact. Scented candles complete the concupiscent adventure.

Can you hear and feel the Shepherd's admiration, respect, and love for the Shulammite? I can. Like the Shulammite, his words make me want to praise God for preserving such a vibrant picture of masculinity and femininity to bless the lives of those who dare to serve him with all their mind, heart, body, and soul.

Secret 5: Sip the Divine Wine of Passion

Song of Solomon 5:1b:
"Eat, friends;
Drink and imbibe deeply, O lovers
[and drink, until you are drunk with love! – CJB]"

God gives a 3-step formula that contains the keys for a couple to delight in an ecstatic lifelong sexual relationship. It's very simple: (1) eat, (2) drink, and (3) get tipsy on love. The Song of Solomon has preserved this wine-based formula for over 3000 years. It gives the Divine answer to the Shulammite's prayer. This is similar to the behind-the-scenes discussion God had with Satan when he maligned Job (Job 1-2).

Teetotalers Don't Get It

In his inspired Song of Solomon, God uses the metaphor of drinking wine to tell the Shulammite and the Shepherd to get married and to increase their bond through frequent, playful lovemaking. Many times as Christians, we are teetotalers and don't know much about drinking except for the ugly drunken scenes we see in the movies and on television, or perhaps endure with relatives or friends. Such was my case for nearly 40 years of studying, teaching, and writing about the Song of Solomon. While I thought I understood the tipsy part, I completely missed the significance of the metaphors about wine and drinking.

I didn't even realize I was missing something important until I spent some time with my brother Ted Snodgrass on his longhorn ranch in the East Texas Hill Country. For weeks, I was bombarded with advertisements about Texas wine and offers for touring the wineries. For example, the Piney Woods Wine Trail boasts, "The heat, humidity, and the acidic red dirt of East Texas produce some of the best sweet wines you have ever tasted."

Finally, I asked Ted about drinking wine apart from getting drunk. He explained that spices and herbs help give the different wines their distinctive appeal. Wine choices range from robust dinner wines to sweet mellow dessert wines. Red and white wines reflect the special flavors of the different grapes. Even the soil the grapes are grown on gives it brand-name-building flavor. Not only is taste important to enjoying wine, but smell also adds a whole new dimension.

The Song of Solomon begins with appeals to both wine and smells, "Your love is better than wine. Your oils have a pleasing fragrance.

Therefore the maidens love you" (Song 1:2-3). It ends with the wedding taking place after the grape harvest (Song 8:11). As I did the word studies for this verse, with my background teaching on sex and the Bible, I realized God was giving the Shulammite and the Shepherd a Divine formula for a wonderful sex life through the imagery of wine.

Alcoholics Don't Get It

Non-alcoholics who are familiar with drinking wine and other stimulating beverages understand the wisdom of God's three-step formula. In a nutshell, the string of events goes like this: (1) first *eat* a real meal so the food in your stomach will slow down the alcohol hitting your bloodstream, (2) order a *drink* and sip it slowly, and (3) *keep drinking and savoring the wine until you're tipsy,* or feeling a pleasant buzz, but not mind-numbing drunk.

This is the opposite of what alcoholics do. They drink instead of eating. Generally, they drink the cheapest stuff they can get—the rot-gut stuff. It has a high alcohol content and can taste putrid. The higher the alcohol content, the better—that's why they drink Mogen David Mad Dog 20/20. It's wine enhanced with alcohol. They drink it because their whole purpose is to get a drunken buzz—not to enjoy the flavor.

It takes much longer to get drunk on the good stuff—the alcohol content is what makes you drunk. When you eat a meal, it absorbs some of the alcohol and slows down how long it takes you to get drunk. This lets you enjoy the flavors and smells of the various spiced and sweet wines along with different fruit wines.

If you're on a bad drunk, you'll wind up with a hangover. What does a hangover feel like? You're dehydrated, have a terrible headache with a filthy taste in your mouth, and your whole body aches like you have the flu. You vomit a lot. You've consumed so much your body can't handle it. Your body has to get rid of the toxin. It's alcohol poisoning.

Alcoholics abusing wine isn't what God is talking about. Alcoholics don't know how to drink wine. And they don't get it about true love.

The Friends and Lovers Get It

Although some people treat sex like winos and alcoholics treat their drinks, that's not God's metaphor for an exciting love life. Teetotalers and winos may not get it, but the Shulammite and the Shepherd did. The Israelites abhorred drunkenness more than we do. They appreciated sane, healthful wine drinking. Their firsthand experience of growing grapes for processing and drinking wine enabled them to understand God's message. It's time we caught up with this 3000-year-old epiphany.

God addresses the Shulammite and the Shepherd as "friends." He ends by calling them "O lovers." The main difference between the two expressions is intensity. They build their friendship in courtship, get married, apply God's formula, and end as lovers.

God applies the 3 aspects of a wonderful love life to (1) eat, (2) drink, and (3) get tipsy equally to the Shulammite and the Shepherd. Thus the couple performs the 3 steps in sync as an intimate dance of intellect, emotions, sensations, and worship of God. Now listen while God teaches us the secret of enjoying an exhilarating lifelong love life.

Step 1: Eat Honeycomb and Honey, Friends

"Eat" is the same verb the Shulammite uses when she invites the Shepherd to eat her choice first fruits (Song 4:16). Then the Shepherd uses it when he foresees actively eating and consuming her honeycomb and honey (Song 5:1a) (Strong 12).

"Friends" means "an associate (more or less close):--brother, companion, fellow, friend, husband, lover, neighbour" (Strong 109).

Being "friends" reflects the Shepherd calling the Shulammite "My sister." God acknowledges and approves of the intellectual intimacy of siblings that the couple brings to their marriage. But their union will grow into much more than just sibling-quality friendship.

The Shepherd identifies in the first part of this verse what he and the Shulammite will eat together in marriage—honeycomb and honey. It's impossible for him to eat it without her loving participation. He uses this same metaphoric imagery earlier in the Song of Solomon to reveal that eating honeycomb and honey is a double aphrodisiac.

The sweet, sticky nectar increases stamina and libido for vigorous lovemaking, and it represents the sweetness of friendship. The Shepherd pleads, "Let me hear your voice; for your voice is sweet" (Song 2:14). He explains, "Your lips, my bride, drip honey; honey and milk are under your tongue" (Song 4:11). The Shepherd enjoys kissing her tender mouth that says sweet, comforting, supporting words to him. She is his sweet friend in every sense of the word.

In the last verse of this chapter, the Shulammite makes a similar statement about the Shepherd. She tells the Virgins, "His mouth is full of sweetness. And he is wholly desirable. This is my beloved and this is my friend" (Song 5:16). Both the taste of his kisses and the tender words of his love and admiration make him wholly desirable.

Sweetness and tenderness build between lovers who are first friends. One husband said, "My wife and I finally got our sexual act together. I couldn't believe how tender I felt all the time and the loving words that came out of my mouth. I had to watch it at work because, without thinking, I was trying to call my male associates, 'Sweetheart.'

Good lovemaking made me feel compassion and love for everyone I came in contact with because of my Sweetie at home."

What does this say about having sex without building a friendship first? It's like the alcoholic going to a bar and skipping the meal. The alcohol hits his empty stomach. The undiluted beverage sets him up for headaches and vomiting; stomach and liver problems. As he slowly poisons himself, it creates an unhealthy addiction.

God says, "First, friends, eat a meal to have something in your heart and mind to absorb the intoxicating wine of lovemaking. Developing a friendship first lets you sip and savor more wine throughout a lifetime. That's part of the way I designed for a man to be with a maid."

Get to know each other. Find out if you even like each other. If you can't be friends before sex, sexual hormones may get in the way of you ever developing a true friendship.

Step 2: Drink Wine and Milk

The verbs "drink" and "imbibe deeply" present a wordplay as they are the opposite ends of the primary root *shâqâh* that means "to quaff [drink something, especially an alcoholic drink heartily], i.e. to irrigate [the ground]" (Strong 120).

"Drink" (*shâthâh*) means "drink, imbibe (literally or figuratively)" (Strong 122).

"Imbibe deeply" (*shâkar*) means "to become tipsy; in a qualified sense, to satiate with a stimulating drink or (figuratively) influence:--(be filled with) drink (abundantly), (be, make) drunk (-en), be merry" (Strong 116).

As we saw earlier, wine and milk are both aphrodisiacs. God instructs the Shulammite and the Shepherd to drink the wine of sexual love. He says, "After you've eaten a hardy meal of friendship, order a *drink* and slowly sip sexual love. Let your imagination and love for each other guide you in ways to serve it. Experiment with the different robust flavors. Taste the various sweet spiced dessert beverages. I've designed so many pleasures for you to enjoy in each other's arms. You'll be amazed how proficient you'll become sipping my beautiful language of love that transcends words."

The Shepherd said in the first part of this verse that he's drinking his wine and milk with the Shulammite. According to bartender Darcy O'Neil in "Cocktails and Dairy Products," adding milk to alcohol is tricky. The key seems to be using rich cream, not our 2% milk, and adding it last. Drinking milk and then alcohol on top of it can curdle the milk in your stomach and start a night of endless vomiting (3/2011).

If we're going to practice good Bible hermeneutics, we must

understand what this verse meant 3000 years ago and not get hung up on what happens in a bar. The issue is the difference in the *fermented* wines the Shulammite and the Shepherd drank and our modern *fortified* drinks. The fermented fruit juices in the Song of Solomon were mixed with water. The Israelites used different ratios from 20 parts water to 1 part wine all the way down to 3 parts water to 1 part wine. Wine made the water safe to drink and added nutrients. Drinking wine straight was considered barbaric. Yet this verse and others talk about strong drink.

The young couple readily understands what God means when he tells them to drink wine and milk. He wants them to savor the different aspects of sexual love by bringing their 5 senses into play. They'll see, hear, and feel the joyous liquid swirling in their hands as they relish the delicate smells and tastes of the abundant fruited wines of their country. We can understand God's message, too...even if we're teetotalers.

Step 3: Until You Are Tipsy, O Lovers

Dôd is used 39 times in the Song of Solomon. All but 6 are translated "beloved" with the Shulammite referring to her Shepherd boyfriend or the Virgins asking about him. *Dôd* never refers to Solomon.

> *"Your love [dôd] is better than wine" (Song 1:2).*
> *"We will extol your love [dôd] more than wine" (Song 1:4).*
> *"How beautiful is your love [dôd], my sister, my bride!" (Song 4:10).*
> *"How much better is your love [dôd] than wine" (Song 4:10).*
> *"Drink and imbibe deeply, O [sexual] lovers [dôd]" (Song 5:1).*
> *"There I will give you my [sexual] love [dôd]" (Song 7:12).*

Other passages that translate *dôd* as "love" also refer to sexual love. God said Judah was "at the time for love" (Ezekiel 16:7-8). Ezekiel said the Babylonians came to God's people "to the bed of love" (Ezekiel 23:17). And the harlot told the young man, "Let us drink our fill of love until morning" (Proverbs 7:18).

In the third part of the formula, God says, *"Keep drinking and savoring the wine until you're tipsy, O sexual lovers.* Take the time to feel a pleasant buzz, but don't get mind-numbing drunk." What do tipsy people do? They are uninhibited. They laugh a lot. They love everyone. They experiment with different wines to see which ones they like best and for what occasion. They savor the flavors and smells. They use any and every excuse to celebrate with a glass of wine. They love wine. Wine growers drink responsibly.

The Shulammite and the Shepherd talk about wine so much, they are obviously connoisseurs of wine. As expert judges in matters of taste, no doubt they'll want to enjoy lovemaking, prolong it, and cherish it, like a glass of pomegranate wine. They understand God's 3 steps because of their healthy upbringing and their knowledge of wines.

A reader said, "It takes a long time to get drunk." How do you take a long time to get drunk? You enjoy a nice meal. You order wine. You sip it, you enjoy it. Then you order another glass and repeat the process.

You don't act like the drunk. He can't walk; he gets obnoxious; he can't perform. All he can do is go home and pass out on the couch. To sober up, he needs to go somewhere and get some food in his stomach. Food absorbs some of the alcohol and helps sober him up. The Shulammite and the Shepherd eating first keeps them sober as they sip the strong drink of married lovemaking over and over.

Like wine, lovemaking mellows you out and gives you a sense of euphoria. Preachers point to the very worst examples of drinking to demonize liquor. It's not the liquor's fault, but the person who lacks willpower. The fact that God asked for strong drink to be given to him as a sacrificial offering shows the problem is not the wine.

Binge drinking is going to the bars to get drunk and to act crazy. Older people go out to enjoy a few drinks and each other's company. Binge drinking is selfish because you're not any good for anybody — not even yourself. The girls in the Hookup Culture make the liquor the scapegoat. They get drunk to have sex. They don't choose their partners — it's just sex with whoever wants to take advantage of them.

Decanting the Wine of Lovemaking

As a vineyard keeper, the Shulammite knows how to decant wine — how to mix it with water and serve it to bring out its best flavors. New wine requires a different technique than older wines. In the following verses, I'm going to use the example of decanting new wine for the honeymooners and decanting the older wines for their golden years.

Awaken Love Before Marriage

Song of Solomon 2:7:
"I adjure you, O daughters of Jerusalem,
By the gazelles or by the hinds of the field,
That you will not arouse or awaken my love,
Until she [it – NASB footnote] pleases."

This is the theme of the Song of Solomon which we've seen twice when the Shulammite begs the Virgins not to force Solomon on her before they fall in love with each other (Song 2:7; 3:5). She will repeat the message one more time give a summary (Song 8:4-7).

A country girl, the Shulammite learned from her mother that even the gazelles and hinds of the field go through elaborate courting rituals to win over the emotions of the intended female before mating. Thus the Maiden gives Solomon's Virgins a lesson in biology that reveals God's design for husbands and wives to awaken love before they marry.

The Maiden and the Shepherd have already spent time together building an intimate friendship of love. Not a foreplay ritual, this arousal of love comes from deliberately joining the man's and the woman's minds before they join their bodies — soulmating before physical mating. No wine being mixed during this stage of eating to prepare for drinking.

Get Tipsy as Newlyweds

Deuteronomy 24:5: "When a man takes a new wife, he shall not go out with the army, nor be charged with any duty; he shall be free at home one year and shall give happiness [cheer up-KJV] to his wife whom he has taken."

"Give happiness" or "cheer up" means "to brighten up, (make) blithe or gleesome, cheer up, be (make) glad, (have, make) joy (-ful), be (make) merry, (cause to, make to) rejoice" (Strong 118).

Ideally, God plans for a year-long honeymoon to start the happy couple on their journey to a lifetime of sexual compatibility and joy. Through the Law of Moses, he instructed the bridegroom to "be free at home," to spend the first year of his marriages "giving happiness" to his bride. It takes time and practice to lay a good foundation for a lifetime of loving and sharing the problems of life. For this reason, God told the new husband not to leave with the army, or to take on work responsibilities such as a traveling job or extra duties in the camp.

God commanded young bridegrooms to stay home for a year making love to their brides, being playful, experimentive, and joyful. A year of frequent passionate lovemaking strengthens their emotional and physical intimacy to protect them from the normal trials of life.

When I teach this verse in Bible classes, sometimes a wife will blurt out in front of everyone, "I was cheated! I want my year!" A modern bride should be so fortunate as to marry a husband who spends the first year making her blithe, gleesome, glad, joyful, merry, and full of rejoicing as only a husband knows how! And what a wonderful language of love their bodies learn to speak for a lifetime!

This is like decanting new wine. Decanting is simply pouring the wine into another bottle (the decanter) before serving. Careful decanting improves the flavor of most any wine as the process aerates it or mixes it with oxygen. "This triggers the release of more aromatic compounds. In addition it is thought to benefit the wine by smoothing some of the harsher aspects of the wine (like tannins or potential wine faults like mercaptans)." This is sometimes done on "a smaller scale by swirling the wine it the drinker's glass" (Wikipedia.org "Decanter").

Wine expert Joseph Nase says after decanting let new wine sit for twenty minutes or more. Then when you serve it, "You'll likely notice a dramatic increase in subtlety and complexity." He advised to keep tasting it for hours as it "may keep evolving and improving" (2014).

God chose the metaphor of wine to portray the 3 steps for a lifetime of wonderful lovemaking. Think about tasting the ever-improving flavor of decanted new wine over a period of hours, days, weeks, and a year. One of the beauties of enjoying a vaginal orgasm is that it changes and deepens with a woman's thoughts and experiences. She's like new wine in the beginning that ages into wonderful delectable sweetness. The more a couple makes love and experiments, the richer the flavor becomes. A vaginal orgasm is the most glorious gift a couple can share with each other.

Stay Tipsy During the Middle Years

> *Ecclesiastes 9:9: "Enjoy life with the woman whom you love all the days of your fleeting life which He has given to you under the sun; for this is your reward in life, and in your toil in which you have labored under the sun."*

"Love" is the same word used throughout the Song of Solomon and means "to have affection for (sexually or otherwise)" (Strong 9).

After the honeymoon, God instructs the husband to keep his priorities straight. The normal man takes his responsibilities to provide for his wife and children seriously — probably more so than most women comprehend. However, Ecclesiastes warns the man about the dangers of making his career, rather than his success as a family man, the purpose of his life. The chief reward God gives the man for working to make a living is enjoying life with the woman he loves.

This requires spending time with her to share both the problems and joys of life. God created a woman to satisfy the man's need for someone to confide in, to share his triumphs as well as his disappointments, and to believe in him when the world doesn't understand or take the time to see his point of view.

Failure to build this emotional bond during courtship and the first years of marriage makes a man susceptible to emotional affairs with women he works with. John Sandford calls this "spiritual adultery" in *Why Good People Mess Up: Keys to Upright Living in a Seductive World*. These affairs of the heart lay the groundwork for physical adultery when the opportunity arises. God intends for soulmating to enhance sexual gratification and to take place in the home, not the office (14-20).

Many wives will identify with the wife's pain in Sandford's book as they recognize their own husband's emotional neglect while he gives what belongs exclusively to them to other women. God wants husbands to work at soulmating and confiding in their wife so that the wife, not the other woman, is their best intimate friend.

In *Male Sexuality, The Truth about Men, Sex, and Pleasure,* Dr. Bernie Zilbergeld says many men find it difficult to leave their work at the office. Bringing their job worries, pressures, and frustrations home kills their desires and numbs their pleasures. He says men need to learn how to relax (150, 157).

He explains that sexual joy increases with age for couples who work at promoting trust, cooperation, and understanding each other. Other couples, however, become bored with each other after a few years. He said the most common reason for a lack of sexual interest was "relationships with little feeling left in them" (217-9).

Joseph Nase explains that careful decanting can improve most any wine. He says, "Occasionally, you'll come across a young wine with sediment," even well-made wines can exhibit this trait. You can decant it the same way you do older wines, only you must "allow extra time for the wine to breathe and develop" (2014).

Three thousand years ago, God told the man to spend time enjoying his wife — that the time he spent loving her was part of God's reward for subduing the earth. This formula for happiness during the middle years still promotes a healthy emotional bond along with ecstatic sexual experiences — even in the 21st century. Fancy cars and houses bought at the expense of time with one's wife can't satisfy for long the emotional hunger in a marriage. Only decanting out the sediment lets the wine breathe and bloom into full flavor to unite two lovers' bodies and minds in supreme sexual love.

Stay Tipsy in the Golden Years

Proverbs 5:15:
"Drink water from your own cistern,
And fresh water from your own well."

Proverbs 5:18-19:
"Let your fountain be blessed,
And rejoice in the wife of your youth.
As a loving hind and a graceful doe,
Let her breasts satisfy you at all times;
Be exhilarated always with her love."

"Drink" in verse 15 is the same Hebrew word the Shepherd uses in Song of Solomon 5:1a, where he says, "I am *drinking* my wine and my milk." It's also the same word God uses to say, "*Drink…O lovers.*"

"Breasts" (*dad*) "apparently [comes] from the same [root] as *dôd*; the breast (as the seat of love, or from its shape):--breast, teat" (Strong 29). *Dôd* is translated "love" and means "properly to boil [like a boiling pot], i.e. (figuratively) to love; by implication a love-token, lover, friend; specifically an uncle:--(well-) beloved, father's brother, love, uncle" (Strong 30). See Song 7:12.

"Satisfy" means "to slake the thirst (occasionally of other appetites):--bathe, *make drunk [emphasis added]*, (take the) fill, satiate, (abundantly) satisfy, soak, water (abundantly)" (Strong 107).

"Exhilarated" means "to stray (cause to mislead) usually (figuratively) to mistake, especially (morally) to transgress; by extension *(through the idea of intoxication) to reel [emphasis added]*, (figuratively) be enraptured" (Strong 112).

"Love" (*'âhab*) is the same word we've seen throughout the book and means "to have affection for (sexually or otherwise)" (Strong 9).

The "wife of his youth" is the girl a man married as a young man. Ideally, he laid the foundation for a good marriage and a happy love life during their courtship, and devoted the first year of marriage to experimenting with all the glorious ways to express love in each other's arms. With strengthened emotional and physical bonds, they worked together as a loving team to raise their family while he advanced in his career. Now he enters the golden years rejoicing in the sexuality and femininity of the grey-haired wife of his youth.

This passage parallels the Shepherd's proposal comparing the Shulammite's sexual favors to a pure spring overflowing with love (Song 4:12). Then God blessed their future, telling the couple to eat, drink, and get tipsy on love. Notice all the verbs of continuing to get tipsy in their golden years—drink from your own cistern, her breasts satisfy at all times, and be exhilarated with her sexual love.

Brain-imaging research pioneer and marriage and family therapist Dr. Earl Henslin says in *This is Your Brain in Love, Scientific Breakthroughs for a More Passionate and Emotionally Healthy Marriage* that older lovemaking is often better than the hot sex of youth. He observed over the years that twenty-year-olds rarely enjoy the same kind of passion that couples in their golden years are capable of experiencing (12).

Indeed, older wives make the best lovers of all because of a lifetime of soulmating during the day fulfilled in each other's arms during the night. How wonderful for men and women to end their lives with love radiating from their eyes, voices, and bodies because they understood the way of a man with a maid throughout their marriage.

Joseph Nase cautions that decanting older wine is a little more involved than pouring new, young wine. Older wine has more sediment and requires more talent to bring out its best flavor. Since the older wine has been aging for a while, its flavor doesn't need any, if much help. Too much oxygen can spoil it. Nase recommends, "You should decant older wine immediately before serving, before it begins to change" (2014).

It's like Conway Twitty singing "I'd Love to Lay You Down" to his older wife. He appreciates her charms, her graying beauty, and the life they've lived together. The wine of new love can't compare to older love that's aged for a lifetime with the sediments of living in the real world.

I love the analogy that the older wine "doesn't need any artificial boost" and "you should decant older wine immediately before serving." A wife who has enjoyed decades of vaginal orgasms in the arms of her husband doesn't require the foreplay of a young bride trying to figure it out. She's ready to get frisky at a moment's notice. If her husband needs help, she knows how to decant his sparkling elixir. Obviously, God knew the difference between new and older wine when he chose the metaphor of sipping Divine wine to teach couples about *SPEAKING HIS BEAUTIFUL LANGUAGE OF LOVE* for a lifetime.

God's Stamp of Approval

God who inspired the recording of this true story put his stamp of approval on the proposal of the Shepherd rather than the sensuous appeal of Solomon. Then he gave us his 3-step plan for how a couple can enjoy true intimacy for a lifetime. Imbibing deeply implies making love frequently to release the joyous sexual hormones that will bind their hearts even firmer to each other. Essentially, God tells us to eat, drink, and become tipsy on married love during the honeymoon year and don't stop drinking until death do we part.

In a marriage built on mutual respect for each other's role in life and inherent abilities, blessings abound from God. He created marriage and the marriage bed. He designed the hormones of love to glue a husband and a wife together as a soulmating union. And as they engage in robust lovemaking, it mellows them out to the normal stresses and disappointments of life. God cares about who a person marries, just as he hovered over the Shulammite as she agonized over her dilemma.

God inspired the Song of Solomon to teach us how to pick the right marriage partner for a lifetime of glorious merriment in the arms of our beloved. He wants us to be giddy with happiness too good to be true. He designed lovemaking to bless us every day of our lives as a couple.

If our marriage has gone astray, through understanding the many-faceted intimacies of love, we can build a foundation of true love to get tipsy on, even in our golden years. It's never too late to begin obeying God in our bedroom. And we're never too old to praise the God of heaven with our minds, emotions, bodies, and souls. To God be the glory forever and ever for his great love and compassion for us.

God tells the Shulammite and the Shepherd, "Get married and drink your fill of married love! Savor and experiment with the different spiced and sweet wines of sex. Laugh yourselves silly. Then drink some more until you fall asleep in each other's embrace!"

Then God tells the older couple, "Continue to get intoxicated on married lovemaking as long as you both shall live!" God wants the exhilaration of lovemaking to last all of a couple's life together—from their honeymoon through their golden years. And he saves the best sex of all for the older couple.

Two men love the Shulammite for different reasons. One loves her body; the other loves her person. The Shulammite must make the choice every bride must make. She must choose between sensuous love with Solomon and intimate love with the Shepherd. Although God has given his stamp of approval and the choice seems obvious to us, the Shulammite is emotionally involved in her dilemma. She's living it, and the right choice isn't clear. Nor is the choice easy for any woman or man in the midst of dating and strange new feelings of love and passion rising within their loins.

The curtains close on the garden as the Shulammite and the Virgin walk slowly back to the palace. Tomorrow, she meets the Queens….

Study Exercise

Answer all questions in your own words.

1. How should the Shulammite's prayer be every man's and woman's prayer before marriage? Is it a good prayer to make during marriage? Why?
2. Did God approve of Solomon or the Shepherd? Why?
3. What does God using the metaphor of wine to refer to sexual love mean to you? Why?
4. How does the Song of Solomon help solve the #1 marriage complaint of being in a sexless marriage?
5. How did the Shulammite and the Shepherd plan to celebrate true love in their marriage?
6. Why did God want the Shulammite and Shepherd to get tipsy on lovemaking for a lifetime? Does God still want couples to do this?
7. How did God answer the Shulammite's prayer to help her make a healthy choice for a husband?
8. How does the Song of Solomon help a couple develop healthy attitudes toward lovemaking?
9. Do you disagree with anything in the lesson? If so, explain giving

scriptures for your reasons.

Research Exercise

Analyze the account of Tamar and Amnon in 2 Samuel 13 in light of what the Song of Solomon teaches about the 4 parts of love, i.e., establishing intellectual and emotional love while honoring spiritual love before starting a sexual relationship. If you need to, review the appendix chapter "The 4 Parts of Love Parallel the 4 Parts of One Flesh." Write a two-page paper giving a brief review of the story, then exploring what teenagers today can learn from the account.

In past classes, teenagers enjoyed doing this project with their parents. It gave them an opportunity to talk about dating and sex in a non-personal and un-embarrassing manner. It also established a relationship with their parents for asking personal questions.

Personal Exercise

Write a paper to describe each part of God's 3-step formula for a wonderful love life. Conclude with two paragraphs about what God's plan means to you. Tell what you need to change to comply with God's plans for you and your relationship.

Stacey's Story:
The Verbal Abuse in This House Is Gone!

Dear Patsy Rae,

When I think of what my marriage and home life were like just one year ago at this time I have to thank the Lord for leading me to your Fighting Fair and marriage books. The pain and tension last year at Thanksgiving was so stressful--and it would only get much worse before it got better.

Let me back up a bit and explain. Almost a year and a half ago I finally faced the fact that we had a serious sexual problem in our marriage. I knew it could be solved if we could only communicate about it, but I was fearful of Joe's angry response. I didn't know where to begin. I found your website and contacted you for some advice on how to proceed.

You recommended the *Challenges in Marriage* material and told me to pay particular attention to the "Fighting Fair" class and *God's People Make the Best Lovers*. I began the hard work of unlearning a lifetime of how not to communicate and deal with problems. For six months, I studied and tried to practice the "How to Fight Fair" rules.

Then the weekend before Thanksgiving was a doozy around here. I don't remember how it started, but it exploded when I was straightforward with Joe regarding his sin. He became violently angry, but I kept my cool, stood my ground, and did not let my fear show. My children were devastated by what we witnessed in their dad. We gathered in one of their rooms. They were fearful, but we prayed and quietly sang hymns and praise songs.

We could hear Joe bustling about the house, going in and out to the car. He had threatened to leave and was packing things. He destroyed many precious belongings of mine. (He burned one copy of each of your books. I found encouragement in this because he hadn't burned both copies of the books. He amazingly left me with a copy of each. Go figure.)

Anyway, to make a long story short, I fought fair and relied on my mirror lines. Joe was stunned. I wasn't intimidated by his verbal abuse or angry outbursts and threats. Yes, I was crying inside, but the Lord upheld me. How could this mild-mannered man treat me, the woman who loved him so much, with such vile, wicked anger?

I followed the example you gave and e-mailed him an itemized bill for all my things he ruined. He tried to blame me for his breaking them. I continued to fight fair. I used my mirror lines and insisted he stay on topic instead of changing the subject. I told him I had been working very hard to not reply to him in kind. When he again tried to change the subject, I told him:

- You are missing my point and insist on changing the subject. You broke my stuff, again. I want to be reimbursed for it.
- If we are going to have a disagreement, then I expect you to fight fair. No name calling, no attributing motives, no destruction of property, stay on the one topic at hand. I will do the same.
- The argument/disagreement is finished when a viable solution has been reached and not until then. Things need to be resolved, not continually brushed under the rug 'til the next time when they are dragged back out again.
- If you are going to continue to break and destroy my things, then I expect to be reimbursed. Period.

Joe came home quiet. We ended up having a lovely Thanksgiving. God is so good. Please understand me. I was not deluded into thinking that all was well. I knew the journey had finally really begun, and God had much to work in me before He could work through me. Joe had the long weekend off from work and at one point early on he hugged me and told me he wanted to stop hurting me.

He never really repented for all that had transpired. It has always been very hard for him to apologize. I knew at this point that he was embarrassed and ashamed by his behavior. He eventually reimbursed me for everything including your books.

Since that awful night things have progressed slowly but surely around here. The Lord is showing me so much about myself and I realize how I have been distant from Him. I've been angry at the Lord, and I've blamed Him for my predicament. But He is so patient and merciful with us. He has given me glimpses of hope.

By God's grace, I persevered and continued to study your materials. I found myself having to go back to them over and over again. Just reading something one time does not suddenly "fix" things or make them easier. I better understand what the Apostle Paul meant when he wrote in Philippians 3, "To write the same things to you is no trouble to me and it is safe for you."

Your materials continually pointed me to scripture and little by little, God's Word began to make the necessary changes in me. At times, progress was painfully slow (and still is), but I continued to plug away at it. The cost was very high and eventually we hit rock bottom. Joe was angry with the changes that were taking place in me. He didn't know what to make of it. I think maybe he felt threatened.

Joe put the children and me through a painful, verbally abusive ordeal that lasted for months. I thought it would be the end of our marriage. It broke my heart to see our children suffer through such a time, but praise God, He turned things around.

As I began learning how to communicate and fight fairly, I taught the children what I was learning. And when their dad finally came and repented to me for the verbally abusive ordeal, he was willing to look at the "Fighting Fair" materials. Finally, we began to communicate.

Don't get me wrong. It takes lots of practice, practice, practice and then more practice to put a new and better habit into place! I wish I could say I have it down pat, but I don't. I fail more often than I care to admit. But repentance comes more quickly and easily now, on both our parts, when we do fail.

The effect on our children has been wonderful. They realize their parents aren't perfect. But seeing us learning to communicate properly and to readily repent when wrong has had a tremendous effect on them. It used to be that the tension would hang over us like a cloud and the children lived in a perpetual state of anxiety over what would happen next. Now they see us learning to fight fair and problems getting resolved quickly. This has lessened their fear, and they eagerly join in a hug when they see their dad and mom embracing.

I'm teaching them to put the same principles into effect in their relationships with each other. My prayer is that this will be a great blessing to them in their marriages because of having the benefit of learning God's principles and putting them into practice at an early age.

I know we have a ways to go. We're a work in progress and the growing and learning never really ends. Sometimes I get discouraged because my eyes get on the problem and not the solution. I forget to look at how far we've come. But when I do, I am humbled and amazed.

Here it is, Thanksgiving a year later. I was struck by the fact that the verbal abuse in our marriage has vanished. Praise God! It's just gone! What a difference from last year. When I get discouraged at the seemingly slow pace of growth, I need to remind myself of this remarkable fact.

I am thankful for the trials the Lord has sent my way because they have increased my faith in Him and shown me that He has indeed given us "all things pertaining to life and godliness" in His word.

Thank you so much for all the study and hard work you put into your Fighting Fair materials and your *Marriage: A Taste of Heaven* books. Thank you for continually pointing your listeners and readers to God's word and principles! He has not left us to flounder on our own. He has given us all the teaching on marriage and communicating we could ever need. It's all there in His word if we only take the time to dig into it and do the hard work of studying it and applying it.

Your materials are wonderful resources for learning where to find the answers in God's word on marriage and proper communication, and how to apply those answers. God has significantly used them in my life, marriage, and family. I heartily recommend them! I literally can't recommend them enough. They have been the catalyst for change in my marriage. It is imperative that those who choose to use them realize that hard work is involved. And the best solutions don't come fast and easy, making them that much more precious when they do come!

I find myself continually going back to your materials as references and reminders of what I need to be working on in my life and marriage. I look forward to teaching our children what I'm learning so they can start their own marriages on a good and solid foundation!

I pray the Lord continues to bless others, as He has me, with the fruits of your labor. I also pray that He continues to bless and strengthen you as you seek to encourage fellow believers in their marriages and Christian walk. Thank you for being an encouragement to me! I've gone from being angry at the Lord and blaming Him to increased faith and confidence in God. My heart is singing His praises.

Stacey

Secret 6: Surrender to Your Wet Dreams of Love

Solomon's Siren Song: Solomon Makes It Hard

The Shulammite and one of the Virgins stroll along the path in Solomon's garden. "Oh, Abby, what a long tiring day it's been. This was the first time I've ever ridden in a traveling couch. The hypnotic crunch, crunch of the soldier's feet trudging along the road, and the swaying of the compartment made me drowsy. Every time I nearly dozed off, a new batch of women would show up trying to see me."

"I know. Their shrill chattering got on my nerves. It's that way every time we bring someone back from one of these trips."

"I need to rest now that we're finally here. You'd think Solomon would be tired, too. I couldn't believe how he kept pulling out of line to race his chariot ahead of our caravan, and then he'd race it back into place. I don't know how many times he did that."

"The King loves his toys. He doesn't deny himself anything."

"I couldn't believe it, Abby. When we got here, the King insisted on talking to me. All I wanted to do was to go to bed and sleep without my body rocking."

"I know. Me, too."

"He didn't say anything new. Ha! I guess that's not exactly right. He keeps finding new ways to tell me how beautiful I am. I'm starting to feel like that's all he cares about—how beautiful I am. Is he going to like me when I get older like my mother? She's still a beautiful woman."

"You have classic good looks. You'll age very gracefully."

"Oh, Abby, that's not the point. I'm so tired of people inspecting me," she fiddles with her opal necklace. "This really is pretty." She looks into the distance, and then continues, "Thank goodness when I told the King I wanted to go to the garden and think about his proposal, he agreed. I'm glad he let you come along to show me the way."

"I enjoyed singing for you while you rested. You looked like you were deep in thought."

"Yes.... Lots of things are going through my mind. The Shepherd and I want to start a large family soon." She picks a cluster of bright pink blossoms and presses them to her nose.

"These smell so sweet—it's almost sickening…. But the fragrance still draws me in. I wonder what it is. I've never seen a bush like this."

"Solomon is always importing trees and planting them in his gardens. Isn't this the most beautiful garden you've ever seen? His servants work in it all the time so we can enjoy it year round."

"Yes, I love this garden, but I don't want to marry the King if we don't love each other as much as the Shepherd and I do…. I wonder how many children Solomon will want with me. He has so many wives. I love babies and little children. They make me laugh."

"Oh, you'll have so many fun things to do around the palace, you won't mind not having a house full of children. Tomorrow you'll be busy meeting the Queens and Concubines. You'll be surprised at how many of us Virgins there are. My folks promised me to the King when I was only seven. He paid a huge dowry for me. Look at my dowry necklace." Abby lifts the heavy chain with many different colored precious stones hanging on small ropes to form a half moon of wealth.

"It's beautiful! How do you stand wearing something so heavy? I like to feel free, not weighed down.

"Oh, I don't mind the weight. It reminds me that I only have two more years to go before I marry the King."

"Well, if that's all you've ever known…maybe that would be okay…. This is so hard! I don't know whom to marry…."

"I can hardly wait for my turn. My parents plan to come live here when I become one of Solomon's brides…. Your folks can come, too."

"It would be easy to live here. My mother would love this garden…. Right now the only thing I want is sleep."

Song of Solomon 5:2-7:
The Love Aphrodisiac Wakes Up the Maiden

ACT TWO, SCENE FOUR
SECOND DAY - NIGHT

The curtains open with the Shulammite in bed. She tosses and turns as her subconscious agonizes over whom to marry. The night before she slept in Solomon's tent in the country surrounded by his portable luxuries. Now her room is even more extravagant, bordering on gaudy with comforts she could never have imagined.

A Wet Dream Wakes Up the Shulammite

Although God cares who the Shulammite marries, he lets her continue to struggle over making the right decision. God doesn't force his will on her. Likewise, God cares who we marry. But just like the Shulammite, he doesn't force his will on us.

Praying to God doesn't transport us to a magic bubble where we can be lazy, stupid, or spineless without consequences. Even when we pray from the depths of our souls, we must still follow through and do our part to make it happen. The more we pray and bare our soul to God without trying to spin our faults into assets, the healthier we become. Only when we work at becoming emotionally whole can we hope to choose a loving mate and solve problems as they occur.

She Dreams of the Shepherd

Song of Solomon 5:2a:
"I was asleep, but my heart was awake.

"Awake" is the same word the Shulammite uses for both "arouse" and "awaken" in the theme of the Song of Solomon when she begs the Virgins not to "*arouse* or *awaken* my love, until it pleases." Review Song of Solomon 2:7, 3:5, 8:4.

All nine times "awake" is used in the story, it refers to a call to action. Earlier, the Shulammite called to God saying, "Awake, O north wind" (Song 4:15). She pleaded for God to wake up and act as he hears her urgent prayer. She is in the midst of a dilemma trying to decide whom to marry. She asked for God's blessing as she works to present herself as an emotionally and sexually healthy bride to her husband. Then she beseeched God to help her choose a husband who is capable of both giving and receiving love.

Now she tries to sleep; tomorrow she meets the Queens. But her heart wakes her up demanding action on her part. We see this same call to action in the ninth time this word is used. When the Shulammite cites the theme of the Song of Solomon for the third time, in the next verse she tells how she obeyed the theme with the Shepherd (Song 8:5).

The Shepherd Values Her

Song of Solomon 5:2b:
A voice! My beloved was knocking:
'Open to me, my sister, my darling,
My dove, my perfect one!'"

In her first dream, the Shulammite missed the Shepherd and went searching for him. This time, he searches for her, knocking at the door, two lovers passing in her dreams. In the previous verse, when the Shulammite visualizes satisfying the Shepherd in marriage, he calls her, "my sister, my bride." This time, in the Maiden's dream, he drops "my bride" and calls her, "my sister, my darling, my dove, my perfect one."

Their relationship has changed. The Maiden is no longer in the country with the Shepherd close by. She can't go to him at any time. Now she sleeps in one of Solomon's opulent guest rooms. The King's sensuous proposals and the environment are starting to sway her emotions.

The Shepherd's salutation of the Shulammite echoes the change in her status. He no longer acknowledges their promise to each other and doesn't call her "my bride." She is about to become another man's wife.

Thus the Shepherd appeals to the only things left of their relationship—the deep soulmating of siblings and the genuine affection of sweethearts. He calls her "my sister"—they share the honesty and comradeship of loving siblings. They can talk about anything. They freely share their problems and don't have to pretend to be perfect.

He beseeches her as "my darling"—he delights in his sweetheart's presence. He wants her to accompany him through life as his lover. He appeals to her as "my dove"—he views her as his sanctuary and refuge from the world. To him she is "my perfect one"—he respects and values her purity. He knows a glorious woman awaits him once she unlocks her garden...for him—not Solomon.

While both Solomon and the Shepherd call the Shulammite "my darling," they use the term in different ways. Solomon always uses the expression in the context of telling her what a beautiful body she has. He never addresses the Maiden with a more permanent term than "my darling." He comes across as a conman trying to broker a deal.

On the other hand, the Shepherd uses "my darling" in a string of adorations which reveal that he views her as a whole person—not just a body. The names he calls her demonstrate intimacy, affection, respect, and desire for a permanent relationship with the Maiden. But she's rejecting him and their promise to each other.

The Shepherd Needs Her

Song of Solomon 5:2c:
For my head is drenched with dew,
My locks with the damp of the night.

His head "drenched with dew and damp from the night" refers to his work as a shepherd. During dry spells, shepherds rise before the sun comes up and herd their sheep out to graze on dew-saturated grass. As the sheep eat the grass, their thirst is quenched by the dew. After the sun comes up, the sheep spend the rest of the day sitting in the shade chewing their cud (Keller 51-3).

While the Shulammite slept in, the Shepherd went to work early.

Now he comes home, he needs her. He wants her to comfort him. Rather than a passing fancy, she gives purpose to his life.

Begging, he pleads, "Open to me!" He wants her to say she'll end this affair with Solomon and become his bride and be the joy of his life. "Please, I love you! I need you!"

She Refuses to Get Dressed

Song of Solomon 5:3:
"I have taken off my dress,
How can I put it on again?
I have washed my feet,
How can I dirty them again?"

The Shulammite hears the Shepherd's plea to come back to him. But she is in the palace now. She has spent the evening strolling through a fragrant garden of imported plants and trees. She's sleeping in obscene extravagance. Singers fill the air with soothing melodies. Servants take care of her every need. Far away from the familiar sights, sounds, and smells of the country, she easily dismisses her longing for him.

Solomon has proposed, why should she get excited because a hard-working Shepherd can't live without her? Does he really want her to give up the glamour of the palace? Does he expect her to say, "Yes," to him?

With the excessive flattery and attention of the King making her unsure of her desires, the Maiden resists the Shepherd's plea. In her dream, she impatiently tells the Shepherd, "Go away! I'm already in bed. I don't want to get up and get dressed. I've already washed my feet for the night. Go away!"

The cascades of kingly flattery are muddling the Maiden's emotions and hampering her ability to think. God knows Solomon is the wrong choice. We do, too. And she should know she'll never be truly happy with him. Yet she is ready to accept Solomon's proposal. Then something happens to jar her back to her senses.

She Sees the Shepherd's Hand

Song of Solomon 5:4:
"My beloved extended his hand through the opening,
And my feelings [literally bowels — NASB footnote] were aroused for
him."

"Feelings" or "bowels" (*mê'âh*) comes "from an unused root probably meaning to be soft; the intestines, or the abdomen, figuratively sympathy; by implication a vest; by extension the stomach, the uterus (or of men, the seat of generation), the heart (figuratively):--belly, bowels" (Strong 69). The *Theological Wordbook* says *mê'âh* refers to "the male and female sexual apparatus" (518). The Septuagint translates *mê'âh* with the Greek *koilia* which refers to "the womb, the place where the *foetus* is conceived and nourished until birth" (Dickey "Song 5:4").

"Aroused" is a primary root that means "by implication to be in great commotion or tumult, to rage, war, moan, clamor" (Strong 33).

These definitions describe a feminine wet dream. Although the Shulammite is trying hard to reject the Shepherd, the sight of just his hand arouses her body. Her subconscious recognizes the sexual impulses of true love that her conscious brain denies. And in response her sexual organs cause her to cry out for him.

In recounting her dream, the Shulammite doesn't need to say anything else to enlightened women who enjoy vaginal orgasms. They'll chuckle and nod their heads. They recognize this graphic, yet delicate, description of a virgin's sexual awakening as a feminine wet dream.

Indeed, sexually active wives continue to enjoy wet dreams during their entire marriage, although a bit subdued in comparison to their own virginal experiences. These marital wet dreams keep wives in tune with their sexual hormones and motivate them to look for opportunities to initiate lovemaking with their husbands.

To a woman in love, the sight of her beloved's hand is enough to trigger sexual desire. He caresses her face with his hand when he kisses her and evokes all kinds of erotic sensations. Twice the Maiden longs for marriage and sexual fondling by the Shepherd (Song 2:6; 8:3).

Wet dreams are not synonymous with masturbation or using porn. They often occur without much, if any, forethought on the part of the pubertal girl and don't require her to do anything to herself. The dreams spring from desires deep in her subconscious. These involuntary natural sensations show God's brilliance in his design of the female's body to prepare her for marriage and lovemaking.

A virgin may not recognize these wet dreams as preparing her body and mind for vaginal orgasms. Later in the arms of her husband, as his powerful thrusts of love bring her to climax time and time again, she knows. *Oh! That's what I was feeling.* She laughs out loud. *A real man is so much better than a dream!*

She Opens to the Shepherd

Song of Solomon 5:5a:
"I arose to open to my beloved."

The half-asleep Shulammite tells the Shepherd, "Go away!" Then her nocturnal vision of the Shepherd's hand affects her as God intended.

It revives her deep feelings for her beloved—her soulmate—the one she loves emotionally and intellectually. In the palace, she tried to forget him—now the unwanted wet dream makes her realize she can't live without him. She bolts out of bed.

Loving wives enjoy a similar experience with their husband. The touch of his hand on hers or on her check or neck can make sexual twinges run through her body as it remembers their nights of passion. Even the playful tone of voice he uses when making love can cause her nipples to shiver and stand erect when he innocently voices those same inflections. God's design of the way of a man with a maid offers daily sensational remembrances of the beauty of their love.

The King's Aphrodisiac Misfires...Again

Song of Solomon 5:5b:
"And my hands dripped with myrrh,
And my fingers with liquid myrrh,
On the handles of the bolt."

Earlier when Solomon had the Shulammite brought to his tent so he could begin wooing her, he had the Virgins use the aphrodisiac spikenard on her (Song 1:12). Instead of relaxing her and making her receptive to Solomon's outrageous salivating over her body, it misfired. She spent the evening remembering the Shepherd's special smells and how much she adored him. Then she dreamed about him that night.

She Uses the Aphrodisiac Myrrh

Myrrh is an aphrodisiac for women—not for men. Remember how the Shepherd compared marriage to the Shulammite to a special blend of his-and-her love-enhancing aphrodisiacs—myrrh for her and balsam for him (Song 5:1). Japanese researchers discovered the warm, musky scent of myrrh is for ladies only. It increases a woman's passion by raising her testosterone, but it lowers the man's testosterone ("Chanel" 8/15/2008).

Solomon knows the power of myrrh. Esther took beauty treatments with it (Esther 2:12), and his father David sang about it as an oil of gladness (Psalms 45). Solomon likely furnishes his ladies with plenty of expensive myrrh to help prepare them for his advances. But once again, his attempt to create a romantic moment with the Maiden misfires.

Wide awake with her passions revved up for the humble Shepherd, the Shulammite lavishly splashes the aphrodisiac myrrh on her neck as she races to open the door to the Shepherd. A warm musky aroma fills the air and swirls along behind her.

Finally, her eyes open. She sees clearly the solution to her dilemma concerning whom to marry. Happy anticipation tingles through her receptive body as her hand touches the handle.

The aphrodisiac myrrh is used eight times in the Song of Solomon and alluded to twice. Balsam is mentioned seven times and pomegranates and wine six times each. The Shulammite is obviously familiar with myrrh since she refers to its different forms.

1. The Shulammite wore a pouch of myrrh (Song 1:13). To be able to wear a pouch of myrrh around her neck, the substance needs to be either rolled-up balls of the resin from the bark or dried flower petals. The delicate aroma helps promote sleep and keeps mosquitoes and other bugs away during the night.

2. Columns of smoke perfumed with myrrh led the Shulammite to Jerusalem (Song 3:6). When Solomon took the Maiden to Jerusalem, servants walked ahead of his traveling couch throwing up handfuls of perfumed myrrh and frankincense. These scented powders of the merchant served similar purpose as our car fresheners do to dispel the odors of a hot climate.

3. The Shulammite went to the mountain of myrrh (Song 4:6). After the Maiden arrived in Jerusalem, she told Solomon she needed to go to the mountain of myrrh and the hill of frankincense. She wanted time to think about his marriage proposal. At least two different species of myrrh grew all over the mountains in Palestine. The two most common varieties were C. villosus with pink petals, and the C. salviaefolius with white petals. These local varieties may have been an inferior form compared to the powders of the merchants.

4. The Shulammite's shoots included myrrh (Song 4:14). The Shepherd praised the Maiden by telling her he knows she'll be a wonderful, loving mother. As the Israelites referred to their children as tender plants, he named a houseful of herbs as their future offspring. He recognized how different children of the same parents are.

5. The Shepherd looks forward to "gathering" his myrrh (Song 5:1). Nearly every word in this verse refers to some aspect of the sexual relationship in marriage. Certainly, the Shepherd anticipates enjoying myrrh in all its forms and varieties as he experiences all of the Maiden's charms. The verb "gathering" shows he expects to continually partake of an aphrodisiacal union with his fervent maiden.

6-7. The Shulammite's hands and fingers dripped with liquid myrrh (Song 5:5). This verse refers to liquid myrrh twice. It creates the picture of the Maiden splashing herself with the warm earthy aroma as she rushes to the door to let the Shepherd in. She uses so much, it drips from the door's handle and lock. She eagerly looks forward to becoming his wife and lover.

8. *The Shepherd's lips drip liquid myrrh (Song 5:13).* After the Shulammite's dream the Virgins ask why she loves the Shepherd instead of Solomon. She says the Shepherd's lips drip with liquid myrrh. We learned kissing deposits testosterone into a woman's mouth which increases her sexual desire (Song 1:2). Then the Maiden tells Solomon that the Shepherd's kisses increase her passion (Song 7:9b).

Two verses allude to myrrh:

9. *The Shulammite is black but lovely (Song 1:5).* A common use of myrrh during this time was to protect the skin from the sun. The result was the most beautiful dark tan imaginable. The Shulammite's description of her sun-tanned skin implies that she knew how to protect her beauty while working under the sun.

10. *The Shulammite is the rose of Sharon (Song 2:1).* This is a different Hebrew word than the others for myrrh. Reputable scholars believe the rose of Sharon is actually the rock rose of Sharon. It may have been a local substitute, or knock-off, for the more expensive imported myrrh.

She Can't Find the Shepherd

Song of Solomon 5:6:
"I opened to my beloved,
But my beloved had turned away and had gone!
My heart went out to him as he spoke.
I searched for him, but I did not find him;
I called him, but he did not answer me."

By the time the Maiden reaches the door, her beloved Shepherd has left. Her heart aching, she searches and calls out for him. She can't find her beloved anywhere.

The hormones of romance and love come into play here. Brain-imaging expert Dr. Earl Henslin says a brain in love looks eerily similar to a brain on cocaine. In fact, it's hard for neurologists to tell the difference between brains in love and brains on cocaine by looking at brain scans.

When loving couples touch, whether kissing or making love, oxytocin releases endorphins that shower their brains. A man's oxytocin increases five times its normal level during sex. A woman's level can quickly rise even more because this is the female bonding hormone. However, in the male oxytocin joins his bonding hormone — vasopressin. Together, these hormones create both emotional and sensual memories which increase the man's love for the woman (7-9).

The Shulammite's love for her Shepherd is stirring up an amorous cocktail of hormones. Her body woke up aching for the Shepherd—not Solomon. She resisted the message of her subconscious only for it to flash a vision of the Shepherd's hand. All the intellectual and emotional love she felt for him plus the memories of his deep kisses propelled her out of bed. In the rush for the door she splashed on myrrh to increase and sustain the heat of her passions. Although she now knows her own mind, her dilemma has changed. She knows whom she wants to marry, but she is still in Solomon's palace wearing his expensive liquid myrrh. And the love of her life is missing.

The Watchmen Stop Her

Song of Solomon 5:7:
"The watchmen who make the rounds in the city found me,
They struck me and wounded me;
The guardsmen of the walls took away my shawl from me."

In his proposal, the Shepherd called the Maiden, "My sister, my bride" making a lifetime commitment to her. Now she is in Solomon's palace and he only calls her, "My sister." They share emotional intimacy. But if she stays in the palace that's all it will ever be. She is the perfect one for him, but whom she marries is her choice.

The full implication of her choice hits the Shulammite when the watchmen strike her and take away her shawl. In her previous dream, the watchmen helped her find the Shepherd. Now the situation is different. Once she marries Solomon, she can never go back to her beloved, her soulmate, and his way of life. If she wants the Shepherd, she must decide now before entering into a covenant with the King.

While both the Shepherd and Solomon earnestly seek a wife, the similarities end there. The Shepherd craves to *end his loneliness* with his true love. Although his Maiden satiates all five of his senses, he's intellectually committed to her for a permanent relationship. Likewise, he values her commitment to him.

On the other hand, Solomon cares only about satisfying his own 5 senses. He doesn't make any commitment to the Maiden or ask any from her except for sexual activity—at his convenience. He desires only her body to *fill his emptiness*. He assumes her physical perfection will stop his obsession with deflowering virgins.

The dream forces the Maiden to acknowledge that Solomon isn't the one for her in spite of all his great wealth and prestige. She turns to the Shepherd, the one she has spent time with building an emotional soulmating bond. He values her as someone to work alongside him to subdue the earth, to bear their children, and to glorify God. Even knowing how hard he must work to provide a living, he offers her more than the King ever could. To Solomon, she is only a body—a plaything. To the Shepherd, she is a valuable lifelong emotional and sexual companion.

But alas, the Maiden is still in Solomon's palace in Jerusalem. The Shepherd is still in the country. What can she do now that she has chosen true love over wealth and prestige?

Secret 6: Surrender to Your Wet Dreams of Love

God's great love and concern for his people's sexual happiness is evident in his design of both the male and the female minds and bodies to experience wet dreams. These nocturnal orgasms showcase their subliminal love and sexual desires wrought through their soulmating. God's ordained yearnings of the subconscious help prepare them to enjoy wonderful, ecstatic lovemaking with their chosen mate.

Dreams of marriage comprise a natural part of a young girl's transition into womanhood. After she starts dating, her dreams center on her boyfriend as she visualizes life with him. Sexual dreaming helps her sort out her feelings and prepares her for marriage. Every sexually healthy woman enjoys these feminine wet dreams as the awakening of her sexual love as she bonds emotionally with her man.

Due to childhood trauma, exposure to Victorian hang-ups, or lack of proper sex education, some girls and women fear their developing sexuality. They refuse to acknowledge these God-given urges of their forthcoming sexual bonding and delight. However, the Song of Solomon reveals the Shulammite's mother taught her about courtship, marriage, and lovemaking. As a result, the young Maiden displays healthy attitudes and responses to both Solomon and the Shepherd. This allows her to analyze the implications of her sexual dreams.

God preserves this very clear description of the Shulammite's wet dream to show his approval of them and his desire for women to learn from them. This feminine wet dream sets in motion the turning point of the Shulammite's dilemma of whom to marry.

This chapter is short to give you time to read the appendix chapter "Wet Dreams, Laws of Cleanness, and Masturbation." That material came from my critique group asking questions about the Shulammite's wet dream. It allows teachers to discuss as much or as little of the subject as they're comfortable with and gives you the chance to pursue your own interests.

In my book *God's People Make the Best Lovers,* I devote two chapters to tracing the Church Father's ignorance about sex and their hoax on the

Song of Solomon. Ignorance of wet dreams contributed to their false sexual teachings regarding priests, nuns, and married couples. They did great damage to men, women, and their children through their Dark-Ages attitudes toward married lovemaking.

Misconceptions about wet dreams continue to cause problems even today although young women talk about wet dreams in their blogs. You'll read in the appendix chapter how wet dreams are God's answer to masturbation for both men and women. God provides a safe outlet to protect his people and to prepare them for marriage.

Love Is the Best Aphrodisiac

The word "aphrodisiacs" conjures up all kinds of thoughts such as the Asian habit of drinking cobra blood laced with alcohol...if the imbiber survives catching the deadly snake. Or a cup of sea cucumber soup—soaked, seasoned, and boiled for days might light the fires of those who can wait until it's done. Ah, the $1 Filipino fix: a duck egg complete with a fetus designed to turn on the cheapskate with a cast-iron stomach. And then there's the Spanish fly that irritates a person's genitalia into performing if it doesn't send the lover to the hospital or the morgue ("World's" 2/2010).

According to neuroscientist, psychiatrist, and brain imaging expert Dr. Daniel G. Amen, mankind has searched for aphrodisiacs for over 5000 years beginning with the Egyptians. Some substances benefit both men and women. Yet others have killed and hurt people and cost the lives of animals as the above examples show (151-2).

Dr. Helen Kaplan, a widely respected pioneer in the study of the brain's role in love, states the "best aphrodisiac" known to modern man isn't oysters or vitamin E. *It's love!* Love increases both sexual desire and pleasure. She says in *Disorders of Sexual Desire* that without love, the sexual organs of both men and women become less sensitive and require more stimulation for arousal to take place (13-4, 61).

The Song of Solomon uses aphrodisiacs to teach the secrets of intellectual, emotional, sexual, and spiritual love. If we miss the emphasis on love, then no love potion can turn a lack-luster marriage into a steaming romance, which will bless the couple and create an affectionate home for their children. Without love, we might as well grab a machete and head into the jungle to slay a cobra, scuba dive for a sea cucumber, or find a vendor peddling his fetal wares chanting, *"Baluuuut* is very good for your sex life!"* Learning to truly love our mate is so much better than swallowing a green blister bug and suffering a screaming, clawing death.

Can VIAGRA Cure a Sexless Marriage?

Can a visit to the doctor for VIAGRA restore romance to a sexless marriage? It depends on why the marriage doesn't have enough sex to keep both the husband *and wife* satisfied. If it's a medical problem, then perhaps the little blue pill can revive the passion of yesteryear. But if the problem originates between the man's ears instead of between his legs, then VIAGRA probably can't offer much help.

When men flocked to their urologists' offices for the magic love potion, a major truth emerged about the drug and male sexuality. Dr Abraham Morgentaler, director of Men's Health Boston, associate clinical professor of urology at Harvard Medical School, gives the news in *The Viagra Myth, The Surprising Impact on Love and Relationships*. He recounts copious examples where VIAGRA failed because most erectile problems stem from the relationship—not the body. Men need an emotional connection with a loving partner to enjoy great orgasms.

The miracle drug for erectile dysfunction can't throw fairy dust over an unloving *or unloved* male organ to miraculous turn it into a pulsating love machine. Pfizer's "Patient Information" insert warns that "VIAGRA...helps a man get and keep an erection only when he is sexually excited (stimulated)" (3/2015). In other words, VIAGRA "has little effect" on men who aren't emotionally turned on to their wife.

Even the pharmaceutical companies recognize that healthy sexual activity is first an expression of love in the man's brain, not the flow of blood to his organ of pleasure. Science doesn't have a magic pill to force a husband and wife to love each other. They must make that choice.

Can Addyi Bring Passion into a Dead Bedroom?

Addyi, the first commercial drug to improve female libido, bypasses the woman's genitals and acts on her brain chemicals. The drug was originally studied as an antidepressant. Like Pfizer states about VIAGRA, the FDA News Release says Addyi is ineffective in dealing with inhibited sexual desire and pleasure in regard to "problems within the relationship."

Even when the drug is given only to ideal women candidates, the success rate for women in their mid-thirties is a dismal 10% for achieving any improvement. That small percentage experiences an increase in the "number of satisfying sexual events" by only 1/2 to 1 additional monthly sexual encounter. The score for an increase in sexual desire is an even lower probability of 0.3 to 0.4 over a placebo.

Women risk "severely low blood pressure and loss of consciousness." And "because of a potentially serious interaction with alcohol, treatment with Addyi will only be available through certified health care professionals and pharmacies." Professionals must assess if patients can "reliably abstain from alcohol" (FDA 8/18/2015).

VIAGRA and Addyi can't compete with true love for liberating our bodies and minds for *SPEAKING GOD'S BEAUTIFUL LANGUAGE OF LOVE* that transcends spoken words. Great lovemaking begins with flooding the brain with love. Then hormones released during sex relieve depression to bathe the lovers with happiness and increased desire.

True Love Is the Scrumptious Choice

Repeatedly the Song of Solomon emphasizes using your 5 senses as aphrodisiacs coupled with intellectual, emotional, sexual, and spiritual love. Notice how potent the 5 senses are when infused with love:

1. The smells of love stimulate sexual arousal through pleasant fragrances that pull one emotionally into the moment. Some aromas help relieve stress and prepare the mind to enjoy lovemaking. Other scents create longing by releasing pleasant memories of the loved one.

2. The tastes of love appeal to the 4 senses of smell, touch, sight, and of course, taste. Hearing is sometimes involved in the sounds of cooking and decanting (the art of pouring) fruited wines. Food gives both emotional and intellectual stimulation. The best benefits of aphrodisiacs and the tastes of love are their health benefits. Some aphrodisiacs promote the production of the hormones testosterone and estrogen. Other foods improve circulation, strengthen the heart, and revitalize the genitals. Increased stamina is always welcome in the bedroom.

3. The sights of love stimulate the imagination and arouse desire. Solomon is a master at analyzing a woman's body for how thrilling it will be to him as he wants to "Climb the palm tree, and take hold of its fruit stalks" (Song 7:8). His descriptions all begin at the woman's head and stop at her luscious bosom revealing his fetish for virgin breasts (Song 4:5; 7:3, 7, 8). The Shulammite's resolve about whom to marry pivots on her dream when just the sight of the Shepherd's hand arouses her passion for him (Song 5:4).

4. The touches of love draw the reader into the opening verses of the Song of Solomon when the Shulammite pleads, "May he kiss me with the kisses of his mouth!" (Song 1:2). Later she longs for the Shepherd's intimate touches in marriage (Song 2:6; 8:3).

5. The sounds of love present a major factor in helping the Shulammite choose a lifelong sexual partner. She continually compares Solomon's sensuous proposals to the Shepherd's pledges of true love. These enticing potent smells, tastes, sights, and touches of love pale beside the Shepherd's verbal commitment to soulmate in love with her.

The Shulammite Surrendered to Her Wet Dream

Throughout the story, the Shulammite resists Solomon's efforts to seduce her. Although he tries to make her body tingle with desire for him, she refuses to swoon over him until he falls in love with her (Song 1:9-15). She never totally disengages her intellect and repeatedly rejects his rehearsed spiel. This is evident the 3 times she reinforces the theme of the book—soulmating before lovemaking (Song 2:7; 3:5; and 8:4).

She continually remembers how the Shepherd demonstrates all 4 parts of true love for her. Both are committed to using the smells, tastes, sights, touches, and sounds of love after marriage to keep their sexual love exciting and fulfilling. Love is truly the best aphrodisiac of all.

Love is even more powerful than Solomon's use of spikenard and keeping fancy bottles of expensive myrrh in the Shulammite's room. Just the sight of the Shepherd's hand told her conscious mind what her subconscious knew about love. Thus, she surrendered to her wet dream and chose the Shepherd. Her wet dream foiled Solomon's best efforts to use the forces of nature to seduce the young, inexperienced Maiden.

But the Shulammite still has problems. She's in Solomon's palace while her beloved Shepherd is pasturing his sheep.

Optional Exercise

Surrender to your wet dreams of love: For many people, this will be their first exposure to feminine wet dreams of love. Read the appendix chapter "Wet Dreams, Laws of Cleanness, and Masturbation" for more in-depth information. Then answer the questions below.

Study Exercise

Answer all questions in your own words.
1. How did the Shulammite's location influence her two dreams?
2. Why did the Shulammite resist the Shepherd when he first appeared in her dream?
3. How did the manner in which the Shepherd addressed the Maiden in her second dream differ from the way Solomon talked to her? What was the significance to the Maiden?
4. What did the Shulammite's dream tell her about marrying Solomon?
5. What can women learn from the Shulammite's two dreams to apply to their own love life?
6. What can men learn from the Shulammite's two dreams to apply to their own love life?

7. What caused the Shulammite to jump out of bed when she didn't want to get her feet dirty? What can you learn from her reaction?
8. What have you learned about using aphrodisiacs to keep romance alive in marriage?
9. Do you disagree with anything in the lesson? If so, explain giving scriptures for your reasons.

Stacey's Story:
Fighting Fair Leads to Incredible Lovemaking

Hello Patsy Rae,

It's been six months since I've written you. I've been hesitant to write before I had something concrete to share. I was a bit hesitant to believe it myself. But the good news is that my husband has agreed to go through your book *God's People Make the Best Lovers* with me.

We've agreed to set aside one night a week as our "together night" making sure the kids are in bed and we have no interruptions. We're each going to read a chapter on our own during the week (and do the homework) and then on our night discuss it together as you suggest. We begin reading this week and our first "together night" will be a week from tomorrow. This is what I've hoped for all along, but it still doesn't seem real to me.

I am cautiously optimistic. Please pray for us. I know this is major progress.

Oh, a few weeks ago, the whole family went for a ride in the country and we popped your *Secret of the Woman of Great Price* into the CD player and listened to the whole thing. That's another big step. It was a good introduction to Patsy Rae Dawson for my husband. Our eldest daughter enjoyed it, too. Oh that I had exposure to this kind of teaching at eighteen!

Anyway, I'll keep you posted as to our progress. Blessings to you.

Formerly angry at the Lord and blaming Him,
Now reaping His joys of marriage,
Stacey

P.S. I'm a bit shy about sharing this information (and although there still seems to be a pattern of infrequency in lovemaking) the intimate times we have shared together in the last few months have been some of the most incredible we've ever had together. The mind really does matter as you teach in *God's People Make the Best Lovers!*

Secret 7: Turn On Double-Dose #10 Orgasms

Solomon's Siren Song: "Dear Lord, I'm Only 13!"

After tossing, turning, and dreaming all night, the Shulammite lays in bed a while longer half awake. A little bit later, she realizes she's actually talking out loud as if her mother were sitting in the chair beside her bed. She continues the conversation as it helps clear her head. "Mom, you told me to make the family proud. I think you wanted Solomon's soldiers to hear you say that, because you whispered in my ear, 'Don't forget what I always told you about the gazelles and the hinds of the field. And take time to think....'"

The Maiden sighs, "Mom, I know the King's money would help you and my brothers if we all moved to Jerusalem. But ever since I can remember, you've pointed to the animals and told me how they always bond with each other before they mate. I think that's what you meant when you told me to make the family proud.... You gave me your blessing and you expect me to have enough sense to think it through and choose the right husband. I want real love like you and Dad always had.... I really miss Dad. I know you do, too."

Silence fills the room. Slowly she gets out of bed and kneels beside it. "Dear Lord, thank you for Mom and Dad and the example they've given me of a loving family. And thank you for my brothers. They work hard to take care of Mom, baby sis, and me.... And...thank you for giving me the time to realize how Solomon with all his wealth and so-called wisdom can't compare to the Shepherd."

Her eyes moisten as tears threaten to run down her cheeks. She stills her emotions by covering her mouth with her hands. She swallows hard and continues, "Dear Lord, I'm only 13. But you've given me a woman's body and emotions. Go with me today and give me wisdom and courage to look King Solomon in the eye and tell him how I really feel. Dear Lord, speaking so boldly to the King will be hard, but I know I can do what needs to be done with you beside me."

Standing up, she looks for her own clothes and realizes the Virgins didn't bring them. She slips on the plainest dress they've given her.

Leaving Solomon's dowry, the gorgeous jewelry, laying on the table, she sits down on a chaise lounge. She lays her head back and closes her eyes in prayer to await the morning…and the Virgins.

Song of Solomon 5:8-6:3:
The Maiden Exclaims, "I'm Ready for Love!"

ACT TWO, SCENE FIVE
THIRD DAY – EARLY MORNING

The Shulammite stands in front of a bedroom window. The sun streams in. Her arms spread out to embrace its warmth. She turns around when the Virgins knock. They enter bringing a tray of food and the fanciest dress she has ever seen. She motions for them to put the food and dress down on her bed.

The Maiden Sends the Virgins to Find the Shepherd

Song of Solomon 5:8:
"I adjure you, O daughters of Jerusalem,
If you find my beloved,
As to what you will tell him:
For I am lovesick."

"Adjure" is the same word we've seen earlier in the theme of the Song of Solomon. It means "properly to be complete; to seven oneself, i.e., swear (as if by repeating a declaration seven times):--adjure, charge (by an oath, with an oath)" (Strong 112).

"Lovesick" is the same compound word used in Song 2:5 where the Shulammite told the Virgins, "Refresh me with apples, because I am lovesick" or weak with love (sexually or otherwise) for the Shepherd.

The Shulammite's wet dream clarified her thinking and signaled the turning point in the drama. Now she tells the Virgins, "I no longer want the attentions of the King. The Shepherd is the one I want to marry. But I can't leave right now…. The King is expecting me and I have to tell him why I can't marry him."

She demands that the Virgins promise to find the Shepherd for her. Then she implores them to tell him she is in anguish with love for him. "Please go find him now! Tell him to come get me! Tell him to hurry!"

"What Kind of Beloved Is Your Beloved?"

Song of Solomon 5:9:
"What kind of beloved is your beloved,
O most beautiful among women?
What kind of beloved is your beloved,
Thus, you adjure us?"

The Virgins' attitude has changed from staring at the Shulammite's dark skin and mocking her reluctance to say, "Yes," to Solomon. Why? What made the difference?

Twice now, the Maiden beseeched the Virgins not to force her to marry Solomon before they fell in love with each other (Song 2:7; 3:5). While Solomon has spoken only about ravishing bodies joining in sex, the Shulammite has begged to put off marriage until their hearts bond in love. With her example of the loving hind and graceful doe, she helped the young girls to stop and think about the role they are assuming as the King's virgins in waiting. She is the first to care about them, and they now see the inner beauty of her person.

Even so, the Virgins cannot believe what they hear. Now instead of mocking her, they ask what kind of man is her beloved to cause her to give up Solomon. Surely, no man deserves such a sacrifice! What kind of woman yearns for a shepherd over a king? A beautiful one, but a silly one, no doubt! They view the Maiden with the same amazement popular girls regard a girl who turns down a date with the captain of the football team or the president of the student council to date an obscure poor boy.

It's the same way, girls who are in a friends-with-benefits relationship often ridicule other girls who save themselves for their husband. Yet girls with high standards place more value on the happiness of their future lives than on the fleeting pleasures of their courting years.

The Maiden Shares the 4 Parts of Love in Her Heart

The Maiden answers the Virgins with a simile similar to the one she used in Song 2:3-6 to portray the Shepherd as being like an apple tree among the trees of the forest, only with one major difference. Earlier she was still in the country and she used elements of nature to describe her love for the Shepherd.

Now she's surrounded by wealth, splendor, and gold in Solomon's palace. She paints a picture of the Shepherd that the Virgins can visualize. With her flair for words, she describes him as being like gold and jewels with a touch of the country thrown in.

Thus, the Maiden reveals a woman's attitude when the 4 parts of true love fill her heart. If a girl doesn't feel this same way about her boyfriend, she should examine her feelings toward him. Perhaps they haven't soulmated enough or they're not right for each other.

Likewise, a married woman needs to examine her attitudes toward her husband. If the wife doesn't view her husband the same way the Shulammite thinks about her Shepherd, her marriage can't be all God desires Fortunately, a wife can learn these attitudes in marriage, just as a husband can choose to truly love his wife.

1. Intellectual Love—"My Beloved Is Outstanding Among Ten Thousand"

Song of Solomon 5:10:
"My beloved is dazzling and ruddy,
Outstanding among ten thousand."

The Shulammite esteems the Shepherd as the greatest man alive. He is dazzling and ruddy. Hess says commentators believe "dazzling" refers to heat as in glistening with perspiration from hard work (181).

"Ruddy" is used to describe the young shepherd David (1 Samuel 16:12; 17:42). David was "ruddy, with beautiful eyes and a handsome appearance." Ruddy is a complementary term that has something to do with the sun's effect upon the skin. Shepherds used various essential oils for protecting their skin from the sun. This may be similar to the Shulammite telling the Virgins she was black but lovely, "swarthy" from the sun's effect upon her skin while she worked in the vineyards.

Now she tells the Virgins, "You can line up ten thousand of the best men in Israel, and none of them can compete with my dazzling and ruddy Shepherd! You can pick him out in an instant! He's the most perfect Hebrew who ever lived! And I am lovesick for him!"

Older women often respond, "That's what all young girls think when they're dating. Love can make you think he's wonderful. But after you get married, you may find out he's not Mr. Wonderful after all!"

The description of the woman of great price in Proverbs concludes with the same warning:

Proverbs 31:30:
"Charm is deceitful and beauty is vain,
But a woman who fears the LORD, she shall be praised."

After praising his older wife, the husband of Proverbs 31 says, "Charm is deceitful." In other words, a young fellow might propose to a woman who admires everything he does only to discover she complains about everything he doesn't do after marriage. The tender feminine words which seduce a man can trap the unlucky husband in a loveless marriage to a shrew.

Emotionally and sexually healthy husbands and wives heap lavish compliments on each other. Vocal admiration is so important for a successful marriage that God commands husbands to cherish and celebrate their wife's glory (Ephesians 5:27-29) and to honor her (1 Peter 3:7). He instructs women to do the same for their husband by showing respect, reverence, and admiration for him (Ephesians 5:33; 1 Peter 3:1-2).

Many loving husbands and wives let life get in the way and fail to feel and express admiration and love for each other. And in the process, they rob each other out of enjoying amazing orgasms for a lifetime. Consequently, they must learn once again to feel the excitement and devotion of their courtship days. As they emulate the Shepherd's and the Maiden's delight in each other that radiates from their hearts, they can turn on #10 orgasms for them both.

Secret 7: Turn On Double-Dose #10 Orgasms

On a scale of 0 to 10, the secret for exceptional #10 orgasms starts in the man's and the woman's brain with mutual admiration for the mate. Here's what science says about the brain and male and female sexuality:

2 Pathways in the Brain Lead to Double-Dose Ecstasy

Rosemary Basson, M.D., a Clinical Professor and the Director of the University of British Columbia Sexual Medicine Program, compares male and female sexuality in her 2003 article "Rethinking Low Sexual Desire in Women." She combines several research studies beginning in 1986 to 1999 to demonstrate two different forms of sexual stimulation for men. Then she makes application to women to show the similarities and where women miss out on sexual pleasure.

These pathways send signals from two distinct areas in the man's and the woman's brain to their genitals for an explosion of ecstasy:

Pathway 1: Emotional arousal comes from the "limbic centres" or the emotional center of the brain. The limbic brain reflects our emotions, behaviors, motivation, long-term memory, and olfaction function (our sense of smell is the only one of our 5 senses that is connected directly to our emotions) (McKenna 10: 157-183). "There is moment-to-moment feedback from the emotions" (Anderson 63: 891-906). "This feedback may be positive: one of enjoyment, pleasurable mood, self-affirmation, or it may be negative: one of embarrassment, shame, or guilt" (Basson 7).

Pathway 2: Physical arousal comes from a different area of the brain that controls the pelvic organs of reproduction and elimination. This stimulation leads to recognizable engorgement with blood of the erectile tissues (penis and clitoris) marking sexual excitement and possible readiness for sexual activity (Barlow 54: 140-157). Sadly, this is the main part and *often the only part* of a man's and a woman's sexuality that science and society recognize.

Emotional arousal plus physical arousal leads to engorgement arousal. The whole body is affected by engorgement along with mounting muscular tension during sexual stimulation. Even the ear lobes and the mouth may become thickened and swollen with blood. And nearly all of a person's muscles are affected.

Both men and women experience whole body orgasms. For women, "from head to toe, the muscles contract and relax, in steady or more convulsive rhythms" (Deutsch 91-2). For men, "the primitive pain nerves throughout their body become sexual triggers ready and waiting" for their wife's passionate touches and nibbles (Eichenlaub 21).

The engorgement sensations are "accurately detected and enjoyed" as tingling and other intense responses. This increases the man's and the woman's readiness for sexual activity and pleasure. "Only men with chronic situation erectile dysfunction typically under-rate their physical response" (Barlow 54: 140-157). Many women don't recognize these sensations at all, perhaps because they don't expect them or know they are theirs to claim.

Double-dose arousal equals #10 orgasms (emotional + physical = #6 to #10s). When a husband loves his wife with all his heart, soul, and mind as the Shepherd did the Maiden, the emotional and physical sensations combine for supreme pleasure. Review the Shepherd's esteem for the Maiden in "Secret 4: Grow the 4 Parts of Intimacy and Love."

Refusing to soulmate and take care of the emotional part of sex is why Solomon was never satisfied sexually. He spent his life searching in vain for a more perfect feminine body than his last wife had. He stayed stuck in single-dose physical pleasure by not taking the time to bond emotionally with any of his wives (emotional + physical = #0 to #5s).

Likewise, when a wife imitates the Maiden by loving her husband intellectually, emotionally, sexually, and spiritually, she frees her body to partake of amazing orgasms.

Ronald Deutsch says in *The Key to Feminine Response in Marriage:*

Heightened tension during intercourse must be actively *sought* by the woman, not passively awaited. For most women, no amount of skill or technique on the part of the husband will suffice. The woman must not merely surrender to her husband, she must surrender to her own drive, a drive to seek stimulation emotionally and physical, to seek tension until tension becomes release. Some women are enabled to attain orgasm simply by adopting this attitude (93).

Many of my students began to enjoy orgasms after understanding and embracing double-dose arousal, paying attention to both their own emotional and physical cues.

Science Teaches Single-Dose Physical Pleasure for Women

Dr. Basson, in "The Female Sexual Response: A Different Model" addressed the problem of poor research regarding female sexuality.

Referring to pioneer researchers William Masters and Virginia Johnson's model of female sexuality (1957-1990s), she wrote:

> The focus on genital responses and traditional indicators of desire, including sexual fantasies and a need to self-stimulate, *ignores major components of women's sexual satisfaction: trust, intimacy, the ability to be vulnerable, respect, communication, affection, and pleasure from sensual touching* [emphasis added].
>
> The absence of these components, according to the *Diagnostic and Statistical Manual of Mental Disorders,* 4th edition (DSM-IV (American Psychological Association, 1994), which relies heavily on the traditional human sex response cycle, is *apparently unimportant* [emphasis added]. Consequently, [university and medical] studies on women's sexuality in health and disease *rarely include these aspects* [emphasis added].

After exposing how researchers labeled a woman's emotions and attitudes as "unimportant" and "rarely included these aspects" in their reports on sex, Dr. Basson disagreed and explained:

> Women's sexual arousal is a subjective mental excitement that may or may not be accompanied by awareness of vaso-congestive [engorgement arousal] changes in her genitalia and other physical nongenital manifestations of arousal (*Journal* 52).

In other words, science promotes physical techniques for women to the neglect of the emotional aspects of lovemaking. Thus they dish out single-dose genital techniques (~~emotional +~~ physical = #0 to #5s). They do not understand sexuality any better than King Solomon did. And they get the same results he did—unsatisfied, frustrated women.

Women Embrace Single-Dose Emotional Pleasure for Themselves

Dr. Basson specialized in examining the emotional aspects of female sexuality, especially in long-term relationships. After discussing in "Rethinking Low Sexual Desire in Women" the man's pathways to sexual pleasure, she said most women focus on the emotional aspects of intercourse to the neglect of the physical—the opposite of science. The women may not even recognize their physical needs:

> If women are asked the reasons for agreeing to or instigating a sexual experience with their partner, their list is extensive. Reasons include wanting to be emotionally close, to show love and affection, to share physical pleasure for the sake of sharing, to increase a sense of attractiveness and attraction, to

increase a sense of commitment and bonding, *but only sometimes to satisfy a truly "sexual" need* [emphasis added]. These intimacy-based reasons appear particularly important in the longer term monogamous relationships.

Although the Song of Solomon emphasizes the role of the emotions or soulmating for increasing the woman's sexual pleasure, Dr. Basson's women didn't get it. Reread the emotional reasons above for initiating and agreeing to sex. How many of them sound like "Just doing my duty for noble reasons"?

The women are locked into single-dose "duty" pleasure (~~emotional + physical~~ = #0 to #2s). Their emotional reasons aren't the same as the Shulammite gives when the Virgins ask her why her Shepherd is so special. Enjoying a #10 is not about a woman doing her duty—it's about experiencing sex for her own emotional and physical enjoyment. It's about bonding with her husband who gives her so much pleasure.

The attitude that starts a woman's body on the pathway to #10 orgasms begins with thinking, "My husband is 1 in 10,000!" In fact, it's physically impossible for a woman to enjoy vaginal orgasms, let alone #10s, without *feeling* the same exceeding adoration for her husband that the Shulammite *expresses* for the Shepherd. A wife must take care of her attitudes before hopping into bed for supreme ecstasy.

Likewise, all orgasms aren't the same for a husband. Some are an expression of the love in his heart and consume him with physical pleasure. Others come strictly from his body and aren't so satisfying. The latter reflects the single-dose orgasmic boredom the young men in the Hookup Culture expressed.

Both the husband and the wife *require admiration in their heart for the mate* to enjoy #10s together. For men, review how the Shepherd said the Maiden was a refreshing orchard of amazing plants and life-giving springs ("Secret 4: Grow the 4 Parts of Intimacy and Love").

For women, keep reading as the Shulammite has only begun to share the secret for female attitudes. Similar thoughts liberate a woman's body for amazing emotional and physical arousal and whole-body engorgement and pleasure in the arms of her husband.

Dr. Marie N. Robinson, a contemporary of Masters and Johnson, in *The Power of Sexual Surrender* (1959) emphasized the role of the brain over physical sensations. *She advocated double-dose sexual pleasure.* She taught women how to recognize their sexual neediness by understanding the physical nature of their orgasms and taking charge of their attitudes. This leads to sexual aroused with both emotional and physical anticipation of the joy to come.

Men and women activate #10 orgasms exactly the same way. They turn on their bodies to ecstasy by paying attention to both the emotional and the physical aspects of sex. Such amorous bonding comes to fruition in the #10 — the most climatic sensation a couple can ever relish together.

True Admiration Faces Problems

Proverbs 27:6:
"Faithful are the wounds of a friend,
But deceitful are the kisses of an enemy."

Displaying admiration for your mate doesn't mean covering up problems and sins in the marriage. Instead, honest respect and devotion helps create an environment where it's easier to solve problems. Honoring your mate and avoiding false flattery improves the husband's and the wife's basic relationship and increases their sexual delight.

Male and Female Orgasms Are Relationship Barometers

A woman's orgasms change from day to day along with the daily stresses of life. Although she continues to experience orgasms, sometimes the degree of her internal sensations are stronger than at other times. She doesn't always enjoy the hot glow of a #10. But once a woman experiences firsthand how her attitudes affect her sexual reflexes, it becomes a powerful motivation to keep the lines of communication open and to solve problems quickly. She gladly works to build an emotional bond filled with love and esteem for her husband.

Dr. Zilbergeld in *Male Sexuality* and the Sarrels in "What Men Need from the Women Who Love Them" state that the same is true for men. A husband's attitudes toward his wife, himself, children, home, and work determine how strong his physical pleasure is. His sensations can range from monotony and a total lack of pleasure to an explosion of ecstasy.

God regulates the bodies of the husband and wife by designing them to respond wonderfully to the right attitudes toward each other. *The better Christian you are, the better lover you will become to your mate, and the more your body will respond in the act of love with glorious #10s.*

Christianity is about growing our ability to love others, especially our mate and children. The sexual joy God gives us testifies to his great love for both men and women. Truly, God's people serve a wonderful Creator!

Because vaginal orgasms are a barometer of the relationship and a woman's healthy attitudes, her enjoyment of lovemaking is the highest compliment she can pay her husband. Likewise, a man's ability to love his wife intellectually, emotionally, sexually, and spiritually is the highest compliment he can pay her. Frequent lovemaking keeps a couple in tune with each other and strengthens their bonds of love.

For more in-depth information about the 4 types of love, you can continue your study in *God's People Make the Best Lovers* to fine tune your *sexual and emotional love*. Then read *God's People Appreciate Marriage* to perfect your *intellectual and emotional attitudes* for ecstatic lovemaking. Learning more fully God's secret for marital passion helps you apply *spiritual love* to your marriage.

Sex with an Intimacy Anorexic Is Mechanical

Dr. Weiss emphasizes that sex for male and female anorexics is mechanical and unemotional—even when they're in the midst of an affair or pleasuring themselves. Double-dose #10 orgasms elude them as they've severed the emotional pathway to their mate and their genitals.

The Shulammite's Intellectual Love Continued— "My Beloved Is Like Gold, Pure Gold"

After stating how much she admires the Shepherd, the Shulammite describes him from head to toe to prove he is outstanding. First, she turns to his masculine appearance, which satisfies her 5 senses. Then she talks about his character and how he accepts responsibility for her.

Although this poetic description easily fits a 200-pound body builder, it also portrays a 96-pound weakling who possesses an important quality—respect for hard work. When a man uses his body to provide for his wife and to protect her from harm, he makes her rich. Her wealth doesn't depend on the size of his paycheck or his muscles, but on his ability and desire to work—how industrious he is.

The Shepherd savors honest labor. Any man who takes his place among men should fit this manly description in the eyes of his wife. The Shulammite glories in the Shepherd's masculine appearance that reflects his work. She demonstrates her intellectual love for his person and work.

Head of Gold and Beneficial Herbs

Song of Solomon 5:11-13:
"His hand [head—KJV, ASV, NIV] is like gold, pure gold;
His locks are like clusters of dates,
And black as a raven.
His eyes are like doves,
Beside streams of water,
Bathed in milk,
And reposed in their setting.
His cheeks are like a bed of balsam,
Banks of sweet-scented herbs;

His lips are lilies,
Dripping with liquid myrrh."

Most translators render verse 11 "his head is like gold, pure gold." A few translate it "his hand." Since the rest of the section talks about the Shepherd's head and his hands aren't mentioned until verse 14, "head" fits the context and pattern better than "hand" does.

The Maiden describes her beloved from the top of his head down to the bottom of his feet. She lavishly decorates the Shepherd with gold.

"His head is like pure gold." The Maiden's first experience with gold probably came from using Solomon's gold cups and eating utensils in his tent. Now she's surrounded by gold in the palace because Solomon thought silver was too common and didn't use it. Thus the Shulammite begins and ends the description with an appeal to the beauty of kings — like pure gold.

Since she is a playful wordsmith, no doubt the Maiden makes a deliberate connection to King Solomon whom she has now rejected in her heart. The Shepherd is the embodiment of pure gold — outstanding among ten thousand of the best men.

Then she displays brashness, irony, and a sense of humor as she decorates the Shepherd's kingly head with ornaments from the country. To her, the Shepherd manifests the value of the King, but he is real and touchable as he radiates humility and true love. She peppers the Virgins with a cascade of sensuous admiration and desire for her beloved.

"His locks are like clusters of dates and black as a raven." She praises his curly, black hair. And when they kiss, her fingers cradle the back of his head and find their way into his lustrous locks.

"His eyes are like doves, beside streams of water, bathed in milk." The whites of his blue eyes make them brighter. "Reposed in their setting," his eyes radiate peace and tranquility. She feels enveloped in softness and tenderness when he looks at her. Sometimes the affection in his eyes makes her blush.

"His cheeks are like a bed of balsam and banks of sweet-scented herbs." The Shulammite's picture captures the sweet olfactory sensations of balsam blended with other herbs for the Shepherd's unique personal fragrance. We've seen how different fragrances turn her thoughts to intense longing for the Shepherd.

One commentator suggests the words "bed" and "banks" of balsam and herbs refer to his beard. Certainly, the poetry suggests a well-kept fragrant beard. But whether he sports a beard or not, the Maiden likes the way he smells and looks.

"His lips are lilies dripping with liquid myrrh." His lips are perfectly shaped and inviting. The Shulammite pairs the lily's characteristics of joy and comfort with myrrh's ability to increase testosterone in a woman. In the first chapter, we learned that deep kissing deposits testosterone into a woman's mouth which increases her sexual arousal. Thus the thought of the Shepherd's lips touching hers sends shivers of happiness and desire up the Maiden's spine as she begs the Virgins to go find him.

The Shulammite's description of the Shepherd can be universally applied to all husbands. She combines the refined gold of kings with the herbs of the countryside. Although she points out individual features that attract her, the main point is that the sight of the Shepherd stirs her passions. She swoons over his sun-kissed ruddy complexion, curly black hair, and bright eyes. She likes the unique way he looks. Yet other women might find different physical traits attractive, such as red hair and brown or green eyes along with a fair complexion.

Body of Gold, Ivory, and Precious Stones

Song of Solomon 5:14:
"His hands are rods of gold
Set with beryl;
His abdomen is carved ivory
Inlaid with sapphires."

"His hands are rods of gold set with beryl." His hands portray the riches of royalty. They are fingered rods of gold with beryl fingernails and rings in the Shulammite's love-filled picture. Rods symbolize strength and protection whether used by a shepherd to protect his sheep or by a peasant to provide for his wife. A mechanic's hands are often stained with grease, but they look beautiful to an appreciative wife since he earns a living with them. A doctor's hands may seem soft and smooth, but they emulate precious gold if they provide for a wife and protect her from harm.

"His abdomen is carved ivory inlaid with sapphires." Describing the hippopotamus God said, "Behold now, his strength in his loins, and his power in the muscles of his belly" (Job 40:16). The Maiden pines for the Shepherd's muscular chest with nipples of blue gems. His self-confident posture and muscles shaped by hard work are earthly rewards denoting strength and power.

This is a very sensual description. "Hands" is the same word used in the Shulammite's second dream when the Shepherd extended his hand through the opening in the door (Song 5:4). The sight of his hand aroused her deep sexual longings for him so that she jumped out of bed and ran after him. Twice she longs for his left hand to be under her head and his right hand to embrace her (Song 2:6; 8:3). Then when his hands are paired with his chest, it presents the picture of the Shepherd wrapping his strong arms around her in an embrace of love. Pressing against the Shepherd's chest, their tender hugs will be an enjoyable expression of love all through the day and night for the Maiden.

Legs of Alabaster and Feet of Gold

Song of Solomon 5:15a:
"His legs are pillars of alabaster
Set on pedestals of pure gold."

"His legs are pillars of alabaster." They are dependable and capable of doing their work. The Jews stored precious liquids in alabaster jars. Oils stored in these containers often retain their fragrances indefinitely. When archaeologists opened some of the ancient tombs of Egypt, 4000-year-old alabaster jars often contained sweet-smelling substances as fragrant as the day they were poured into the containers.

"His feet are pedestals of pure gold." Pure gold, refined with fire to remove all impurities, symbolizes preciousness and piety throughout the Bible as in Job 23:10 and 1 Peter 1:7. The pedestals hold her Shepherd upright and firm. He is dependable and sturdy.

The Shulammite overlays the Shepherd from his head to his feet with pure gold and precious jewels from the everyday life of King Solomon. With her play on words and sense of humor, she personalizes her Shepherd's face with the herbs of the Northern streams.

From head to toe, the Shepherd is the embodiment of loving masculinity. Wow! Is he hot! Her passions simmer just below the surface, longing…. No! Insisting that the Virgins bring him to her.

"My Beloved Is Choice as the Cedars on Lebanon"

Song of Solomon 5:15b:
"His appearance is like Lebanon,
Choice as the cedars."

The Shulammite leaves the comparisons to royalty and turns to the country to restate that her Shepherd is outstanding among ten thousand. She summarizes, "His appearance is like Lebanon, choice as the cedars." An impressive, scenic, snow-capped mountain range, Lebanon is plush with rare cedars—no one compares to her beloved. Not even King Solomon in the prime of his own youth.

She began by saying he was "outstanding among ten thousand."

Now, as if being so distinguished among men were not enough, she ends her description by saying he equals the most majestic and awesome sight in nature—the strong, beautiful rare cedars standing tall and proud on Lebanon. As God's creation, he embraces all of the best traits of manhood—strength, determination, purity, dependability, resourcefulness, endurance, wealth in character, and especially a loving disposition.

Together, the Shulammite and the Shepherd represent femininity and masculinity as described in Proverbs 11:6: "A gracious woman attains honor, and violent [strong—KJV] men attain riches." The Maiden is graciously a haven of comfort, for the Shepherd views her as both a refreshing garden stream and as his honey preserved with honeycomb. He presents a picture of strength as an adoring leader, protector, and provider for her. Together, they possess all the qualities necessary for a loving marriage and to adorn the earth with succored children.

2. Sexual Love—"My Beloved Is Wholly Desirable"

Song of Solomon 5:16a:
"His mouth is full of sweetness.
And he is wholly desirable [lovely – KJV]."

"Desirable" means "delightful, hence a delight, i.e., object of affection or desire:--beloved, desire, goodly, lovely, pleasant (thing)" (Strong 64).

Dr. Rosemary Basson says sexual desire is "manifested by sexual thinking, fantasizing and conscious sexual neediness." To this commonly recognized cycle of human sexual response, she adds, "Continuous modulation of this cycle occurs as feedback obtained from genital and non-genital physical responses, as well as from emotions and perceptions [soulmating]" ("Rethinking").

In her sexual thinking, fantasizing, and conscious sexual neediness, the Shulammite began the account of her dilemma longing for the Shepherd's deep kisses (Song 1:2). Now that she's chosen the Shepherd, her thoughts return to his mouth, full of soft, tender, sweet kisses and words. She longs to taste him.

She has yet to experience sexual love with the Shepherd, which remains a deeply anticipated mystery of coming splendor. So she focuses on his mouth as the memories stir her passions and tingle her body.

The Song of Solomon begins with the Maiden saying, "May he kiss me with the kisses of his mouth!" and adds, "Your oils have a pleasing fragrance" (Song 1:2-3). Any man who fails to learn this lesson from the Shepherd about satisfying a woman's 5 senses, especially her sense of smell, which is connected to her emotions, shouldn't be surprised if his wife acts less than enthusiastic to his advances. But the Shulammite is not silent about how the Shepherd appeals to all of her senses. She tells him what pleases her.

To the Maiden, the Shepherd is completely desirable with nothing detestable about him. She looks forward to satisfying his sexual needs because he is the object of her own yearnings. Love builds within her a desire to give her whole self to him. Her romantic description of the man of her dreams unashamedly reflects her own deep longing to begin *SPEAKING GOD'S BEAUTIFUL LANGUAGE OF LOVE* with #10 orgasms in the arms of her Shepherd.

3. Emotional Love—"This Is My Beloved and My Friend"

Song of Solomon 5:16b:
"This is my beloved and this my friend,
O daughters of Jerusalem."

"Friend" means "an associate more or less close)." It comes from a root word meaning "to tend a flock, i.e., pasture it, to graze, generally to rule, to associate with (as a friend)" (Strong 109).

The Shepherd revealed his emotional love by describing the Maiden as "my sister." They share the emotional intimacy of siblings. She acknowledges their soulmating bond by calling him "my beloved and my friend."

Many times lovers are only lovers—not friends. For a marriage to survive the bad times as well as the good, the lovers must cultivate true friendship. They must delight in each other and enjoy each other's company during the day as well as the night. They must trust each other with the bonds of siblings so that they are free to confide their deepest secrets to one another.

The Maiden shares such a relationship with the Shepherd. He genuinely cares about her welfare and doesn't exploit her for his own selfish purposes. She can share her most private feelings and fears knowing he'll respond with true empathy. She doesn't dread his leadership because he isn't drunk with power. He won't dominate her as a tyrant, nor talk to her as to a child, nor treat her as a feeble-minded slave. She can confidently call him "my friend" because he is full of sweetness, kindness, and consideration.

The Virgins Ask, "Where Has Your Beloved Gone?"

Song of Solomon 6:1:
"Where has your beloved gone,
O most beautiful among women?
Where has your beloved turned,
That we may seek him with you?"

The Maiden started the morning by asking the Virgins to find the Shepherd for her. She asked them to do this rather than doing it herself because she has unfinished business with the King. Thus she implores them to find the Shepherd and tell him she is ready to marry him. After first doubting her sanity and then listening to a beautiful, romantic description of her beloved, the Virgins eagerly want to befriend the Shulammite and find the Shepherd for her. They are finally paying attention to her message about awakening love before marriage.

"My Beloved Is Pasturing His Flock"

Song of Solomon 6:2:
"My beloved has gone down to his garden,
To the beds of balsam,
To pasture his flock in the gardens
And gather lilies."

The Shulammite knows exactly where to find her beloved. As a responsible person, he is taking care of his flocks. A wise girl wants her future husband to be a dependable worker.

One girl felt uneasy about the work habits of a boy who proposed to her. He habitually worked a few months, then quit his job and lived on his earnings for several months. When his money ran out, he found another job and worked a few more months. This pattern repeated itself over and over. When he asked her to marry him, she told him she didn't want to live with constant uncertainty. The boy promised after marriage he would change. The girl wisely decided not to take a chance on him.

Deeply ingrained childhood work habits often require much effort to change. Promises made before marriage are often forgotten afterward by the person who made them. But the person to whom the promises were made doesn't forget which leads to bitterness.

Many parents become upset when their son or daughter marries a lazy, shiftless person. With forethought, parents can often avoid such tragedies. Parents can instill a good work ethic in their children by admiring and associating with hard-working people.

My father, Ray Snodgrass, did this without lecturing any of us. Not only did he set an example of working hard himself, at meal times he praised his employees who delivered honest labor. He often bragged about a high school boy who always found something to do to stay busy. He said, "If Jimmy doesn't have anything else to do, he cleans the restroom." Dad's praise of Jimmy made me desire to do the same quality of work by always looking for jobs to stay busy. I also wanted the same characteristic of hard work in my husband.

One father said, "Before my daughter begins to date and becomes emotionally involved with boys, I plan to take her to dinner from time to time to discuss what kind of man would make the best husband. It should be easy to help her think through her plans and to get her to agree that her future husband must possess certain qualities."

Before emotions become aroused and create a chance for hurt feelings, a father and daughter can make a pact to find the best possible husband for her. Mothers can help their sons choose a loving wife in much the same way.

If parents wait until their children begin dating to try to teach them how to choose a marriage partner, they may find their children will reject any suggestions they make. Parents should begin preparing their children for marriage before they even begin school. The Song of Solomon story presents the perfect beginning place.

4. Spiritual Love—"I Am My Beloved's and My Beloved Is Mine"

Song of Solomon 6:3:
"I am my beloved's and my beloved is mine.
He who pastures his flock among the lilies."

A powerful feminine wet dream has awakened the Maiden. As she listens to the cravings of her body, she realizes that she feels no sexual desires for Solomon. He has not attempted to get to know her as a person. Nor has he shared any of his goals or fears with her. All he talks about is how beautiful she is and how he craves to fondle her breasts. His mouth is not full of sweetness and he is not her friend. Her subconscious rejected him before her conscious mind got a chance.

Yet her body cries out for the Shepherd. They share kindred hearts, minds, and purposes—they belong together. Their mutual bond of love and respect is so enduring no one else can intrude. They share all 4 parts of true love, which offers a husband and wife the highest form of happiness.

She honors God's plan for the way of man with a maid as she looks forward to being united with the Shepherd for a lifetime of passion. She follows God's design of soulmating before lovemaking. She understands how God, love, and sex are intimately linked.

The Shulammite begs the Virgins to leave the palace where Solomon is waiting for her and go find her beloved who is pasturing his flocks outside Jerusalem. She is confident the Shepherd has followed her. Perhaps she even saw him keeping a safe distance as Solomon's caravan brought her to Jerusalem.

"Tell him I've made my decision. I am lovesick for him. Tell him to hurry! I'm on my way to meet with the King to end his infatuation with me. I need the Shepherd here now! Please hurry and bring him to the palace to get me and take me home!"

Study Exercise

Answer all questions in your own words.

1. What does "charm is deceitful" refer to? How can a person avoid being taken advantage of by courtship flattery?
2. Why is mutual admiration so important for a marriage?
3. Was it reasonable for the Shulammite to say the Shepherd was one in ten thousand? Explain your answer.
4. Why did the Shulammite describe everything about the Shepherd as being like pure gold?
5. What advice would you give an engaged couple so they may enjoy a loving marriage?
6. What was the Shepherd's attitude toward work? Are a man's work habits an important consideration? Why?
7. Why is it important for a woman to be able to say her husband's or boyfriend's mouth is full of sweetness?
8. Why is it important for a woman to be able to say her husband or boyfriend is her friend?
9. Do you disagree with anything in the lesson? If so, explain giving scriptures for your reasons.

Personal Exercise

Explain how the Shulammite's description of the Shepherd is of universal application. Write two paragraphs for each characteristic.

If you are a woman, discuss your attitude toward your spouse or boyfriend in regard to each area. How do these characteristics satisfy your 5 senses? How do they reflect the 4 parts of love?

If you are a man, how do you showcase these characteristics to your wife or girlfriend—be the kind of man who would make a great husband? Discuss these qualities as they apply to you.

1. Outstanding among ten thousand
2. Appearance is like purified gold
3. Choice as the cedars
4. Kisses turn her on
5. Wholly desirable
6. Her beloved and her friend

Personal Exercise

Women: You can learn what the men in your family are most proud of and would like to be admired for by listening. Spend the next week listening to your husband, sons, father, or boyfriend. When they start talking, stop what you're doing, and listen. Watch their eyes and facial expressions. Be prepared to give one example in class of a man or a boy asking for admiration.

Men: The chapter "Secret 4: Grow the 4 Parts of Intimacy and Love" shows how a loving husband or boyfriend compliments his family members. If you need to, review that section. Men can learn what the women in their family are most proud of and what they would like to be admired for by listening. Spend the next week listening to your wife, daughters, mother, or girlfriend. When they start talking, stop what you're doing, and listen. Watch their eyes and facial expressions. Be prepared to give one example in class of a woman asking for admiration.

Personal Exercise

Read the appendix chapter "Orgasms of Love with Cervical Kisses." Many readers who do the homework at the end of the chapters, if they're not already experiencing powerful orgasms, will be close to enjoying such euphoria. Sometimes just reading what to expect is all husbands and wives need to begin enjoying double-dose #10s.

Stacey's Story:
We Had an Over-the-Top Setback

Hello Patsy Rae,

I know I have much for which to be thankful. We've had our struggles this year (I haven't shared them all with you, but we have worked through them). I've seen the Lord bring my husband to the point where he was willing to study your book with me.

But before we could get started, Joe got upset with me. His reaction was over-the-top. He immediately used it as an excuse not to read the book with me. I didn't push it. I used the fighting fair techniques and my mirror lines to point out how he was being unjust in his reaction, and left it at that.

He came to me several days later and repented. He looked me in the eyes and told me he'd read the book with me. I could see his eyes were watery. I know this is a big step for him. I think deep down he has been a bit scared about reading the book together and that's why he was resisting so much.

His over-the-top reaction made it so clear to me. That's why I know we have to keep our problems out of our study and just learn God's Word together. I am looking forward to it. I know the Lord has much to work in me, too. I'm also looking forward to Joe sharing his insights.

I appreciate your reminder that our study is not a time to bring up problems. It's easy to forget that sometimes when you want everything fixed now. But there are no instant fixes and God's perfect timing brings about growth that we didn't even know we needed.

I can't tell you how much I've learned from our trials these past two years. I do wonder if there is something in Joe's past. It seems that sometimes when we talk, he seems to shut down at a certain point as if we might be getting too close to something. I don't push it, and I certainly don't want to surmise.

I just pray that the Lord will work and heal. I know we might have some rocky spots. I'm ready and willing to face them, but I am a bit intimidated by it, too. More reason to lean fully on the Lord through all of this. He is able!

I'll let you know how the studies go. Please keep us in your prayers.

Blessings, Reaping His Joys,
Stacey

I closed out our e-mail exchange with some encouragement:

Hello Stacey,

You and Joe have developed good communication skills and are still working on them. I think you'll be able to get through this. Sometimes letting go of the past and stepping out into the full light is hard to do. Mental housecleaning is the hardest work of all. I'm finding that we never really complete the job. We just keep growing to new heights.

You're both in my prayers,
Patsy Rae

P.S. To my readers: I had no idea just how true my last two concluding sentences to Stacey were, and are, for my own life—that we never really complete the mental housecleaning to let go of the past. But the more we work, the brighter the light becomes.

I'm convinced God intends for us to learn by hindsight, by examining what we did right and what we did wrong, so we can continually make future corrections. We never grow old enough that we don't make mistakes. But we can learn how to correct them more easily and quickly.

The Apostle Paul alluded to this when he said mature Christians have learned how to identify good and evil through practice—through life's experiences (Hebrews 5:13-14).

Secret 8: Avoid the 12 Love-Defying Traits of a Sexless Spouse

Solomon's Siren Song: Solomon's Bachelor Party

"Aviva, the eunuch, Noam, wants to see you."

"Help me freshen up a bit first." Aviva sits down at her dressing table.

The servant scurries to arrange Aviva's hair and puts oil of gladness on her face. "You look beautiful. I'll send him in and leave."

Noam bows before Aviva. "My lady, the King is on his way back to Jerusalem. He sent a messenger ahead to request that you accompany him in his private chambers tonight."

"Tonight? But he hasn't sent for me since I finished my wedding week. That was two months ago. I thought he didn't like me."

"Ohhhh, he likes you alright. Slave girls are his favorite. He's bringing a free woman to the palace this afternoon. He'll ask for a concubine every night until he begins the new girl's wedding week."

"He's never asked for me before. What do I do?"

Noam walks around Aviva looking her over. "You don't have much time. Report immediately to the beauticians. They know their job. They'll bathe you in a tub with milk to soften and silken your skin and myrrh and rose petals to stimulate your romantic juices. The King likes a strong fragrance of desire on his women." His hollow laugh echoes off the walls.

"The hair stylists will wash your hair and fix it the way he loves it— long and flowing with a few braids…. You don't have to worry about anything…except pleasing the King tonight to put him in a good mood when he introduces his new bride tomorrow morning."

"Oh, oh, oh! I can hardly wait to be with the King again."

"Don't get your hopes up. It'll be months before he asks for you again…. He likes to keep his women on edge and eager. The last thing he wants is a woman bored with sex. If you ever pout because it's been too long, he'll never send for you again. Several girls learned the hard way not to try and make the King feel guilty."

"Oh, I'm more than ready. I'm so glad he likes me after all."

"During daylight hours, he goes for spontaneous sex. The gyrations of his dancers always stir up his passions…. So you never know when he'll summon you. But he's more pensive when choosing his nighttime lovelies."

Noam walks to the door, turns around. "He'll want you to spend the night. It'll be like your wedding night all over again. So choose an alluring negligee that shows off your breasts. The servants will take your selection to the King's chambers."

"What's his favorite color?"

"He won't care about the color as long as the gown emphasizes your breasts." Naom snickers under his breath as he exits her room.

A smile spreads across Aviva's face as she dances and twirls around the room. "He likes me! He likes me!" Then she stops abruptly, "Beauticians, here I come. I have a hot date tonight!"

Song of Solomon 6:4-7:5: Solomon Reigns Over Sexless Marriages

ACT TWO, SCENE SIX
THIRD DAY – MORNING

The meeting with Solomon takes place in the Great Hall to accommodate Solomon's 140 wives and the maidens without number. It's an impressive room with many lavish golden works of art.

Solomon's Third Proposal

The night before Solomon gave the Shulammite time to think. While she strolled in the garden, he partied with one of his wives. As the Maiden lingered in the garden, she remembered the Shepherd's pledge of lasting love and how it differed from Solomon's proposal. That night she fretted over a dream about life without her Shepherd. Reaching the turning point in her affections, early that morning she sent the Virgins to find her beloved Shepherd to tell him she wants to marry him.

When Solomon summons her, she's dressed simply, but elegantly with her long sheer veil covering her head and breasts to protect her modesty. Solomon meets her at the door of the Great Hall and leads her to a chaise lounge. Solomon tries a third time to persuade her to marry him as he describes her with flattering and erotic terms of passion—the best proposal a sensuous lover can ever make. With fancy words, he attempts to seduce her in joining his harem.

In spite of all his wealth, prestige, and glory, Solomon is a perfect example of how to fail in love and marriage. Sensuous love focuses on the external and lacks the in-depth emotions necessary to sustain it over a long time. Notice the shallowness of Solomon's proposal:

She's as Beautiful as Tirzah

Song of Solomon 6:4:
"You are as beautiful as Tirzah, my darling,
As lovely as Jerusalem,
As awesome as an army with banners."

"Beautiful" means "beautiful (literally or figuratively):--comely, fair (-est, one)" (Strong 51).

Solomon looks the Maiden up and down, and he's more than pleased. Her simple dress and lack of jewelry contrast with the gaudy costumes of his wives. The soft flowing fabric accentuates her curves as he focuses on her body instead of her character and personality.

"Ah," he smiles, "the villagers will come from miles around to gawk at you like they do when they visit my royal cities. Tirzah and Jerusalem are eclipsed by your beauty." He walks slowly around her taking in every detail. "My darling, you're as stunning as my army parading through the streets with banners and flags flying high. Wow! I can see the jealous eyes ogling such a beautiful trophy wife as you."

Her Eyes Confuse Solomon

Song of Solomon 6:5:
"Turn your eyes away from me,
For they have confused [disturb – RSV, overwhelm – NIV] me."

"Confuse" is a primary root that means "to urge severely, i.e. (figuratively) importune, embolden, capture, act insolently" (Strong 107).

Solomon notices the Maiden's eyes watching him through her veil. Shocked that he no longer sees the look of eager trust shining in her eyes he briefly falters. Before her dream, the King's flattery charmed her. At last her eyes are open and she sees him for who he is—a man who uses women for his own pleasure. She is immune to his polished words. Her eyes speak volumes about what she feels.

He has witnessed plenty of women swooning over his graceful speech—140 to be exact. Her piercing look rattles and disheartens him, "Turn your eyes away from me. They're confusing me and making me forget what I want to say."

Yet the Shepherd told the Shulammite, "You have made my heart beat faster with a single glance of your eyes" (Song 4:9). The love and admiration radiating from the Shulammite's eyes turned him on. It made him want to be with her and to partake of her succoring nature.

She's Exceedingly Beautiful

Song of Solomon 6:5-7:
"Your hair is like a flock of goats
That have descended from Gilead.
Your teeth are like a flock of ewes
Which have come up from their washing,
All of which bear twins,
And not one among them has lost her young.
Your temples are like a slice of a pomegranate
Behind your veil."

Solomon continues his description after the Shulammite turns her eyes away. No ordinary beauty, her features appear perfect in every way. "Oh, you are the most beautiful woman I've ever seen! I made a wise choice in bringing you to the palace."

But something is wrong!

Didn't Solomon describe her this same exact sensuous way yesterday (Song 4:1-5)? He rattles off the words as if he's well practiced at seduction. Can this be a line he's perfected on other women? His next words take away the mystery of why he repeats himself.

Solomon Introduces His 140 Wives

Song of Solomon 6:8:
"There are sixty queens and eighty concubines
And maidens without number."

His First Two Wives

Solomon took at least two wives during his four-year co-reign with his father David. The daughter of the Pharaoh of Egypt became his first wife soon after he started his co-reign (1 Kings 3:1). She is the only wife named in a list of wives Solomon loved (1 Kings 11:1-2). Likewise, she is the only wife he built a house for (1 Kings 7:8). This indicates she was not only his first, but also probably his favorite wife.

He also married Naamah the Ammonitess who bore him a son, Rehoboam. He followed Solomon to the throne at age 41 (1 Kings 14:21). This would have made him 1 year old when David died and Solomon was anointed king the second time to begin his official 40-year reign.

His Next 998 Wives

Solomon married 998 women during his 40-year reign in addition to the two he married during his co-reign. These 1000 women average out to be 25 wives per year. This limited Solomon to spending a little over two weeks on each new wife including the courtship, the marriage festival which usually lasted a week, and the honeymoon. Then he moved on to deflowering the next virgin. This scenario fits his 3-day whirlwind pursuit of the Shulammite.

When Solomon died, his harem contained 700 free women and princesses along with 300 slaves or concubines. Rather than these being strictly political wives that Solomon didn't have sex with, 1 Kings 11:2 says, "Solomon held fast to these in love."

> *1 Kings 11:1-3: "Now King Solomon loved many foreign women along with the daughter of Pharaoh: Moabite, Ammonite, Edomite, Sidonian, and Hittite women, from the nations concerning which the LORD had said to the sons of Israel, "You shall not associate with them, nor shall they associate with you, for they will surely turn your heart away after their gods." Solomon held fast to these in love. He had seven hundred wives, princesses, and three hundred concubines, and his wives turned his heart away."*

"Held fast" is the same word translated "cleave" in Genesis 2:24 where Adam said, "A man shall leave his father and mother and *cleave* to his wife." Cleave means to "stick like glue."

"Love" is a common word throughout Proverbs and means "to have affection for (sexually or otherwise)" (Strong 9).

Solomon treated these women as true wives in every sense. He cleaved to them as a husband and had sex with them. God warned Solomon against marrying foreign women stating if he did, they would turn his heart away from God.

Solomon's pagan wives were already involving him in idolatrous worship by the time of the Song of Solomon. We'll see this when the Queens and Concubines meet the Shulammite and praise her appearance with idolatrous descriptions. They assure the King they will accept her into the harem by reminding him of their idols of both virginity and prostitution.

The Shulammite is the only Israelite the Bible ever connects with possible marriage to Solomon. At the time of the Song of Solomon, the Hebrews still had healthy attitudes toward marriage and lovemaking. When Solomon's 40-year reign ended the Jews' view of women, children, and marriage had deteriorated into disrespect.

His 60 Queens and 80 Concubines

David possibly arranged Solomon's first marriage to Pharaoh's daughter as a political union to help protect his young son when he began his solo rule. Solomon brought her to the city of David while his father was still alive. She lived there until Solomon completed his own house and a separate house for her (1 Kings 9:24; 2 Chronicles 8:11). The 12-year-old boy king gained political benefits from this marriage:

> To strengthen his position among contemporary princes, Solomon sought marriage with the daughter of Pharaoh. Egypt was at this time the most wealthy and therefore the most powerful country in the world. Solomon's marriage, accordingly, with the daughter of Pharaoh was an event of great importance. The Delta would henceforth defend him. It was a political marriage, quite unlike anything that had happened in Israel before. His union with Pharaoh's daughter meant that he was allied with the strongest monarch then ruling upon any throne. By it he also won the Canaanitish city of Gezer, about midway between Joppa and Jerusalem (ISBE "Solomon").

Doing the math on Solomon's wives at the time of the Song of Solomon shows that although some of Solomon's marriages may well have been political unions, the majority were all about sex. Here's the breakdown on the 140 wives in Song of Solomon 6:8:

> 60 Queens (political and commoners like the Shulammite) = 43%
> 80 Concubines (slaves did not include Jewish women) = 57%

In the early years, Solomon acquired concubines (slave wives) faster than he married free women. All the concubines would have been pagans because the King could not keep Israelite slaves. With 57% of Solomon's wives being slaves, more than 50% of his early marriages were primarily about satisfying his raging hormones. Sometimes the concubines belonged to the wives who ruled over them. Any children born to a concubine also belonged to her mistress. The stories of Leah, Rachel, and Sarah provide examples of these differences.

Additionally, the Shulammite was a free woman with no political benefits for Solomon. We have no way of knowing how many of the Queens were also commoners whom Solomon lusted after. With the huge political benefits from marrying the daughter of Pharaoh and keeping her as his favorite wife, Solomon's need for other political alliances would have decreased. This allowed the playboy king to pursue any beautiful body that aroused his passions.

His Maidens Without Number

In addition to the queens and concubines, Solomon's harem included "maidens without number" (Song 6:8). The fact that these Virgins are listed along with Solomon's queens and concubines implies they were either promised or betrothed to Solomon.

A promise to marry was more like modern engagements—it could be broken easily. A person might break a number of "promises" before marrying. On the other hand, a betrothal was a formal covenant which required a divorce to break it even though the marriage was never consummated. The betrothal period before the wedding for a virgin was set by law to be 10 months to a year while it lasted only 3-6 months for a widow (Wight 129-30).

Solomon's 3-day whirlwind romance with the Shulammite indicates he probably preferred to dispense with the long wait of a formal betrothal. Likewise, the Shulammite's pleadings with the palace Virgins to wait for love to grow naturally suggest she considered them promised to Solomon rather than betrothed to him.

However, some parents may have betrothed their daughter to Solomon for a large dowry which went to the parents of the bride. A handsome dowry gift was also given to the virgin to support her if the marriage ended in divorce (Wight 127-8).

Solomon Promises She'll Be His #1 Wife

Song of Solomon 6:9a:
"But my dove, my perfect one, is unique:
She is her mother's only daughter;
She is the pure child of the one who bore her."

Solomon's speech reveals his third ploy to entice the Shulammite to marry him. He began his seduction in the countryside by addressing her with flattering lewd compliments. She was so beautiful, she was like a mare in heat stampeding pharaoh's chariots. She would turn everyone's head.

When that didn't work and she asked for time to think, Solomon moved on to Plan B—the Virgins offered her fine jewelry and clothes for an expensive dowry and he displayed his magnificent wealth in the traveling chair. Now he impresses her with his opulent palace and furnishings. Once again she asked for time to think.

Not dissuaded from his pursuit of her as wife number 141, Solomon launches into Plan C. He promises the Shulammite that she will become his #1 wife (Réville 21). Indeed, many commentators have fallen for this line and assume the Shulammite was Solomon's favorite wife. However, instead of swooning, the maiden's eyes continue to open because of what Solomon is revealing about himself.

She recognizes that Solomon doesn't profess to love her. Instead, he offers her the power and prestige of becoming his primary wife—superior to all the others. Many women sell out for power, prestige, and money. But the Maiden wants something money can't buy — true love.

Solomon puts Plan C into action when he introduces the Shulammite to his wives. He pays her his highest compliment. He waves his hand over 140 of the most beautiful women in the land from kings' daughters, to slaves, and to peasants like the Shulammite with numerous virgins waiting for their chance to marry him.

Then Solomon brings his hand back to his chest promising from his heart, "There are sixty queens and eighty concubines, and maidens without number; but my dove, my perfect one, is unique: she is her mother's only daughter; she is the pure child of the one who bore her."

In essence, Solomon says, "None of these beauties can hold my attention for long. But you, my dear, are different. Their beauty pales beside yours. You are perfect — even your sisters — daughters of your mother — cannot compare to you. After you, I'll stop searching for the perfect feminine body and settle down. You'll be my favorite wife and get privileges the others don't."

What a line Solomon feeds the Shulammite! All his other gorgeous wives failed to satisfy him for long, but he promises the Shulammite, "It will be different with you!" How many times has he used this same ploy? Perhaps as many times as he used the one to describe her beauty — 60 queens plus 80 concubines equal 140 wives plus maidens without number! Can the Shulammite believe him? Dare any woman believe any man who tells her, "It'll be different with you"?

Solomon Was a Prototype of Sexual Addiction

At the time of the Song of Solomon, Solomon had 140 of the 1000 wives he would eventually marry. The true story reveals he was already developing warped attitudes toward women and the sexual relationship. Indeed, listening to sexual addicts talk about their attitudes toward women, sex, and marriage is like listening to King Solomon.

Solomon proposes to the young maiden four times, and each time he eloquently praises her sexual charms. He never sees her as a person with a brain and a personality, or as a person with needs and desires of her own. His four proposals expose his views of the Maiden as only the most ravishing female body he's ever seen. Her bountiful breasts stir up wild and overwhelming sexual urges craving to be released.

This same characteristic of Solomon, of a purely physical attraction without the intimacy of soulmating, is the common thread that runs through all sexual addiction. Dr. Patrick Carnes in his book *Out of the Shadows: Understanding Sexual Addiction* uses such words as isolation, abandonment, loneliness, cut off from reality, self-preoccupation, pain, anxiety, lack of emotional balance, alienation, anger, distrust, and despair to describe both male and female sexual addicts. The almost total lack of a proper intellectual and emotional relationship with the spouse is at the core of the sexual addiction (1992).

Solomon is the perfect man for studying sexual addiction. He enjoyed access to the most beautiful women in the known world! If sexual addiction's promise of supreme pleasure and fulfillment were true, Solomon would have found it with the abundance of his wealth to spend on his addiction. Although no pornographic movies, magazines, or Internet connections were afforded him—Solomon heaped his lusts upon the real bodies of the most desirable women of his time including princesses, slaves, and peasants. He relished all the sexual techniques his foreign wives brought with them as part of their idolatrous worship. If ever a man could find true sexual happiness and fulfillment in variety, techniques, and glorification of the body, Solomon was that man.

Howard Hughes Was a Modern Solomon

If Solomon's search for true love and his resulting harem seem unreal, many men of wealth and prestige try to find happiness with the exact same formula. Perhaps the most famous in modern times was the multibillionaire Howard Hughes. Soon after his death, newspapers and magazines published articles about his habits and lifestyle. He resembled Solomon in a tragic way.

Solomon and Howard Hughes used women in much the same manner. Only Hughes employed modern technology to locate the most perfect bodies known to man. When he found a picture in a newspaper or a magazine of a woman with all the right dimensions, he launched an investigation complete with a background study and blown-up pictures of her. If the woman still met his specifications, he sent for her. Hughes kept the woman on call twenty-four hours a day to satisfy his sexual desires. Even with this intense, painstaking search to find the perfect body to turn him on, he quickly became bored with the women.

Neither Solomon nor Howard Hughes were fictitious characters. Each was a real, warm-blooded man who spent his life searching for the perfect body to find fulfillment and supreme happiness. But all their intelligence, resources, and fame proved useless in the pursuit of love.

Men of more limited means still try Solomon's formula to a lesser degree by constantly changing girlfriends. Many of them claim it's impossible for a man to find satisfaction by restricting himself to one sexual partner for the rest of his life. However, countless poor, common, and obscure men succeed where playboys flounder. *The secret isn't in finding the perfect body to make love with, but in making love with a woman you're emotionally intimate with.*

A study of the Song of Solomon shows a poignant contrast between true love and sensuous love. True love builds an intellectual and emotional bond with the lover which liberates both their bodies in a rapturous sexual union. Sensuous love looks only at the physical body and traps its participants in a lifelong compelling search for the perfect combination of bodies. At whatever age a person studies the Song of Solomon, it teaches a powerful lesson on how to lay the foundation for true love and sexual satisfaction that lasts a lifetime. Ideally, that foundation should be laid in one's youth. Regardless of a person's age and past sexual history, no one is too old to learn the secret of true love and find supreme sexual pleasure.

Solomon Becomes the King of Sexless Marriages

In the first chapter, I let Dr. Douglas Weiss who wrote *Intimacy Anorexia, Healing the Hidden Addiction in Your Marriage* and coined the expression "intimacy anorexia" define the disorder. He explained it as a hidden addiction of avoiding sex with the mate—not necessarily avoiding sex, but *avoiding sex with the mate*. Sexual anorexia is a *withholding addiction* manifested in a dysfunctional marriage. When sex occurs, it's mechanical and emotionless.

Then I defined sexless marriages from the Song of Solomon:

The Song of Solomon's Definition of Sexless Marriages: The inability to love the mate intellectually, emotionally, sexually, and spiritually.

Next I defined sensuous love:

The Song of Solomon's Definition of Sensuous Love: Satisfaction of the 5 senses without intellectual, emotional, sexual, and spiritual love.

Finally, I gave the definition of true Love:

The Song of Solomon's Definition of True love: Satisfaction of the 5 senses with intellectual, emotional, sexual, and spiritual love.

Secret 8: Avoid the 12 Love-Defying Traits of a Sexless Spouse

Weiss lists 11 characteristics of an unloving person in *Intimacy Anorexia*. I added a second part to financial abuse to make 12. We've covered enough of the Shulammite's dilemma that we can quickly recognize how Solomon displays all of them. See if you don't agree that Solomon is, indeed, the King of Sexless Marriages.

1. Solomon Blamed 1000 Wives for His Failure

Blaming the spouse is a nearly universal characteristic of people who withhold love. It usually appears in the first few months of the marriage alongside the surprise dead bedroom syndrome. They blame the spouse for their lack of sexual interest in them. Over time, this spills into every area. No matter what happens, they blame the spouse. They fail to see or take any personal responsibility for what happens around the house or in the relationship. This continues to get worse as they eventually despise the spouse.

Solomon had 1000 wives, and he blamed them all as utter failures in Ecclesiastes 7:27-29. The word "woman" is the same Hebrew word translated "wives" in other passages. The context determines what kind of woman she is. See the chapter, "Solomon Never Had Great Sex with 1000 Virgins," for more information on how "woman" is used in this passage and Proverbs.

We also see Solomon blaming his wives for not being beautiful enough when he tells the Shulammite all the other women are thorns compared to her (Song 2:2). He continually praises the Maiden's beauty as superior to his wives (Song 6:9). His blaming cycle may have lasted about two weeks as he averaged spending only two weeks from courtship, to marriage, to moving on to deflowering the next virgin. Blaming a woman for not being pretty (or a man handsome) enough for the intimacy anorexic to desire sex with her (or him) is a common tactic.

2. Solomon Was too Busy to Be a Husband

Always being busy is a common characteristic of most anorexics. By staying busy, this leaves them little time to spend with the spouse. They find lots of ways to be too busy such as always cleaning, helping the kids with homework, pursuing hobbies, working in the yard, fixing the car, whatever they can do to avoid spending quality time with their spouse. Handhelds and computers present many opportunities to be too busy. Even when they're riding in the car or eating at a restaurant with the spouse, they can be texting, talking on the phone, reading email, playing games, or looking at porn.

Obviously, Solomon was always busy looking for new virgins to court, marry, and deflower. This left little personal time for any of his wives. The more wives he added, the less time he had for any of them. His three-day courtship of the Shulammite shows he probably wasn't interested in a real bond with any of them.

3. Solomon Withheld Love

This characteristic isn't just about withholding love, it also involves the aspect of how love is expressed to the mate. If the spouse has to analyze whether or not the anorexic loves them, then love is being withheld. When one wife asked her husband, "Why do you never say, 'I love you,' anymore?" the anorexic replied, "I buy food and clothes for you don't I? If I didn't love you I wouldn't do that." The spouses of anorexics often describe themselves as love starved.

While Solomon pursues the Shulammite, he never expresses love for her. Instead, he admires her perfect body. She's so beautiful she's like a mare in heat running among Pharaoh's chariots distracting his stallions. He shows zero interest in her as an intelligent, caring person. He doesn't even seem to desire love from her. His reason for making her his #1 wife is not because he'll enjoy her company, but because she's more beautiful than all his other wives.

4. Solomon Withheld Praise

Another almost universal characteristic of anorexics is withholding verbal appreciation for what the spouse does for them and what the spouse means to them. One wife told her husband, "I hear you compliment other women all the time, but you never compliment me."

The husband replied, "You do have beautiful hair." That was the only compliment she ever got from him. He didn't have a clue to how her soul hungered to be celebrated for who she was.

The Song of Solomon records many of the compliments the Shulammite and the Shepherd gave each other. But other than continually admiring her breasts, Solomon didn't offer the Maiden a single compliment on his own. When she told him she was the rose of Sharon, he agreed, but he didn't think of it on his own.

5. Solomon Withheld Sex

Withholding sex from the spouse is the most obvious characteristic of anorexics. It has three parts in marriage: (1) withholding sex, (2) sabotaging sexual opportunities, and (3) not connecting emotionally during sex. Weiss lists many ways unloving people master these three areas of withholding sex (*Intimacy* 43).

Commentators on the Song of Solomon don't know what to think of Solomon having 1000 wives and trying to keep all of them sexually happy. Obviously, there was no human way to accomplish that feat. But his conduct with the Shulammite and the fact that he kept marrying more and more women demonstrates how sick he was. He essentially practiced all three ways of withholding sex.

For example, (1) the more women Solomon added to his harem, out of necessity, the more he withheld sex from all of them. (2) While Solomon was busy completing his wedding week with each new bride, he was sabotaging sexual opportunities with the rest of them. He was out of commission every other week since he added a new wife about every two weeks. (3) Solomon's conduct with the Shulammite shows he didn't even consider connecting emotionally with the women.

Once we understand Solomon was an intimacy anorexic, his sexual relationship with all his wives is no longer a mystery. Commentators experience a problem when they try to view him as a normal husband who had an emotional relationship with each wife. While Solomon loved his wives sexually and cleaved to them, he never desired a real marriage with any of them.

6. Solomon Withheld Spirituality

Even preachers, elders, and spiritual leaders who withhold sex also withhold spirituality from their spouse. Weiss says, "The anorexic might be religious to the hilt, but spiritually not authentic in the presence of their spouse." In other words, what you see is not what you get. The anorexic is not transparent to the spouse.

What an amazing irony with Solomon! He was building the Temple in Jerusalem for God. At the same time, he was building altars on the high places in the country for his wives to worship their idols. Wherein is his loyalty? With God or his wives? Or is he faithful to none of them?

7. Solomon Didn't Share Feelings

Anorexics are undeveloped emotionally. Many grew up in homes where they were prevented from showing emotions. Not only do they not express their feelings, they also don't know how to feel in the first place. When they're in crisis mode, they may briefly share feelings, but it doesn't last for long.

From the first time he sees her to his last sensuous plea, the only feelings Solomon shares with the Shulammite are those of lust for her beautiful body. He's not bashful about admiring her breasts and declaring his desire for her. But he never professes his love for her.

8. Solomon Criticized All His Wives

This is ongoing and ungrounded criticism of the mate. It doesn't need to be spoken or have anything to do with reality. When verbalizing or giving the look, the anorexic uses criticism to avoid emotional and physical intimacy. This problem gets worse over time and eventually grows into unfounded hatred of the mate.

Certainly, Solomon disparaged his 1000 wives and, as Ecclesiastes 7:26-29 shows, his disdain for them grew worse over the years (reference the chapter "Solomon Never Had Great Sex with 1000 Virgins").

Likewise, he described all of his maidens as thorns compared to the Shulammite (Song 2:2).

9. Solomon Exhibited Anger and Bitterness

This is a natural result of failing to share feelings and indulging in constant blame of the mate instead of solving problems. The unloving person never invests energy in learning how to get along with another human so he or she can grow up into emotional maturity.

In Ecclesiastes 7:26, Solomon said, "I discovered more bitter than death the woman [literally wife] whose heart is snares and nets, whose hands are chains." He went on to say that not a one of his 1000 wives gave him lasting pleasure.

10. Solomon Abused People with Money

Dr. Weiss says this characteristic is rare. However, respondents to my *Sexless Marriages Self-Assessment Survey* identified 12 ways sexless spouses frequently use money to control and abuse their mate. Examples include secret spending, refusing to discuss or share control of money, saying, "I show my love by taking care of you, I don't need to say I love you," and complaining about spending money on necessities. Both male and female deprivers even promise, "If you earned more money, I would have sex with you."

No doubt, Solomon had money issues. He nursed a huge sense of entitlement in taxing the Israelites to pay for his extravagancies and to support his wives. When he died, the kingdom was in financial ruin.

11. Solomon Substituted Collections for Love

This is a different application of "lovers of money." I've observed many times that when the relationship is love-starved that one or both partners maintain huge collections. It's more than not being organized or not throwing things away. The unloving person often openly loves things or pets more than people. The love-starved enabler can also be a collector because he or she feels, "My spouse doesn't love me. My things do." Things become a distraction from emotional loneliness.

Solomon lavishly outfitted his home with gold as silver was too common. He treated silver like gravel. Obsessed with building, he drafted young Israelite men to work on his grandiose projects. He collected huge herds of horses and chariots along with beautiful women.

12. Solomon Pursued Roommate Relationships

This is a common characteristic of anorexics. Instead of being lovers, they pursue being just roommates, business partners, spiritual friends, joint parents, partying buddies, debate partners, or a slave-master relationship. Essentially, they want a trophy spouse and family.

Avoid Solomon's 12 Love-Defying Traits of a Sexless Spouse

Solomon was a royal intimacy anorexic who didn't know the first thing about loving a woman intellectually, emotionally, sexually, and spiritually. He tried 1000 times, but he never got it right. He pursued a friends-with-benefits or roommate relationship with his wives. The Maiden wisely rejected him as a potential mate.

If you're single, avoid these characteristics in a date like the plague. If you're married to a loving spouse, hug his or her neck and tell your mate how lucky you are. But if you're married to someone with these traits, it's time to deal with these love-defying sins that destroy families.

My free *Sexless Marriages Self-Assessment Survey* will help you examine your marriage regarding these 24/7 character flaws that surround being without natural affection for family. Once your eyes are open, you can begin to work at bringing true love into your life.

The Queens Praise the Shulammite

Song of Solomon 6:9b-10:
"The maidens saw her and called her blessed,
The queens and the concubines also, and they praised her, saying,
'Who is this that grows like the dawn,
As beautiful as the full moon,
As pure as the sun,
As awesome as an army with banners?'"

The Queens Are Religious Prostitutes and Perpetual Virgins

Solomon built high places throughout the Israelite countryside for his foreign wives to burn incense and sacrifice to their gods. In his old age he followed their influence by going after their gods.

Some of his wives served Ashtoreth, the goddess consort of Baal. The women were required to sacrifice either part of their hair or their virginity. These male and female gods of fertility were also worshipped with prostitution (1 Kings 11:4-8; 14:22-24; 15:11-12; 2 Kings 23:1-14):

> There was apparently a strong sexual aspect with regards to the worship of Ashtaroth in every culture in which she appeared. In Erech, in Babylonia, prostitution was practiced in her name, with groups of men and women who were employed apparently as priests and priestesses and practiced immoral rites

with worshippers ("The Doctrine" 5).

Some commentators argue that Solomon would not have had sex with 1000 women because it would have been impossible to keep them all satisfied. Perhaps his wives' religious service of prostitution eased his burden. Interestingly, he eventually worshipped Ashtoreth with them. The scriptures don't record the sexual atrocities of Solomon and his wives which more than likely included ogres in which his wives pleasured each other. (See chapter 13 for the implication in Ecclesiastes of orgies under the heading "A Harem — The Delights of Men.")

The Bible says Solomon loved them, and they led him astray into following their gods. Worshipping their idols provided varied sexual experiences for him. Understanding the normal progression of sexual addiction, Solomon's slide into idolatry and the accompanying orgies is more likely than not. Because he had limited emotional involvement with his wives, he would have needed greater thrills to satisfy him just as sexual addicts today constantly go deeper into their sexual obsessions.

Worshippers served Molech and Baal with animal, vegetable, and human sacrifices. In the last days of the kingdom when the Israelites became desperate to win back God's protection, they sacrificed their own children (Jeremiah 7:31; 19:4-6; 32:35; Isaiah 57:3-5a).

Some commentators speculate that the reason we read about only three of Solomon's children may be due to his wives sacrificing their own children. However, generally it takes a significant amount of sexual activity to impregnate a woman (Reece n.d.). Solomon may not have given his individual wives enough sexual attention to father many children. For example, his three known children were born when Solomon didn't have many wives (1 Kings 14:21, 4:11, 15).

Additionally, virgins served some of the idols. "Celibacy was an essential condition in a few of the orders of [pagan] priests, and in several orders of [pagan] priestesses" (Lecky, 1338-9). By the time of Christ, idolatrous worshippers highly revered virgins:

> Intense sanctity [was] attributed to the vestal virgins whose continence was guarded by such fearful penalties [such as death], and supposed to be so closely linked with the prosperity of the state, whose prayer was believed to possess a miraculous power (Lecky, 1351-3).

Even with all of his wives and his sinful flaws, King David continued to love and serve God. But Solomon and his queens lived in a different world from his father David and the other Israelites. As Solomon dotted the countryside with diverse places of worship for his pagan wives, both he and his people succumbed to their influence.

The Queens Welcome the Shulammite

Understanding the idolatrous religions of the Queens lends new insights to their praise of the Shulammite who will share their husband and lover if Solomon gets his way. When the Queens see her, they ask Solomon, "Who is this?" Then they describe her beauty in glowing terms from their idolatrous view of marriage and femininity:

> The image here may owe something to graphic representations of the goddess Ishtar, who is often portrayed surrounded by sun, moon, stars (v. 10). Ishtar was worshiped as the patroness of war as well as love. (The combination of sex and violence was as compelling for ancients as it is for us.) Her Canaanite counterpart Astarte was worshiped in Israel even by Solomon, as the biblical historians note disapprovingly (1 Kings 11:33). It seems that some Judeans continued to worship her, as "the queen of heaven" (Jer. 44:17-19, 25), up to the time of the Babylonian exile. Perhaps the poet is intentionally creating a positive counter-type to that ancient goddess of love and war with this larger-than-life figure of a woman who combines sex appeal with *peace* (Davis 286).

These women's marriage to Solomon is like a big sorority with sensuous partying. The King supports their allegiance to prostitution by building their altars and temples. And he eventually joins their revelry.

The Queens Are Primary and Casual Wives

Evidently, as stated earlier, the daughter of the Egyptian Pharaoh, was Solomon's favorite and primary wife (1 Kings 7:8, 9:24; 2 Chronicles 8:11). This is similar to what many girls put up with today with their boyfriends. In the Hookup Culture, teens and college students talk about "primary and casual sex partners." This refers to tacit approval of promiscuity and experimentation by dividing partners into two groups; primary partner and casual sexual hookups.

The *New York Times* bestseller *Restless Virgins, Love, Sex, and Survival at a New England Prep School* reveals this kind of thinking today. It is the "riveting real-life story of the intimate lives of seven teenagers." After a sex scandal in 2005, authors Abigail Jones and Marissa Miley interviewed students to paint a true picture of life on campus. The young women weren't much different from Solomon's queens and concubines.

For example, one teen, Annie, considered the pros and cons of becoming a "friend with benefits." She knew she'd rather have a real boyfriend, but she didn't know if that was possible. She might have to settle for much less and become part of a modern harem:

The girls [Annie, Isabel, and Jillian] knew about the times when Brady showed up at parties, knocked on the door, and barged right in. Behind him stood a harem of young DSGs [day school girls as opposed to boarders], fresh out of the Volvo wagon [Brady's car], made up, bright-eyed, smiling as if they were the lucky ones (87, 93).

If the Shulammite marries Solomon, she will share him with the 140 women he already has and the maidens without number. Solomon isn't a one-woman man. He doesn't know how to love a woman intellectually, emotionally, and sexually. Solomon's wives probably aren't able to love him emotionally either as demonstrated by their approval of the Maiden.

A girl should determine if her fiancé is monogamous before marriage rather than risk finding out later he cannot be true to his vows. When a young man makes a sensuous proposal to a girl, she will find it next to impossible to satisfy him completely. When a relationship rests on a sensuous foundation, love requires variety and perfected techniques to keep its base from crumbling. A man needs more than a glamorous body for sexual satisfaction. A sensuous husband places an impossible burden on his wife to keep him interested. In Proverbs 27:20, Solomon observes that the eyes of a man are never satisfied.

Solomon's wives ask, "Who is this? She is so beautiful, she reminds us of our gods. Where did you find her?'"

Solomon Is Overcome by Lust at First Sight

Song of Solomon 6:11-12:
"I went down to the orchard of nut trees
To see the blossoms of the valley,
To see whether the vine had budded
Or the pomegranate had bloomed.
Before I was aware, my soul [desire – NIV; lust – KJV] set me
Over the chariots of my noble people."

"Aware" (*yâda'*) is a primary root that means "to know (properly to ascertain by seeing); used in a great variety of senses, figurative, literally, euphemism [for sex], and inference [both good and bad]" (Strong 47). The *Theological Wordbook* says *yâda'* is used for intimate knowledge including sexual intercourse as "Adam *knew* Eve his wife" (Genesis 4:1). It is also used for sexual perversions (Genesis 19:5) and rape (Judges 19:25) (366-367).

"Soul" is used to refer to the Shulammite's extreme sexual longing for the Shepherd. Here Solomon likewise uses "soul" in a sexual context. See Song 1:7 and 3:1-4 for a complete definition of the word.

Hess explains the significance of "chariots of my noble people":

The term for chariot is in the plural, suggesting a squad of chariots that go to battle. The passion of desire translates into the excitement of the most adventurous and dangerous experiences known to the author. Such chariotry traditionally made up the elite of the army, those who could afford to maintain the required horses and all the trappings for the vehicle. Since a chariot served as a mobile firing platform for an archer, there normally were two or three individuals on a chariot, including at least a driver and a master of the weaponry. Thus, the female lover's sense of a place on board this instrument of terror is part of a fantasy of danger and excitement, which provides the climax of this experience. Away from the peaceful gardens, the chariotry of the nobles, whether in war or in procession, heightens the drama and fuels the passion of the lover (208).

Solomon uses a different form of the word "garden" from what the Shepherd used to praise the Shulammite. The King tells his wives that he first saw the Maiden in the "orchard of nut trees." He brags about being overtaken by lust at first sight by her beauty (Song 6:11).

Solomon tells them the same thing he told the Maiden when he dined with her in his tent (Song 1:9). But now in retrospect, he makes a play on two sexual words with "before I was aware [knew sexually], my soul [my desire or lust] set me" to draw a colorful pun with the simile he used earlier of a mare in heat running among Pharaoh's war chariots.

Solomon says, "I wasn't even aware of any sexual urges until I saw the most beautiful body in the land. I was instantly transported into full-lust mode with an erection that equals Pharaoh's stallions enduring the barbed whips of the chariot drivers to chase after a mare in heat. I made plans to deflower the young virgin and had her brought to my tent."

Only Solomon left out the part about the mare in heat for his wives. He says simply, "My soul set me over the chariots of my noble people." In other words, "When I saw her, it was lust at first sight and it made my heart beat faster than an army of chariots racing to war. Her appearance completely captivated and overwhelmed my sensual desires!"

Finally! The Shulammite gets it about Solomon comparing her to a mare in heat running among the chariots of Pharaoh. His lewd sensuous proposals without love or regard for her as a person repulse and alienate her. For the first time she understands his depraved intentions. She doesn't need to hear more. Disgusted, she turns and flees for the door.

The Queens Beg the Shulammite to Stay

Song of Solomon 6:13a:
"Come back, come back, O Shulammite;

Come back, come back, that we may gaze at you!"

Solomon, the Queens, and the Concubines can't understand why their flattery fails to impress the Shulammite. Doesn't every woman want to feel sexually attractive? Who desires her more than they? The Queens beg, "Come back, come back! We want to lust for you!"

The Queens' plea sickens the Shulammite even more. Surrounded by Solomon's wealth and his glamorous wives, she is the only woman in the room who sees through Solomon's lecherous desires. She stops, slowly turns around, and throws their lewdness back at them.

The Shulammite Mocks the Queens

Song of Solomon 6:13b:
"Why should you gaze at the Shulammite,
As at the dance of the two companies?"

Richard Hess says the word "dance" comes from a root that means "to turn or whirl." It carries the "sense of an exuberant dance [such as] the Israelites performed before the golden calf (Exod. 32:19).... Usage elsewhere dictates a whirling dance of ecstatic joy" (209f).

The rose of Sharon ridicules Solomon's wives by asking if they want to gaze at her in the same way they watch someone dancing wildly and seductively. She asks, "Do you only want me to amuse you with the movements of my body? Is my physical beauty all you care about?"

Solomon's Queens answer with a resounding "YES! What's wrong with that?" To prove their point, they proclaim how perfect she is to stir up their passions with a tantalizing dance.

The Queens Want to Gaze at Her Seductions

Song of Solomon 7:1-5:
"How beautiful are your feet in sandals,
O prince's daughter!
The curves of your hips are like jewels,
The work of the hands of an artist.
Your navel is like a round goblet
Which never lacks mixed wine;
Your belly is like a heap of wheat
Fenced about with lilies.
Your two breasts are like two fawns,
Twins of a gazelle.
Your neck is like a tower of ivory,
Your eyes like the pools in Heshbon
By the gate of Bath-rabbim;

Your nose is like the tower of Lebanon,
Which faces toward Damascus
Your head crowns you like Carmel,
And the flowing locks of your head are like purple threads;
The king is captivated by your tresses."

Solomon always describes the Shulammite by starting at her head and moving down until he stops at her breasts. Now as she stands before the Queens wearing a veil of royalty (Song 6:7), they start at her feet and move up to her head. They worship idols of prostitution and virgins. They've already said she looks like a goddess. They describe her in sensuous detail—a perfect seductress to dance for the King…and them.

Just as the Virgins mocked the Maiden when Solomon had her brought to his tent, his wives throw in their own barbs. "O prince's daughter! For a peasant who works in the vineyards aren't you acting high and mighty? Don't you know your place? Here in the palace you even have sandals for your bare feet."

The wives verbally undress the Shulammite. Her navel never lacks mixed wine—an erotic attention-getter then and now. Many commentators think "fenced with lilies" probably refers to her pubic hairs—a beautiful cushion for young bodies. They know how her soft, well-developed breasts will command Solomon's attention.

Her long slender neck gracefully supports her head. Her eyes are seductive like the harlots enticing their clientele down by the pools in Heshbon. Like the tower of Lebanon, her nose reveals her native beauty. Her long flowing hair captivates the King as she sways her head from side to side in their vision of lascivious delights.

They can't wait for her to tantalize them with an energetic belly dance! "Yes!" they want to watch as the Shulammite stirs up their passions. The Queens' eagerness suggests that Solomon and his wives indulge each other in sexual orgies—perhaps somewhat like the Hookup Culture's theme parties. (See chapter 13 for the Bible's allusion to their orgies.)

Her hands cover her mouth in horror, the Shulammite spins around, and runs for the door. Solomon hurries after her. When he calls to her, she stops, and faces her king.

Taking her elbow, he leads her to the chaise lounge inside the door and motions for her to sit. He claps and the musicians start playing. She recognizes the melody from the night he wined and dined her in his tent. One of the Virgins begins singing of desire and fulfillment.

Solomon sits beside her and smiles, "My darling…."

This is it. He has no clue. Her stomach churns as bile races up between her breasts and scorches her throat. *Dear Lord, please give me the strength to see this through.*

Study Exercise

Answer all questions in your own words.

1. What is the difference between a person who flatters and a person who gives compliments? Which one did Solomon and his wives do?
2. What is the difference between a person who spends money on the spouse and a person who values the mate? Which one did Solomon do?
3. What is the difference between a person who lusts after a spouse and a person who loves the mate? What did Solomon do?
4. What is the difference between a person who has intimacy anorexia and a person who loves the mate intellectually, emotionally, sexually, and spiritually? Which one did Solomon do?
5. Name three ways Solomon demonstrates intimacy anorexia. Give an example of each.
6. Why did the Shulammite's eyes confuse Solomon? What did he ask her to do? Why?
7. Why do you think the Queens and Concubines praised the Shulammite when she would share their husband?
8. Why did the Shulammite try to get away from Solomon and the Queens?
9. Do you disagree with anything in the lesson? If so, explain giving scriptures for your reasons.

Family Exercise

Youngsters of all ages love the Song of Solomon when exposed to the exciting drama about true love versus sensuous love. Visit Michael Cole, MD's modern rendering of the Song of Songs to share during family time. This account of the Song of Solomon provides the perfect vehicle for supplying age-appropriate details beginning with young children through young adult and beyond. Dr. Cole states:

> This is a true story about a fair maiden who developed a sexually pure relationship with a young shepherd. Then one day, unexpectedly, the king noticed her beauty and desired to have her. The king could provide pleasure and luxury, while the shepherd was capable of building an emotional connection. The shepherd cared about the maiden's heart and soul, while the king cared only about her body. She must make her choice between a common laborer who offers her true love and a wealthy king who can only offer sensuous love.

(View at Westarkchurchofchrist.org/library/songofsongs.htm)

Personal Exercise

If you're single and didn't start a dating notebook after reading "Secret 3: Practice Your Sensuous-Love Mirror Lines," now is the time to do it. List Solomon's 12 characteristics of being an intimacy anorexic. Spend some time getting familiar with each defect so you can begin to recognize red flags in potential dates. Keep practicing your mirror lines, "I need time to think about it. I'll get back with you later."

If you're married and recognize any of the 12 characteristics in your sexless spouse or in yourself, you need to delve deeper into the love sins than we can in this book. I highly recommend you work through my free *Sexless Marriages Self-Assessment Survey*. It will open your eyes to the daily manifestations of these issues in yourself and your companion.

Learning more about what you're dealing with will help you make healthy decisions for your spouse, children, and yourself. You can learn more about the survey at my website: PatsyRaeDawson.com

Personal Exercise

If you believe you can rescue a defective person through courtship and marriage, I urge you to take Dr. Karyl McBride's survey. She is the author of *Will I Ever Be Good Enough?* and works with the adult children of a narcissistic parent. It will help you analyze your upbringing.

If you grew up in a defective home as Solomon did, you may be living in denial. You may think you can fix others even when they have no desire to change. Take the survey "Is Your Mother Narcissistic?" at WillIEverBeGoodEnough.com. The survey applies to men and women.

Stacey's Story:
Real Problem Solving Begins

Hi Patsy Rae,

It's been awhile since I've been in touch, but I wanted to give you an update on how we're doing. I last shared with you how we had gotten to the point where my husband agreed to go through your *God's People Make the Best Lovers* with me. Then we had a major setback when we had an argument and he said he wouldn't study with me.

Well, I've often read that, generally speaking, most men are not the ones to seek out the self-help books or do the research when it comes to marriage improvement. That it's the women who are the readers. This is true in our case. (Of course, if the man isn't even willing to admit there is a problem in the first place why would he go searching for help?)

But Joe did come round to the place where he was willing to work with me to keep our marriage together and have it be better than we could imagine.

Joe is not an avid reader, and he's not an eager reader either. A large portion of his work involves reading and writing long technical reports and such, so I was a little doubtful he'd follow through on our reading plan, and I was right. The last thing he really wanted to do was pick up a book in the evening and do more reading.

So we came to a compromise that worked for both of us. We set aside about an hour of private time where I read aloud many of the sections in your book that we could apply to our situation and then we discussed them.

We usually curled up on our bed or the couch in the evenings. We often talk curled up on our bed even in the daytime. Our room is a comfortable room and with kids around, it affords us the most privacy for personal conversation.

We studied a chapter over a week or two with two to three sessions each week. I continued to do all the reading and then we discussed what I read. I noticed changes very shortly after starting. I think Joe actually enjoyed learning the material as much as I did. It wasn't anything we'd ever been taught before, and it was so nice to finally have a compass and direction for what God intended. It was freeing. Both of us became more vulnerable and transparent with each other which quickly translated into our intimate life.

We did like you suggested and made sure to keep our problems out of our study and just have it be a time of learning together what God's Word teaches about marriage. Your book was a real eye opener for both of us and it was a great catalyst for opening up our communication.

We both began to see how little we knew about God's purposes for marriage and how neither of us ever had it modeled for us in our homes growing up. It paved the way for us to begin to share a new and deeper intimacy than we'd ever experienced before in our marriage!

I am so grateful for all the Lord has been doing in our marriage and home, and once again, I am grateful for all the hard work you put into your books so couples like us can grow in the knowledge of what God wants for us—both individually and as a couple.

We still have more progress to make, of course, but being pliable in God's hands along with doing the hard work has certainly been worth the effort. The blessings far outweigh the pain and struggle.

Thanks again, Patsy Rae, for all your encouragement and counsel.

Pressin' on!
Stacey

Secret 9: Layer Your Hormones to Intensify Emotional Ecstasy

Solomon's Siren Song: "Queen Mother! Wake Up!"

"Queen Mother! Queen Mother! Wake up! I'm sorry.... Please wake up!"

"Oh, Sarah...what's wrong? It's barely daylight."

"I know, my lady. But we have an emergency! It's that new girl!"

"Get me some water. Then tell me what's going on."

When Sarah returns, Bathsheba is sitting on the side of the bed rubbing her eyes. "Here." Sarah hands a golden goblet to Bathsheba, then kneels in front of her. "It's terrible! It's that new girl from the northern vineyard...she's been a pain in the *tuchis* from the beginning. She says, 'I'm old enough to decide for myself.' She keeps jabbering on. Pleading, 'Don't force Solomon and me to wed before we fall in love!'"

"Oh! How ridiculous! What does love have to do with it? If I'd waited 'til I fell in love, Solomon wouldn't have ever been born."

"I know, my lady, but it's gotten worse. She summoned us early this morning.... She demanded we go find the shepherd, her true love."

"She loves a shepherd?"

"Yes, my lady. She talks about him all the time."

"This is getting more insane! Doesn't she like the jewelry Solomon gave her for a dowry? A shepherd can't ever afford anything so precious!"

"She gave it back to me this morning. Said she couldn't accept it."

"A peasant girl gave back expensive jewelry! Unbelievable!"

"I know, my lady. I was shocked myself."

"Then she told us, 'I've made up my mind. I won't marry Solomon! Go find my Shepherd! Hurry! Bring him here! I want him to take me home.'"

"Didn't anyone try to talk her out of such a crazy notion?!"

"Some of the Virgins asked, 'Why's this shepherd so special?' The loving way she described him and the syrupy look in her eyes...I knew it was hopeless.... She said, 'He's one in ten thousand.' Can you imagine?"

"Oh! None of his chosen have ever been so impossible! No one has ever rejected Solomon! I don't know what his reaction will be…."

"It won't be *gut!* That's why I hurried to awaken you. The other Virgins left to go find the Shepherd."

"You did the right thing, Sarah. Solomon is so radical and compulsive about everything—all his infernal building. He's obsessed with erecting a temple for his god and a new wife every few weeks…. If only he could have been a little older before we crowned him king. His harem of misfits is going to be the death of me."

"Yes, my lady, of that I'm sure."

"I'd hoped by marrying an Israelite, he might settle down. That's why I suggested he go inspect his vineyard in the North. They spawn the most beautiful women in the kingdom."

"Yes, my lady. And this Maiden is by far the most exotic we've ever seen."

Bathsheba stands up and paces back and forth for a few minutes, then turns to Sarah. "It'll take a special Virgin for his wedding week to soothe him after the Shulammite rejects him. I hope she does it gently."

"That'll be a miracle! She tells us exactly what she thinks…. I don't think she's intimidated by the King either. She's already told him she's promised to the Shepherd. And she told the King, 'I'm very particular about whom I marry.'"

"Such nerve! I was hoping an Israelite bride would calm him down. When will the Virgins get back?"

"I'm guessing they'll be back with the Shepherd about noon."

"We don't have much time to prepare. Send ten of the most beautiful Virgins who have come of age to me for inspection. Don't tell them any details. Just tell them I need their help welcoming Solomon's new bride. Then I'll pick a replacement."

Bathsheba walks to the window. "Bring me my shawl, Sarah. There's still a chill in the air."

Sarah wraps a long shawl around Bathsheba's shoulders. "There you are."

"Ever since his brother talked me into asking him for Abishag in marriage, Solomon has been obsessed with marrying a woman from Shunem. He's going to take this hard…. I don't think he'll be satisfied with only one substitute. We're going to have to throw him a wedding week he'll never forget…. It'll take at least three exquisite virgins."

"I know, my lady. He told me how much he wants to marry a virgin from Shunem…. Queen Mother?"

"Yes, Sarah?"

"Can I be one of the girls? I've been waiting a long time to be called into the King's chambers."

Bathsheba turns from the window and takes Sarah's hands, "I'm sorry, my dear. You are very lovely and you will make a beautiful bride for Solomon someday. But he knows you and trusts you. He will be too upset to appreciate your charms…. We need new girls he's never seen before to totally slay his misery. And I need you to oversee this…and make sure the girls are ready as soon as the Shulammite tells him she won't marry him."

"I understand…." Sarah's eyes mist and she bites her lip as her head and shoulders sag.

"Sarah, you are like a daughter to me." Bathsheba touches Sarah's cheek and looks into her eyes. "Let's get through this. After the girls finish out their week with Solomon, then I'll make sure he takes you for a wife. You won't have to share your wedding week with anyone. And Solomon will be in a better mood. I need someone in the harem I can trust to keep me informed."

"Yes, my lady," Sarah stands erect. "I'll go wake the girls and send them to you."

"Sarah, I can't over emphasize the necessity of us keeping all of this hush hush. We don't want any of the other Virgins or Solomon's wives suspecting what's going on. We don't want any of them alerting Solomon so they can connive special favors from him. This must be a surprise, or it won't work."

"Yes, ma'am. You can depend on me."

"Hmmmm…. Bring me a variety of nationalities and religions…and a couple of Hebrew girls to choose from. We need someone who worships the virgin goddess so Solomon can delight in arousing her sexual charms…. Ah! Also a fem fatale. Someone who has tutored with the prostitute priestess and knows all her fine arts…but remains a virgin. She'll slaver Solomon in sultry seduction…. Then I want a needy Hebrew. Solomon loves to be admired…. It's even more important to him than sex. Bring me someone who'll gush over him building the temple in Jerusalem. The mushier the better. This smorgasbord of feminine minxes will keep him so occupied sampling their charms, he'll thank the moon and stars that the little Shunem girl turned him down."

"Anything else, my lady?"

"Yes, Sarah…. Solomon has a thing for *brosts*…. He can't take his eyes off 'em. Send only buxom virgins to me.

"Yes, my lady! I'm on it right now."

Oh! One more thing…. While I'm selecting the right virgins, set the bridal chamber up with plenty of our very best hard apple cider for Solomon and the girls. He dearly loves hard apple cider. Now hurry! We don't have much time!"

Song of Solomon 7:6-13:
The Shulammite Jilts King Solomon

ACT TWO, SCENE SIX CONTINUES
THIRD DAY – MORNING

When the curtains open, Solomon and the Shulammite are sitting on a chaise lounge in the Great Hall. The Queens, Concubines, and Virgins without number are seated in the background. Musicians play softly. A Virgin sings a tender love song, and then fades into the background.

Solomon's Lewdest Proposal of All

The previous chapter ends with Solomon's unashamed declaration that the first sight of the Shulammite working in the vineyard sent him into a lustful frenzy of animalistic desire. Horrified, the Shulammite turns to flee when the Queens and Concubines call her back. They don't want her to leave. They describe her in sensuous detail, admitting that they want to watch her twirling and writhing in a seductive dance.

Solomon has no clue why the Maiden wants to get away from him. He catches up with her and motions for her to sit on the chaise lounge with him. She sits on the end, dressed very simply compared to the gaudily-jeweled Queens. It adds to her mysterious allurement as her eyes look at him through her sheer veil. Visualizing her disrobing, her modesty enhancing her appeal as she dances provocatively, he tells her what he wants. He's saved his most lewd proposal for last.

She's Beautiful and Delightful

Song of Solomon 7:6:
"How beautiful and how delightful you are,
My love [O love – KJV], with all your charms!"

"Beautiful" is the same word defined earlier and refers only to her outer appearance.

"Delightful" means "luxury:--delicate, delight, pleasant." It comes from a primary root that means "to be soft or pliable" (Strong 125, 89).

"My love" (*'âhab*) is the same word we've seen before that means "to have affection for (sexually or otherwise)" (Strong 9).

"Charms" is a primary root that means "to be agreeable (literally or figuratively):--in beauty, be delight, be pleasant, be sweet" (Strong 79).

The Shulammite's beautiful and delightful feminine charms that fascinate and captivate Solomon most assuredly aren't her personality and character. He sees only her body and excitedly says, "You've got such a sexy body! You've got everything it takes to make a man happy!"

In contrast, the Shepherd briefly mentions her looks. He praises and enjoys the femininity of her mind, emotions, and body. Such is true love.

She's Like a Palm Tree

Song of Solomon 7:7:
"Your stature is like a palm tree,
And your breasts are like its clusters.
'I said, 'I will climb the palm tree.'"

Solomon's seductive words are reminiscent of modern-day phone sex. He tells her exactly what he wants to do to her body. He designs his graphic talk to fuel a wild fire of desire in her for his passionate embrace.

He doesn't refer to her stateliness when he compares her to a palm tree. Instead, he takes his lewdness in their first meeting to a new low. When he first met her, he said she was like a mare in heat driving Pharaoh's war stallions crazy with lust. Now he makes it personal saying she heats up his loins with throbbing desire.

Joseph Dillow explains the sensuousness of Solomon's expression in *Solomon on Sex*. "Climbing the palm tree" refers to the Oriental method of fertilizing palm trees. Since the male and female flowers were born on separate trees, someone had to climb the female trees and tie some of the pollen-bearing male flowers among their blossoms (136).

Solomon declares, "I said [past tense], I will [future tense] climb the palm tree." From the moment he saw her, Solomon began making plans to add her body to his harem. Notice what he wants to do to her.

Her Breasts Are Like Clusters of the Vine

Song of Solomon 7:8b:
"'I will take hold of its fruit stalks.'
Oh, may your breasts be like clusters of the vine."

Every time Solomon speaks of the Shulammite's breasts, he uses the biological term to describe her physical maturity. Solomon is what women call "a breast man." This is not necessarily a derogatory expression. The Maiden makes it clear she's looking forward to the Shepherd enjoying her breasts. Most wives enjoy their husband being "a breast man," but they want him to be a much better lover who is enamored with their whole *je ne sais quoi*.

By now, Solomon has handled 140 pairs of breasts. His previous descriptions of the Maiden stopped at her breasts. The Queens' description started at her feet and went up to the top of her head. They admired her breasts, too, saying, "Your two breasts are like two fawns, twins of a gazelle." All of Solomon's wives have been on the receiving end of his admiration of breasts. They know what turns him on. But with Solomon, it's a fetish, what he hones in on with women. He's always looking for the next luscious bosom.

He says, "I said, I will take hold of its fruit stalks. Oh may your breasts be like clusters of the vine." From the moment he saw her, Solomon's mouth began watering at the thought of tasting and plucking at the ripe clusters of her soft, bountiful breasts. In his lewd sexual spiel, Solomon tells the Maiden, "As soon as I saw you, I knew I had to fondle, kiss, and press my face into your bosom."

What do you think the King's eyes are looking at while he speaks?

Obscenely blunt, Solomon expects his words to stir up the Maiden's sexual juices and throw her into his arms. No wonder the priests and early Church Fathers who understood the King's graphic language were uncomfortable with a book of the Bible celebrating a woman's sexuality. Therefore, they invented the allegorical position.

By covering up the sexual teachings of the book, they glorified Solomon to make their allegory make sense. As they did so, they hid from God's people the empty, lonely pain of intimacy anorexia before Weiss coined the expression. God used Solomon as an example to warn his people about the consequences of being unloving. The priests and Church Fathers altered God's morality play to suit their own agenda. (See Chapter 13, "Solomon Never Had Great Sex With 1000 Virgins," for the scriptures and epilogue of Solomon's shameful life.)

Some of it makes me uncomfortable, too. I've asked myself many times, "Do I share what the word definitions and the customs plainly teach, or do I dilute it to make it more palatable for a wider readership?" But I don't have the nerve to question God's wisdom in preserving this sexually-explicit book to show us how to love. And God teaches older women to instruct young women to love their husband and children as the Shulammite's mother did her daughter (Titus 2:3-5; Song 8:2).

Solomon was the perfect man to demonstrate for future generations that physical beauty alone can never truly satisfy the deepest yearnings of a man's heart. Our current three cultures: Purity, Hookup, and Sexless Marriages are just reruns. It's time we move out of the Dark Ages into God's marvelous light to embrace his proudest creation—the way of a man with a maid.

Her Breath and Mouth Are Like Apple Wine

Song of Solomon 7:8c-9a:
"'And the fragrance of your breath like apples.

And your mouth like the best wine!'"

"Mouth" means "the sense of tasting; properly, the palate or inside of the mouth; hence, the mouth itself (as the organ of speech, taste, and kissing):--(roof of the) mouth, taste" (Strong 39).

To clinch his phone-sex-type spiel, Solomon moves from her breasts up to her mouth. After telling the Maiden what he wants, he promises to give her what he thinks every woman wants. Solomon has observed with all of his wives that open-mouth kissing turns a woman on.

Dr. Jack Schafer agrees. He says men can easily manipulate casual dates into having sex with them through deep kissing and tongue play (12/28/2012).

Solomon compares kissing the Shulammite to the aphrodisiac of wine. The wine of kisses works on women more than men. Solomon expects it to lower her inhibitions and make her pliable in his arms. Review chapter 2, Song of Solomon 1:2 on how open-mouthed kissing deposits testosterone into a woman's system which immediately increases her libido.

Many commentators question if real apples are mentioned in the Song of Solomon claiming, "None grew in the area at this time." However, Aryeh Naftaly, one of Israel's leading Hebrew/English translators, disagrees in *The Song of Songs, A Messiah's Confession:*

> Professor Zohar Amar, expert on natural history and the Bible from Bar-Ilan University, assures me that the apple (*tapúah*) mentioned in the Bible is just that—an apple (111).

Neuroscientist and psychiatrist Dr. Daniel G. Amen says in *The Brain in Love* that the health-building and aphrodisiac attributes of apples are well known. They increase libido and symbolize fertility in nature. They enhance lovemaking by freshening the breath, cleansing the teeth, and increasing the flow of saliva for deep kissing (156-7).

Compared to grape wine, apple wine takes less time to process— two to four months for a rich, delicate flavor. Also, it can be fermented after the grape harvest to make good use of the winery in a less busy season. Using a variety of aromatic and moderately acidic apples, including crabapples, produces a more pleasing apple wine (Dharmadhikari n.d.).

Beer expert Bryce Eddings says considering apple cider as a wine is a "tad controversial." Fresh apple juice ferments easily with any wild yeast and is more like making grape wine than making beer. Consequently, Eddings reasons that the wine maker gets to choose if he'll label his product apple cider or apple wine (n.d.).

Solomon's mouth waters over the thought of the Maiden's kisses being like fragrant apple wine. Or perhaps since he wants her to become wife number 141, he slobbers over the sensations of hard apple cider as he tastes her open-mouthed charms. Oh! He knows when she's finally his, she's going to be the best wine ever.

Solomon's Sexual Depravity

The lewdness coming from Solomon resembles the indelicate remarks characteristic of dirty ol' men. Men who've lived their life as a sexual addict and intimacy anorexic, as they age, their frontal lobes shrink and they lose a lot of their inhibitions and common sense. They think the ladies are turned on by their risqué comments.

Every woman knows the difference between a mutual hug with an old male friend and a surprise hug from a dirty ol' man. The latter usually comes up and grabs her from behind. Then he pins her against him too long and too tightly in a position where she cannot easily get away from him. Here's a letter from a concerned wife and my reply:

Dear Patsy Rae,
My husband accuses me of being jealous when I object to him hugging and touching all the young girls and single older women at church. Am I wrong to object?
Signed,
Am I really jealous?

Dear Are You Jealous,
Before I address your problem, answer a question for me: Is your husband sexually attentive to you?
Patsy Rae

Most of the wives with a similar problem that I've asked how their husband treats them sexually gave similar answers. "We seldom have sex." Or "He became impotent many years ago." Intimacy anorexics and sexual addicts often become impotent with their wives. They become emotionally worn out from all the pretending and blaming necessary to excuse their lack of sexual love. Read my full reply, "Is my spouse engaging in harmless hugging...or is it flirting...or is it more?" on my website at EmbarrassTheAlligator.com under Ask PatsyRae.

One woman said, "When I stayed with my mother in a retirement-apartment building, I had to avoid two old men. The worst offender needed a walker to get around. Yet he tried to maneuver himself so he could accidently elbow my breasts. Then he told me, 'Babe, I want to kiss you.' Can you believe that old man?"

Although Solomon is about 21 years old, he's already gone through 140 women with a lineup of virgins waiting for their turn. In the next 35 years, he'll go through 860 more women. If Solomon became king at 16 as many historians assume, that means he was only 56 when he died. At 21, he already sounds like a depraved old man slobbering over women.

In Proverbs 5:14, preceding the passage telling older husbands to be ravished with their older wife's breasts and love, the writer warns about what happens when a man spends his life pursuing women. He says, "I was almost in utter ruin in the midst of the assembly and congregation." Sexual addicts and intimacy anorexics age badly as their brains shrink. They make fools of themselves with women in doctors' offices, at parties, and family reunions; and especially, in church vestibules.

The Shulammite Jilts Solomon with the Metaphor of Wine

Song of Solomon 7:9b:
"It goes down smoothly [sweetly – KJV] for my beloved,
Flowing gently through the lips of those who fall asleep."

"Smoothly" means "evenness, i.e., (figuratively) prosperity or concord, also straightness, i.e., (figuratively) rectitude:--agreement, aright, that are equal, equity, (things that are) right (-eously, things), sweetly, upright (-ly, -ness)" (Strong 65).

"Flowing gently" means "to move slowly, i.e., glide:--cause to speak." It comes from a word which means "to be sluggish, i.e., restful, quiet:--strength" (Strong 29).

Revolted by Solomon's intentions toward her without building a relationship of love, the Shulammite interrupts his crude, erotic attempts to possess her body. She raises her head. Then in character with her personality and spunk, she lifts her veil up over her head. Her gesture jerks Solomon's eyes up from her bosom. He sees the fire in her eyes and the vexation on her mouth that he longs to kiss.

Looking him in the eye, she rebuffs him in an even voice with terse palm-tree and wine metaphors. In essence, the Maiden tells the King, "Great sex is like sweet palm and apple wines—oh it goes down so smoothly, flowing gently through the lips of those who fall asleep."

Since he lusts to climb her as a palm tree, she flaunts the aphrodisiac-effects of good palm wine. Her beloved Shepherd is so much finer on her palate. What nerve for a 13-year-old virgin!

William Patton, an expert on Bible-times wines, says palm trees abounded in Jericho and En-gedi. The sap of any palm tree, including date and coconut palms, can be used to make a very sweet toddy wine. The sap begins to ferment almost immediately. When fresh, it is sweet like honey, but if allowed to age, it quickly turns to vinegar (9).

Like playboys today, Solomon craves to get well-developed bosoms into bed. The Maiden's beautiful breasts and sweet breath will make the sexual embrace much more tantalizing—just like the smooth taste of good wine. In essence, Solomon tells her, "Baby, you've got a beautiful body, and we'll enjoy a great time in bed!" But the young virgin thinks differently.

Sex with the Shepherd Will Go Down Smoothly

Since "smoothly" refers to "things that are right" and "righteous," the Shulammite describes sexual love as a righteous act for loving husbands and wives. Lovemaking presents the perfect means of telling the other, "I love you! I need you! And I appreciate you!"

"Smoothly" means "evenness, equal, equity." Sexual contact between true lovers produces equal enjoyment and mutual blending of emotions. Throughout the Bible, God makes no distinction between the sexual desires of men and women or their abilities to experience supreme pleasure. The Shulammite looks forward to delighting in the sexual embrace with her beloved as much as he does because of their soulmating during courtship.

Sex with the Shepherd Promotes Sleep

She boldly tells Solomon, "Sexual love will flow gently through the lips of true lovers who fall asleep." The Shulammite and the Shepherd will work hard for their living. An orgasm, especially a vaginal orgasm, affects the adrenal glands of both the husband and the wife. This in turn determines how they handle stress. Thus the union of love relaxes lovers after a day of hard work.

Although God fashioned the human body for hard work, he also built within it a pleasant method of relaxation. Ecstatic lovemaking may be habit forming, but it has none of the harmful side effects of many sleeping pills. It can even boast that it has fewer calories than raiding the refrigerator!

One wife confessed, "I used to have a problem going to sleep and then I'd feel irritable the next day. Now we make love more often and that problem is gone. We even go to bed earlier so we won't be too tired to enjoy each other. If one of us wakes up in the middle of the night and can't get back to sleep, we know the other is ready for us. We both sleep better as a result of making love more often."

Unfortunately, many couples don't use sexual love in the same manner as the Shulammite and Shepherd intend. Instead, they allow nervous tensions to rob them of sleep and hamper their ability to work effectively and creatively. A husband and a wife seeking each other to ease strain and stress use sexual tenderness in a godly way. The thoughtful Creator of such a naturally soothing tranquilizer that's better than wine should be cheerfully thanked by husbands and wives for his great love of mankind.

Two lovers in the backseat of a car seldom experience the gentleness of sexual love. Fear of being caught and pregnancy destroys intimacy. On the other hand, a husband and a wife can enjoy each other as long as they desire. All the while, their bodies release hormones which help both of them sleep peacefully.

The Shulammite Jilts Solomon with the Metaphor of the Mouth

Song of Solomon 7:9b:
"It goes down smoothly [sweetly – KJV] for my beloved,
Flowing gently through the lips of those who fall asleep."

After Solomon tells the Maiden he wants to kiss her deeply, she says her kisses are reserved for her beloved – the Shepherd. She used the same Hebrew word when she sent the Virgins to find the Shepherd. She told them, "His mouth [palate] is full of sweetness." She continues Solomon's metaphor of her mouth being like wine by saying, "With my beloved Shepherd the wine goes down smoothly and gently."

The Shulammite had a powerful wet dream the night before which made it clear to her that she loves the Shepherd – that she feels no sexual desires for the King. She is looking forward to becoming sexually active in marriage. We'll learn in the next chapter that her mother has given her a liberal sex-education on how to please a husband. She is not ignorant of the pleasures that await her in marriage like our young women of today who are caught up in the Purity and Hookup Cultures that reinforce negative views of men and sex.

Wives who enjoy their femininity and their husband's masculinity recognize two common actions of the mouth and lips during lovemaking in the Maiden's metaphor of the mouth and wine. The mouth is a sensitive erogenous zone. A loving woman delights in expressing her own brand of passion with her mouth.

Passionate Kisses During the Act of Love

Solomon got it right about kissing. Kisses do turn a loving woman on. The dose of testosterone from her husband's mouth as he smothers her with tender soft kisses while teasing her with tongue play can make a loving wife ready for action in seconds. And she's not the least bit intimidated that her man knows his power to make her swoon in his arms. She relishes it!

Oh, the best kisses of all! Passionate kisses on the lips with tongues teasing each other…and kisses, nibbling on the neck, and elsewhere…. Oh! How delicious and arousing. But soft, tender, prolonged kissing with tongue play while deep in the embrace of love…. Wow! Wow! Wow! A woman who has never been kissed this way has never really been kissed.

We now know why kissing during lovemaking is so delightful. It's because sexual excitement leads to whole body engorgement. When the lips swell with blood, both their softness and sensations increase. (Review "Secret 7: Turn On Double-Dose #10 Orgasms" for more information.) No other kissing quite compares with passionate kissing during the act of love. Try it and relish the difference for yourself.

What About Oral Sex or Blow Jobs?

A teen girl emailed, "I can't ask my mother about this, but is oral sex really sex?"

Yes, dear, it is.

A wife emailed, "My husband wants me to give him a blow job. I'd like to, but isn't it a homosexual act, and thus forbidden by God?"

Bruce Allan gives a great answer to this question. He uses two verses to make a simple argument — what God forbids is a man treating another man like a woman:

Leviticus 18:22: "You shall not lie with a male as one lies with a female; it is an abomination."

Leviticus 20:13 "If there is a man who lies with a male as those who lie with a woman, both of them have committed a detestable act; they shall surely be put to death. Their bloodguiltiness is upon them."

These two verses in Leviticus imply that anything a husband and wife do together sexually that gives them both pleasure is part of "the way a man lies with a woman." If we state that a man lies with a woman as a man would lie with another man, then we make these verses mean the opposite of what is condemned. The unnatural act is having sex with a person of the same sex rather than *what* a man and a woman do as an act of pleasurable foreplay or intercourse (6/3/2014).

This parallels a similar statement in the New Testament:

Hebrews 13:4: "Marriage is to be held in honor among all, and the marriage bed is to be undefiled; for fornicators and adulterers God will judge."

Once again *who a person has sex with* defiles a marriage between a man and a woman — not *what* they do in the marriage bed that gives them both pleasure. If they engage in sex with someone they're not married to, they become fornicators and adulterers. They can fornicate with a single person, the spouse of someone else, a homosexual, or a lesbian. A homosexual or lesbian couple can only try to imitate *what* a heterosexual couple does naturally.

These three verses necessarily imply that anything a man does with a woman that gives them both pleasure is a normal heterosexual act. God never condemns a husband and wife enjoying each other's body.

Here's the answer to the wife's question, "Isn't a blow job a homosexual act, and thus forbidden by God?"

"No. A blow job is a heterosexual act. Sitcoms and movies portray homosexuals kissing. Does that condemn kissing between husbands and wives just because homosexuals do it? No. Kissing is a heterosexual act of both foreplay and lovemaking that homosexuals mimic."

For a woman who has learned the secret of the vaginal orgasm and how it's a barometer of the relationship (see the next chapter for details), using her body to express love to her husband is very natural. At some point in their relationship, she enjoys fondling her husband's genitals with her hand. It is part of the man she loves and desires. It is his organ of love that gives her so much pleasure and which he uses for *SPEAKING GOD'S BEAUTIFUL LANGUAGE OF LOVE* to her.

As their relationship matures and their passions excite and satisfy each other, she feels a comfortable, enjoyable desire to kiss him—to kiss all of him. And as they age together, using her mouth, her palate, to express her fascination with him becomes a loving way to arouse him to keep their romance active. Experiencing all of him arouses her as well.

Love should be the guide. A blow job becomes a problem when that's all the husband wants. He's not willing to give his wife oral sex or a vaginal orgasm. When that happens, insisting on a blow job becomes an intimacy anorexic's venue to deprive his wife of sexual pleasure.

The Shulammite Jilts Solomon
with the Promise of Great Sex with the Shepherd

Song of Solomon 7:10:
"I am my beloved's,
And his desire is for me."

"Desire" means "stretching out after, a longing:--desire" (Strong 126). It comes from a root word which means "to run after or over, i.e, overflow:--overflow water" (Strong 114).

The Shulammite repeats the commitment she and the Shepherd made to each other three times. After telling the Virgins about having to postpone marrying the Shepherd, she said, "My beloved is mine, and I am his" (Song 2:16). Then that morning when she sent the Virgins to find the Shepherd, she switched the order, "I am my beloved's and my beloved is mine" (Song 6:3).

Now she adds a barb to emphasize to Solomon how defective he is as a prospective husband. Both sentences say the same thing with intensity added to the second one, "I am my beloved's, and his desire is for me" (Song 7:10). In other words, "The Shepherd claims me as his own, and he truly loves and desires me." The Shepherd longs for her as a person—not just as a body.

Great Sex Obeys God's Law of Compatibility

Joseph Dillow suggests in *Solomon on Sex* that the three parallel pledges of love and desire in the Song of Solomon 2:16; 6:3; and 7:10 correspond to 1 Corinthians 7:3-4, God's law of compatibility (144):

> 1 Corinthians 7:3-4: *"Let the husband fulfill his duty to his wife, and likewise also the wife to her husband. The wife does not have authority over her own body, but the husband does; and likewise also the husband does not have authority over his own body, but the wife does."*

Paul states a wife doesn't possess what it takes to satisfy her own sexual desires—it takes a husband loving her with his emotions, body, mind, and spirit to satisfy a wife's deepest needs. Likewise, a husband doesn't possess what it takes to satisfy his own sexual desires—it takes a wife engaging her mind, emotions, body, and spirit to truly satisfy him.

The Shulammite and the Shepherd gladly recognize their obligations to satisfy each other with great sex. In marriage, their whole being belongs to the other. She pledges to fulfill this duty by releasing her own desires to arouse him. Likewise, she accepts his promise to pursue her.

This shows the importance of a couple determining *before marriage* to always satisfy the other's sexual needs. The couple doesn't plan to leave sexual happiness to chance. A robust sexual relationship between soulmates deepens their existing love while expressing affection. *God's People Make the Best Lovers* devotes a chapter to God's compatibility law.

Secret 9: Layer Your Hormones to Intensify Emotional Ecstasy

When God gave his blessing to the Shulammite marrying the Shepherd, he told them, "Eat and drink until you're tipsy with love." (Review "Secret 5: Sip the Divine Wine of Passion" for the details.") From newlyweds to senior citizens, God promotes active lovemaking.

Following God's command for frequent sex effectively layers your hormones and emotions. As a result, your orgasms and emotional intimacy keep getting better and stronger for both you and your mate.

Layering love works like this: you engage in sex Monday night. Tuesday morning you get up energized from the emotional connection and all the hormones flooding your body. If you don't have sex again for a week, the tenderness and hormones will continue to make you happy as they slowly evaporate.

But suppose you enjoy sex again on Tuesday night. You'll lay down another layer of soulmating and hormones on top of the fading ones from Monday.

Then you initiate sex again on Wednesday. After all, God said get drunk on love, and it takes a while to get tipsy on wine. So you add a third layer of emotional bonding and hormones on top of the two fading after glows.

You get the picture. When a couple stays in soulmating mode and layers lovemaking, the sensations in his penis and her vagina keep increasing until they're deliriously happy and emotionally connected.

Sex Is More Emotional for Men Than for Women

Based on 44 years of working with both men and women, when I launched my *Sexless Marriages Self-Assessment Survey* in 2016 I knew that sex is emotional for men. Many of the husbands I worked with shared their emotional pain of being rejected by their wives. They struggled with feeling like a beggar and being unloved. The husbands longed for affectionate touching, lingering playful kisses, and back-rubbing hugs. Instead, their wives accused them of being sexual addicts because they weren't content to live in celibacy or to "go take care of themselves."

Thus, when I started the survey, I knew it takes more than the physical act of sex to satisfy a man's masculine hormones. Even so, I was shocked to learn something I didn't expect:

Husbands suffer more emotionally from sexual rejection than wives do.

In other words, for a loving husband sex IS NOT an animalistic action as the Victorian moralists and doctors insisted. Likewise, sex IS NOT a "beastly" activity as the young evangelical men claimed in the University of Washington study regarding the effect of virginity pledges on boys. Also sex IS NOT just a physical release of pent up semen as our modern society asserts.

In contrast to these false assumptions, I was surprised at how Millennial and baby-boomer husbands answered the survey questions about emotional pain from sexual rejection. They checked nearly double the number of painful emotions than the women participants marked. That's not to discount the wives' emotional pain, because they checked plenty of pain points. But the husbands checked more! Notice their searing pain:

- ✓ Your masculine spirit is crushed
- ✓ Your soul has been killed
- ✓ You're drowning
- ✓ You're fighting for emotional survival
- ✓ You can't think straight
- ✓ You never rise to your full potential as a spouse
- ✓ Your never rise to your full potential as a parent
- ✓ You never rise to your full potential as a Christian
- ✓ You never rise to your full potential as a worker

The Pain of Sexual Rejection Never Goes Away

The baby boomers' checkmarks on the survey show the pain of sexual rejection and being unloved never goes away—not even after a person's hormones slow down. Both men and women checked that their feminine or masculine spirit was crushed. Although most of the wives did not check "Your soul has been killed," many husbands did. The men checked they were drowning more often than the women did. The husbands indicated that being without sexual love affected them in all areas of their lives with the wives checking fewer areas.

Both male and female baby boomers said they tolerated the pain of rejection better after their hormones slowed down, but they were more emotionally lonely than ever.

On the essay questions, some of the men described their feelings this way:

- *I feel like I'm not a real man.*
- *Worthless and can't be who I really am anymore.*
- *It's very lonely—not just sexually, but in terms of being valued as a human being.*
- *Overall, the refusing has seeped into every waking facet of my life and manhood and poses a constant, never ending, soul-crushing reminder that I am unattractive and a failure as a man, husband, father, and spiritual being.*

Sex Is More Emotional for Men Than Previously Thought

When I first taught marriage classes nearly half a century ago, I didn't discuss the sexual relationship. Yet after a few weeks, two older women sat across my kitchen table asking for help with their sexless marriages. So many women approached me in those early years about this problem that I began to wonder, "Are there any red-blooded Christian men out there who enjoy sex with their wives?"

Years later when *God's People Make the Best Lovers* came out, men started talking to me about their sexless marriages. I recognized the same emotional despair in these husbands as the women expressed. As a result, I updated the profile on desperate marriages to include men. See "The Profile of Desperate Husbands & Wives" at my website. In that article, I concluded:

> The husband often experiences overwhelming bitterness against his wife. One desperate husband described this time as an emotional breakdown where he could not stop crying for several weeks. While women's emotional nature changes as they lose their ability to cry over the problem, men's emotional nature also changes as they easily cry over the situation. A preacher, who counsels couples, said he often has men in his office sobbing while their wife is dry-eyed and hard as stone.
>
> The husband's depression deepens as he feels more and more that the situation is hopeless. He desperately strives to survive as a whole person.

Now the survey takes understanding male sexuality to a new level. Christians have had male sexuality wrong ever since a 3rd-century-theologian by the name of Origen tried to put marital lovemaking into a religious straitjacket. He hid the sexual teaching of the Song of Solomon under the guise of being an allegory about Christ and the church.

Rather than being an animalistic drive,
sex is an emotional bonding necessity for loving husbands.

As such, sexual rejection *damages* men more emotionally than it harms women. The survey demonstrates that both loving husbands and wives suffer tremendously from sexual rejection, but men experience greater emotional pain than women do.

Society Gets Male Sexuality Exactly Backwards

Victorian morals caused society to assume that sex is just a "beastly" experience for men as the young Evangelical virginity pledgers assumed. The truth is, sex is more emotional for men than it is for women. Men just hide their emotions better than women do.

By not recognizing the emotional nature of sex for men as an expression of love, both men and women are harmed. Many sexless Christian women say and do things to their husbands that are outright cruel such as, "Just go take care of yourself" or "Are you done yet?"

Some husbands check the box that their wives say things that cause them to lose their erections. One husband no longer has confidence to initiate lovemaking with his wife because of what she has said to him.

Layering Your Hormones Creates Deep Emotional Ecstasy

In "Secret 5: Sip the Divine Wine of Passion" we learned that God instructs husbands and wives to get tipsy on lovemaking. Frequent sex binds husbands and wives together emotionally. This layering of their hormones satisfies the deepest emotional needs of them both for SPEAKING GOD'S BEAUTIFUL LANGUAGE OF LOVE that transcends human words.

The Shulammite Begs the Shepherd, "Take Me Home Now!"

Song of Solomon 7:11a:
"Come, my beloved, let us go out into the country."

The Maiden steps back after rejecting Solomon's lewd proposal. *Where is the Shepherd? The Virgins left hours ago. I need him to rescue me from Solomon's sensuous lair. I meant it when I told Solomon, "I am my beloved's, and his desire is for me." If only I could see my beloved, I would tell him how much I love and desire him!"*

She turns around, "Look! The Shepherd!" Ignoring Solomon, she runs to the Shepherd as he enters the room. She wraps her arms around him as he lovingly embraces her. He bends down and kisses her mouth and lingers to gently tug her lower lip.

"Ahhhhh," she shivers as her body longs for the promised pleasures of last night's wet dream.

Pulling on his arm, she heads toward the door. "Come, my beloved, take me away from all this mockery! I've made up my mind. You're the one I want to marry. Take me home now!"

She pauses as she looks deep into his eyes, "I want to spend the rest of my life with you and caring for our children. A simple life and hard work appeals to me more than all this luxury without love." She waves her other hand around the Great Hall.

Until now the Shulammite and the Shepherd have spoken to each other only through the Maiden's memories. From now on, they speak directly to each other in the same way any courting couple pledges their love and devotion as they prepare to marry.

"We Can Spend the Night in the Villages"

Song of Solomon 7:11b:

"Let us spend the night in the villages."

Although the translations soften the Shulammite's words by adding, "Let us," Hess says all the verbs in Song 7:11-12 are commands. They carry the same force as the Shepherd's verbs in Song 2:10-13 when he says "Arise!" and "come along." Hess clarifies, "The female gives her orders to the male" (225).

After her ordeal with Solomon, the Maiden doesn't shrink into helplessness. Early in the morning, she sent the Virgins to find the Shepherd. She had time to think, and she knows what the two of them must do. She implements the second phase of her escape from Solomon.

It's about noon. The Maiden doesn't know how Solomon will react. The longer they tarry, the more dangerous the situation may become. "Come on! Let's go now!" she pulls on his arm. "I know we don't have enough daylight to make it very far. We'll walk as long as we can. With all the villages, we'll find a safe one to spend the night in. Come on!"

The verses don't give an idea of how many days it will take the Shulammite and the Shepherd to walk from Jerusalem to Shunem. On the map, it's about 55 miles almost straight north of Jerusalem through some valleys. More than likely, the reason the Virgins found the Shepherd so quickly was because he followed her to Jerusalem. Now he'll get her home safely. Of course, the people for whom this play was first presented knew the territory and this wasn't a question for them.

"I Must Check on the Vineyards"

Song of Solomon 7:12a:
"Let us rise early and go to the vineyards;
Let us see whether the vine [vines – NIV] has budded
And its blossoms have opened."

The Shulammite says, "We'll get an early start in the morning. We'll be home before we know it. I need to check on the vineyards as soon as I can and make sure everything is okay."

This statement shows the Shulammite's take-charge and get-it-done attitude. Her acceptance of responsibility is one reason her brothers insisted she become the caretaker of the vineyards while they labored on Solomon's projects. Putting their can-do sister in charge guaranteed that the work in the vineyards was as good as done. The word "caretaker" in Song of Solomon 1:6 refers to an overseer, not a laborer.

It's been a few days since she last checked the blossoms, and this is a critical time for the grapevines. "If the little foxes jostle the newly opening blossoms the plants won't produce as many grapes," she tells the Shepherd. "I need to hurry home and check on them."

"I Need to Check on the Pomegranates"

Song of Solomon 7:12b:
"And whether the pomegranates have bloomed."

Apparently the Shulammite is taking care of a pomegranate orchard along with the grapevines. Earlier Solomon said he had gone down to the valley to check on the land he leased to tenant farmers (Song 6:11). He wanted to see if the vine had budded and if the pomegranates had bloomed. Now the Maiden worries about the pomegranates as well. Both Solomon and the Shulammite associate a vineyard and pomegranate trees to the place where Solomon first saw the Maiden.

Later the Shulammite tells the Shepherd, "After our fall wedding, I'll give you spiced wine to drink from the juice of *my pomegranates.* They'll be ripe soon after we marry."

After the pomegranates bloom, the fruit ripens in six to seven months. The fruit keeps well all winter. With their wedding four months away, the Shulammite and the Shepherd can look forward to eating the refreshing fruit and making pomegranate wine to enjoy during the long cold winter.

For the Shulammite to worry about the grapevines and the pomegranates on the walk back to Shunem is very common for farm families. To do otherwise is irresponsible. They constantly accommodate the weather.

When my dad was in hospice with only a few weeks left to live, he told me many times, "Patsy, I need to get out of here. I need to be planting the cotton seed right now for it to ripen on time. It has to be in the ground by April 27th. I need you to get me out of here!"

My dad grew his first crop of cotton the previous year at age 82. Cotton, a complicated crop, had recently been genetically modified to grow well in the short growing season of the Texas Panhandle. Dad went to cotton school once every week at a local gin to learn its peculiarities. He studied how it bloomed and when to have a crop-dusting plane spray defoliant on it to make all the bolls mature at the same time.

He hired harvesters and his field was the last cotton they stripped. The large modules of cotton, the size of a semi-truck bed, sat exposed to the weather for weeks before the gin picked them up for processing. Determined to be the first to the gin the next year, he special-ordered quick-maturing seed. But it had to be planted earlier than the slower growing variety.

Dad spent one entire day of his last good ones discussing with my brother Tom what the seed and crop would require. He instructed Tom on the special cotton stripper he'd decided to buy so they could harvest their own crop. He wasn't going to risk losing the cotton because it sat in the field too long waiting for the harvesters and the gin.

The Shulammite trying to get home to check on the crops gives us a glimpse of her character. Her brothers knew what they were doing when they made her the overseer. Their livelihood depends on her protecting their crops during this vulnerable first stage.

"Our Fall Wedding Is Still On"

Song of Solomon 7:12c:
"There I will give you my love [breasts – Septuagint]."

"Love" (*dôd*) comes "from an unused root meaning properly to boil [like a boiling pot], i.e. (figuratively) to love; by implication a love-token, lover, friend; specifically an uncle:--(well-) beloved, father's brother, love, uncle [feminine ending is for aunt]" (Strong 30). *Dôd* is connected to breasts (*dad*) in Proverbs 5:19 which speaks of the older wife's breasts. "Breasts (*dad*) apparently [comes] from the same [root] as *dôd*; the breast (as the seat of love, or from its shape):--breast, teat" (Strong 29).

The Septuagint (Greek translation of the Hebrew Old Testament that Jesus and the apostles quoted from) translated *dôd* with the Greek *mastos* which means "to knead, the breasts (nipples) of a man; breasts of a woman" (Thayer 392). It comes from the root word *masaomai* which means "(to handle or squeeze); to chew:--gnaw. 1. To chew, consume, eat, devour" (Dickey "Song 7:12").

Ignoring for the moment the peering eyes and listening ears of the Virgins, the Shulammite speaks from her heart to the Shepherd. "Let's go home. Let me take care of my responsibilities with the vineyards and pomegranate trees. We'll get married in the fall. And then I want to experience the full sweetness of loving you. There I will give you my breasts as an expression of my love."

The Shulammite's Promise to Initiate Sex

Imagine the Virgins overhearing this beautiful declaration of love that will continue with God's blessings. Perhaps they clasp their hands over their mouths in shock, contrasting such devotion to Solomon's infidelity. Now the Maiden who jilted Solomon is embarking on a love life that will never be theirs if they stay in the palace subservient to Solomon's lust. Later when the Shulammite turns to speak to them, they will pay careful attention.

A Young Wife's Breasts of Love

The Old Testament Hebrew uses many words for "breasts" to convey different aspects of this part of a woman's anatomy. Earlier the

Virgins heard Solomon tell the Shulammite how he longed to climb her palm tree and take hold of her breasts (Song 7:8). He used a biological term which indicates a girl is transitioning into sexual maturity.

Now they listen as the Shulammite uses a different word as she promises to initiate lovemaking by giving her breasts to the Shepherd as the seat of her love. This word for "breast-love" (*dôd*) is used fifty-eight times in the Old Testament with thirty-eight of them occurring in the Song of Solomon. The Shulammite begins the story of her dilemma by using this word to describe her longing for the Shepherd's passionate kisses of love (Song 1:2, 4).

She uses *dôd* to call the Shepherd "my beloved" thirty-four times. The Septuagint translates "beloved" as "kinsman" (*adelphos*) which means "1. a brother, 2. having the same national ancestor, belonging to the same people, countryman, 3. any fellowman, 4. a fellow-believer, united to another by the bond of affection, 5. an associate in employment or office, and 6. brethren of Christ" (Thayer 10).

Thus the Septuagint recognizes *dôd's* portrayal of the love of family as it refers to an uncle or aunt. This corresponds with the Shepherd calling the Shulammite "my sister, my bride." Both the Shepherd and the Shulammite treasure an intellectual and emotional intimacy common to siblings and kinsman. It also reflects the Shulammite later telling the Shepherd he is like a brother who nursed at her mother's (biological) breasts (Song 8:1). They share deep committed love common to families.

Dôd is a multi-faceted word for love. Yet all the parts, love for family and breasts as the seat of love, combine to express a very active, touchable kind of love. The Shepherd is the Shulammite's breast-love — the love of her breasts.

This makes sense to a wife who regularly yields to vaginal orgasms. One wife laughed at this definition and said, "I guess you could say my husband is my breast-love. I like it when he enjoys my breasts during lovemaking. He has a certain tone of voice he uses sometimes when he's talking animatedly or when he's teasing me. As soon as I hear his playful tone, my nipples become erect and tingle. It's involuntary and has nothing to do with what he's saying. It's all about his voice. I always tell him, 'You're making my breasts tingle.'"

She laughed again, "I never thought about it before, but I guess he's my beloved — my breast-love. I can't wait to tell him the next time I hear his playful tone of voice."

Wives who depend on vibrators to achieve an orgasm probably will never experience this sensation. When a woman learns how to yield to the joys of regular vaginal orgasms, her whole body becomes sensitive to her husband's presence. He can touch her thigh and her vagina will jump for joy. The inside of her body becomes sensitive to his presence.

Using a vibrator to climax is an annoying nuisance for such a woman.

A Vintage Wife's Bosom Amour

A similar message is found in Proverbs 5. A wife giving her breasts as part of her love for her husband is contrasted with the biological breasts of a harlot (Proverbs 5:19-20). Only Proverbs 5 speaks of an *older* wife's sexual charms as compared to what a sweet-young thing offers a husband facing a mid-life sexual crisis. The older wife continues to give her breasts to her older husband as an expression of her growing love for him over the years.

God's People Make the Best Lovers devotes a chapter to Proverbs 5 titled "The Older Wife—An Exciting Lover." It makes a simple point: God designed for a wife to be an exciting lover her whole life—for the whole marriage. Indeed, couples who actively loved each other through the hot-hormonal years of their youth say the slowed down lovemaking of their senior years are the best times ever. Older couples make the best lovers! Barring illnesses such as diabetes, God has wonderfully designed the male and female so that frequent lovemaking keeps their bodies expressing love in each other's arms well into their golden years.

A survey of 2930 men and women 45 and older commissioned by the AARP, The American Association of Retired Persons, shows that sexuality remains an essential element in older couples' lives. Approximately 49% of those with a regular partner engage in sex once a week or more. Most of these adults say "a satisfying sexual relationship is important to their quality of life" (1999).

The AARP update six years later reported basically the same facts about sexual love being important to older couples. The main difference was that six years later both men and women were more open in talking about sex. They shared that a fulfilling sexual relationship makes for a more positive outlook on life for both husbands and wives.

In addition to limitations from poor health, the #1 reason for sexual dissatisfaction from the older participants is *a lack of initiative from their partner* when it comes to having sex (2005). The AARP studies reveal that no matter how old a loving person gets, a sexless marriage is pure misery until the bitter end.

My experience of nearly a half of century also shows that *a lack of interest in sex* is the #1 reason for marital unhappiness of both men and women of all ages. If a couple regularly expresses sexual love to each other, their emotional bond grows stronger over the years. As they age, the affection their bodies speak to each other deepens. The hot impatient hormones of youth give way to the mellow sweetness of a lifetime of loving intimacy in each other's arms.

While physical health may change the way a couple expresses love, their emotional and intellectual bonds stay strong. And their hugging, kissing, and snuggling keep the hormones of love flowing. But sexless marriages don't have a foundation of emotional, intellectual, sexual, and spiritual love to sustain them during the years of infirmity.

The Shulammite's Promises for Youth and Old Age

The Shulammite promises the Shepherd, "You'll never wonder if I love you. I'm looking forward to initiating lovemaking. My breasts tingle and ache for you. My nipples stand erect at the thought of your touch."

Many husbands long for a wife like the Shulammite to approach them for lovemaking. They often complain, "I feel so unloved because my wife never initiates sex. When I try to arouse her passions by caressing her breasts, she accuses me of groping. This has gone on for years. I've reached the point where I'm afraid to show her how much I love her. I never know how she'll react."

Sometimes a husband or a wife refuses to learn how God designed lovemaking to bind a man and a woman's hearts together. Spouses of such unloving people may look forward to their hormones slowing down to get some relief from sexual frustration. They don't know the anorexic is foisting the greatest sexual fraud ever on them. The anorexic is once again cheating them—this time out of the best sex of their entire life. Anorexics often use their senior years as an excuse to become impotent or frigid with the spouse of their youth.

The Maiden pledges that she won't be an intimacy anorexic in her youth or her senior years. She knows a feminine lover doesn't lie still like a prude to let her husband show all the affection. God created the woman as an active participant in lovemaking. Promising to follow God's plan, she assures the Shepherd she looks forward to initiating the act of love. With such an attitude, her wedding night and honeymoon will generate many delightful memories of shared love. And she will carry forth these godly attitudes toward lovemaking into her old age. All her days, she will both entice and love her shepherd with her breasts.

The Blessings of Children

Song of Solomon 7:13a:
"The mandrakes have given forth fragrance."

The Shepherd used the metaphor of a wife's garden filled with springs to encompass both love of her husband and children (Song 4:12-15). Now the Shulammite enhances his comparison when she tells him, "The mandrakes have given forth fragrance, and over our door are all choice fruits." Since the time of Leah and Rachel, the Israelites viewed mandrakes as increasing fertility (Genesis 30:14).

The Maiden speaks of her desire to bear many children with the Shepherd as the mandrakes release their erotic fragrance. She also talks about the many choice fruits she's saved for him in her hope chest. She associates loving her future children with loving the Shepherd — their father-to-be. She appreciates the connection between a woman truly loving her husband with being a wonderful, affectionate mother.

The Shulammite's mention of mandrakes held special significance for the Shepherd and the Maiden as the Jews regarded it as a plant with the powers to insure conception. Dr. Robert Pettus describes the plant in *As I See Sex Through the Bible:*

> Mandrakes are called "May apples" and "devil's apples." It is a plant which grows about a foot high, has purple blooms in May, has a tubular root, and is akin to the potato family. The plant blooms with a purple flower in May which turns into a two-inch large apple. The roots of the plant and the fruit of the plant both have been used to promote fertility in the female (122).

Dr. Pettus tells the story of Jacob and his wives, Rachel and Leah, in Genesis 30:14. Reuben brought his mother Leah some mandrakes in the days of the wheat harvest, the same time the mandrake's apples ripened. Then Rachel bargained with Leah for the mandrakes by allowing Jacob to spend the night with Leah. Soon Rachel conceived. Dr. Pettus explains how the mandrakes may have helped Rachel become pregnant:

> Rachel's desire to have a child bordered on the psychotic. She "said unto Jacob, 'Give me children or else I die'" (Gen. 30:1). If not psychotic she was certainly irrational. We know anxiety, tension and worry will affect fertility. Perhaps the mandrakes Rachel obtained from Reuben and Leah served no purpose, however, it is interesting to me as a physician to think about it in the light of the following. Mandrake roots and "May apples" have been used throughout the ages as sedatives, soporifics and fertility potions. A nervous, tense, worried woman sometimes does not conceive. When the tension over being childless is relieved by the adoption of a child, these women frequently conceive. Perhaps the sedative effect which the mandrakes had, helped Rachel conceive (123).

The Maiden assures the Shepherd they will enjoy a happy home. The fragrance of the fertile mandrakes will mingle with the aroma of love when they're in each other's arms. Children will abound for her to nurture and to bless their union. And the fruit of their union will thrive in a home where an abundance of open love is shared with everyone.

The Blessings of Exciting Sex

Song of Solomon 7:13b:
"And over our doors are all choice fruits,
Both new and old,
Which I have saved up for you, my beloved [same Hebrew word as
breasts in 7:12]."

The Shulammite stores up new and old delights for the Shepherd. He is already enamored with her intellectually and emotionally and eaten her honey and milk. Soon he will taste the new fruit of uniting physically with her as he drinks from her pure garden spring.

As we saw earlier, God instructed the Israelites to spend the first year of marriage giving sexual pleasure to each other to build a healthy foundation to weather the normal trials of life (Deuteronomy 24:5). Sexual love is designed to grow more fulfilling as the couple experiments and plays with each other their first year. A timid bride may quickly become more assertive in her flirting with her husband. She may entice her lover by getting in the shower with him. And as for his organ of love which gives her so much pleasure? Oh, how her desire will manifest to touch, kiss, and swirl her tongue around his uniqueness.

Only the limits of their imagination control the way a husband and wife express love to each other. Their physical displays of affection will expand over the years. Together they will learn the art of *SPEAKING GOD'S BEAUTIFUL LANGUAGE OF LOVE* in each other's arms.

```
ACT TWO, SCENE SIX TO BE CONTINUED
THIRD DAY - NOON
```

Still in the Great Hall, the Virgins listen to every word the Shulammite says to the Shepherd. They've never heard such declarations of love in Solomon's palace. They look around to see if the King is watching them. Not seeing him, they turn their attention back to the Shulammite.

The curtains close for an intermission.

Study Exercise

Answer all questions in your own words.

1. How do a woman's eyes either comfort or confuse a man?
2. Why did Solomon tell the Shulammite he wanted to climb the palm tree?

3. Why did the Shulammite reject Solomon?
4. What did the Shulammite mean when she said, "Sex goes down smoothly for my beloved?"
5. What does "beloved" mean? Give an example of how a woman can treat her husband as her beloved.
6. Is it feminine for a woman to initiate lovemaking with her husband? Explain your reasoning for your answer.
7. How can a couple determine if they are sexually compatible in courtship without engaging in sex?
8. How important is kissing to a marriage? Explain your answer.
9. Do you disagree with anything in the lesson? If so, explain giving scriptures for your reasons.

Family Exercise

Boys and men view purity differently than girls and women. To help girls and women better understand male thinking on this subject, if you are a female, ask some of the men or boys in your life how boys think and talk about girls and sex. Write their remarks down. If you are a male, write down some of the remarks you've heard. Be prepared to turn your paper in and to share the comments in class.

Research Exercise

For your weekly study of the Song of Solomon, read it in the Septuagint, the Greek Old Testament translation of the original Hebrew. We've finished our study of the first seven chapters of the Song of Solomon, and you'll find the Septuagint to be a quick, pleasant read. You'll find it at ecmarsh.com/lxx.

Beginning with Song of Solomon 1:1, notice the Septuagint's translation of the word "beloved" (*dôd*) for the Shepherd as "kinsman." Contrast this with the word "king." A casual reading of the Septuagint makes it easy to see how the Song of Solomon speaks of two men—a king and a kinsman (beloved) who works as a shepherd.

The Septuagint was translated prior to 285 BC. This was over 500 years before Origen's allegory. Before the destruction of Jerusalem in 70 AD everyone took the Song of Solomon literally with two men vying for the attention of the young vineyard keeper (ISBE "Septuagint, 1").

Keep in mind that the Septuagint is a translation. It's not the inspired word-for-word Hebrew of the Old Testament scriptures. But the Septuagint tells us how the Jewish translators viewed the original Hebrew words. Jesus, the apostles, and New Testament writers cited the Septuagint. They also used the original Hebrew text when it contradicted the Septuagint. We need to do word studies with the Septuagint just as we do with our English translations.

If you want to learn more about the Septuagint, read Sir Lancelot C. L. Brenton's introduction to his translation of the Greek Septuagint, "An Historical Account of the Septuagint Version" at the above website where you'll find the Septuagint's rendering of the Song of Solomon.

Stacey's Story:
My Relationship with My Son

Good Morning Patsy Rae,

You asked about my journey with my son. As you know, in those early days of our struggle when I let Joe speak disrespectfully to me, my young son was starting to ignore me when I talked to him. He was imitating his dad in the way he treated me.

I have to tell you the Lord has done more than I could have imagined. My son and I now have a wonderful, special relationship. He is a Christian and one of the kindest, most gentle young men I know.

He is very close with his sisters and they all love him dearly and value his opinion and respect. My son can (and does) feel free to talk to me on any subject and I am amazed at what the Lord has done in his life and all our lives!

Through learning how to fight fair, all five of our kids learned very young how to communicate and work out their problems and disagreements in a respectful, mature way. They all love each other so much and our home is free of the sibling rivalry and bickering that permeates so many homes today — and that we grew up with.

Clear out of the blue, our nineteen-year-old son turned to Joe and me one summer day, and said, "You two are good parents. You really are, and I just want you to know that." When that happens, you know you're truly blessed! And all the pain was worth it to get here.

Our children know we love them; they love us and are respectful to us. They all love each other too, and are the best of friends. Could any parent ask for more? I have to pinch myself sometimes when I realize the fruit the Lord has grown in all of our lives through our trials! I am very grateful for all the Lord has done and continues to do!

Thanks for asking and letting me share with you how blessed our family has become over the years. I'm looking forward to watching my children in their own marriages.

I am so loving the Lord,
Stacey

Secret 10: Face Your Past to Get Fired Up About Sexual Love

Solomon's Siren Song: By the Gazelles or By the Hinds

The 7-year-old Shulammite pulls open the flap of their tent door. "Mama! Mama! Aunt Edith is having her baby!"

"Slow down, Missy. Who's with her?"

"All the women are headed for her tent. I asked Old Martha what was happening. She told me, 'Hurry up! Tell your mama it's time for Edith's birthing party.'"

"I'm on my way."

"Can I come this time? Please, Mama! Please! Aunt Edith won't mind. She let me feel the baby move in her tummy lots of times. Please, let me come this time. I'm old enough now."

"Well, I don't know...."

"Please, Mama, I know all about how babies get here. You told me about the gazelles and the hinds."

"Oh, sweet daughter," Mama laughs, "If you only knew half as much as you think you do."

"Please, Mama! Please! Please!"

"Okay, miss-know-it-all, tell me about the gazelles and the hinds."

"Everything, Mama? I want to get there before the baby's born. Do you think they'll let me be first to hold him and kiss him after Aunt Edith?"

"Well, Missy, tell me one thing. And quit jumping up and down. This is a serious question, and I want a serious answer. If you give me the right answer, then you can go kiss your first newborn baby."

"Oh, Mama, thank you! Thank you!"

"Stop jumping up and down.... That's better.... Now here's the question. How does a virgin know when it's time for her and a young man to get married and start having babies?"

"That's so easy, Mama. You've shown me the gazelles and the hinds being romantic in the field behind the tent. Us virgins are particular about who we marry and have babies with. Boys are yucky until you get to know them! I'm never going to have a baby with a yucky boy!"

"I understand. But what makes a boy not be yucky anymore?"

"Well!" Missy Prissy uses her adult voice, "First he has to show me he loves me…just like the gazelles and the hinds do. They never just get married and start having babies. They spend time together schmoozing. The doe is very particular. She doesn't have babies with just any old gazelle. She makes him prove he loves her! And she has to fall in love with him first. Now can we go?"

"Not yet. You need to tell me a little more."

With her nose in the air, Missy rapid fires, "And when the mama and the papa really love each other, their kids grow up in a loving home just like my brothers, me, and my baby sister. Now can we go now, Mama? Please now, Mama! I don't want to miss a thing!"

"You'll soon be developing your breasts," Mama laughs. "And you've been paying attention to the gazelles and the hinds. I guess it's time for you to see how babies come into the world. Aunt Edith's baby will be your first one to hold and kiss, even before he's cleaned up."

An hour later, Edith still reclines on a birthing stool as her relatives and neighbors sit around cheering her on. Then the midwife says, "I see the head!" The baby slides into her waiting arms. She holds him up for everyone to see. "Someone go tell Gabe he has another fine Israelite son." She hands the squirming baby to his mother for the first kiss. "Edith, who gets to give him his second kiss?"

"Missy. Only she has to sit down and quit jumping up and down."

Everyone laughs as Missy quickly sits beside her aunt and holds out her arms. "He's so tiny. He looks just like Uncle Gabe." She kisses his forehead and gently uncurls his finger around her own.

"Okay," the midwife takes the baby and hands him to the next woman. They pass him around the room with everyone exclaiming over his good looks and kissing him. "Bring Gabe in to kiss his son hello. Then we'll rub him with salt, put some oil on him, and swaddle him. It's time for Edith to feed him. They both need to sleep."

Missy runs to door, "I'll tell Uncle Gabe," and she's gone.

Song of Solomon 8:1-4:
The Maiden Promises to Be Passionate

ACT TWO, SCENE SIX CONTINUES
THIRD DAY – NOON

The previous scene in the Great Hall continues. Solomon left after the Shulammite rejected him. The Queens and Concubines are still in the background. The Virgins and the Shepherd gather around the Maiden as she continues her declarations of love.

The Shulammite Honors Their Loving Mothers

Song of Solomon 8:1a:
"Oh that you were like a brother to me
Who nursed at my mother's breasts..."

Solomon offered the Shulammite only sensuous love, but she expects to experience real love for a lifetime with the Shepherd. Why? Because they both grew up in affectionate homes, so similar, the Shepherd could pass for one of her brothers who nursed at her mother's breasts.

Nursing and breastfeeding aren't always the same. Breastfeeding, the simple act of offering a baby the breast instead of a bottle, differs from nursing, which includes tender loving care. Some breastfed babies are not surrounded by tenderness while some bottle-fed babies receive lots of emotional nourishment. The Maiden states, "Both of our mothers provided loving homes for us to grow up in and to bless our marriage."

The Shulammite credits her mother with not only teaching her verbally about love, but also setting an example by letting the love of her husband spill over onto loving her children. The Maiden understands that the more a mother loves her husband, the more she surrounds her children with emotional love.

God Designed Breastfeeding to Teach Love

God ordained the important role the nursing mother plays in the developing child:

Psalms 22:9-10:
"Yet Thou art He who didst bring me forth from the womb;
Thou didst make me trust when upon my mother's breasts.
Upon Thee I was cast from birth;
Thou hast been my God from my mother's womb."

The love conveyed by a mother's breasts is so powerful; God used the example of a nursing mother to describe his own love for the Israelites:

Isaiah 66:11-13:
"'That you may nurse and be satisfied with her comforting breasts;
That you may suck and be delighted with her bountiful bosom.'
For thus says the Lord, 'Behold I extend peace to her like a river,
And the glory of the nations like an overflowing stream;
And you shall be nursed, you shall be carried on the hip
And fondled on the knees.

As one whom his mother comforts, so I will comfort you;
And you shall be comforted in Jerusalem.'"

One of the tenderest scenes of parental love is when a father lets his baby hold his finger while nursing at his wife's breast. The emotional love softening the faces in this three-way bonding says more than words ever could. No wonder God chose a nursing mother as a cherished example to portray his own love for his people.

Parents Lay the Foundation for Their Children's Marriage

The Shulammite recognizes that when parents lay the proper foundation for affection through marital example and parental love, their children reap the natural blessings of the parents' sexual love. This foundation begins to form in infancy as the mother nurses, cuddles, plays with, and talks to her children. As the children mature, the foundation continues to build through the free rein of love in the home. As the parents flirt, kiss, and hug each other, their open expression of love overflows to envelop their children.

One mother said, "My husband was unaffectionate and showed almost no sexual interest in me. I thought, 'If I can just quit caring about sex, then I'll be like him, and we'll have a perfect marriage.' I worked hard to turn off my desires. One day I realized, 'My feelings are turning off for my kids!' I was horrified! I loved my kids. So then I had to work very hard to turn my feelings back on."

She continued, "I learned the hard way it's impossible to turn your intimate feelings off for your mate and be a loving parent at the same time. I deceived myself by thinking we'd have a perfect marriage if I became sexually cold like my husband was. I'm glad I figured it out when I did. My ex never figured it out. He was not a good father, and none of our kids have anything to do with him."

The Shulammite Promises to Be Passionate

Song of Solomon 8:1b:
"If I found you outdoors, I would kiss you;
No one would despise me, either."

Sometimes a wife considers it unfeminine to make the first move toward tenderness. But the Bible teaches the woman sets the loving atmosphere in the home, and the man responds to it (Titus 2:4-5). A wise wife doesn't wait for her husband to create the mood for love. Instead, she bestows her affections upon him as the Shulammite promises to do.

If she finds him outdoors or in front of company, the Shulammite will still kiss him. And no one will despise her either—especially not her husband! The woman's tender emotions make her the perfect one to fill the air with love. And so many love-starved husbands yearn to respond in kind to an emotionally and physically loving wife. Children delight in seeing their parents show love to each other — and to them.

Many a husband embarrasses his wife by becoming cranky when company visits. This usually doesn't happen because the company overstays their visit, but because the couple refrains from their usual hugs and kisses. He misses those wonderful, passionate hugs that promise more. And a wife who falls into bed exhausted from being the perfect hostess makes him fight resentment toward the company he thinks robbed him of her special refreshments. Such a husband often becomes irritable.

But when a wife puts her husband's needs first by openly kissing him and patting his knee, he enjoys the company more. Likewise, the company sees an example of an affectionate wife and a happy husband and children. When the man of the house gets grouchy, no one relaxes or has a good time.

The Blessings of a Loving Mother's Sex Education

Song of Solomon 8:2a:
"I would lead you and bring you
Into the house of my mother, who used to instruct me."

"Instruct" (*lâmad*) means properly, to goad, i.e., (by implication) to teach (the rod being an Oriental incentive)" (Strong 60).

Lâmad is translated "expert" in Song 3:8 where Solomon's guards are described as "expert at war." They were highly trained to protect the King and his traveling party. "Instruct" is used in a sexual context in Proverbs 5:1-14 where the young man regrets not listening to the voice of his teachers or heeding the words of his "instructors" (verse 13). The chapter continues to admonish middle-aged husbands to delight in the sexual blessings of their older wife.

God's plan has always been for sex education to take place in the home in the context of the mother's and the father's open love for each other. Then their instruction is not hypocritical words, but a way of life for the whole family. The Maiden credits her mother with giving her such a thorough sex education that she is now an expert at distinguishing the differences between sensuous and true love.

Indeed, at the time of the Song of Solomon Israelite women were known for their passionate attitudes toward lovemaking. Even today, Jewish wives don't suffer from the sexual inhibitions of many Christian women who falsely assume God is anti-sex. Unlike Jewish women who have always known God loves sex and sexually active couples, many

Christian women have been duped into believing the hoax that sex is a necessary evil for producing children. And their husband and children pay a terrible emotional price from living in a cold, unloving home.

The Shulammite and the Shepherd grew up in loving homes and looked forward to a passionate marriage. However, as the King of Sexless Marriages, Solomon wasn't so fortunate.

Solomon Grew Up in a Dysfunctional Home

Solomon didn't grow up in a loving home as did the Shulammite and the Shepherd. His father and mother, David and Bathsheba, began marriage on the basis of sensuous lust and murder. After watching Bathsheba bathing, David committed adultery with her. Later when she discovered she was pregnant, he killed her husband to cover up his sin. After they married, God took the life of their first child as punishment for their wickedness. Then Bathsheba, one of David's many wives, gave birth to Solomon (2 Samuel 11:2-12:24).

The scriptures record jealousy, fighting, and rape among David's children by his different wives. Two sons killed one of the brothers. In fact, Solomon killed one of his brothers whom he thought was trying to steal his throne. Although Solomon was probably breastfed by either his mother or a wet nurse, nursing alone cannot replace an emotional void in the home. Not seeing his parents set a monogamous example of love and devotion to each other and growing up in a home filled with malicious sibling rivalry, Solomon never learned how to build an emotional relationship with any woman.

Many Couples Grow Up in Dysfunctional Homes

Of the over 200 people who worked through my *Sexless Marriages Self-Assessment Survey* since edition one of this book was published, with the exception of one person, their sexless spouse grew up in a narcissistic or alcoholic home or in a combination alcoholic/narcissistic home. And only a few of the husbands and wives who married a sexless spouse grew up in a loving home.

Generally speaking, the answers to the checklists show that both people in a loveless marriage are often an adult child of a dysfunctional parent and home. They don't know what true love looks, sounds, feels, tastes, and smells like. They don't recognize and act on the 4 parts of love. As a result, they make an unhealthy choice for a marriage partner.

But all is not lost. The Apostle Paul tells us not to stay stuck in our childhood, but to grow up into love and do away with "childish things" (1 Corinthians 13:11). We can follow the Shulammite's example and candidly look at each home. What kind of love did the couple witness between their parents? How affectionate were their parents to each other and the children? If a parent failed to show love to the family, the adult child should expect to encounter more than the usual adjustment problems.

During courtship the adult child can say, "I've never seen my parents kiss. And I can't remember them ever telling me they loved me. I don't want to be like them. I want to show affection to you and our children. I probably won't overcome 20 years of upbringing overnight, but I know I need to work at it. I pledge to do my part to overcome my upbringing. I hope we can always talk to each other without accusing the other of not being loving or caring." If this honest discussion didn't take place before marriage, then it needs to happen after marriage.

Sometimes we think we grew up in a loving home, but it's easy to be fooled because we were inexperienced children who thought like a child. More than likely, we naively believed everything our parents told us...until we turned into teenagers and began questioning everything they said and did. Even so, we still carry around a lot of inaccurate views of our childhood home unless we have carefully examined it as an adult.

My free *Sexless Marriages Self-Assessment Survey* helps you examine both yours and your spouse's home of origin. It also guides you in evaluating the sex education you received growing up. The purpose of the checklists is to open your eyes to core problems so you can make loving decisions for yourself and your family. You can learn more about the survey at PatsyRaeDawson.com/sexless-marriages-checklists/.

Queen Victoria Made Sexual Love Politically Incorrect

Christopher Hibbert's excellent biography *Queen Victoria: A Personal History* gives new insights into Queen Victoria. Although brought up by a prudish mother who was herself scandalized by King William's illegitimate children, Queen Victoria was not a prude:

> She spent the evening after their wedding [to Prince Albert] lying down with a headache, but wrote ecstatically in her diary:

> I NEVER, NEVER spent such an evening!!! MY DEAREST DEAREST DEAR Albert.... His excessive love & affection gave me feelings of heavenly love & happiness I never could have *hoped* to have felt before! He clasped me in his arms, & we kissed each other again & again! His beauty, his sweetness & gentleness—really how can I ever be thankful enough to have such a *Husband!*...to be called by names of tenderness, I have never yet heard used to me before—was bliss beyond belief! Oh! This was the happiest day of my life! (123).

The Internet abounds with examples of how Queen Victoria and Prince Albert frequently gave gifts of nude paintings and sculptures to each other. In recent years exhibits of their extensive collection have gone on display. Never shy about romping with the Prince, the Queen bore him nine children.

Royalty set different standards for the common people than what they practiced. Queen Victoria under Prince Albert's influence created a politically-correct atmosphere in her court that idolized sexless marriages. In the beginning, the colonists snickered at Queen Victoria's obsession with political prudery. But the young United States wanted to be recognized as a world power by the old European governments. Since Great Britain wielded political clout and Queen Victoria refused to see any divorced person in her court, the young country knuckled under to be taken seriously by Europe (Lewinsohn 295).

Politically-Correct Prudery Became Medically Correct

About this same time many doctors took up their pens and turned out volumes of medical books to warn the public of the physical dangers of excessive intimacy — even in marriage. Who could dispute so-called medical facts by the respectable scientific community? Even people who cared nothing for politics or religion believed the medical dogma. These doctors exerted the greatest influence of all; and as a result, caused tremendous damage to marriage and sexual love.

Sylvanus Stall, D.D. fell under the influence of these doctors. At the turn of the 20th century, he published an eight-volume set of books called *Self and Sex Series.* He wrote four books to tell "what a man ought to know" at each period of his life: a young boy, a young man, a young husband, and a man of 45. He viewed life as nearly over for a man of 45. Mrs. Mary Wood-Allen, M.D. wrote the two books to cover the first part of a woman's life: a young girl and a young woman. Mrs. Emma F. A. Drake, M.D. wrote the remaining two books for women: a young wife and a woman of 45.

Altogether, these books contained over eighty recommendations from prominent men and women and newspapers in the United States and England. Doctors, authors, editors, mayors, governors, judges, educators, and religious leaders lavishly praised the books. The front of one book claimed, "More than a million copies in English sold. Two thousand new readers daily. Translated into six languages in Asia and in as many more in Europe. None of these foreign publishers was solicited. Each sought the privilege to translate. In two countries, publishers contended for the privilege."

Stall relied heavily on existing medical books to prove his various points. He and the doctors he quoted branded other doctors who disagreed with their views as "charlatans." The *Self and Sex Series* represented the thinking of responsible people and respectable doctors of the time in regard to sexual intercourse.

Men and Women Condemned God's Morality

Banning the writings of poets and authors didn't keep the Victorian moralists busy enough. Soon they began to examine the Bible. Richard Lewinsohn explains in *History of Sexual Customs*, "They reaped an abundant harvest. The Bible turned out to be the most dangerous book to fall into the hands of anybody of unchaste mind" (292).

During this time, atheists sprang up because they refused to believe in a God who promoted sexual love because his morals failed to measure up to their own. One typical atheist wrote a book protesting the recording of true stories about David and other men who committed adultery. Even though God condemned these acts, the atheist objected to telling people about them. He found the book of Ruth especially distasteful. This man denied the existence of God because God's love of sex for husbands and wives contrasted with Victorian avoidance of lovemaking. In short, this atheist treated his morals as if they were better than God's. Not intimidated, God said:

Isaiah 55:8-9:
"'For My thoughts are not your thoughts,
Neither are your ways My ways,' declares the Lord.
'For as the heavens are higher than the earth,
So are My ways higher than your ways,
And My thoughts than your thoughts.'"

In 1898, prominent feminist Elizabeth Cady Stanton organized a committee of 30 women to publish their own version of God's scriptures called *The Woman's Bible.* The effect of Victoria's morals on Stanton shows in the brief treatment she gave the Song of Solomon—a total of 184 words. She refused to see any sexual teaching in the book for husbands and wives. She concludes the section:

The Church, as an excuse for retaining this book as a part of "Holy Scriptures," interprets the Song as expressive of Christ's love for the Church; but that is rather far-fetched, and unworthy the character of the ideal Jesus. The most rational view to take of the Song is, it was that of a luxurious king to the women of his seraglio. E.C.S (Part II 100).

Such ignorance of God's love for sex and his preserving the Song of Solomon in the Bible caused Victorians to go to an extreme in trying to eradicate all references to sex in every area of their lives and religious beliefs. When public morality begins to condemn God's morality and censures the Bible as unfit literature, let alone a book to base one's life on, something is wrong. Something is horribly wrong! Since the sexual relationship originated within the mind of God as his proudest creation, sexual love has a proper and righteous use.

Don't Victorianize and Americanize the Shulammite

About a year before I started studying the Song of Solomon nearly half a century ago, I read Dr. Marie N. Robinson's book, *The Power of Sexual Surrender*. I learned the difference between clitoral and vaginal orgasms. Because I had immersed myself in studying the scriptures relating to marriage I recognized that the psychological facts Dr. Robinson taught were in the Bible. Her description of the vaginal-orgasmic woman resembled the woman of great price in Proverbs 31:1-31. The attitudes she attributed to the clitoral-orgasmic woman were the same ones the female cougar of Proverbs 7:6-27 displayed toward her husband and the young man she seduced.

Dr. Robinson's book changed my life and my teaching. My book *God's People Make the Best Lovers* devotes several chapters to discussing the differences between these two women and their respective orgasms from the scriptures. It provides medical and psychological proof for the existence of a vaginal orgasm. It also demonstrates how a woman's thoughts determine which orgasm she enjoys — that her mind is her most powerful sexual organ. Women like me who've enjoyed both responses to their husband agree the vaginal orgasm is a much superior experience.

I gave copies of *The Power of Sexual Surrender* to my students until it went out of print. I was delighted to discover it's now available as an eBook. I highly recommend it.

The Song of Solomon showcases the Shulammite as a young woman with healthy sexual attitudes. Studying the Shulammite's promise to initiate lovemaking after marriage enabled me to accept that it was feminine to initiate sex with my husband. I've brought to this study a long history of personally enjoying vaginal orgasms and teaching other women how to do the same since 1972. The words of the Shulammite prepare women to embrace glorious lovemaking with their husbands.

Ignorance of female sexuality and failing to recognize the healthy sexual attitudes of the Israelite women in the early Solomon era leads to an erroneous view of the Shulammite. She wasn't like many Victorian and American women when it comes to sex. We need to allow her to teach us instead of trying to force her into our modern-day mold of requiring her husband to coax her into being an exciting lover.

The Song of Solomon is a story of two men and a woman who is in love with one suitor and not the other. Naturally, some of the passages are going to sound like she's turned off. In the end, she was repulsed by Solomon. We saw in the previous chapter how when Solomon made his final sensuous plea for her breasts the Maiden said, "Solomon, I can't stand the thought of your lips on mine." Then she told him, "But lovemaking with my beloved Shepherd will be wonderful because we belong to each other." (For more information about the vaginal orgasm, please see the appendix chapter "Powerful Vaginal Orgasms of Love.")

Lovemaking Is as Righteous as Partaking the Lord's Supper

I often tell women, "Making love to your husband is as holy and righteous as partaking the Lord's Supper." God spends more time extolling the virtues of a wonderful love life than he does teaching about any other aspect of marriage.

The Shulammite got it! Christian women often miss it. Husbands and wives along with their children suffer greatly from this neglect to practice the whole counsel of God. The ignorance of Victorian politicians, doctors, atheists, and feminists often rules in the cold, dead bedrooms of many Christians whom God said are to be the lights of the world.

The Maiden's Second Promise to Be Passionate

Song of Solomon 8:2b:
"I would give you spiced wine to drink from the juice of my pomegranates."

The Shulammite is ready to obey God's command to get married and get tipsy on frequent married lovemaking (Song 5:1). She promises to serve the Shepherd mulled pomegranate wine enhanced with bold spices. She teases him with the not-too-sweet liquid dessert and entices him with her tamed tartness. She will seduce him with her own aromatic beverage.

After marriage the Maiden promises to serve her Shepherd one of the most powerful and healthy aphrodisiacs of all—pomegranate juice, which increases the libido of both men and women. She wants to marry a virile man and will prepare foods and drinks to help him maintain his vitality for a lifetime. No telling her man, "Go take care of yourself."

The Internet abounds with articles and university studies about the benefits of pomegranates as an aphrodisiac, perhaps more than any other mentioned in the Song of Solomon. Notice these titles: "Heat Up Your Sex Life with Pomegranate Aphrodisiac" and "Who needs Viagra? The secret to enhancing your sex drive could be a daily glass of pomegranate juice."

Parabens and Painful Sex

Jennifer Smith in *The Unveiled Wife: Embracing Intimacy with God and Your Husband* recounts how her marriage was not consummated for 4 years because of sex-stopping vaginal pain. Finally, her husband Aaron researched toxic ingredients, especially parabens. Learning how they cause problems with estrogen, he asked her to replace her face wash that she's used faithfully for 6 years with something natural.

After only 3 days, she "felt different down there." They waited 6 days before attempting intercourse. When they made love for the first time, she burst into tears. When Aaron asked if she was okay, she replied, "I'm fine! I'm just so happy, babe. I can't believe this is what sex is like!"

As Jennifer shared this information on her blog, many women wrote to tell her eliminating products with parabens had solved their painful intercourse problems, too (170-5). As we've seen, the Israelites paid attention to foods and essential oils to help ensure a robust sex life long into old age.

As part of the Purity Culture, Jennifer and Aaron were both taught that sex is sinful. Even after they started enjoying sex, they had a lot of mental housecleaning to do to overcome their negative upbringing. They didn't get to start marriage with healthy attitudes as the Shulammite and the Shepherd did.

The Maiden Learned From Her Mother the Art of Sex

Lovemaking was so important to the Israelites in their obedience to God that they gave careful attention to preparing their children for sexual love. Dr. Robert Chartham describes in *Mainly for Wives: The Art of Sex for Women* how the Israelites prepared both their sons and daughters before marriage to be expert lovers. However, the girl received a much more elaborate sex education than the boy did. Older and experienced women taught her the art of how to give pleasure to her new husband while enjoying lovemaking for herself (24-5). This corresponds with the Apostle Paul's instruction to Titus that the older women are to encourage the young women to "love their husbands and to love their children" (Titus 2:3-5).

This cultural attention to sex education for the girl contrasts vividly with the Victorian concept that nice girls don't even feel sexual desires. The extreme prudery of the past has falsely made women think sex is a man's pleasure for the woman to endure.

In contrast to the thorough sex-education of young girls, the Israelites taught "a few very simple caresses" to the boys. The bridegroom assumed he was the dominant bed partner, which the bride allowed him to think. She quietly practiced the art of love on him that the older women taught her. Through practice and erotic experimentation, the couple quickly advanced to skillful lovemaking for their mutual pleasure. As a result, they greatly appreciated the love and techniques they each brought to the marriage bed (25).

Thus the Israelites learned from their parents the art of lovemaking. They entered marriage with a great capacity to enjoy complete marital bliss. Loving parents, especially mothers, taught their children how to build their marriages on this solid foundation of true love so they could reap all the blessings of marriage — the soulmating of two hearts fulfilled in each other's arms.

Many times getting similar instructions as the Hebrew mothers gave their daughters is all a wife needs to step over the threshold into the glorious world of vaginal orgasms with her husband. The main reason they haven't experienced one is that they don't understand how their vagina and brain function in sync with one another. Just reading what a vaginal orgasm feels like allows a woman who deeply loves her husband to relax and yield to the experience instead of trying too hard.

I often hear from these students who email me saying, "You are so right about how wonderful a vaginal orgasm is and how the brain is the key."

One wife whom I explained the sexual and emotional dynamics to called the next day exclaiming as soon as I answered the phone, "Patsy! I did it! I did it!"

The Maiden Expects to Enjoy a Passionate Husband

Song of Solomon 8:3:
"Let his left hand be under my head,
And his right hand embrace me."

The Shulammite repeated these same words earlier in Song of Solomon 2:6. Twice she shares her expectation that the Shepherd will be a loving husband with both the desire and the ability to fulfill her sexual needs. She rejected Solomon who couldn't give her sexual love.

Part of the leftovers of Victorian morals has been to give the husband a free ride sexually and blame all the problems on the wife. Before the proliferation of computers and easy Internet access, sexual hang-ups of men often went unrecognized. Now the epidemic spread of sexual addiction, especially among Christians, has brought these problems to the forefront.

Unloving husbands like Solomon don't understand how to bond with a woman to enjoy great sexual pleasure. Men and women have been duped by the Victorian notion that sex is just an animalistic release of hormones for the man. The Song of Solomon debunks this hoax and shows thrilling lovemaking comes from a man and woman joining their minds, emotions, bodies, and spirits in the embrace of love.

The Maiden Expects to Enjoy Vintage Amour

What's the main difference between young and vintage sex? Young lovers first get aroused and then enjoy sex. Older lovers start the process in each other's arms and then become aroused. Many older couples say the sweet, mellow sex of their last years is the best of all.

As the lovers age, we witness God's wisdom unfolding as the couple's sexual desires relax while still present. The husband's responses slow down. As the children leave the home, the wife's lightened family responsibilities bring her physical desires closer to the surface. If she's kept a loving attitude toward her husband throughout the years, she arrives at this age prepared physically and mentally to ravish him like the loving vintage wife of Proverbs 5. She possesses the qualities to pleasure her vintage husband with sexual delights which are even greater than they enjoyed in their youth.

Sometimes the husband needs more physical stimulation from his wife than before—not the young body of a mistress or porn star parading before him, but the loving mind of the wife of his youth beside him. As his body slows down, the sexual union takes on new characteristics, which according to many older couples makes for the best lovemaking ever. Carol Tavris analyzed a *Redbook* questionnaire in the article "40,000 Men Tell About Their Sexual Behavior, Their Fantasies, Their Ideal Women, and Their Wives." She learned that teenage boys tend to want a passive woman. But mature men find their wives' passiveness unappealing (176).

Unfortunately, Victorian morals took away many an older woman's freedom to enjoy her husband's body. She may view his penis as something she shouldn't talk about let alone look at or touch. But it's part of him—part of the man she loves. It's his organ of pleasure for both her and him.

Now the husband occasionally gets too tired to do all the work of initiating sexual intercourse. Yet he still deeply desires to make love with his wife. It gives the wife great joy to bypass his tiredness to speak the language of love directly to his organ of pleasure. She appreciates his years of adolescence when his mindless organ worked independently from his brain. Now his penis listens to her tender expressions of adoration. Great joy swells in the wife's heart as her husband's body comes to life in response to her love.

The key for success is relaxation with a total absence of pressure to perform. If it happens, great; if not, tomorrow will be even better. For the moment, the husband simply relaxes and lets his wife charm his receptive body. And a tired masculine body finds energy and a throbbing desire for union with the wife who gives him so much joy.

Experiencing rapture in the arms of a loving husband motivates a wife to pleasure him the very best she can—oral sex, or a blow job, becomes her delight rather than her wifely duty. As they mature, their sexual desires change and continue to adapt to each other's needs. The husband seeks a stronger mental involvement with her while she enjoys the physical union more than ever. God blends them in perfect harmony in their golden years.

Secret 10: Face Your Past to Get Fired Up About Sexual Love

Someone always asks during class about how to overcome a sexual past. The obvious question is, "I've done things I'm not proud of. How do I overcome a sexual past so I can have a great marriage now?"

The not so intuitive question is, "I was raised in the Virginity Culture. How do I overcome my shame and fear of sex?"

In the first classes I taught on the Song of Solomon, two young women asked each version of this question, one married with a promiscuous past and the other single and scared witless of having sex in marriage.

The Promiscuous Wife

The young wife, I'll call her Judy, had been married three years. She stayed after class to talk about her problems and said, "When I went to college this boy told me, 'If you love me you'll prove it.' I loved him so I proved it. Then he dropped me. I was so upset, I slept with any boy who came along. I went from bad to worse until I married my husband."

Every time her husband made love to her, all she could do was lay there and cry from the pain. She knew nothing was wrong physically; that the pain came from guilty feelings over her past. She said, "After I was baptized, I knew my sins were forgiven and washed away. Our sex life is better. I enjoy the sexual relationship more, but I still have pain. It isn't what it should be."

Judy came to the classes regularly and listened. She often said, "That makes sense. I agree with that." But when she went home, she wouldn't study her Bible or look at the class handouts. She refused to do the homework. She made no effort to help herself, except to come to class. She wanted her marriage to become wonderful without any effort on her part. It never happened.

The Perpetual Virgin

The single girl, I'll call her April, attended the same classes. One night she stayed after class. She said, "This class has torn me up and really upset me."

I asked, "Why would the Song of Solomon upset you?"

April replied, "This boy wants to marry me. I love him and I want to marry him, but I'm scared of sex. My father raped my older sister and he tried to rape me. I made up my mind he'd have to kill me first. My mother was very Victorian and harped about the evils of sex. Our father tried to make us loving by raping us. I was caught in the middle. Sex just looks like a horrible, nasty relationship—men are just beasts who think about nothing but sex. I told this boy about my feelings and why I feel like I do. He is very understanding and says he won't push me. He's willing to wait up to three weeks after we get married to have sex."

I said, "My husband is going to be out of town for a week, why don't you come over some evening for supper. We can talk all night long if we want to."

April came over. She had already been through the classes on Victorian morals and turned in the homework. But she had not been able to change her attitudes about marital sex. As we talked, she shared her views about sex and men and things her mother and father said. Then we examined the scriptures that applied to each one. That night April mentally cleaned house and deliberately threw out many false impressions from her upbringing. She just needed someone to help her apply the scriptures to her situation.

Soon afterward, April married the young man, and we invited the new couple over. She gushed, "Marriage is so great! And I'm married to the most wonderful man there ever was!"

My husband teased her, "That offends me. My wife says I'm the most wonderful man there ever was, and you think your husband is that man. We can't both be that man."

April averted the potential for a tragic marriage by doing the homework and then asking for help to apply the principles. She put in the mental effort to free her mind of all the inhibiting beliefs she accumulated while growing up and dealing with two unloving parents. Best of all, she became a happily married wife who thoroughly enjoyed satisfying her husband's deepest needs.

Take 2 Steps to Face and Overcome a Sexual Past

Many men also have a past that interferes with their sexual enjoyment. The Purity, Hookup, and Sexless Marriages Cultures affect both men and women. The following two steps for overcoming a sexual past help men and women embrace God's glorious plan for lovemaking.

Step 1: Become Sanctified or Transformed

Sanctification or becoming transformed is an important concept for overcoming both one's upbringing and sexual problems. Sanctification takes the thing sanctified (in this case, the sexual relationship) and separates it from the common use and views of the world. Sanctification makes the thing sanctified better than what people of the world enjoy. Here's an overview of verses, which teach how to become transformed.

1 Thessalonians 4:4: This verse admonishes Christians to *sanctify their sexual lives.* God commands his followers to avoid sexual immorality by possessing their own vessels unto sanctification and honor. As discussed in chapter 1, "Sexual Happiness for God's People," in *God's People Make the Best Lovers,* this means Christians are to know how to delight in a better love-life than the Gentiles who know not God.

1 Timothy 4:1-5: Paul says Christians are to sanctify their marriages by the word of God and prayer. Rather than forbidding to marry as Origen's hoax does, God's people are to go on to enjoy wonderful marriages. This is possible by (1) going to the word of God to learn the truth about marriage and how God loves passionate sex, (2) praying to God in an interview-type prayer for help in implementing that truth, and (3) giving God thanks for creating the way of a man with a maid. All sins that invade the home and destroy the harmony between husbands and wives can be overcome with sanctification by following this formula. *God's People Appreciate Marriage* devotes chapter 2, "Solving All Marriage Problems" to studying the mechanics of God's problem-solving formula.

1 Corinthians 6:9-11: Paul told the Corinthians they had overcome fornication, adultery, prostitution, effeminacy, homosexuality, drunkenness, and reviling (or verbal abuse). How did they do this? They followed a 3-part formula: (1) They were *washed.* They received forgiveness of their sins through baptism. (2) They were *sanctified.* They obeyed 1 Thessalonians 4:4 and 1 Timothy 4:1-5 and studied God's truths about marriage and the sexual relationship. (3) They were *justified.* God accepted them into fellowship with him because they had received forgiveness and put in the mental work to learn from the heart how to love their families. *God's People Make the Best Lovers* devotes chapter 14, "The Sin Against the Whole Body" to these scriptures.

Romans 12:2: This parallel passage shows how Christians are sanctified. God's people are not to be conformed to this world, but are to be *transformed by the renewing of their minds.* "Transformed" means "to change into another form, to transfigure, transform" (Thayer 405). This word was used when Jesus was transfigured on the Mount of Olives.

The modern word "metamorphosis" comes from this Greek word. In the English language the word refers to the insect larva as it spins a cocoon around itself to undergo drastic change and maturation. After a certain time the ugly caterpillar emerges as a beautiful butterfly — a transformed insect. Both the insect's outer appearance and its function change. The butterfly leaves behind the caterpillar's compulsion to eat plants and destroy foliage. Instead, the butterfly pollinates flowers and makes the world lovelier. This verse is why I use a butterfly for my logo with the tagline "Transforming Lives with the Power of the Scriptures."

Step 2: Master the Song of Solomon

If you haven't read the article at my website, "Your Marriage and Your Love Life Will Never Be the Same If…You Do the Homework Exercises," please do so now if you want to break the cycle of your past. See the assignment at the end of the first chapter, "God Loves Passionate Sex" to begin making the Song of Solomon belong to you so it can influence your love life by helping you get fired up about lovemaking.

The above 4 verses are more important than space allows for discussing them here. Most have a whole chapter devoted to them in other books. I encourage you to complete your study by reading those books and doing the homework. You will experience the power of the scriptures to transform your life. It makes no difference if you start with *God's People Make the Best Lovers* or with *God's People Appreciate Marriage*.

The Maiden Repeats "Secret 2: Insist on Soulmating Before Lovemaking"

Song of Solomon 8:4:
"I want you to swear, O daughters of Jerusalem,
Do not [Why should you — NASB footnote] arouse or awaken my love,
Until she [it — NASB footnote] pleases."

"Swear" is the same word translated "adjure" in 2:7 and 3:5 and means "to be complete, to seven oneself, i.e., (as if by repeating a declaration seven times)" (Strong 112).

Now the Shulammite turns to the Virgins who are still listening wide-eyed to her pledges of love to the Shepherd. She makes a final plea to them to wait for true love before marrying. The theme changes a little bit. The New American Standard footnote says, "Why should you arouse or awaken love until it pleases?" Most of the commentators agree with this translation.

After seeing how she almost fell for Solomon's practiced lines, the

Shulammite turns from the Shepherd to ask the Virgins, "What good reason can you give for forcing love in your own lives? Can't you learn from my experience with Solomon? Swear you will wait for true love in your own lives."

The italics on "my" in the translations show the scholars added it to make the meaning clearer. But "my" limits the secret of the book to the arousal of just the woman's heart. The main difference between Solomon and the Shepherd was the Shepherd's love for the Shulammite had been awakened while Solomon only lusted for her body.

Both males and females need time to get to know each other before their love can become truly aroused. If sexual activity begins before this happens, as in premarital sex, the relationship may well be destroyed before it even begins.

Many a girl writes to an advice columnist, "I gave in to having sex to keep him, then he left. How can I win him back?" The girl lost her virginity and her boyfriend; and she probably won't be able to win him back because she violated the secret of the Song of Solomon. She gave in to pressure for sex before he developed an emotional bond with her that demanded he marry her. So he left to continue his search to find the perfect feminine body to satisfy his desires.

A renowned psychologist in the field of male sexual problems, Dr. Bernie Zilbergeld, states in *Male Sexuality* that a man must feel an emotional attraction for a woman before sexual contact is meaningful or even highly pleasurable. After sexual intimacy without love, most men quickly became bored and lose interest in developing an emotional bond with the woman (Chapters 1-4, 10).

In addition, George Gilder says in *Men and Marriage* that sexual purity in women is the greatest gift they can give their boyfriends. Rather than saying "because all men want to marry virgins," he states that if women don't say no to sex, then men are never forced to make serious choices about women. When sex is easy, the man isn't motivated to make a long-term commitment to marry. He often yields to his sex drive, which drives him from body to body. He gets locked into an unsatisfying search for variety and excitement that avoids settling down to take care of a family (47).

Nearly all men who rise to the top of their professions are married. Men need wives! But without sexual purity on the part of women, men often aren't motivated to seek marriage and its responsibilities. So without purity which encourages soulmating and eventually marriage, women cannot fulfill the desperate need in men for wives.

Hence, the Shulammite implores the Virgins, "Can't you learn from my experience not to force love? True love leading to marriage is too wonderful a gift. Do not throw away your chance for happiness by forcing love."

Then the Shulammite hugs each of the Virgins and says, "Thank you for bringing my beloved Shepherd to me." Taking the Shepherd's arm, she says to him, "We've stayed too long—we need to leave. But I just had to tell you how this experience has made my heart swell with love for you. I know we will enjoy a wonderful marriage." The curtains close on the Great Room in the palace.

Study Exercise

Answer all questions in your own words.
1. How do you know the Shulammite and the Shepherd grew up in loving homes? Why is the kind of home you grew up in important?
2. What kind of home did Solomon grow up in? How did his home of origin affect the way he treated women and marriage?
3. How does nursing teach a baby to love?
4. How did the Shulammite's mother teach her about love and sex?
5. How did Queen Victoria damage lovemaking for a lot of people? What should a person do to overcome Victorian morals in their life?
6. Do you believe lovemaking is as righteous as partaking of the Lord's Supper? Explain your answer.
7. Should every wife expect her husband to be passionate like the Shepherd? What should she do if he isn't?
8. Should every husband expect his wife to be passionate like the Shulammite? What should he do if she isn't?
9. Do you disagree with anything in the lesson? If so, explain giving scriptures for your reasons.

Research Exercise

True Love Versus Sensuous Love Charts: The Shulammite has made her decision about whom to marry. Finish the charts you began in chapter 2 to help you analyze the differences between true love and sensuous love. Write a one to two page summary of what you've learned. Be prepared to share one or two paragraphs with the class.

Remember, the 5 senses plus intellectual, emotional, sexual, and spiritual love equal true love. The 5 senses plus only sexual attraction equal sensuous love.

Family Exercise

If you have teenagers or young adults at home, do this exercise with them. A television special on teenage sex said a boy may ask, "Why?" when a girl tells him, "No," to sex. If the girl stumbles around, it makes him think he can keep pursuing her and maybe she'll give in. The special emphasized a girl needs to have clear reasons in her mind for saying, "No," to protect herself. If she doesn't, some boy may come along with what seems like a good argument, and she'll say, "Yes."

Although the special didn't cover this, a boy also needs clear reasons in his mind for saying, "No." These days a girl is just as likely to try to initiate sex. Boys need clear guidelines for protecting themselves from getting intimately involved with a pushy girl. I personally know several boys who fell for a girl's sexual pass only to discover her agenda was to get pregnant so she could collect child support.

To help both our girls and boys make healthy choices, list the reasons for saying, "No," to premarital or extramarital sex. Create a second list of the reasons for saying, "Yes," i.e., "Everyone is doing it" or "If you love me, you'll prove it." Analyze your pro and con reasons and write a concluding paragraph. Be prepared to share your lists and concluding paragraph in class.

Stacey's Story:
Vaginal Orgasms Make My Eyes Sparkle

Hi Patsy Rae,

Thanks for letting me read your chapter on wet dreams and the laws of cleanness. I agree with what you wrote about vaginal orgasms. God is so good!

Experiencing vaginal orgasms does put a spring in my step and a sparkle in my eyes, not to mention a smile on my face. Since regularly experiencing them, I've had people comment on how good I look when I run into them, and it's more than just a polite comment. They actually seem to step back and take a good look at me as if there's something new that wasn't there before. It's as if they're trying to figure out my secret. It takes me by surprise; and of course, it makes me feel good.

Also, my youngest daughter (who is not yet fourteen) regularly tells me that my eyes sparkle. I guess I never really made the connection until after reading what you wrote. I have found that I cannot help smiling after experiencing a vaginal orgasm. Even the memory of it makes me smile when I think about it.

I am so thankful for the knowledge I've gained from God's Word. It has made me able to speak openly and knowledgeably with my young adult children about all of these things. I am especially thankful to be able to speak openly with my teenage son about wet dreams so he can start out in purity without any unnecessary hang-ups or confusion.

We serve a great God who provides for our every need if we just take the time to seek out His wisdom.

I'm so thankful,
Stacey

Suggestions for Spicing Up Your Marriage

No matter how long a couple has been married, they can improve the intellectual, emotional, sexual, and spiritual intimacy of their relationship if both partners are willing. Here are some suggestions:

1. Attend a Retrouvaille: A Lifeline for Marriages Weekend (HelpOurMarriage.com). "The program offers tools needed to rediscover a loving marriage relationship…. It is for couples with marital problems including those who are considering marriage separation and those who are already separated or divorced that want marriage help."

   I highly recommend this program. You will come away with tremendous skills for communicating on an emotionally intimate level. If every minister and elder went through this program with their wife, not only would it change their marriages, but it would also greatly improve their teaching and counseling of others.

2. Start a yearly habit of attending a marriage retreat to keep your relationship finely tuned and running smoothly. You do this for your cars. Soulmating with your mate is more important and needs some special attention on a regular basis.

Secret 11: Pay Passionate Love Forward

Solomon's Siren Song: Unfinished Business

"Well, Mother…I guess you think you're terribly clever?!" Solomon enters Bathsheba's apartment carrying a gold goblet and sits down on a chaise lounge. "If it hadn't been for you, I would have slaughtered those traitors! That Shulammite! Her Shepherd! And those back-stabbing Virgins! Squashed 'em all into paté!"

"Son, if I weren't clever, you and I would be dead already. Or have you forgotten so soon how I finagled the crown out of your brother's greedy hands?"

"Yeah, I know…. More than anything, she wounded my pride. But when I saw those giggly Virgins leading that Shepherd down the hall…. Then that Shulammite ran to him, snuggling into him with her bountiful *brost* and kissed him…I was infuriated!"

"I know, Son. But I was protecting you and your crown once again. If you'd slaughtered 'em, we'd had an uprising."

"The orgy you arranged for me…. We're still sore after a week…. It was absolutely marvelous! What a coven of crazed vixens! Such creativity! I could never have imagined such a sexual smorgasbord! The little Hebrew gal was especially luscious!"

"Sarah is the one who made it all come together. She's very intelligent."

"I know. I can't manage my affairs without her."

"How about you giving her a wedding week, something nice and relaxed…. Tutor her in what pleases you. Then you might get the high priestess of the prostitutes to mentor her. Make her a superb hostess in charge of all your extreme sexual extravaganzas. She could make you ecstatically happy!"

"Hey! What a great idea! And you're right. Marrying 'em three at a time is the way to go…at least for a while. I might have to up the ante before long!"

"Son, we're going to run out of room to house all those women if you start marrying them by the gross! You need to slow down. Keep the ones you've already got happy so we don't have a revolt on our hands."

"I guess you're right, Mother." Solomon sips his wine.

"What about the Virgins who brought the Shepherd here? You can't trust them now."

"I know. Noam's already packed 'em up and sent 'em home. They're not welcome in my palace anymore! Every time I think about how they betrayed me, it drives me crazy! I can't believe Abby who played her lyre for me so sweetly turned against me like the others!"

"You did right to send them home. If the Shulammite slaughtered their allegiance to you in just three days, think of the shambles she could have turned our palace into. You're lucky she left."

"I guess so.... But I haven't given up on marrying a beautiful virgin from Shunem. I sent Noam to find another one. He knows what I like. I told him to close the deal before he brings her back. I told him to pack up her family and bring them with her. There'll be no more betrayals. I'm done with virgins who need time to think." Solomon walks to the window, then turns and faces his mother.

"When I go to collect the rent for the vineyard from that Shulammite, I'll show off the new Shunem maiden. I'll bedazzle that little village when my new bride's gussied up in the finest royal attire. I might even take her resplendent folks along to rub it in real *gut!*"

Song of Solomon 8:5-14:
The Maiden Answers the Wedding Riddle

ACT TWO, SCENE SEVEN
FOURTH DAY – AFTERNOON

The curtains open to reveal the same backdrop of vineyards dotting the countryside at the beginning of the play. Instead of Solomon's multi-room tent center stage, peasants' one-room mud-brick houses sit in a row beginning center stage and continuing off stage right. A small group of peasants gathers stage right to watch the Shulammite and the Shepherd walk into town, arm in arm. The Maiden still wears the gown and shoes from her ordeal with Solomon.

"Who Is This Leaning on Her Beloved?"

Song of Solomon 8:5a:
"Who is this coming up from the wilderness,
Leaning on her beloved?"

Wilderness refers to the uninhabited area between Jerusalem and the Shulammite's home in Shunem. After the long walk home from

Jerusalem, the couple enters the Shulammite's village. The people come out to see what is going on. Earlier these same country folks witnessed Solomon and his traveling party take the Maiden to Jerusalem to marry the King. Now they can't believe what they see.

They ask, "Who can this possibly be leaning on her beloved? They are so obviously in love." The town folks whisper among themselves, "What could have happened to cause the vineyard keeper to give up Solomon and all his riches? Why is she coming back home? And with the Shepherd? We expected that her mother, brothers, and little sister would soon join her in Jerusalem."

Some of them shake their heads, "What would make any woman give up wealth and prestige to marry a common shepherd? Or maybe Solomon didn't like her...."

Then someone notices, "Look! She doesn't look sad at all. She's radiant! I've never seen her look so beautiful. And she's certainly not bashful about letting us see how much she loves the Shepherd. What could have happened?"

The Secrets of the Song of Solomon Expanded

Her dilemma over, the Maiden understands her mother's lessons about the gazelles and the hinds of the field better than ever. She is eager to share the secrets of love that lasts for a lifetime with anyone who will listen. She stops in the street, turns to the Shepherd, and speaks loud enough for her friends and neighbors to hear.

"I Awoke Your Love Under the Apple Tree"

Song of Solomon 8:5b:
"Beneath the apple tree I awakened you."

"Awakened" is the same word used in the theme of the book quoted for the third time in the previous verse (Song 2:7, 3:5, 8:4). It means "(through the idea of opening the eyes); to wake" (Strong 86). Martin revealed it's the idea of waking from sleep to action.

Three times, the Shulammite told the Virgins what she learned from her mother, "By the gazelles and the hinds of the field, don't force love. Let love grow naturally." Now she expands on the theme.

"Listen up everyone while I tell the Shepherd what I learned in Jerusalem and why I chose to marry him."

Speaking to the Shepherd she says, "Remember how I awoke your love for me under the apple tree?" She lets her arm fall from his to clasp his hand as she turns to face him. Soft brown eyes caress him. "I came to your house often and you came to mine. We spent lots of time together getting to know each other...and our siblings and parents."

She laughs at the sweet memories. "I remember the first time you called me, 'my sister.' We do get along well don't we? We can talk about anything. I dearly love that I can tell you my deepest fears and you won't think less of me. And I can share my faults with you, and you give me such wonderful emotional support instead of rebuking me."

The Shulammite claims she's the one who awakened and nurtured the Shepherd's love for her. She said no to sex and yes to spending time together in each other's homes. Because she was a frequent visitor in the Shepherd's home, she observed firsthand how he grew up in a loving home like her own.

"I Watched to See If Your Parents Love Each Other"

Song of Solomon 8:5c:
"There your mother was in labor with you,
There she was in labor and gave you birth."

Wow! What a different statement from what many American kids today say. Some have been heard remarking, "I wanted to throw up at the thought of my parents having sex."

Contrary to this view, the Shepherd and the Shulammite celebrate their conception and birth. She says to the Shepherd, "I love that old apple tree. Your mother gave birth to you there and all the neighbor women and relatives welcomed you into this world with kisses. I paid attention to how your mother and father talk to each other and how they treat each other. I love the way they tease and flirt. I want the same kind of home for us and our children."

Now the Maiden calls the Shepherd to open his eyes to his love for her and respond with action in a faithful marriage of hearts, souls, and bodies.

"Put Me Like a Seal Over Your Heart"

Song of Solomon 8:6a:
"Put me like a seal over your heart,
Like a seal on your arm."

"Seal" refers to "a signature-ring:--seal, signet" (Strong 38). It comes from a primary root that means "to close up; especially to seal:--make an end, mark, seal (up), stop" (Strong 45).

Sometimes the word "arm" is used for the whole arm including the hand and fingers.

God used the metaphor of a signet ring to show his relationship to different individuals. In Haggai 2:23, he says, "'On that day,' declares the

LORD of hosts, 'I will take you, Zerubbabel, son of Shealtiel, My servant,' declares the LORD, 'and I will make you like a signet ring, for I have chosen you,' declares the LORD of hosts." In Jeremiah 22:24, he says, "'As I live,' declares the LORD, 'even though Coniah the son of Jehoiakim king of Judah were a signet ring on My right hand, yet I would pull you off.'"

The Shulammite brings the Shepherd's hand up and spreads his fingers on top of hers, "Pledge that you will never hide your love from me—that you will make your love as obvious as wearing a signet ring for everyone to see."

Earlier she told him, "If I found you outdoors, I would kiss you. No one would despise me, either" (Song 8:1b). Now she tells him, "Make your love for me apparent, so everyone will know it as if you wore a signet ring with my name carved in it."

"True Love Is as Strong as Death"

Song of Solomon 8:6b:
"For love is as strong as death."

"Love" is the same word all through this section. It is a primary root that means "to have affection for (sexually or otherwise):--(be-) love (-d, -ly, -r), like, friend" (Strong 9).

"Love" is not the same Hebrew word for breast-love. This word is only used eleven times in the Song of Solomon. The Maiden uses this same word the three times she recites the theme to the Virgins, "Do not arouse or awake love until it pleases."

Now that she has awakened the Shepherd's love for her, she speaks to the power and passion of true love. Looking into his eyes, she tells him and the country folks, "Someday you and I are going to die. There's no way we can avoid it. We can choose to love, but we can't choose death; it chooses us. But true love is as strong as death. Because we have awakened each other's love, our love can survive any heartache or disaster life throws at us. And if we live very long, we'll face many challenges together."

"Jealousy Is as Severe as Sheol"

Song of Solomon 8:6c:
"Jealousy is as severe as Sheol;
Its flashes are flashes of fire,
The very flame of the Lord."

"Sheol" refers to destruction in either this life or the life to come. The Shulammite rapid fires strong words to make her point about betraying one's marriage vows—flashes of fire and the very flame of the

Lord — anger that cannot be appeased or stopped.

These three lines appeal to much more than the jealousy the Maiden witnessed among the Queens and Concubines as they jockeyed for Solomon's attention. She appeals to God's jealousy over Israel — its flashes of fire, the very flame of the Lord. A similar passage sheds light on this verse as it shows God's jealousy when Moses tried to lead the Israelites to the Promised Land:

> Deuteronomy 32:21-22: 'They have made Me jealous with what is not God; They have provoked Me to anger with their idols. So I will make them jealous with those who are not a people; I will provoke them to anger with a foolish nation, For a fire is kindled in My anger, And burns to the lowest part of Sheol, And consumes the earth with its yield, And sets on fire the foundations of the mountains."

The verses in Deuteronomy and the Shulammite's words show anger is a godly reaction to unfaithfulness to one's marriage vows. Many times, a person responds to infidelity with hurt feelings. Hurt feelings are worthless for solving problems because they cause us to focus on restoring the relationship instead of eradicating the sin in the home. Taking care of the sin should happen before restoring the relationship.

The Maiden cautions the Shepherd, "I will honor our marriage vows and keep myself pure for you. But I won't put up with infidelity. God's example in the wilderness with Moses shows how God handles betrayal with anger."

She takes both of the Shepherd's hands and brings them to her lips. "My mother taught me well about the rewards of a husband and a wife, if they keep themselves pure for each other. To enjoy wonderful orgasms of love we must truly trust each other and valiantly surrender our passions. I love you, but our marriage won't survive infidelity."

"We Can't Destroy True Love"

Song of Solomon 8:7:
"Many waters cannot quench love,
Nor will rivers overflow it."

Although this seems like a long speech, it's not any longer than most wedding ceremonies. Indeed, it's the Shulammite's pledge from her heart to the Shepherd. She tells her beloved, "Many waters cannot quench my love, nor will floods drown it. My love for you will only grow in the coming years. My love can stand the test of time, the good and the bad, until death do we part."

The POWs who came back after up to nine years of imprisonment in Vietnam demonstrate the strength of true love. Some men came home to the loving arms and tender sympathy of their wife who truly loved them and who remained faithful during their ordeal. Sadly, other men came back to find their wife had divorced them and started new families. Powerful enough to withstand pounding rains and raging floods, true love weathers the tortuous tests of life and marriage.

"We Can't Buy True Love"

Song of Solomon 8:7:
"If a man were to give all the riches of his house for love
It would be utterly despised."

The Shulammite laughs and says, "Wow! Did I ever learn from Solomon that we can't buy love! He offered my mother and me an expensive dowry. It would have made such a difference in our lives. Everything would be easier. But I saw firsthand how empty he is and how void of love his palace is."

Growing serious, she continues, "O my beloved, if I'd married Solomon, I would have given up a lifetime of passionate lovemaking for what? For money? How can money compare to the love we share?"

Her eyes moisten, "I have so much love for you, and it overflows to make me want children to share our love. I so want children. Solomon didn't love me. How could he? He didn't even know me. What kind of father would he have been?"

Then she takes the Shepherd's arm once again, "I dreamed about you the last night in the palace. I realized if I gave away my love for Solomon's riches, I would grow to despise them. And you know...Solomon seemed to utterly despise all his wives. He didn't have the kind of love we have...or that our parents have. He introduced me to his wives right before you came. They all wore expensive dowry jewelry on their head gear. He had bought them all! But not a single one made him happy.... He told me I would be his last and best wife, but I knew better when I saw his harem."

Tugging on his arm, she says, "Take me home, my beloved.... I want to thank Mama for the lesson she taught me over and over since I was a little girl about the gazelles and the hinds of the field."

The curtains close.

ACT THREE, SCENE ONE
FOUR MONTHS LATER — LATE AFTERNOON

When the curtains open, a wedding festival is taking place in a well-kept garden of fruit trees and herbs (Song 8:13). The audience still sees the same backdrop of vineyards dotting the countryside. Wine pots and serving pottery from an earlier banquet sit on a table stage right. Center stage sits the Shulammite dressed in typical wedding finery. The Shepherd is nearby and wears his wedding garments which include a silken girdle. Seated around them are the guests wearing wedding attire.

The Harvest Is Over and It's Time to Get Married

An obvious time change highlights the importance of this event. When the Shulammite left with Solomon, the grapevines were just beginning to bud. When she returned to the country with the Shepherd, the blossoms were still just starting to open. Now the story ends after the grapes are harvested and sold which creates a gap of three to four months—the normal time (depending on the weather) it takes for the blossoms to turn into ripened grapes.

When the Shulammite and the Shepherd returned home from Jerusalem her brothers were still working on Solomon's building projects. They came home for two months, then left again for another month—right when the grape harvesting needed to start. The Shulammite oversaw the care of the vineyards at the two most critical times—when the vines were in bloom and when the grapes were harvested. Finally her brothers come home for two months before the cycle starts all over again. With the grapes harvested and her brothers home the Shulammite and the Shepherd's wedding day has arrived.

What the Shulammite and Her Family
Learned from Hindsight

With turning 70 years old this fall, I'm convinced the primary way God expects us to learn is from hindsight. He allows us to be tested in various ways. Then he expects us to meditate on our life and figure out what we could have done better, so we can do differently in the future. The past illuminates the present and the future. Since it has been twenty years since I updated my Song of Solomon chapters, I've been pleasantly surprised at how much hindsight has increased my insights as I've studied the scriptures anew. That is especially true with the Shulammite's conclusion.

The Song of Solomon didn't end with her pledge of undying love for the Shepherd and them living happily ever after as we know they did (Song 8:7). Instead, verse 8 continues with what authors call an epilogue, playwrights call ACT THREE, and inspirational writers call the take away. It's the most important part of the story.

Solomon taking the young vineyard keeper to Jerusalem and her coming back with the Shepherd was a news-breaking event in Shunem. For the last four months the Shulammite, the Shepherd, her family, and the town folks have talked about little else. They've drawn some powerful conclusions. Now at her wedding, they are ready to share their hindsight. It's God's grand finale.

Her Brothers Ask a Wedding Riddle

Song of Solomon 8:8:
"We have a little sister,
And she has no breasts;
What shall we do for our sister
On the day when she is spoken for?"

Israelite weddings were very festive affairs. The Shulammite and the Shepherd's wedding was no exception. Dr. William Smith explains:

> The inhabitants of the place pressed out into the streets to watch the procession (Cant. iii.11). At the house a feast was prepared, to which all the friends and neighbors were invited (Gen. xxix.22; Matt. xxii.1-10; Luke xiv.8; John ii.2), and the festivities were protracted for seven, or even fourteen days (Judg. xxii.11), and the feast was enlivened with riddles (Judg. xiv.12) and other amusements (382-3).

The Bible reveals that Israelite brothers were usually very protective of their sisters' chastity and honor (Genesis 34; 2 Samuel 13:22-33). The Shulammite's brothers are no different. They use the custom of asking a wedding riddle to show how seriously they take their responsibility to protect their sisters.

Her oldest brother says what's been on everyone's mind, "Hey! Sweet Missy, we're thrilled you're marrying the Shepherd. But you're leaving home and our baby sister is growing up way too fast. Right now, little Raizel doesn't care anything about boys. But one day her hormones will start to develop her *brosts* and she'll start thinking about boys."

Her middle brother chimes in, "Yeah, Sis. We want to know, how can we protect Raizel from making a terrible mistake...like you almost did?"

While teaching a class, a preacher told how boys flatter girls and tell them they're beautiful. A little girl who had no breasts was sitting with her father. She turned to him and said, "If a boy ever tells me I'm beautiful, I'm going to slap him!" Of course, when puberty hits this little girl's attitude toward compliments from boys will completely change. How can her parents protect her when the change takes place?

That is what her brothers and the wedding guests want to know. It's what all parents need to know. Then the brothers answer their own question to see if the Shulammite agrees. After all, she made the choice between sensuous lust and true love. They value her opinion.

If Our Little Sister Can Say, "No"

Song of Solomon 8:9a:
"If she is a wall,
We shall build on her a battlement of silver."

A "wall" symbolizes security because the walls around a city keep the enemy out. A "battlement," a parapet built on top of the wall, protects the soldiers who guard the wall. The battlement usually contains small openings for the soldiers to see through or to fight. Sometimes it serves mainly as decoration for the wall. In addition, lattice-type battlements adorn the tops of the flat-roofed houses as protection against falling off the roof.

The Shulammite's youngest brother Mark offers an answer to see if they've figured out the answer to the riddle. "If Raizel is a wall, if she can say, 'No,' to boys who want to have sex, we should build on her a battlement of silver."

"In other words," her oldest brother says, "We need to teach her like Mama did you. We need to show her the gazelles and the hinds during mating season. The cows and the sheep, too. Every chance we get, we need to talk to her about being as smart as the animals. Being fellows, we can tell her how important building an emotional bond is to a man before he marries. A woman holds the key to make it all happen."

Mark adds. "We won't let her run all over the village. We'll know where she is and who she's with. We'll give her only the amount of freedom she can handle."

Her middle brother says, "We've thought about this ever since you came home from Jerusalem and we learned what Solomon tried to do. A battlement of silver conveys just how precious Raizel is to us. She can still do things, but we won't give her privileges she can't handle."

"Yes, brother dears," the Shulammite replies. "Teach her like Mama did me. Before the soldiers took me away, Mama whispered in my ear, 'Remember about the gazelles and hinds of the field.'" The Maiden laughs, "She made me repeat the lesson to her every chance she got since I was younger than Raizel. I was starting to get sick of it." She laughs again, "But Solomon's Virgins were so smitten with him they thought I should be thrilled to enter his harem. I was glad I'd heard and seen the lesson so many times of the beautiful does when the stags came a calling. It was second nature to me. Not once did I have to stop and think, 'What should I do now?' I'm sure those Virgins got tired of me telling them I wouldn't marry Solomon until we fell in love."

She grows somber, "And Mama also whispered, 'Take time to

think.' Every time I told Solomon I needed time to think, he said, "Okay," but I don't think he was happy about it. I think he expected us to get married soon after he introduced me to his wives."

Her oldest brother wraps his arm around her shoulder and looks at their mother as he says, "No doubt about it, Mama built a beautiful silver battlement around you. It's what we need to do for Raizel…. And we all want to have the same kind of marriage Mama and Dad enjoyed…. Now Mark is ready to ask you the second part of the riddle."

If Our Little Sister Can't Say, "No"

Song of Solomon 8:9b:
"But if she is a door,
We shall barricade her with planks of cedar."

By providing entrance into something, a "door" represents a gullible, naive girl who remains open to all the boys' suggestions. The Israelites considered the doors the weakest part of their defense. As a result, they used strong bars of wood or bronze to secure the whole gate by passing them transversely into sockets in the gateposts.

Mark smiles at her. "Okay, Missy, here's the second part. If Raizel is like a door, if she can't say, 'No,' then we'll barricade her with planks—"

"OF CEDAR!" Her middle brother interrupts. "And if there's one thing her brothers know how to do, it's how to cut down cedar trees and saw them into planks. We can build a barricade of cedar around her like you never saw before!"

All the guests laugh at his pun.

"What we want to know," her oldest brother sums it up, "is do we treat Raizel one way if she's a wall and another way if she's a door? In other words, Missy, just because you were a wall and able to handle Solomon, it doesn't mean your baby sister won't be a door. We don't know if she'll go totally boy crazy when the time comes."

The Shulammite Could Say, "No"

Song of Solomon 8:10a:
"I was a wall, and my breasts were like towers."

"Yes, brother dears, you've learned the same thing from this experience I have. I feel so sorry for all those Virgins who can't wait for their turn to become one of Solomon's wives. They have no idea what they're missing. I want something much better out of life."

She turns to her oldest brother, "You're right, I was a wall. And my *brosts* were like knockers."

The guests gasp and the men burst out laughing when the Maiden turns bright red.

"Oops!"

The women join in the laughter. An embarrassed Missy continues, "That's what that slum dog Solomon called 'em. He couldn't take his eyes off my *brosts,* and it's all he talked about. That's not the worst he said, but that's the worst I'm going to tell you...."

She sighs, "The point is, I've become a woman. I'm more than ready for love. I was starting to dream about being married to my Shepherd." All the women nod knowingly as she smiles at her beloved.

Then looking at her mother, she continues, "I had more than just a battlement of silver around me from Mama and Dad's example and Mama talking to me so plainly about sex and pleasing a husband...." She shakes her head yes and whispers, "Thanks again, Mama. I love you."

Looking back at her brothers, she continues, "But I had towers built on my battlement for extra protection. I thought a lot about marriage and what I wanted." Her eyes mist, "Especially after Dad died. I was determined not to settle for anything less than what Mama and Dad enjoyed." Her voice stronger, "I was fortified to protect my body from unwanted advances...even when they came from the King."

Biological Breasts Versus the Seat of Love

The Shulammite uses two different words for breasts. She uses breasts as the seat of a woman's love when she tells the Shepherd she will give her "love" or "breasts" to him after marriage (Song 7:12). She had thought well about the role her breasts would play in expressing love in marriage.

But her brothers use the biological term for the wedding riddle and the Shulammite uses it for her answer. They refer to the shape (bulging) and function (nursing) of a woman's breasts. Using the biological term for Raizel's and the Shulammite's breasts shows their development in puberty.

In contrast, Solomon used only the biological term for breasts—he never described them as expressions of love. Even though he eloquently used poetic words, he viewed a woman's breasts as a toy or a play thing. The sight of luscious breasts fired up his lusts—his fetish.

Breasts Are Part of a Woman's Virginity

Moreover, the Bible clearly views a woman's breasts as part of her virginity—to be saved for her husband in marriage. Ezekiel stated this:

Ezekiel 23:3: "And they played the harlot in Egypt. They played the harlot in their youth; their breasts [biological term—Strong] were pressed, and there their virgin bosom [seat of love – Strong] was handled."

Even if a man touches a woman's breasts outside of marriage because they love each other and plan to marry, it still violates her virginity. Thus the Shulammite built towers on her battlement by saving her breasts for marriage. She looked forward to the Shepherd caressing her at the beginning of the story and the end (Song 2:6; 8:3).

As a girl thinks about keeping her body 100% virginal for her husband-to-be, one of the nicest memories she can cherish is the first time he caresses her breasts. It's a wonderful memory to remind him of occasionally. If a man has touched lots of girls' breasts, his wife won't get the thrill of providing his first experience. Likewise, if many boys have explored a girl's breasts, she won't enjoy the same reaction to her husband's first touch as a virgin would.

The Shulammite Finds Peace

Song of Solomon 8:10b:
"Then I became in his eyes as one who finds peace."

"Peace" (*shâlôm*) means "safe, i.e. (figuratively) well, happy, friendly; also (abstractly) welfare, i.e. health, prosperity, peace" (Strong 116).

"You know, brother dears, I worry about Raizel, too. Look at her over there playing with the other children. She doesn't have a clue about how complicated life will get when she starts developing breasts."

The Shulammite sighs deeply. "The last night in the palace I went to the garden...TO THINK...Mama," she laughs. "I prayed to God and asked him to help me make the right decision. I laid my soul bare and asked his north wind and south wind to swirl around me. I told him I wanted to be a good wife and enjoy everything marriage offers a woman. Ohhhh, I felt his peace deep within my soul. And the happiness I feel today is so much greater than I ever imagined. I'm ready to enjoy all the amenities of being a wife." Love sparkles in her eyes as she gazes upon the Shepherd.

Saying, "No," doesn't mean a girl misses all the fun in life. A lifetime lasts much longer than the few courting years spent battling the temptations to join the crowd. Each time a girl says, "No," she makes a wise investment in her future happiness.

Secret 11: Pay Passionate Love Forward

I used to think the Song of Solomon was preserved to teach teenagers how to choose a mate. And it is. But that's the secondary purpose. It's primarily for us as their parents and grandparents to teach us the proper kind of home in which God expects us to rear our children. Because of Victorian morals and the sexual revolution—we often don't know how to foster a loving family.

Chapter 8 of the Song of Solomon addresses what we can learn from the Shulammite's and her family's hindsight and our own. It's to teach us how to help our children enjoy a wonderful life after they leave our home. It's the wisdom of the ages. We just have to open our hearts to God for our families to reap his bountiful blessings and rewards.

1. Build a Battlement of Silver on Our Girls and Boys

The battlement of silver is the foundation of a healthy marriage and sexual life that extends from a couple to their children and grandchildren. God said, "Indeed, may you see your children's children" (Psalms 128:6a). Life doesn't get any better than that. The Song of Solomon contains two elements for this foundation to support ones children. The first is creating a loving home for them to grow up in. The second is helping them learn about lovemaking from two experts—Mom and Dad—through the Song of Solomon.

Provide a Loving Home

God created the way of man with a maid as his proudest creation. Then he says the fruit of their wonderful union of love is both a gift and a reward from him (Psalms 127:3-5). Our children deserve to be raised as a gift and a reward from the Lord—in a home where Mom and Dad's love for each other brims over onto their children.

Throughout this book, we've seen how Solomon was an intimacy anorexic without natural love for anyone. We've read the Shulammite's and the Shepherd's pledges to each other. Their healthy attitudes toward love and sex stir our hearts to rejoice with them and exclaim, "I want the same for my own marriage as well as for my children's."

Stacey's story at the end of this chapter shows the difference it makes in a home when Mom and Dad know how to love each other. Likewise, Charla Muller's story reveals the effect of frequent lovemaking on children (review "Secret 5: Sip the Divine Wine of Passion"). People often talk to me about how their children don't want to have much to do with them after they leave home. I always ask, "Was there abuse or emotional neglect in your family when they were growing up?" Every time, the answer is "Yes."

Often one parent tries to compensate for the unloving, sometimes cruel, parent. But unloving mates don't try as hard to fool their children as they do to keep the mate in denial about their being without natural affection. Children often see the abuse better than the victimized parent does. They frequently suffer tremendously from being love starved.

I've made this point many times throughout this study. I don't want to belabor it here. I simply want to remind you that the Song of Solomon closes by praising the Shulammite's and the Shepherd's mothers with teaching them about love from their inception. The greatest asset this couple brings to their marriage is the fact that they both grew up in loving homes with parents who loved each other intellectually, emotionally, sexually, and spiritually.

If you are trying to survive marriage to an intimacy anorexic, then step back from your pain. Look at your children's pain. Look at their school pictures. Do you see sadness in their eyes? Now look at their person. What do their eyes tell you? Don't live in denial about what is happening to your children because your mate chooses to be unloving.

If you deny your mate's sin of being without natural love for family, you condemn your children to a lifelong struggle to live a normal happy life. They either learn to be enablers from your example and marry an intimacy anorexic like you. Or they become like your unloving mate and Solomon, hollow on the inside without normal emotions and the inability to truly love others. They don't know how to love their mate nor their children. Many become atheists and skeptics.

Your children are worth fighting for. They have their whole life ahead of them. If you don't fight for them while they are still living at home, they will suffer from your neglect for the rest of their life.

God doesn't trap anyone in marriage to a person without natural affection. Read Stacey's story at the end of this chapter, then go back and study chapters 6 and 8. You have your work cut out for you. But your children are worth your efforts. And so are you.

Teach the Song of Solomon

The Song of Solomon is God's answer to sex-education in the schools. The beautiful poetic language permits parents to use it to teach their children about sexual love at each stage of their development. For example, parents can teach the drama of the story to very young children. They can tell them a true story about a young farmer's daughter who loved the Shepherd. Then one day the rich and powerful King came and took her to his palace. He wanted to marry her but she still loved the Shepherd. And on the story goes catching the interest of young children and teaching them age-appropriate lessons of true love.

Guides children as they mature. The poetic form allows the parents to insert more details. When the children ask questions about lovemaking, the parents can use the Song of Solomon to supply the answers. This helps the parents protect their children from bad choices when they begin their search for romantic love. In addition, the story protects students when they must attend sex-education classes that teach biology devoid of the role that the mind and emotions play in true love.

Thus God's wondrous preservation of the Song of Solomon is for parents to use with their children regardless of their age. Sex-education classes in the schools can't begin to compare with such a marvelous book! And studying the book together helps parents and teenagers establish a forum for talking about sex without embarrassing each other.

Guides teenagers through their dating years. The Shulammite was probably about 13. The Israelites married earlier then than we do now. They considered an unmarried 16-year-old girl an old maid.

Jahnna Beecham's *Writer's Digest* article about writing for teenagers demonstrates the attraction for teenagers God packed into this book. She advised to never forget that young adults are "emotions, emotions, emotions." She attributed the ups and downs of teenage emotions to "hormones going wild" (4/90).

God inspired the writing of the Song of Solomon in the form of poetry and dialogue which impacts the emotions and speaks directly to teenagers. During courtship emotions and hormones rage which can cause young lovers to act irrationally rather than logically. By appealing to the 5 senses and emotions, the story captures the intellect and makes readers think in a different way.

Another writing technique Beecham advocated was to let the story get into the head of the young adult and deal with her or his inner fears and thoughts. Part of adolescence is continual self-examination and self-criticism. She described this as the "monster critic" who is always second guessing the teen with, "You should have...." or "You shouldn't have...." or "Everyone will notice your..." (4/90).

That God knows teenagers and their self-doubts is easily seen in the Shulammite's self-consciousness about her appearance since she is burned by the sun. But she displays a healthy self-image and stands up for herself when the Virgins look aghast at her (Song 1:5-6). The whole book is mainly about the Shulammite's conversations with herself as she tries to decide whom to marry.

When children learn the Song of Solomon at an early age, it speaks directly to them and helps them analyze their dates. A girl asks herself, "Is he like Solomon or the Shepherd? Do I really love him or is this just hormones affecting me?" A boy wants to know, "Does she have the qualities of a good wife? Do I really love her, or do I just want her body?" In this way the book helps teenagers successfully cross the bridges from parental love to romantic love and finally to married love.

Teaching the Song of Solomon to young girls. When my daughter was 11 years old, I taught the Song of Solomon in a ladies' class. Afterward I approached all the mothers who had daughters 11 to 13 and asked if they would like their daughter to attend an age-appropriate class on the Song of Solomon. Only one mother thought her daughter was too young.

Eight young girls took the class. We sat around a large table with our Bibles open. I covered one chapter in the Bible each week. I just taught them the story. I concentrated on helping them understand the scriptures and the young Shulammite's emotions and what the experience must have felt like to her. We had no need to go into the lewd innuendos of Solomon's proposals. You can imagine the fun we had discussing his descriptions of her body. The only discussion about sex was saying things such as, "Solomon didn't care about the Maiden as a person. All he wanted was her body."

One mother said, "My daughter loves your class. And because you've already taught it to us, I'm able to discuss it with her. Thank you so much for teaching this to the girls. I will always be grateful that we can now talk about this important subject."

Teaching the Song of Solomon to teenage girls. I had the opportunity to teach the Song of Solomon at two other congregations when my daughter was 14 and 16. I taught the material for "Teenagers, Their Mothers, and Grandmothers — For Ages 11-99." The ladies all had my books *God's People Make the Best Lovers* and *God's People Appreciate Marriage.* Some of the details about orgasms and lovemaking that I include in this book, I assigned to be read outside class.

The first thing I noticed was the difference in the body language of the teenage girls from the preteens. The teenagers leaned back in their seats with their arms folded. They looked at me like, "The only reason I'm here is because my mother made me come. I already know about boys. You're not going to teach me anything." But the preteens were soaking up the material, just like in my earlier class.

I spent significant time talking about abusive boyfriends and sweetheart murders. The teenage girl whose body language was the most hostile about having to come to the classes became teary eyed, leaned forward, and put her hands in her lap. I knew something about her boyfriend and was concerned. Several days later I told her mother, "I don't know if she's in an abusive relationship, but you need to find out."

As a result of watching how these older worldly-wise teenage girls responded to the Song of Solomon, I now encourage congregations and parents to start teaching their daughters as preteens while they're the most receptive and looking forward to dating.

Teaching the Song of Solomon to boys. A mother listened to the cassette tapes of the third time I taught the Song of Solomon with her children on a car trip. Afterward one of her sons asked to keep the tapes in his room. Several years later he asked me for the documentation to the class on sex education in the schools to use in writing a high school English report on arguing effectively. The teacher was so impressed with his report that she asked to listen to the series. Years later he and his bride-to-be planned their wedding around the beautiful poetry and concepts in this true love story. I published the documentation *Safe Sex: What They Don't Tell You* at SongOfSolomonLoveTriangle.com in the Book Shelf.

A teenage boy emailed me, "i'm agd 16. a friend of my grandfather recommended the dawson book [*Safe Sex*] to me to help fight against sexual/genital temptation. at the moment i'm using lots of devotions/prayer/scripture to make sure i overcome inappropriate, selfish, sinful desires : wanting to gratify bodily lusts (re. kissing girls, masturbation etc) – so it was good, chastening discipline for me to see God's Word on sexual morality spelt out so plainly and clearly. thanks."

One of my greatest regrets is I didn't teach my son the Song of Solomon like I did my daughter. A lot of churches have scruples against women teaching boys after a certain age. The fact that the Song of Solomon is the words and thoughts of a woman to teach the world about love and sex questions the soundness of their doctrine. At any rate, I could have taught my son and his friends in our home, especially when I was unable to get any men to teach the boys.

2. Build Planks of Cedar on Our Girls and Boys

It doesn't matter what older siblings got to do on dates. It doesn't matter about anything big sister and big brother did. What matters is how much responsibility little sister and little brother are ready to accept—are they a wall or a door?

The parents should look at each child individually. Where they see weaknesses, they must build reinforcements—battlements of silver and planks of cedar—whatever it takes to protect their children from sexual harm. Wise parents either grant or deny privileges for each child on the basis of their personal maturity.

Both girls and boys need their parents' protection because when sexually excited, people do many foolish things. A joke writer compared irrational sexual desires to the man who jumped off a ten-story building. As he went by each floor he said, "All is going fine so far."

Protect from Sexual Addiction

Our youth are in crisis. When taught frank material about sexual addiction, high-school boys often ask, "Why didn't someone tell us these things when we were in junior high before we developed bad habits that require lots of work to overcome?" This question was often asked of Oscar Miles, a teaching and counseling minister who frequently taught at teen retreats. His surveys show:

9-10th graders (age 14-16)
20% Never viewed Internet porn
33% Viewed on accident
47% Viewed on purpose
20% Still viewing occasionally or somewhat regularly
13% Admitted viewing homosexual porn on the Internet

11-12th graders (age 16-19)
100% Viewed Internet porn ON PURPOSE
67% Still viewing occasionally or somewhat regularly
22% Viewing it "somewhat regularly"
22% Admitted to viewing homosexual porn
11% Admitted to having interest in homosexual porn

The damage done by instant Internet porn is much worse than any of us can imagine. The proliferation of cell phones and tablets provides the opportunity for young people to carry the dancing graphics with them everywhere.

Protect from Incest and Pedophilia

Our body is racing toward maturity from the time we're born preparing us for mating and reproducing. The emotional part is what we need to learn. That's why I tell people, "If you take care of your attitudes, your body will take care of itself." Our body is programmed for proliferation. Adding emotional bonding to sex transports the mechanical aspects into another realm of ecstatic pleasure.

The most powerful tool a pedophile or rapist has to trap our children in an abusive sexual relationship is to take advantage of the body's innate ability to respond sexually. Most pedophiles and incestuous family members spend time giving the child pleasure before seeking their own. This way they can tell the child, "See! You liked that didn't you! If you tell anyone, I'll tell them you liked it as much as I did." They deceive the child and insure his or her silence. They also justify their vile actions in their own warped thinking.

Alfred Kinsey interviewed dozens of pedophiles. He misinterpreted the seeming pleasure the children got from being sexually stimulated by abusers. He was totally ignorant of the way the body of a child, and even an adult, can be made to respond by a skillful manipulator without the person's consent. In effect, their body betrays them. Unfortunately, many of these children suffer from tremendous guilt for the rest of their lives falsely believing they must be an evil person because their body responded with pleasure to rape and sexual abuse.

Fred Littauer and Cecil Murphey, both abused as children, warn about the dangers and offer recovery hope for other victims. Littauer says many sexually frustrated Christians don't view molesting their own sons and daughters as a sin. They seem to think taking advantage of their family protects them from sin. See Cecil Murphey's book *When a Man You Love Was Abused, A Woman's Guide to Helping Him Overcome Childhood Sexual Molestation*. Fred Littauer's books are out of print, but you can sometimes find used copies. Look for *Freeing Your Mind From Memories that Bind, How to Heal the Hurts of the Past*.

Fathers, mothers, and siblings can be sexual deviates, as well as can be church leaders and workers. And sometimes they molest a child of their own sex. We need to teach our children not only that there's good touching and bad touching, but also, "Sometimes bad touching feels good." We must help them feel safe to confide in us. And if we see sadness in our children's eyes, we need to open our eyes and start investigating to find out the source. This problem cuts across all religions, economic groups, genders, and ages.

The Shulammite's Obligations to Solomon

Song of Solomon 8:11a:
"Solomon had a vineyard at Baal-hamon;
He entrusted the vineyard to caretakers"

Her Joke on Solomon

"Vines" and "vineyards" (*kerem*) are translated vineyard (singular) four times and vineyards (plural) five times. The Maiden uses the singular twice to refer to her body, her person (Song 1:6; 8:12). She uses the plural form once to refer to the Shepherd (Song 1:14).

She also uses the singular twice in this passage to describe Solomon's vineyard at Baal-hamon. When the King told the Queens and Concubines he met the Maiden when he went down to the orchard of nut trees to see if the vine (singular) had budded, he used a different Hebrew word (*gephen*) (Song 6:11). *Gephen* is used three other times by Solomon, the Maiden, and the Shepherd (Song 2:13; 7:8, 12).

In contrast to Solomon's singular vineyard at Baal-hamon, each time the Shulammite talked about her work as an overseer, she spoke of plural vineyards (Song 1:6; 2:15; 7:12). Thus the Shulammite takes care of a multitude of vineyards, one of which her family leases from Solomon.

All the commentators I consulted about Baal-hamon say they don't know where it was and some offer guesses. The explanation most consistent with the story and the Shulammite's personality comes from Professor for the Old Testament Ellen F. Davis who sees humor in the expression:

> Solomon is the butt of [her] jibe. We know of no real place named Baal-hamon, but the name itself makes the desired point. It means "master/husband of a multitude" or alternately, "owner of a lot [of wealth]." The Song throughout emphasizes the unique value of "the one" [the Shulammite].... Therefore this name mocks Solomon as the poor rich man, whose silver and gold are only a foil to show up the superior wealth of love.... Wisdom and real happiness lie in shunning too much wealth, too many lovers, and treasuring what is "my very own" (301).

The Maiden doesn't address these two lines to Solomon, but to the wedding guests. It's easy to visualize the Maiden, the Shepherd, and her brothers making Solomon the brunt of a family joke with a pun for the nickname of the vineyard they lease from him. Farmers often name different parcels of land. Indeed, the joke is on Solomon, the poor rich gentleman farmer who never understands that his money can't buy love.

Her Entrepreneurial Duties

Song of Solomon 8:11b-12:
Each one was to bring a thousand shekels of silver for its fruit.
My very own vineyard is at my disposal;
The thousand shekels are for you, Solomon,
And two hundred are for those who take care of its fruit."

The young Shulammite did an excellent job of overseeing the vineyard her family leases from Solomon. But before she pays him, she makes sure he knows where he stands with her. Looking him in the eye, she says, "Solomon, my very own vineyard is at my disposal—I control my body and who I give it to in love. And today I'm giving my body to my Shepherd. I am my beloved's, and his desire is for me."

Then handing him a thousand shekels of silver, she continues, "This is everything I owe you—payment in full—one thousand shekels of silver for the fruit." She turns to the harvest crew and says, "Two hundred shekels are for your labors in the vineyard."

Since her family rents the land from Solomon, she may have felt pressured not to anger him. He could void the family's lease. Instead of winning the lottery, they could lose an important source of income. The young entrepreneur shows clear thinking about peer and financial pressure. She refuses to sleep with the boss to advance her career.

What does her statement say about a girl who thinks she owes her date a good-night kiss or more because he paid for their movie and dinner? What does it say about a boy who expects sexual rewards for taking a girl out? Every girl has the right to protect her virginity as her own private property, regardless of how prestigious or how high up the corporate ladder her boss is or what he expects.

The 13-year-old Maiden has just handled a major financial transaction with the most powerful man in the world—King Solomon. What does this say about the stereotypes of many religions that assume the man takes care of all financial transactions? Many argue, "But she was a single woman. When she marries, she must turn over all control to her husband without question."

The book of Proverbs dates to about the same time as the Song of Solomon. It ends with the woman of great price's husband praising her as an example for young women such as the Shulammite. Her husband was respected as an elder who passed judgment at the gates of the city. An excellent homemaker and an entrepreneur, she manufactured garments and sold them in the marketplace. She earned enough to invest in land (Proverbs 31:10-31). Both the Shulammite and the woman of great price set a high standard for women today to imitate.

ACT THREE, SCENE TWO
FOUR MONTHS LATER — EARLY EVENING

Still in the garden, the Shulammite and the Shepherd sit center stage facing each other. The male witnesses stand behind them waiting to hear the Shulammite agree to become the Shepherd's wife.

The Shulammite's and the Shepherd's Wedding Vows

Modern marriages conclude with saying, "I do," after the couple pledges lasting love. Then they are pronounced husband and wife. The Israelites enjoyed a similar custom with witnesses of the vows:

> The bridegroom now entered into direct communication with the bride, and the joy of the friend was "fulfilled" at hearing the voice of the bridegroom (John iii.29) conversing with her, which he regarded as a satisfactory testimony of the success of his share in the work. The last act in the ceremony was conducting the bride to the bridal chamber (Judg. xv.1; Joel ii.16), where a canopy was prepared (Ps. xix.5; Joel ii.16) (Smith 383).

It's time for the Shulammite and the Shepherd to say their wedding vows. True to custom, the Shepherd speaks first:

The Shepherd's Call

Song of Solomon 8:13:
"O you who sit in the gardens,
My companions are listening for your voice –
Let me hear it!"

The Shepherd is eager to claim his bride. No doubt, his eyes dance with happiness. He calls to his chosen Maiden and is anxious for his companions, the witnesses to their marriage, to hear her intentions.

The Shulammite's Answer

Song of Solomon 8:14:
"Hurry, my beloved,
And be like a gazelle or a young stag
On the mountains of spices [balsam odors]."

She replies, "Hurry, my beloved! My heart has already reserved my body for you. Come! Enjoy the ravishment of all my love I've saved for you." She concludes, "Be like a gazelle or a young stag on the mountain of spices." She begs him to be a man like these male animals. She's ready to experience his prowess in loving her intellectually, emotionally, sexually, and spiritually — the true mark of masculinity.

The Shepherd's virginity pledge ends very differently from the 15 young evangelical Christian men in the virginity-pledge study. They didn't have a clue about how to love a woman. They were naive enough to believe they now had a wife to boss.

The Song of Solomon begins and ends with a woman's desires. Her plans for a spring wedding were thwarted by the King drafting her brothers and then taking her to his tent (Song 1:1-4). Now she has come full circle in the realization of those desires being satisfied with her true love. "Hurry, my beloved!" she says. "And show me the way of a man with a maid on the mountains of balsam."

God inspired this wonderful true love story for us so we can learn from it and use it to teach others, especially our children. Dear Lord, thank you for your love of passionate sex and for teaching us about *SPEAKING YOUR BEAUTIFUL LANGUAGE OF LOVE* that transcends human words. To God be the glory forever and ever. Amen.

Study Exercise

Answer all questions in your own words.
1. Why were her neighbors and friends curious about why the Shulammite was coming home with the Shepherd?

2. How did the Shulammite awake the Shepherd's love for her?
3. What kind of love is as strong as death? Why?
4. What did God do when Israel betrayed him? What does God's reaction tell us about how we should combat infidelity?
5. Why can't a man buy love?
6. List three ways to protect boys and girls who are a wall.
7. List three ways to protect boys and girls who are a door.
8. What should a person do if they are married to an unloving person? Why?
9. Do you disagree with anything in the lesson? If so, explain giving scriptures for your reasons.

Personal Exercise

Answer the following questions about your home of origin.

If you're single, answer the questions for both yourself and all your dates. Start learning to discuss your homes of origin in courtship.

If you're married and have children, answer the questions again as your children would about you.

Finally, write a two-page paper on how the home a person grew up in affects who they marry and what kind of parent they become.

1. How did your parents solve problems?
2. Did they scream at each other or talk calmly about problems?
3. Did you see your parents hug and kiss often?
4. Were your parents playful with each other?
5. Did your parents tell you they loved you?
6. Did they ridicule you and put you down? About what?
7. Did they scream at you? About what?
8. Did you want to leave home as soon as possible?
9. Did you have a loving relationship with your siblings or did you fuss and fight frequently?
10. Were you forbidden to talk about what went on in your home?
11. Do you hug and kiss your parents and tell them you love them?
12. Have you moved across the country to get away from your parents?
13. Were you happy growing up?
14. Have you repressed memories of your home life? If so, why do you think you did that?
15. What have you learned about your home of origin from this exercise?
16. If most of your answers to these questions are negative, what can you do to overcome growing up in a dysfunctional home?
17. If most of your answers for your children are negative, what can you do to help them overcome growing up in a dysfunctional home?

Personal Exercise

Examine your home of origin and how your parents taught you about sex further by going through the free *Sexless Marriages Self-Assessment Survey* at PatsyRaeDawson.com. The checklists of intensely personal simple questions help you evaluate the true state of your upbringing and your relationship so you can make healthy, loving decisions. When you complete the last checklist, you'll receive a free report with suggestions on how to deal with a lack of love in your marriage and home. Everyone in the family suffers, especially the children, when one parent doesn't know how to love the other.

Stacey's Story:
I Can't Believe Our Happiness

Hello Patsy Rae,

Well, here it is 2015 and I am truly humbled and amazed at where the Lord has brought me over the last several years. You asked me to give you an update at how we're doing. As I re-read the letters I sent to you (back in 2007 and 2008 I believe), looking back at where we've been overwhelmed me a bit, to say the least. It was a little hard to believe that I was reading about *my* life. We tend to get so caught up in our day to day living that we can so easily forget where God has brought us.

Where to begin? I must start by giving all the glory and honor to the Lord for all He has done and continues to do, for loving me enough to allow these trials in my life in order to make me the woman He created me to be, and causing me to rejoice in spite of it all.

I never thought I would see the day that I would rejoice over my trials. I can remember only wanting to be rid of them. My constant prayer was "Just fix this, Lord, and do it now!" I wanted the pain and struggle gone. I just wanted my marriage and husband fixed and to get on with the business of living. But praise God, He had other plans!

No, He never left me, He never forsook me, and no, He didn't give me my own way either, but neither did He leave me where He found me. He knew things needed to change and wanted them to, but it had to be in His perfect way and time. He had much for me to learn and blessings in store that I could not foresee.

1 Peter 1:6-7 says, "In this you rejoice, though now for a little while, if *necessary*, you have been grieved by various trials, so that the tested genuineness of your faith—more precious than gold that perishes though it is tested by fire—may be found to result in praise and glory and honor at the revelation of Jesus Christ." Well, it was *necessary* that I face these trials. I *needed* them.

I didn't see it back then when my heart hurt so much I didn't think I could bear any more pain. Every day seemed like a battle for my sanity and very existence. But the Lord gradually took me to the place where I could rejoice through the pain and struggle, and praise Him for what He was accomplishing in my life and the lives of my family. I wanted the quick fix but oh, what I would have been losing out on if I had gotten it!

The theme of our wedding was "He makes all things beautiful in His time" from Ecclesiastes 3:11. My husband and I had dated for more than five years as he really wanted us to wait to marry until he had completed his degree. We figured that He was making everything beautiful now because we could finally marry after waiting for so long.

Oh, how young and naive! Little did I know what awaited me. Far from realizing all the 'baggage' we had brought into our marriage from our upbringings I set out to have the perfect marriage, the perfect husband, and the perfect children, all while being the perfect wife. Things didn't go according to plan—at least not mine—and nineteen years later I ended up a broken-hearted mess living with an angry husband, no intimacy, and wondering what was wrong with me. As you know from all I've written you in the past, it wasn't a pretty picture.

So fast-forward to today and how are we doing?

Well, we've celebrated another wedding anniversary a bit older and a whole lot wiser I think. The constant battling and struggling is gone. Our home is peaceful. Fighting and arguing are a thing of the past. Sure, we have our disagreements and problems to work out like everyone else; but generally, our home is a haven from the storm instead of being the whirlwind in the storm.

The communication between Joe and I has improved immensely and it continues to get better. The more willing we are to be vulnerable with each other the better it gets. He is so much quicker to admit when he's wrong and repent of it. I'm still not used to that. Just when I've worked myself up to a defensive pitch, convinced he'll never change, the Lord takes me down a peg or two and reminds me He's still working when my husband comes to willingly admit his mistakes.

All five of our children have come to the Lord and show a deep desire to love, serve, and know Him better! They are growing and maturing, healing and learning from our mistakes. The relationship that I have with each of them is incredible. We have such open communication! They know they can talk about anything with me and nothing is off the table. And I am amazed at how much they love me—in spite of me! I am a rich woman indeed. In the midst of my worst pain and heartache, the Lord used it all to bring my children to Himself.

And I wanted Him to hurry things along! What was I thinking? He had such bigger and better plans!

And did I mention our sex life? Okay, I'm blushing a little bit as I write this because I'm not one to go around proclaiming these things from the housetops (though sometimes I really wish I could). But the truth is that just one person willing to work through their issues, unloading the baggage they brought into the marriage, and freeing up their mind to enjoy the intimacy improves the sex life for both spouses. And when you both work together—wow!

Joe and I both turn fifty this year and we both agree we have no desire to return to the early days of our marriage when it comes to sexual intimacy. It doesn't even compare to how wonderful it is now. I regularly experience vaginal orgasms and the premature ejaculation for my husband is a thing of the past! And to think that there's always room for improvement in all areas of life, well…who can tell what the future holds? I can say from experience, fifty is pretty nifty!

In the midst of my trials, I had read a statement by a Christian man who said, "My own bride had become the greatest trial of my life, and yet strangely she was significantly used of God as a means of drawing me closer to my Savior." I understood completely what he was saying. I had finally reached the point where I could see that my husband and our marriage problems were the very tools the Lord was using to draw me ever closer to Himself.

I had made an idol of both Joe and my marriage. It wasn't fair to him, and it certainly wasn't fair to God. The Lord had to show me that as noble a desire it is to have a good marriage and to be a good wife, it can't be the most important thing in our life. I had to be willing to lay it all on the altar before the Lord and leave it to Him to do what He would with it. Would I still love Him no matter what?

In the beginning of my trials, I was angry at the Lord and blaming Him for not fixing it. How wrong I was and how much I probably could have spared myself if I had started out from the position of, "This hurts terribly Lord, but I want to know what you want me to learn from this. What do you want to do in my life?"

When I finally reached that point, my eyes were opened and growth began. When I sought His will and wisdom through prayer, the Scriptures, books like yours, Patsy, that are bathed in Scripture, I could start to rejoice in every situation, even the painful ones, because I knew there was a purpose, a way—and hope!

Life is a journey, and even good marriages have room for improvement. There are still things Joe and I need to work through, but I'm much more willing to do it in God's time than my own. I know that the Lord has worked tremendous healing in my own heart and helped me to unload a lot of baggage. And I also know that Joe still has to deal with some of his own. We can't change anyone else, only ourselves. I'm much more willing to leave my husband in the Lord's hands than try to make him into the image I want him to be. I look forward to what the Lord has planned for us next.

I would say that the most important thing to come out of all my marriage trials has been my deepening love for the Lord, my growing desire to know Him and always have Him first in my life, and the desire to be the woman He has created me to be, no matter my circumstances and no matter how anyone else in my life is acting. I praise Him for answering my prayers above and beyond what I could have asked. I've learned that He is a "more than" God!

And I thank you too, Patsy Rae, for all the time and effort you have put into your writing to help enlighten people like me about God's wonderful plan for Christian marriages! He has greatly used your hard work and I hope you are richly rewarded by knowing that!

God bless!
Stacey

* * *

Dear Reader,

Thank you for reading and sharing your time with me. I hope your amazement has grown at God's love for us and our marriages. I pray that the Song of Solomon has touched your heart as it has mine.

If you benefitted from this study, please consider leaving an honest review of this book. Here's a link directly to Amazon's review page:

https://www.rpbook.co.uk/azr/0938855093

A short, honest review of a couple of sentences along with your rating works great. Your words help other book lovers decide what to read.

May God bless you on your journey of love,
Patsy Rae Dawson

P.S. If the message of love in this book resonates with you, please consider teaching or finding someone in your congregation to teach the Song of Solomon. It's my observation that when Bible classes study material such as this, more compassionate, loving congregations are often the result.

SOLOMON'S MATH THEN AND NOW

Solomon Never Had Great Sex
with 1000 Virgins

I moved back to Amarillo, Texas about four years ago to take advantage of the amazing group of writers, programs, and critique groups in the area. One of the first articles I took for critique was "Solomon Made Love to 1000 Virgins But He Never Had Great Sex."

A male screenplay writer observed, "I've never understood the fascination with virgins. Think about that plethora of inexperience."

And I have been thinking about his comment ever since. I'd written about Solomon's inadequacies as a lover and concentrated on the healthy attitudes of the Shulammite maiden whose mother taught her how to please a husband. But I'd failed to take into account the sexual immaturity of Solomon and his 1000 wives and make application to the #1 marriage complaint I get from both husbands and wives — sexless marriages. Infrequent, lukewarm lovemaking sucks the emotional life out of a marriage for both the husband and the wife regardless of which one deprives the other of loving sexual contact.

Essentially, Solomon kept having the same sexual experience over and over — 1000 times to be exact. He stayed locked in immature junior-high backseat-quality lovemaking his entire life. It doesn't get much worse than that.

Now science has proven just how empty Solomon's and his wives' sexual experiences were. Doctors McIlhaney and Bush state that having sex with one woman and then moving on to another woman only to repeat the cycle over and over never lets the brain grow to experience mature lovemaking and orgasm. It limits brain activity to the dopamine rush of sex (42-3). (See chapter 5, "The Shepherd Proposes True Love," to review how our hormones affect our enjoyment of lovemaking.)

A lifetime of glorious lovemaking requires work to get to know the other person intellectually and emotionally while solving the normal problems of living in the real world. Enjoying a happy marriage forces a person to grow up. In fact, growing up in to love is what life is all about.

We spend the first 20 years of life growing up physically.
We spend the second 20 years growing up emotionally.
We spend the next 20 years enjoying a wonderful love life.

But Solomon and his wives stayed locked in sexual immaturity for 40 years. At the time of his death at about 56 years old, Solomon was no doubt still deflowering 12 to 15-year-old virgins trying to satiate his breast fetish. Solomon was unable to enjoy a wonderful marriage and mature relationship with a single one of his 1000 wives. And because of his ignorance of the role of the mind in intellectual and emotional bonding for creating ecstatic sexual contact, he was not motivated to invest the time to learn how to truly love a woman.

What a tragedy! A man, whom God loved and gave wisdom to so that there were none like him, chose to be a fool in his own love life. Even the 13-year-old Maiden knew more than he did about lovemaking. She had the insight to say, "Solomon, I can't stand the thought of your lecherous lips on mine. But it goes down smoothly for my beloved, flowing gently through the lips of those who fall asleep" (Song 7:9b).

In spite of all his wisdom, Solomon never grasped the truth of the young Shulammite's words that she spoke to his Virgins about the secret of sexual happiness: Soulmating before lovemaking leads to *SPEAKING GOD'S BEAUTIFUL LANGUAGE OF LOVE* which transcends words.

The 21st Century's Sexual Experiment

Three thousand years ago, King Solomon tried the 21st century's sexual experiment better than any couple can execute it today. He didn't require grants to fund his experiments—with his great wealth and excessive taxes, he treated silver like gravel. He didn't need a home theater—he frolicked to live bands and singers. He didn't need magazine foldouts or electronic porn to turn him on. He used his political power and prestige to sample the most beautiful and sexually diverse women of his day, from king's daughters to peasants to slaves.

And guilt? When he tired of one woman in about two weeks, Solomon simply added another one to his harem. At the time of the Song of Solomon, he had 140 wives (60 queens and 80 concubines) and virgins without number awaiting his attention. Eventually he went through 1000 women.

If ever the 21st century's experiment was going to work, it should have succeeded for Solomon who gorged on sexual debauchery. He delighted in worldly-wise sex in all its glory—different partners, uninhibited techniques, wild music, beautiful bodies, and hookup attitudes without shame.

Solomon's Math

Commentators have many theories about Solomon's 1000 wives. Progressives point to the number as an example of why the Bible can't be taken literally. Others think Solomon may have actually had sex with some of them, but can't see how he could have kept them happy or even fed them all. Many writers claim most were political marriages without any sexual contact. Those who take the allegorical position assert the wives represent the millennium and Christ's 1000-year reign. Or they say it's not really Solomon, but he's used as a figure for God the father, or Jesus, or a good husband. Consider these facts for a different view:

Solomon's 140 Wives in the Song of Solomon

- 60 Queens (43% were political and free women like the Shulammite. The political wives were idolaters.)
- 80 Concubines (57% were slaves. All would have been idolaters since the Israelites were forbidden to make slaves of Hebrews.)
- Maidens without number.
- 57% were Concubines; and thus, were not political marriages.
- The Shulammite would not have been a political wife.

Solomon's 1000 Wives at the Time of His Death

- 700 Queens divided by a 40-year reign averages 17.5 free women per year.
- 300 Concubines divided by a 40-year reign averages 7.5 slave women per year.
- 1000 wives divided by a 40-year reign averages 25 wives per year.
- 140 wives divided by 25 wives per year equals 5.6 years into Solomon's reign. He was about 21 years old.

Observations About Solomon and His Wives

- He was acquiring Concubines faster than Queens in his early years—57% to 43%. Thus the majority weren't political marriages.
- God said Solomon held fast to all 1000 wives in love [sexual and otherwise] (1 Kings 11:2).
- He was fascinated with bodies, bosoms, and sex; not getting to know the woman.
- He devoted only three days to his polished courtship rituals.
- He married 860 more virgins after the Song of Solomon. This indicates he continued to marry adolescents about 12 to 15 years old even as he and his earlier wives aged.
- He may have gone through women faster than 25 a year in his

early years as he was worn out at the end of his life (1 Kings 11:4).
- He built altars around the countryside for his wives' idolatrous worship of both virgins and prostitutes.
- The wives acceptance of the Shulammite is not surprising. They may well have been like Hugh Hefner's young women who lived in his Playboy Mansion.

King Solomon's Epilogue

Solomon's Sunday-School Persona

We teach our children that Solomon asked God for wisdom. True, he did. And, yes, God gave him wisdom more than any man before or after him. But we often fail to let Solomon grow up and become accountable for his choices. If we remain locked in the Sunday-school version of the boy king, we can draw false conclusions about his role in the Song of Solomon. It's only through the hoax Origen perpetrated on Christians that anyone would ever think of Solomon as a hero.

Solomon's Lack of a Perfect Heart

Before King David died, he asked God to give his son Solomon a perfect heart to keep God's commandments and statutes and to build the temple (1 Chronicles 29:19). But God didn't take away Solomon's freewill.

Obedience without the freedom to choose means nothing. We'd be like a vacuum cleaner that sucks up dirt when you turn it on and quits sucking dirt when you unplug it. In other words, without choices, we'd be like deluxe-model robots that do only what they're programed to do.

Thus when Solomon asked for wisdom after David's death, God reminded Solomon of his accountability to him in the choices he made. If he obeyed God of his own freewill, then God promised Solomon he would give him riches, honor, and a long life (1 Kings 3:13). However, Solomon refused to keep his heart perfect before God (1 Kings 11:4).

Like David, many women and men today pray to God to take away their loved one's freewill and give their mate and children perfect hearts for obeying him. Then they wait for God to take care of everything. God has always held people accountable for their own actions—even men whom God loved very much such as David and Solomon.

Solomon's Limited Wisdom

After David died and Solomon was anointed king a second time, he went to the tabernacle tent in Gibeon to offer sacrifices. That night God appeared to him in a dream and said, "Ask what I shall give you." Solomon asked for wisdom for ruling the people. God said, "You have asked for wisdom and knowledge, that you may rule My people, over whom I have made you king, wisdom and knowledge have been granted you" (2 Chronicles 1:3-12).

We often assume Solomon asked for all encompassing wisdom, but he asked for wisdom in a specific area—in ruling over God's people, stating that he was but a little child. In addition, God gave him wisdom beyond what he asked for regarding trees, animals, birds, creeping things, and fish. He was a walking encyclopedia. Solomon spoke 3000 proverbs and wrote 1005 songs (1 Kings 4:29-34).

God also gave Solomon what he didn't ask for—riches and honor. Then he reminded Solomon that he had not given him a perfect heart and he was accountable for his actions. God told him, "If you walk in My ways, keeping My statues and commandments, as your father David walked, then I will prolong your days"(1 Kings 3:13).

Solomon quickly became a folk hero because of his judgment as a ruler over two prostitutes in 1 Kings 3:16-28:

> Not long after, a test was made of his wisdom. Two mothers stood before him, accusing each other of the same crime; and there were no witnesses. A modern judge would have dismissed the case for want [lack] of evidence. Solomon, however, quickly devised a stratagem which revealed the real mother. From village to village, the story of the incident was repeated, and the king's insight into human nature was everywhere applauded (ISBE "Solomon").

Solomon's Worship of Pagan Idols

Solomon exercised his freedom to disobey God by building altars to his wives' false gods of both prostitution and virginity on the high places among the country farms. Just outside Jerusalem on the Mount of Olives, Solomon built a high place for Chemosh, the odious god of Moab, and for Moleck the detestable god of the Ammonities (1 Kings 11:7). The worshippers of these false gods practiced human sacrifice by burning their infants to death.

After 40 years of Solomon's rule, many Israelites eventually followed the example of Solomon and his wives. They sacrificed their own babies to these hideous false gods. History records that these facilities were in continuous use for 400 years. The rest of the Old Testament is devoted to accounts of God's attempts to purge idol worship from his people.

Solomon's Vanity of Vanities

The Preacher of Ecclesiastes refers to "life under the sun" 29 times. He explores the question, "What is the meaning of life, under the sun on the earth, if there is no God?" He claims to speak for Solomon, the greatest experimenter of all time of what life without God offers men and women:

- King over Israel in Jerusalem — 1:12
- Set his mind to know more wisdom than any before him — 1:16-18
- Tested pleasure, laughter, and wine — 2:1-3
- Pursued luxurious living — 2:4-6
- Bought slaves, flocks, and herds — 2:7
- Hoarded silver and gold — 2:8
- Partied with live singers and women — 2:8
- Became great and didn't deny himself any pleasure — 2:9-10

Then the Preacher rehearses how Solomon's excesses sent his kingdom into decline as he squandered God's gifts and his life under the sun. He wasn't the only one who suffered as his obsessions hurled the Israelite nation into political, financial, and spiritual ruin:

- Wickedness in place of justice — 3:16
- Oppression reigned — 4:1-3
- Bribery was rife — 5:8-10

The Confessions of a King
Who Didn't Know How to Love a Woman

Four passages in Ecclesiastes summarize Solomon's views of women and correspond with the king revealed in the Song of Solomon:

- A harem, the delights of men — 2:8; Song 7:6-9a
- The woman more bitter than death — 7:26
- Not one woman found in 1000 women — 7:27-29
- A joyous life with the woman whom you love — 9:9

A Harem: The Delights of Men

Ecclesiastes 2:8: "Also, I collected for myself silver and gold and the treasure of kings and provinces. I provided for myself male and female singers and the pleasures of men — many concubines [delights of the sons of men, musical instruments, and that of all sorts — ASV, KJV, NKJ]."

"Pleasures" or "delights" (*ta'ănûg*) comes from a primary root that means "to be soft or pliable" (Strong 125, 89). Solomon used this word in describing his lust for the Shulammite, "How beautii *delightful (ta'ănûg)* you are, my love, with all your chari launched into his most outrageous proposal for sex saying climb the palm tree and take hold of her soft, luscious brea 9a). This same word is used in Jeremiah 6:2 for "the comely and dainty one, the daughter of Zion." It is also used in Isaiah 47:1 for the "virgin daughter of Babylon" who will "no longer be called tender and delicate."

"Sons" means "a son (as a builder of the family name)." It comes from a primary root meaning "to build (literally and figuratively):--(begin to) build (-er), obtain children" (Strong 21-22).

"Men" means "ruddy, i.e. a human being (an individual or the species, mankind)" (Strong 8).

"Concubines" or "musical instruments" refer to "a wife (as mistress of the house):--x all sorts, musical instrument [x refers to an idiom peculiar to the Authorized King James Version]." It comes from a primary root that means "properly to be burly, i.e. (figuratively) powerful (passively impregnable); by implication to ravage" (Strong 113).

The confusion over concubines versus musical instruments comes from the translators of the Authorized King James Version inventing an idiom that hid the sexual implications of the Hebrew language. Notice how modern translations render *"the delights of the sons of men, as musical instruments":*

- CJB—"things that provide sensual delight, and a good many concubines."
- NIV—"a harem as well—the delights of a man's heart."
- NRSV—"delights of the flesh, and many concubines."
- RSV—"many concubines, man's delight."
- YLT—"the luxuries of the sons of man—a wife and wives."

Old Testament scholar David Hubbard highlighted the sexual teaching of this verse. He said the male and female singers performed at banquets and parties. He recognized the erotic meaning of "delights" and its connection with Song 7:6. He cited recent translations of "harem" (NIV), and "concubines" (RSV, NASB) as being in keeping with Solomon's 1000 wives (75).

Likewise, another Old Testament scholar Dr. Herbert C. Leupold said Solomon's sensualism needed to be considered in accurately translating this verse (64).

Whatever translation we use, the consensus of the newer commentators is that the verse refers to Solomon's 1000 wives. The male and female singers performed at his orgies. The other three references to women in Ecclesiastes are also made in the context of Solomon's marriages and his unique experiences and obsessions with women.

The Woman More Bitter than Death

Ecclesiastes 7:25-26: "I directed my mind to know, to investigate and to seek wisdom and an explanation, and to know the evil of folly and the foolishness of madness. And I discovered more bitter than death the woman [could be translated wife] whose heart is snares and nets, whose hands are chains. One who is pleasing to God will escape from her, but the sinner will be captured by her."

"Woman" (*'ishshâh*) means "a woman (used in a wide sense):-- adulteress, each, every, female, wife, woman. Often unexpressed in English" (Strong 17).

Since Ecclesiastes says the woman is "more bitter than death and whose heart is snares and nets, whose hands are chains," it's easy to assume she is a prostitute like the adulteress wife of Proverbs 7:10-27. However, Proverbs 7 uses the word for woman plus it says she was "dressed as a harlot." Ecclesiastes doesn't identify the woman as a harlot and we have to assume a lot to make her one.

Proverbs demonstrates that this word for woman or wife needs an adjective to show what kind of person is being discussed:

- The *strange* or *adulterous* woman — Proverbs 2:16; 6:24, 26, 29, 32; 7:5, 10; 30:20; 31:3
- The *older* wife and her sexual charms — Proverbs 5:18
- The *clamorous foolish* wife knows nothing — Proverbs 9:13
- A *gracious* wife retaineth honor — Proverbs 11:16
- A *fair* [beautiful] wife *without discretion* — Proverbs 11:22
- The *virtuous* woman is a crown to her husband — Proverbs 12:4
- The *wise* woman builds her house — Proverbs 14:1
- Whoso finds a wife finds a *good thing* — Proverbs 18:22
- The *contentions* of a wife is a continual dripping — Proverbs 19:13; 27:15
- A *prudent* wife is from the Lord — Proverbs 19:14
- Better to live in a corner than with a *brawling* wife — Proverbs 21:9; 25:24
- Better to live in the desert than with an *angry* wife — Proverbs 21:19
- The wife of *great price* — Proverbs 31:10

Only by the context can we determine whom the woman is that the Preacher describes. Read the characteristics and see if this doesn't sound like the confession of a sexual addict married to an unloving woman.

- Directed his mind to know the evil of folly
- And the foolishness of madness

- Discovered more bitter than death
- The woman (could be translated wife)
- Whose heart is snares and nets (classic description of an intimacy anorexic who manipulates the spouse to starve him or her for love)
- Whose hands are chains (intimacy anorexics become more emotionally bankrupt as they age)
- The sinner is captured by her (God said Solomon was a sinner because of all of his wives. Weiss says it's not unusual for anorexics to marry each other. Then two people deprive each other and neither is happy in their abuse of the other.)

Is this an intimate portrait of one of Solomon's wives times 1000? Is this the kind of wife idolatrous women made for him? Or is this what his aging wives turned in to as he continually supplanted them with young virgins? Obviously, these two verses lead up to the next two. If we don't put them together, then we rip both sections out of their common context.

Not One Woman Found in 1000 Women

Ecclesiastes 7:27-29: "'Behold, I have discovered this,' says the Preacher, 'adding one thing to another to find an explanation which I am still seeking but have not found. I have found one man among a thousand, but I have not found a woman [could be translated wife] among all these. Behold, I have found only this, that God made men upright, but they have sought out many devices.'"

The Preacher said in the previous two verses he wanted an "explanation." While he still hasn't discovered the answer, he has figured out part of the puzzle. Thus at the end of his life, Solomon confided that in marrying 1000 virgins, he had never found great pleasure and happiness, or a wonderful, loving wife.

Could the one man in a thousand be the Shepherd whom the Shulammite loved? Perhaps Solomon spent the rest of his life trying to figure out what the Shepherd offered the Maiden that he didn't. Instead of finding marital happiness, he continued chasing women, bedding them, and then chasing more women. Solomon died saying, "Adding one thing to another to find an explanation, which I am still seeking but have not found, I only know what I chose didn't work." He never got it. Probably the reason he didn't get it was because of all the damage he was doing to his hormones, binding himself to them all, and yet to none.

Sadly, Solomon never learned the simple lesson the Shulammite tried to teach him. Three times she told the Virgins to not force love—to let it develop naturally. Then when she told him she was choosing the Shepherd because they shared true love, he still didn't get it.

A Joyous Life with the Woman Whom You Love

Ecclesiastes 9:9 "Enjoy life with the woman whom you love all the days of your fleeting life which He has given to you under the sun; for this is your reward in life and in your toil in which you have labored under the sun."

"Love" is the same word used throughout the Song of Solomon that means "to have affection for (sexually or otherwise)" (Strong 9).

"Reward" means "properly smoothness (of the tongue); also an allotment:--flattery, inheritance, part" (Strong 40).

It may well be that Solomon honored the Shepherd as the one man in 1000. Perhaps he recognized that the Shepherd enjoyed a relationship with the Shulammite that evaded him with his 1000 wives. Since Solomon owned the vineyard the Maiden's family leased from him, no doubt he was in her hometown yearly. He could have easily kept tabs on her and watched her babies and grandbabies grow up. When he died, she would have been about 47 years old, still a very beautiful, happy wife, mother, and grandmother.

The Shulammite and the Shepherd had it all. Solomon had a palace full of manipulating wives who didn't know the first thing about how to love him. But then he didn't know how to love them either.

We don't know if Solomon figured out the secret of true love before he died. However, this verse corresponds with God boasting that his proudest act of the creation was to create the way of a man with a maid. It corresponds with God declaring:

Proverbs 18:22:
"He who finds a wife finds a good thing,
And obtains favor from the Lord."

The Preacher urges husbands not to follow Solomon's example but to love their wives intellectually, emotionally, sexually, and spiritually. Why? "Because God gave you the woman's love as a reward or an inheritance for working so hard on the earth." Solomon reveled in all his perks—gorgeous women, unlimited wealth, and supreme knowledge. But the Shepherd trumped him by enjoying life with the woman he dearly loved.

The questions remain: Have we figured out love? Are we going to figure it out before we die? Or are we going to choose the miserable life of Solomon who lived and died without ever experiencing true affection?

Here's the math concerning Solomon's women in Ecclesiastes:

- Solomon had 1000 wives
- Solomon recommended 1 wife
- Solomon had 999 wives too many

God's Anger Burned Against Solomon

- Took the kingdom away from Solomon's son (1 Kings 11:9-13, 42-43).
- Took his wealth away.
- Took away the gift of a long life. Solomon died an "old" man at about 56 years old still pursuing young 12 to 15-year-old virgins (1 Kings 11:4, 43; 2 Chronicles 9:31). David was old at 70.
- Solomon turned his heart away from God (1 Kings 11:4). David was a man after God's own heart (1 Kings 11:33, 38).

Solomon's Public Rebuke by God

Before Solomon died, God rebuked him. God was so angry, he ripped the kingdom away from Solomon. Out of respect for his father David, God left a remnant which included Jerusalem and the temple for Solomon's son, Rehoboam. But he waited until Solomon died to do this (1 Kings 11:9-13, 42-43).

After Solomon's death, instead of eulogizing him, God instructed Nehemiah to use his example to curse the people who married foreign women and gave their daughters to foreign men. Nehemiah said, "Did not Solomon king of Israel sin regarding these things? Yet among the many nations there was no king like him, and he was loved by his God, and God made him king over all Israel; nevertheless the foreign women caused even him to sin" (Nehemiah 13:23-26).

Nehemiah chastised the people by asking, "Can't you look at Solomon and learn what not to do in your marriages? Solomon committed a great evil in marrying foreign women" (Nehemiah 13:27).

But Nehemiah wasn't through with his inspired rant about the evils of Solomon's life. He told about driving out the son of the high priest because he married a foreign woman. He berated the priests for defiling their office by following Solomon's example in their own marriages. Then he offered sacrifices for them as he "purified them from everything foreign." Nehemiah asked God to remember him for good because he rebuked the Israelites' spiritual leaders (Nehemiah 13:28-31).

Did God condemn Solomon and then inspire the writing of the Song of Solomon to teach us about his love for the Israelites and Jesus' love for Christians? Or does the Song of Solomon amplify Solomon's marital decadence as it teaches us how to enjoy wonderful marriages?

God preserved the true story of a young virgin of Israel whose mother taught her about love and marriage. He lets us listen to her inner thoughts as she struggles to choose between sensuous love and true love. God pits Solomon's depravity against the Shepherd's love. Dare we not listen and learn? That's the question Nehemiah asked the religious leaders of his time. Can we learn from Solomon's terrible example how we should live our lives?

Solomon's Early Death

Solomon died prematurely about 35 years after the Shulammite rejected him. Instead of the long life God offered Solomon if he'd obey him (1 Kings 3:4-14), Solomon died in his mid-50s, old before his time (1 Kings 11:4). This same word "old" is used to describe how Abraham died in a "ripe old age" at 175 years old (Genesis 25:7-8).

Solomon warned young men in Proverbs about the harlot taking their vigor and life. Although Solomon married all of his women, they still took his vigor. He aged badly because of his excesses with women, his extravagant lifestyle, and his obsession with gaining more knowledge. He left his country in financial ruin.

Solomon's Son Rehoboam

When Solomon died, the Northern tribes asked his son Rehoboam to lighten the yoke of exorbitant taxes his father had extracted from them. Instead of listening to the older, wiser men, Rehoboam heeded the advice of his young friends who advised him to tell his people, "My little finger is thicker than my father's loins [literally penis]! Whereas my father loaded you with a heavy yoke, I will add to your yoke; my father disciplined you with whips, but I will discipline you with scorpions" (1 Kings 12:1-17).

Rehoboam made light of his father's reputation with women by saying something to the effect, "My little finger is bigger than my dad's cock, so you can just imagine what I'm packing." But Rehoboam's threat to the Israelites tells us something important about Solomon. Rehoboam didn't think most of his father's 1000 marriages were sexless political alliances. He knew firsthand that his father continually exacted sexual favors from his harem.

No doubt, he reveled right along with his dad at the orgies in the palace. Thus he didn't make an empty brag that his little finger was bigger than Solomon's loins. He and all his contemporaries knew Solomon indulged in sexual activity with fervor.

Because of Rehoboam's arrogance, the Northern tribes split off from the two Southern tribes. God did what he warned Solomon he would do. He ripped the kingdom out of his hands, but he left a remnant for the sake of his father David.

Solomon's Political Satire

The Song of Solomon reveals the story began to be spread among the Israelites as oral history when the country folks asked, "Who is this coming up from the wilderness, leaning on her beloved? Why did she leave Solomon for the common Shepherd?" (Song 8:5ff) The true account survived throughout the generations because it was sung by the women and young girls in the evenings according to Israelite custom.

The Song of Solomon would have become a popular satire after Solomon's death when the Northern Kingdom split off from Solomon's 41-year-old son, Rehoboam. As a double-edged farce, it exposed the sexual depravity of Rehoboam's infamous father. The wisest king who ever lived was a sexual addict who destroyed his kingdom with his sexual excesses. Read the last section of Albert Réville's book *The Song of Songs, Commonly Called The Song of Solomon, Or the Canticle* for an in-depth discussion of the political nature of the Song of Solomon (59-76).

After the 70 AD destruction of Jerusalem, the statement "which is Solomon's" was added by the Levitical rabbis to identify who it was about and to guarantee its inclusion in the list of inspired scripture (Song 1:1). The contrast in the Hebrew words between their addition and the original text which contains the language and landmarks of the rural Northern Kingdom makes their addition obvious. The Levitical rabbis were always loyal to Solomon as they were protected from his heavy taxes and forced labor. They also invented the Jewish allegory for the book. Not only has the Song of Solomon been preserved intact, but also their manipulations are a matter of record (ISBE "Song of Songs").

Since the Song of Solomon was in the canon of scriptures recognized by the Jews, the Apostle Paul's words regarding the value of the scriptures is applicable:

> *2 Timothy 3:16-17: "All Scripture is inspired [literally God-breathed] by God and profitable for teaching, for reproof, for correction, for training in righteousness; so that the man of God may be adequate, equipped for every good work."*

The Shulammite's knowledge of true love in the story defies modern man's perception of love and sex. It also contradicts the sexual customs of the nations surrounding the Israelites and of Solomon himself. In my book, *God's People Make the Best Lovers,* the first four chapters trace the history of how mankind got to the 21st century with so many sexual hang-ups.

The World's Most Ancient Opera

Aryeh Naftaly is a multi-instrumentalist, singer, composer, lyricist, arranger, and producer. He is also one of Israel's leading Hebrew/English translators in the field of theater, film, and television, having translated over 3000 works. Aryeh wrote *The Song of Songs, A Messiah's Confession, An Explanation, English Translation and Dramatic Adaptation of the World's Most Ancient Opera.*

In his book, he shares his love and understanding of music and the original Hebrew language to demonstrate that the Song of Solomon is indeed the world's oldest opera. It contains "all the elements of opera: a script, characters, music, division into acts and scenes, and most importantly, as we will see, a spellbinding story." He asks, "Why an opera?" then explains that at the time of the Song of Solomon:

> There was no written Bible and all books had to be painstakingly hand-copied.... [An opera presents] a sensuous, captivating musical love story which could be easily memorized and performed for crowds again and again—the best way to guarantee that it would be heard by as many people as possible throughout the ages. Whether it was ever actually performed as an opera we do not know; what we do know is that it has been preserved intact for 3,000 years, read millions of times, and can be performed now (83).

At the Song of Solomon Project website www.thesongofsongs.net you can listen to extensive samples of Aryeh and The Song of Songs Ensemble singers' and musicians' production of *The Song of Songs (Words and Music of King Solomon)*. The tracks are divided into the eight chapters of the Song of Solomon. Although the words are sung in Hebrew, you can determine the different characters by their voices. The music is so beautiful, if you love the Song of Solomon as I do, you will thoroughly enjoy this presentation. Information about Aryeh's fascinating approach to the Song of Solomon as an opera and his book is at the website.

A special thanks to Aryeh for sharing his work with me. He said my online article "Song of Solomon—Evidence that King Solomon Was Not the Shepherd" convinced him the book spoke of two men. His work thrills my soul with its glimpse into the so very precise Hebrew language and music preserved in this beautiful true love story. And thank you, Aryeh, for revealing the political significance of the Song and the unique way it was preserved as oral history through the medium of music.

Take 7 Steps for Sexual Healing

Brain-imaging research pioneer Dr. Earl Henslin observed that regular, fervent lovemaking makes it easier for couples to get along with each other. It helps if the couple views sex as a gift from God to ease the normal stresses of life. He said most men need frequent sexual love to think clearly.

As a marriage and family therapist who specializes in treatment of psychological, physical, and spiritual problems, Dr. Henslin said regular sexual activity affects his job of trying to help a couple overcome problems. He always sighs with relief and joy when troubled couples renew their sexual bonds. When couples start making love on a regular basis, therapists start seeing more playfulness, patience, and a more positive view of their marriage. It makes his job much easier (180).

As we saw in the first chapter, "God Loves Passionate Sex," the unhappy cultures of purity and hookups often transform many a couple's sex life into a sexless marriage. This increases their stress (and their children's) from the normal problems of living in an imperfect world.

God has done everything possible to point us toward enjoying a wonderful lifetime of passionate lovemaking in the arms of our mate. So I want to close our study with seven practical takeaways from the Song of Solomon to help us overcome our stilted, loveless, and Godless views of married sex.

These steps are the advice I'd give the young evangelical husbands and their wives who participated in Sarah Diefendorf's doctoral study and presentation to the American Sociological Association: "Virginity Pledges for Men Can Lead to Sexual Confusion—Even After the Wedding."

I discussed this doctoral study in the first chapter as part of exposing the damage of Origen's hoax against married lovemaking. Now I'm concluding our study with a scriptural answer for the dilemma those husbands and the two young women who made virginity pledges expressed in chapter 1 in trying to merge healthy sexual desires with their view of God and sex.

Step 1: Examine the Love
in Your Home of Origin

I often tell students in my classes, "If you fail to examine both of your homes of origin before marriage, if you're like most people you'll scrutinize your in-laws' relationship when problems arise. Only then, it will probably lead to bitterness."

How do I know this? Nearly every time a man or woman consults me about a marriage problem, they begin with, "When he/she was little, his/her mother did.... And his/her father was...." The resentment toward the in-laws is extreme.

In Isaiah 66:11-13, God uses the example of a nursing mother to describe his own love for Israel. The Shulammite makes the same application when she tells the Shepherd she knows they'll enjoy a successful marriage. Why? Because they both grew up with loving, nursing mothers. Then she assures him she'll build on this foundation to be a loving wife (Song 8:1-3).

In contrast, Solomon grew up in a dysfunctional home. The scriptures record jealousy, fighting, rape, and murder among David's children by his different wives. Solomon killed his own brother to protect his throne.

The evangelicals assured Diefendorf they grew up in good homes. I wonder.... I'd like to ask these men and their wives some questions. How did your parents solve problems? Did they scream at each other or sit down and talk? Did you see your parents hug and kiss? Did they tell you they loved you? Did they ridicule you and put you down? Did they scream at you? Did you want to leave home as soon as possible?

Most telling of all, I'd like to ask: Were you forbidden to talk about what went on in your home? Do you hug and kiss your parents and tell them you love them? Or have you moved across the country to get away from your parents?

If your answers show you grew up in a defective home, expect problems. So Step 1 is to be honest with yourself and your mate. Talk about how love was expressed in your home. Then work together to create a better marriage than your parents had.

Step 2: Talk about Sex Before and After Marriage

Diefendorf said, "There's little support [from the church] in figuring out sexuality in married life, and these men don't know how to talk to their wives about it" (McElroy).

I don't agree with the common religious practice of preaching hell, fire, and damnation to scare people away from premarital sex. Instead, in my Song of Solomon classes for ages 11 to 99, I talk about the positive aspects of lovemaking to create a desire to enjoy a wonderful sex life in marriage. Diefendorf's paper highlighting all the hang-ups these young religious men took to their marriage beds adds credence to my view.

Besides that, I emphasize how the Maiden in the Song of Solomon gave her mother credit for teaching her that sex is for women as well as for men. Her mother taught her how to satisfy her husband when she got married. Instead of listening to a lot of harangues about sex and men, she grew up looking forward to marriage...and sex.

While the Shulammite and the Shepherd remained virginal during the time they were promised to each other (Song 4:12), they talked about sex and what they wanted in marriage. They promised to be passionate lovers for each other.

The Shulammite promised that after they married, she would delight in initiating lovemaking (Song 7:10-13). Before her ordeal with King Solomon and afterward, the Shulammite told the Shepherd she longed for his hands to intimately discover her body (Song 2:6; 8:3). The Shepherd told her he was committed to respecting her virginity (Song 4:12) while he was excitedly looking forward to their sexual relationship (Song 5:1).

This is different from the young evangelical who lamented, "For me to come home from work and say, 'Hey, did you like last time?' I mean that would be—that would be such a weird question for me to ask."

The Shulammite and the Shepherd used premarital-sex talk to lay a foundation for open communication after marriage. Healthy adjustment requires frequent conversation while laughing and sexually playing together.

The thought of a young couple speaking so frankly about sex before marriage strikes horror in the hearts of lots of religious people. Their way may encourage virginity pledges, but it gets in the way of couples enjoying married lovemaking. And it leads to sexless marriages.

If you didn't learn how to talk about lovemaking in courtship, then more than likely, you're going to have problems talking about sex in marriage when someone is unhappy. Then it can result in anger and tears. To help turn the sex talks into a mutual benefit for you and your spouse, move forward to Step 3:

Step 3: Turn the Song of Solomon into Exciting Homework

"Once married, Diefendorf found these men encountered trouble. Instructed by the church to keep problems 'in the dark' after marriage. The men reported feeling like they couldn't discuss sex with their friends and that they didn't know how to comfortably broach the subject with their wives" (McElroy).

Obviously, this is a spiritual problem for these young men and they won't be satisfied with anything less than a Biblical answer. Fortunately, God provides the solution through the Song of Solomon which over the last 10 years has become increasing popular among both Christians and self-declared heathens.

The theme of the Song of Solomon is all about soulmating in courtship before entering into a sexual relationship. That should be the purpose of a purity pledge before marriage—to give the couple time to build uncomplicated emotional and intellectual bonds before they start enjoying sex after marriage.

I've been teaching the Song of Solomon for nearly half a century and am continually amazed at all the sexual teaching that has always been in the book, but has only recently come to light. For example, only in the last 35 years have scientists discovered that the brain is the most important sexual organ. They're still conducting experiments and studies in an effort to better understand the role of the brain in lovemaking.

Yet the Song of Solomon has patiently taught this principle about the intellect for over 3000 years. I teach in my books and classes, "If you develop the right attitudes, your body will take care of itself to give you glorious orgasms, whether you're a man or a woman." In fact, God teaches more about the positive aspects of the sexual relationship than any other area of marriage.

Lovemaking is not a spectator sport—it's two people *SPEAKING GOD'S BEAUTIFUL LANGUAGE OF LOVE* which transcends words. Therefore, to truly find sexual comfort after making a virginity pledge, then marrying, these young evangelical Christian men need to involve their wives in the solution.

If you find sex-talk hard, a good place to start is by studying the Song of Solomon together. This takes the discussion out of the "you always" and "you never" realm and turns it into an intellectual and spiritual adventure with the possibility for some exciting homework in the bedroom.

Make sure you follow the guidelines in "Your Marriage and Your Love Life Will Never Be the Same If... You Do the Homework Exercises" discussed at the end of chapter 1. Then move on to Step 4:

Step 4: Overcome the Beastly by Romancing the Way Animals Do

During their virginity-pledge time, the evangelicals continually lamented over the "beastly" when sex "occurs outside marriage." Diefendorf said, "The newly wedded men also expressed surprise that sexual temptations continued to taunt them" (McElroy). Their "beastly" language is a holdover from Victorian morals. The Victorians had no understanding of the emotional part of sex and viewed a man's sexual desires as animalistic. They also taught that a man was ready for the grave at 45. Now couples can be sexually active in their 80s and older.

Three times the Maiden appeals to the example of animals as she pleads with the Virgins not to force her to marry the King before they love each other. She tells them, "Look at the animals—the gazelles and hinds of the field. They know they must build an emotional bond before they mate." Thus the beastly comparison is ironic (Song 2:7; 3:5; 8:4).

Several years ago, I visited my brother Ted at his longhorn ranch in East Texas. One day as I looked out the window, I asked, "Why is your bull snuggling with that female and licking her face? I've never seen him lean in close to any of the longhorns. I'm used to seeing him bully the females with his horns at the feed trough over the sweet grain."

Ted replied, "He has romance on his mind. After a while, they'll disappear in the trees to procreate."

"Wow! This is similar to the Song of Solomon when the Maiden's mother told her to pay attention to what the animals know about making love. I need to observe these longhorns so I can teach the Song of Solomon better."

The bull continued to lick and snuggle with the cow for a couple of days. Every so often, he tried to mount her. She would have none of it, and he would go back to his licking. Then one day they disappeared. Later that evening I saw them in the pasture again. This time the female was very affectionate and expressed her afterglow by washing the bull's face with her long tongue. He closed his eyes in syrupy rapture.

As for the young bucks who sniffed her wafting hormones and tried to mount her? She didn't even look back as she rejected their teenage-mating attempts by walking out from under them. These animals seemed so much smarter than many humans appear to be.

The theme of the Song of Solomon involves looking at the animals. All the enlightened males know they must romance the female—from birds to snakes and all those in between. The Song of Solomon teaches us to build emotional bonds before sex just like the animals do if we want to enjoy ecstatic lovemaking for a lifetime.

Step 4: Get rid of the beastly by taking time to romance your mate and strengthen your intellectual, emotional, and spiritual bonds. Spend time together talking and listening to each other. Perhaps if you put down your handheld device and quit checking your social media or texting your friends and look into each other's eyes—and really listen—your body will reward you. Why don't you try it and see what happens.

Step 5: Wake Up to Your Wet Dreams

Diefendorf reported, "The newlyweds also revealed that they continued to think of sex in terms of control, and how the so-called beastly elements of sex—temptations by pornography and extramarital affairs—do not disappear with the transition to married life" (McElroy).

Masturbation, pornography, and cheating can be difficult to overcome, and the young husbands may need professional counseling. Experiencing an orgasm through these activities greatly imprints the brain and changes how the person experiences pleasure. Essentially, the body learns to prefer solo sex over coupling with the mate.

Surprisingly the Bible's solution is to yield to wet dreams. As we saw earlier, the Song of Solomon describes two of the Shulammite's wet dreams showing God's approval (3:1-4; 5:2-7). Likewise, the Old Testament doesn't condemn wet dreams, but regulates them with the laws of cleanliness. These laws discouraged teenagers from developing a habit of masturbation and pushed them toward early marriages.

A male's wet dreams release the buildup of semen through nocturnal ejaculation. A female's wet dreams discharge a more subtle form of sexual tension through natural movements of her pelvis for a nocturnal vaginal orgasm. Single males and females often wake up to orgasmic peaks of pleasure which do not require masturbation to complete. The body knows its job. (Read the appendix chapter "Wet Dreams, Laws of Cleanness, and Masturbation" for more in-depth information.)

Now that you're married, give your body permission to enjoy waking up to pleasant, but perhaps less intense wet dreams. This will encourage you to look for lovemaking opportunities. As you stretch and yawn tell your lover, "I woke up horny this morning. Can we shower and go to bed early tonight?" Or smile to yourself and start the morning flirting and touching to create a spontaneous moment of sexual pleasure.

But if your mate is sexually cool, then your wet dreams will likely cause resentment because of the resulting temptations aroused by a body starved for love. 1 Corinthians 7:1-5 says these temptations come from not enough good marital sex.

The young evangelical husbands need to fight the beastly by enjoying more lovemaking with their wives. In their case, it's probably due to the Purity Culture's sexual ignorance on the part of both the husband and the wife. They need to go back to "Step 3: Turn the Song of Solomon into Exciting Homework."

If the sexual neglect comes from intimacy anorexia, the anorexic and /or the unloved mate can go through my free *Sexless Marriages Self-Assessment Survey* to help them analyze what kind of sins they're dealing with. When they complete the last checklist, they'll receive an eReport on how to approach the lack of loving sex in their marriage based on their answers. The plan of action includes suggestions for both the spouse who withholds sex and the one deprived of lovemaking.

Step 6: Have Fun with Breast Orgasms

Diefendorf disclosed, "There's little support [from the church] in figuring out sexuality in married life, and these men don't know how to talk to their wives about it" (McElroy). The truth of the matter is the wives are just as confused about married sexuality as their husbands.

Here's one of the Song of Solomon's secrets about female sexuality that defies traditional church wisdom—a woman's breasts play an important role in expressing her love for her husband. The Old Testament Hebrew uses many words to convey different aspects of a woman's breasts. For example, when Solomon told the Shulammite he longed to climb her palm tree and take hold of her "breasts," he used a strictly biology term (Song 7:8).

But the Shulammite uses a different word when she promises to give her breasts to the Shepherd as part of her love for him (Song 7:10-13). Interestingly, this "love-breast" word is used fifty-eight times in the Old Testament with thirty-eight of them in the Song of Solomon. The Shulammite begins her account of her dilemma about whom to marry by using this word to describe her longing for the Shepherd's love (Song 1:2, 4). She uses a form of this word to call the Shepherd "my beloved" throughout the Song of Solomon.

A similar passage commends an older wife giving her breasts in love to her older husband (Proverbs 5:19). The following verse contrasts her love-breasts with the biological-breasts of a young sweet thing that might tempt a husband facing a mid-life crisis (Proverbs 5:20). The breasts of lustful passion cannot compare to the wife's breasts of love.

The Shulammite promises the Shepherd, "I'll readily initiate lovemaking. My breasts tingle and ache for you. My nipples stand erect at the thought of your loving touch" (2:6 and 8:3).

A wife comfortable with her sexuality grows into a multi-orgasmic woman with many erogenous zones. But her breasts are especially full of love waiting to respond to her husband's touch of affection.

Instead of slapping your husband's hand and telling him to quit groping, embrace this gift from God. And you don't have to save your breast orgasms for bed. Enjoy them any time of the day. Snuggle on the couch and engage in love play while watching a movie. It can be very arousing. Give yourself permission to blend all aspects of your femininity and masculinity together in sexual experimentation and delight.

Step 7: Hey! God Said, "Get Tipsy on Lovemaking!"

"There's an obsession with virginity in this country," Diefendorf said. "And we forget to have informative, successful conversations on sex" (McElroy).

Christians and non-Christians alike may forget, but God certainly didn't! God not only preserved the Song of Solomon for us to learn from, but he also interjected himself into the Shulammite's dilemma right before she realized King Solomon was not the man for her. What did God say in this inspired interruption of the Shulammite's story?

Song of Solomon 5:1b:
"Eat, friends;
Drink and imbibe deeply, O lovers."

God told the Shulammite and the Shepherd, "Get married and get tipsy on married love! Savor and experiment with the different spiced and sweet wines of married sex. Laugh yourselves silly in each other's arms. Then drink some more until you can't stand up!" Review "Secret 5: Sip the Divine Wine of Passion."

Isn't it delightful that God tells even older couples to get tipsy on passionate lovemaking?

Prov. 5:18-19:
"Let your fountain be blessed,
And rejoice in the wife of your youth [now she is older].
As a loving hind and a graceful doe [there's those animals again],
Let her breasts satisfy you at all times;
Be exhilarated [literally intoxicated] always with her love."

The older wife still possesses the ability to satisfy her older husband. As a result, even the older husband can reel or become tipsy with happiness in the arms of his gray-headed lover. Truly, God loves husbands and wives and does his part to ensure their happiness over their whole lifetimes.

One reader emailed, "It takes a lot of wine and a long time to get drunk."

Draw your own conclusions.... Preferably in bed with your mate.

APPENDICES

Wet Dreams, Laws of Cleanness, and Masturbation

In spite of God teaching about feminine wet dreams for over 3000 years, during the last two millenniums religious teachers thought wet dreams were visitations by demons. Then during the Victorian Era, doctors and moralists expanded on those views as they likewise believed wet dreams came from the devil. They warned, "Sexual dreams cause big, fiery-red pimples on boys.

And heaven forbid, if a girl ever has a wet dream—she is doomed to be flat chested."

God preserves the description of two of the Shulammite's wet dreams to show his approval and desire for women...and MEN to learn from them. The word definitions for the second dream make it easy to identify it as a wet dream (Song 5:2-7). Thus we can use that understanding to re-examine the first dream and see that it also has the same characteristics as the second, only it is a milder wet dream (Song 3:1-4).

Since wet dreams reveal the subconscious, the intensity of them varies as the circumstances change. The second dream initiates the turning point of the Shulammite's dilemma of whom to marry. Her powerful physical sensations catch her attention and cause her to pivot and go in a new direction. Please review the two dreams in the verse-by-verse discussion and pay particular attention to the word definitions.

8 Benefits of Wet Dreams

It's past time to stop propagating the ignorance of the early Church Fathers and Queen Victoria's court about wet dreams and to turn to God's word! He has preserved the Song of Solomon to reveal his love for his people to help us enjoy wonderful love lives. Notice some of the similarities and benefits God built into wet dreams for both males and females:

1. Centers on a Real Person

Wet dreams of both males and females normally revolve around a real person. The Shulammite's dreams focus on her shepherd boyfriend to whom she is promised and has an emotional attachment with (Song 3:1-4; 5:2-7).

2. Releases Sexual Tension

A male's wet dreams release the buildup of semen in his body through a nocturnal ejaculation. A female's wet dreams discharge a more subtle form of sexual tension through natural movements and contractions of her pelvic area for a nocturnal vaginal orgasm. Her upper body curves forward and arches back as she gasps to breathe during an intense climax. A woman's breasts physically ache for the touch of her beloved. Twice, the Shulammite shares the aching of her breasts for the Shepherd's touch in marriage (Song 2:6; 8:3).

The Maiden sees just the Shepherd's hand in her second wet dream and her "feelings are aroused for him" (Song 5:4). As shown earlier in the definitions, the Shulammite's sexual organs caused her to cry out for her beloved. While her brain tried to reject the Shepherd, her body jumped out of bed at the sight of just his hand.

The descriptions of the dream are easily recognized as a wet dream by women with a history of vaginal orgasms. On the other hand, male authors work with a severe handicap for even knowing feminine wet dreams exist, let alone understanding them.

3. Wakes Up the Person

Single males and females often wake up to orgasmic peaks of pleasure which do not require masturbation to complete. When a person starts masturbating, it ceases to be a wet dream and the effect on the body and mind is different. All a person needs to do with a wet dream is what the Shulammite did. She lay there and let her body respond automatically while she contemplated the implications of the sensations. The body knows its job and the Maiden wanted to know what her body was telling her instead of her showing her body what to feel through masturbation.

She starts her first dream by saying, "On my bed night after night I sought him whom my soul loves." This is the experience of a woman in love. She is promised to the Shepherd, and these nightly wet dreams are pushing her toward a fall wedding. After Solomon enters the picture, her dream changes to reflect her uncertainty about what life will be like with him in the palace (Song 3:1).

4. Announces Sexual Maturing

Wet dreams reveal physical and mental sexual maturing in both boys and girls. At the end of the Song of Solomon, the Shulammite's brothers ask a riddle about their little sister who has no breasts and isn't mature enough to be interested in boys. She is also too young for wet dreams. The Shulammite replies, "My breasts were like towers," meaning she is sexually mature and ready for love. Her wet dreams demonstrate her sexual maturity (Song 8:10).

5. Reveals the Subconscious

Single men and women can use wet dreams to analyze their sexual attraction to a specific member of the opposite sex. The Shulammite says, "I was asleep, but my heart was awake." Her two wet dreams warn her against marrying King Solomon by exposing her lack of sexual attraction to him. In the second dream, she fully recognizes a life of misery awaits her if she marries the King (Song 5:2-7).

6. Signals the Desire or Need to Marry

Coming from an innate desire and need for regular sexual activity, wet dreams drive men and women toward selection of a mate. As healthy young people, the Shulammite and Shepherd frequently discuss marriage to each other. Recognizing their needs for an active lifelong sexual partner, they examine their attitudes toward sex and pledge to be passionate. The Shulammite even promises the Shepherd she'll initiate sex with him. She will not be like many modern wives and will never make him feel like a sexual beggar (Song 7:10-12).

7. Provides a Natural Release

Wet dreams are not synonymous with masturbation or using porn. They often occur without much, if any, forethought on the part of the person. They spring from desires deep in the subconscious. These involuntary nocturnal dreams show God's brilliance in the design of the male and female bodies as they prepare his people for marriage.

Twice, the Shulammite reveals how she longs for the Shepherd's touch rather than practicing self-stimulation or masturbation. Before her first wet dream she said, "Let his left hand be under my head and his right hand embrace me" (Song 2:6). After her second wet dream, she pledged to initiate lovemaking with the Shepherd and repeated her longing for the Shepherd to touch her body in arousing foreplay (Song 8:1-3). The young couple talks about sex and pledges to satisfy the other's sexual desires (Song 7:10-13).

A virgin may not recognize her wet dreams as vaginal orgasms. Later in the arms of her husband, as his powerful thrusts of love bring her to climax time and time again, she knows. *Oh! That's what I was feeling.* She laughs out loud. *A real man is so much better than a dream!*

8. Arouses for Married Lovemaking

After marriage, wet dreams arouse the husband's and wife's bodies for lovemaking. Healthy lovers enjoy waking up to pleasant, but less intense, wet dreams. This encourages them to look for lovemaking opportunities. As a husband stretches and yawns, he can tell his wife, "I woke up all hot and bothered this morning, can we shower and go to bed early tonight?" Or the wife might smile to herself and start the morning by flirting to create a spontaneous moment of sexual pleasure.

An Epiphany on the Old Testament's Uncleanness Laws

Many people snicker at the Old Testament laws of cleanness and uncleanness as archaic and ignorant. In reality, these laws benefitted the Israelites without the need to teach them the science behind the regulations. These laws of uncleanness offered protection of both men and women. God gave the Jews certain laws of uncleanness in matters of reproduction which covered four basic areas:

1. *Circumcision* — Isaiah 52:1 considered the uncircumcised male unclean. Doctors now recognize circumcision helps protect the man's sexual partner from cervical cancer.

2. *Menstruation* — Leviticus 15:19-33 considered a woman unclean both during her menstrual flow and for seven days afterward. When marital relations resumed, the woman was at her most fertile time. Some modern fertility doctors also recommend a period of abstinence for men to increase the likelihood of conception. This law of cleanness is still good advice today for couples trying to conceive.

3. *Childbirth* — Leviticus 12 considered the woman unclean after the birth of her child for a period equal to the time doctors now recommend a woman avoid sexual intercourse after childbirth. This spared the woman painful sexual relations and allowed her body to heal without the husband introducing germs into the affected organs.

4. *Seminal emission* — Deuteronomy 23:9-11 and Leviticus 15:16-18, 32-33 considered the man unclean because of a nocturnal emission. This is commonly called wet dreams and discharges the buildup of semen in the man's body. It allows the man to continually produce fresh sperm for

healthy offspring. It also offered great protection for the young man's budding sexuality by discouraging him from developing the habit of self-masturbation, but to allow wet dreams to occur naturally.

"Uncleanness" was not synonymous with "sin." Sometimes it was simply an uncleanness that required cleansing before the person could go into the tabernacle compound or associate with others. At the same time, it usually offered health benefits for the Israelites that they had no way of understanding. For example, touching a dead body wasn't a sin, but it exposed the Israelites to deadly germs they didn't know about. The required washing protocol protected them from untimely deaths.

S. I. McMillen, M.D. discusses in *None of These Diseases* how the laws of uncleanness protected the Jews from many of the diseases common in Egypt and other surrounding countries (Exodus 15:26). For example, the high mortality rate of surgery "would not have occurred if surgeons had only followed the method God gave to Moses regarding the meticulous method of hand washing and changing of clothes after contact with infectious diseases." It was not until 1960 when the New York State Department of Health "issued a book describing a method of washing the hands, and the procedures closely approximating the Scriptural method given in Numbers 19" that deaths from infections decreased in hospitals (12-6).

The Ebola virus that killed over 10,000 people in 2014 shows the wisdom of the uncleanness laws (Ross 10/23/2014). It was spread by touching or kissing the corpses at funerals. Peter Piot, director of the London School of Hygiene and Tropical Medicine said, "Traditional cultural and religious beliefs in parts of Africa help spread the virus" (Grundy 9/26/2014).

Likewise, menstrual discharges or wet dreams were not sins. They signaled the ability of the male and the female to bear children. Without giving the Jews science and biology lessons, God's laws of uncleanness protected them in spite of their ignorance about the human body.

Discouraged Masturbation

Labeling the man with a seminal discharge "unclean" until the evening and preventing him from going to work or battle with the other men protected the young man when he was developing lifelong sexual habits. While the passage doesn't refer specifically to masturbation, this law of uncleanness or hygiene controlled self-stimulation, not by condemning it as sin, but by discouraging it through social and moral pressure. The separation from other people during the unclean period exerted tremendous peer pressure on the young man not to develop a habit of self-pleasuring, which would cause him to be in frequent isolation. The unclean period would raise questions and rebuke.

Encouraged Early Marriage

Likewise, the required cleansing ritual applied moral pressure on the young man by focusing his mind on God's laws of sexual conduct. The law also encouraged him to marry at an early age to provide a recognized means for release of the seminal fluid since married sexual intercourse was not unclean. In the meantime, he learned self-control which would benefit him later when his wife was unclean because of menstruation or childbirth.

Promoted an Active Sex Life

A husband could make love to his wife all day long and not be unclean or ostracized by the other men. But if he preferred making love to himself instead of to his wife, then the other men would think he was a pervert. Or they might wonder if the couple fought all the time and didn't know how to kiss and makeup. Either way, a husband's frequent uncleanness made him and his wife a ready topic for gossip.

Essentially, God's laws of uncleanness kept a man's sexual conduct out in the open during his whole lifetime. A husband was either loving his wife or he was getting it on with himself. Think about God's genius in designing this law of uncleanness. He gave men a wonderful organ of love that's very sensitive to touch, especially to a wife's caresses and kisses. Then to make sure men didn't abuse this gift by indulging in selfish self-touch, God ordained the law of uncleanness. If the man did something with his semen other than deposit it in his wife, everyone knew it. God protected men from themselves. Talk about peer pressure!

WOW! Does God love women or not? The #1 complaint I get from wives is in regard to sexless marriages. Their unloving husband would rather have sex with himself than make love to a real woman.

This uncleanness law would also take care of the #1 complaint I get from husbands—trying to survive a dead bedroom. The wife often claims she is too tired, too preoccupied, or too smelly to make love. If the Hebrew husband couldn't go to work because he had a wet dream because his wife had a headache, she'd begin to notice it when she didn't have money for clothes and food. Or if all the other women were talking about what a bad wife she was behind her back.... Well, you get it. Certainly, God is wonderful in the way he loves us in spite of our ignorance and stubbornness!

Don't you love the Bible! I researched the clean and unclean laws 48 years ago. Yet I missed this obvious epiphany until recently. And it's been in the Bible the whole time. Truly, what God said in Ecclesiastes is true:

> *Ecclesiastes 8:17: "And I saw every work of God, I concluded that man cannot discover the work which has been done under the sun. Even though man should seek laboriously, he will not discover; and though the wise man should say, 'I know,' he cannot discover."*

Indeed, the quality of a couple's sex life is always public even though the uncleanness law isn't in effect today. You've heard the old saying, "You can tell a sexually happy woman by the sparkle in her eyes and the spring in her step." Now it's a scientific fact as the next section illustrates.

Affected the Way the Wife Walked

In 2012, Rob Waugh wrote the article "You Can Instantly Know a Woman's Sex History From Her Stride, Claims Study." He shared details from Belgian researchers at the Universiti Catholique de Louvain et de la sexuality in Louvain-la-Neuve, Belgium. The academics demonstrated with a blind study that just by watching videos of the way women walk, sexologists could determine if the women regularly enjoyed vaginal orgasms. The catch? The orgasm had to come from "penile-vaginal intercourse" to affect the woman's gait.

The researchers videotaped two groups of "healthy young Belgian women." The first group had a history of vaginal orgasms with a man. The second group was unable to orgasm vaginally through sex. Just any orgasm didn't affect the way a woman walked. For example, a clitoral orgasm didn't produce the same walking results as a vaginal orgasm.

A group of sexologists viewed the videos to see if the manner in which the women walked could determine their sexual history. The results of the blind study showed that vaginal orgasms improve a woman's walk when other types of orgasms don't because of the way it exercises her muscles, vertebrae, and pelvic floor. The sexologists observed the spring-in-her step as "a gait that comprises fluidity, energy, sensuality, freedom, and absence of both flaccid and locked muscles" (5/2012).

Medical journalist Colette Bouchez clarified that the women's walk wasn't "the old Marilyn Monroe hip swinging, or the obviously provocative Madonna-esque stances" (9/12/2008). Their walk exhibited energetic freedom and confidence. The women radiated innate sexual satisfaction.

Israelite mothers enjoyed vaginal orgasms and taught their virgin daughters the physiological aspects of them (Song 8:2). Although the Oriental women didn't call it the PC muscle, they knew how to contract it during intercourse (Chartham 24-5; Deutsch 62-8). The PC muscle also tenses and relaxes naturally during feminine wet dreams. Thus the Shulammite would enjoy all the health benefits of a loving sexual relationship with her Shepherd.

What about the Shepherd? If movements of the wife's pelvis and contractions of her vagina during lovemaking exercise and strengthen her muscles, what do you suppose the husband gets? As one man put it, "A husband's orgasm is a whole lot more pleasurable with a wife having vaginal orgasms than with one who can only climax clitorally." The husband experiences firsthand that she's not faking it. It'd be interesting if the sexologists would interview the husbands of the women they videotaped.

Put a Sparkle in the Husband's and Wife's Eyes

Another experiment the university researchers might want to consider is videoing the women's faces, especially their eyes. Then they could instruct the sexologists to look at the videos to determine which women enjoyed vaginal orgasms just by studying the sparkle in their eyes. From my work with women, I believe the sexologists could easily determine the women's sexual history by observing their eyes.

To verify this theory, I contacted three students I've kept in touch with over the years. All the women were in sexless marriages when they first emailed me. Each was dealing with a different root problem and spent several years working through it. As a byproduct of turning their marriage around each woman began enjoying vaginal orgasms.

I shared this chapter with the three wives and asked if people noticed a significant change in their demeanor after they began enjoying vaginal orgasms. They gave me permission to share their responses with you. The first wife is Stacey whose reports you've been reading. Check out her response following chapter 11 in "Stacey's Story: Vaginal Orgasms Make My Eyes Sparkle."

The second wife wrote:

Dear Patsy Rae,

When wives have a sparkle in their eyes, others notice. It happened to my husband and I when people at church asked us why we looked so happy all of a sudden. We told them why. That's when they wanted my husband to teach them what we had learned in your marriage book. He taught them the Song of Solomon. He was given this opportunity because we looked happy and must have had a sparkle in our eyes. I like this chapter very much.

Good job on this, Patsy Rae!

(Name withheld.)

The third wife called me and said, "Your chapter made me laugh when I realized why I'm always getting compliments about how my eyes sparkle. My husband and I enjoy a very loving relationship. And people are always telling me I look so happy and younger than ever. And I do feel very young at heart."

Women who experience regular vaginal orgasms with their husbands, sparkling eyes are a given. God generously rewards women when they dare to love their husbands intellectually, emotionally, sexually, and spiritually. They walk with a flowing clip while the glow on their faces catches the attention of everyone they meet.

Explains Why Israelite Women Enjoyed Easy Childbirths

These health benefits to the pelvic floor and surrounding area by strengthening weak muscles and relaxing tight muscles along with strengthening the vertebrae help explain why the Israelite women often gave birth much easier than modern women do (Isaiah 66:7). Hayyim Schauss tells about the Jewish birth experience in *The Lifetime of a Jew:*

> Jewish women had a reputation for natural strength and vitality. For the most part they were delivered easily and quickly, like the Bedouin women, often 'ere the midwife came unto them (11).

Sometimes following a series of vaginal orgasms, a wife naturally curves her upper body forward to bear down on her husband's organ of love. This automatic climax of orgasm built upon orgasm treats the previous orgasms as if they were but warmups for the grand finale. The birth process occurs in much the same way. The wife's multiple vaginal orgasms help prepare her muscles for delivery.

When I taught classes on the many Bible verses regarding giving birth and motherhood, I shared this information. After another class, a woman who was far along in her pregnancy said, "I told my husband what you said about a vaginal orgasm exercising a woman's muscles to help her when she gives birth. Now he puts his arms around me and asks, 'Would you like to do your exercises?'" She laughed, "Exercising is so much fun for both of us."

Vaginal orgasms along with hormones exert a tremendous impact on the woman. Not only do they strengthen her body for giving birth, but they also help her become a wonderful, loving mother. Review the role of the hormones in chapter 5, "The Shepherd Proposes True Love." Chapter 11, "The Shulammite Promises to Be Passionate," has more information about vaginal orgasms and the husband's response.

Three Types of Masturbation

Just as many male authors don't recognize or know much about feminine wet dreams, I must rely on men to fully understand male self-masturbation although there are many parallels with females. The best overview I've found comes from Dr. Douglas Weiss, an expert on sexual addiction. In his book *Sex, Men and God*, chapter 5, "The M Word," he describes three types of masturbation which he labels A, B, and C. His breakdown of masturbation clarifies Bible principles (which I've added) and makes them easier to explain. It's also helpful for recognizing when a person crosses the line from what's normal into sin and becoming without natural affection. While Weiss addresses this issue with men, the same types of masturbation apply to women.

In the overview below, I'm not attempting to thoroughly discuss or prove these points. I'm only introducing them for your further study if you're interested. Please read *Sex, Men and God* by Douglas Weiss and my book *God's People Make the Best Lovers* for more information. Weiss says sexual addicts will not identify with the first two types. In fact, most don't believe Types A and B even exist. Likewise, Types A and B have difficulty understanding the compulsion and lust involved with Type C. Preachers and elders who only engage in Types A and B masturbation often are not very helpful to men trying to overcome Type C as they have no insights into the addictive qualities of lust and masturbation.

Masturbation Type A: Wet Dreams Activated by the Subconscious

Deuteronomy 23:9-11 and Leviticus 15:16-18, 32-33 considered the man unclean because of a nocturnal emission. This is commonly called wet dreams and discharges the buildup of semen in the man's body. It allows the man to continually produce fresh sperm for healthy offspring. It also offers protection for the young man's budding sexuality by pushing him toward marriage and discouraging him from developing the habit of self-masturbation, but allows wet dreams to occur naturally during the night. Wet dreams are not necessarily a sin. This is the topic of this chapter.

Masturbation Type B: Release Controlled by the Mate

1 Corinthians 7:4: "The wife does not have authority over her own body, but the husband does; and likewise also the husband does not have authority over his own body, but the wife does."

"Authority over" means "to have power or authority, use power; to be master of any one, exercise authority over one, to be brought under the power of any one" (Thayer 225).

Often husbands and wives selfishly use this passage on each other by saying, "Your body belongs to me, and I have the right to say what happens sexually. I have the authority over your body." This attitude conveys the opposite of what the verse teaches.

This verse contains two ellipses—two "not-but" constructions with a common verb. An ellipsis, a common Greek word combination, shows a relationship between two things that are both true, but it places the emphasis on the second over the first. In other words, the wife has authority over her own body, but the husband exercises greater authority over her body.

Yet the husband's authority is not to tell the wife what to do with her body. Rather, the husband exercises his authority as "the way of a man with a maid." In other words, he uses his power over his wife's physical sensations *by giving her body sexual satisfaction* in keeping with the context of the passage "because of immoralities." Thus the wife possesses some authority or ability to satisfy her own sexual desires through masturbation.

The passage emphasizes her husband's power to satisfy her in comparison to her own ability—he exerts much more power to satisfy her by making a vaginal orgasm possible which is not possible through self-masturbation. In fact, once a woman tastes of a vaginal orgasm, masturbation seems empty and worthless. It takes a husband to satisfy a wife's deepest feminine needs.

This makes masturbation a sin when the husband uses it to drain off his sexual energies so that he fails to satisfy his wife's needs. Tim LaHaye says a man's heavy use of masturbation is the most common cause of a man's low sex drive for his wife. A man often gets into the habit in his youth and carries it into his marriage. When a couple comes to him for counseling because of a husband's low sexual interest, the first question he always asks is if the man masturbates (LaHaye 169).

The woman wields the same power over her husband as he does over her. The husband, likewise, exercises limited power to relieve his sexual urges in comparison to his wife's power. In the follow-up article on the *Redbook* survey of 40,000 men, "The Sex Lives of Happy Men," Carol Tavris found that the most happily married men didn't enjoy masturbation nearly as much as making love with their wife. They didn't possess the necessary body parts to *fully* satisfy themselves—only their wife could give them the very best of sexual thrills (197).

Times have changed and when a husband complains that his wife is not available sexually, she needs to be asked about her masturbation habits. It's not unusual for wives to masturbate while fantasizing about former boyfriends or movie stars. A flesh-and-blood husband can't compete with these images in a woman's mind. Masturbation that denies either the husband or the wife satisfaction of their God-given sexual needs is a sin against the mate and is adultery of the heart.

While the husband and the wife depend on the other for sexual release, both also find their greatest delight in experiencing the other's enjoyment. The wife delights in seeing her husband's exhilaration through her charms. Likewise, many of the 40,000 men in the *Redbook* survey said the best lovemaking occurred when their wives obviously experienced their own ecstasy (Tavris, "Sex" 195).

Sometimes because of illness, work, travel, etc. the mate is not available to make love. When sexual tensions build, the person may resort to self-masturbation as a temporary fix. The above information comes from my chapter "God's Compatibility Law," in *God's People Make the Best Lovers* where I study 1 Corinthians 7:1-5 in detail. Please see my book for detailed discussion of these scriptures. That chapter and others teach when masturbation crosses the line into sin against the spouse.

Weiss states a man usually starts Type B as a teenager. When he marries, he prefers sexual intercourse with his wife as the superior pleasure and rarely resorts to masturbation. He doesn't use porn or objects. He stays connected with himself and his wife. He doesn't live in a fantasy world or use masturbation to meet his emotional needs. He is simply engaging in a bodily function, the same as with a wet dream, only it's a deliberate act rather than being activated by the subconscious. The husband releases and moves on (*Sex* 77-8).

Masturbation Type C: Driven by Lust

Jesus plainly stated adultery begins with "mental adultery" or lust. He doesn't give men and women free rides in the way they treat their spouses sexually:

Matthew 5:27-32: "You have heard that it was said, 'YOU SHALL NOT COMMIT ADULTERY'; but I say to you that everyone who looks at a woman with lust for her has already committed adultery with her in his heart. If your right eye makes you stumble, tear it out and throw it from you; for it is better for you to lose one of the parts of your body, than for your whole body to be thrown into hell. If your right hand makes you stumble, cut it off and throw it from you; for it is better for you to lose one of the parts of your body, than for your whole body to go into hell. It was said, 'WHOEVER SENDS HIS WIFE AWAY, LET HIM GIVE HER A CERTIFICATE OF DIVORCE'; but I say to you that everyone who divorces his wife, except for the reason of unchastity, makes her commit adultery; and whoever marries a divorced woman commits adultery."

We often wonder why Jesus talked about plucking out the eye and cutting off the hand right in the middle of warnings about mental adultery. We know many religions cut off the hands of thieves. Is that what Jesus warned about in the context of divorce?

This passage suddenly made sense to me when I was counseling a husband and wife about the husband's sexual addiction. He was making passes at women to whom he was trying to teach the gospel. The wife blurted out, "I didn't know you were masturbating to them."

The husband reddened, ducked his head, and quietly said, "Masturbation is part of lust."

This wife recognized her husband's masturbation violated their vows to keep themselves only for each other. The husband went beyond noticing the women were attractive by masturbating to orgasm while visualizing them and thinking about what he wanted to do to them. Most women and some men are naive about the connection of masturbation to mental adultery. I was…until a husband admitted acting out the lust of his eye with his hand. Loving women know they don't like their husband masturbating instead of having sex with them. But they often don't know Jesus condemns it.

Jesus pronounced lustful self-masturbation as mental adultery and grounds for scriptural divorce. Type C masturbation relies on fantasy and lust. A person may become so addicted to pleasuring himself that he can't drive down the freeway without masturbating.

Giving in to masturbation while driving also appears to plague some women. Right before this book was published Hugo Gye for *MailOnline* in the UK helped break the story about feminine sexual compulsions with the headline "Woman Driver Smashed Her Mini into the Back of a Van While Pleasuring Herself With a Sex Toy at the Wheel." In her low-riding Mini Cooper the woman took advantage of being stalled in traffic. After her car lurched forward and hit the truck, she got out and exchanged her information and driver's license with the truck driver. No one would have known what caused the accident except the truck's rear camera captured her quickly pulling up her pants with a Rampant Rabbit-style vibrator in her hand (7/13/2015). The Internet came alive with humorous and vulgar tweets about her sexual exposé.

In addition to grabbing every opportunity for masturbation, sexual addicts also see sex in everything. One man who was struggling with sexual addiction emailed me. After expressing appreciation for my booklet on sexual addiction he asked me to stop abbreviating the book of Titus as the three letters brought sexual imagines to his mind. He said it was a stumbling block for the people I was trying to help (2 Peter 2:14). Many people lose their jobs when sexual addiction takes over their lives.

Rather than recommending actually cutting off the hand and

plucking out the eye, Jesus is using an extreme example. Sexual addiction requires tremendous effort to overcome it. You start by putting in the mental effort to learn what it means to soulmate with the opposite sex so you can enjoy healthy lovemaking.

The Harm of Lustful Masturbation Type C

The rest of this discussion deals with the harm of Masturbation Type C—sexual addiction that thrives on porn and lustful fantasies.

Teaches the Body to Prefer Solo Sex

Experiencing an orgasm through masturbation greatly imprints the brain and changes how the person experiences pleasure. Essentially, the body learns to prefer solo sex over building satisfying intellectual, emotional, sexual, and spiritual bonds with another human. Self-masturbation is nearly always present in serial adultery, sexual addiction, homosexuality, and intimacy anorexia.

In helping couples overcome intimacy anorexia, Weiss insists on frequent lovemaking with eyes open looking at the mate. What the eyes focus on during orgasm, whether in their imagination, on objects, or a real live person, the act and the hormones bind the person to their fantasy, object, or mate. As a couple ages, open-eyed lovemaking increases the beauty of the spouse.

Several husbands who complain about their wife's lack of sexual enthusiasm say, "My wife has body-image issues. I can't make her believe she's beautiful to me. I desire her just the way she is." These men understand the emotional part. Lovemaking makes their wife gorgeous to them no matter how unhappy she is with her changing body.

Ladies, if you can't believe your husband finds you beautiful, then believe Weiss. Frequent open-eyed lovemaking is skinny dipping in the fountain of youth and beauty in the eyes of your aging husband. Plus it gives you both many health benefits to prolong your lives and keep a spring in your step and a sparkle in your eyes.

Self-stimulation lessens the penis' sensations during vaginal intercourse. Likewise, using vibrators and other self-gratifying objects during sexual abstinence decreases a woman's vaginal feelings during lovemaking. Then when sex takes place, the husband's and the wife's bodies fail to respond fully to each other—no matter how much emotional love they feel in their hearts. Simply stated, self-stimulation exacts a precious price from both husbands and wives by greatly decreasing their physical thrills when in each other's arms.

Test it for yourself to see if this is not true. Watch my video "Take the Hand Love Test" on PatsyRaeDawson.com to see the power of the brain over physical sensations. Refrain from masturbation for at least two weeks. Layer as much lovemaking as you can during this time. Pay attention to your little sexual twinges during the day. Allow yourself to surrender to passionate lovemaking. See if you can recognize heightened sensations from before. I don't know if this will work with Masturbation Type C because that person has crossed a line into addiction.

Creates Fetishes

A tremendous body of evidence has surfaced during the last 40 years regarding how masturbation creates fetishes. This includes Tim LaHaye's book *The Unhappy Gays: What Everyone Should Know about Homosexuality* that came out at the beginning of the AIDS scare in 1978. He stated that most homosexuals he worked with had a history of heavy masturbation along with fantasy (81-82). Focus on the Family founder Dr. James Dobson's 1988-89 interviews with the serial killer, Ted Bundy, revealed the role masturbation and pornography played in his serial murders of young women (Dart 1/25/1989).

In 1994, Dr. Archibald Hart exposed in *The Sexual Man: Masculinity Without Guilt* the role masturbation plays in sexual compulsions and fetishes. He gave the example of a 13-year-old boy who stole his older cousin's black panties. He began fantasizing and masturbating to the panties. When he married years later, he couldn't get excited about his wife unless she wore black panties (113).

In 2007, Dr. Vivienne Cass discussed in *The Elusive Orgasm* how masturbation prevents women from enjoying their husband sexually. For example, self-pleasuring while visualizing rough sex gets in the way of tender passionate lovemaking. Likewise, masturbating while trying to be very still and quiet so the rest of the family won't know what's going on becomes an inhibiting fetish with a real man in marriage (130-132).

Not the Same as a Wet Dream

If self-masturbation carries so many risks and harmful side effects, what are teenage boys and men without a responsive partner to do about the buildup of sexual pressure? They can begin by realizing the difference between wet dreams and self-masturbation based on lust.

Dr. Hart says, "Masturbation has taken over what wet dreams used to accomplish." His surveys show that older men have more wet dreams than teenage boys (106-8). This indicates the shift to masturbation from wet dreams probably stems from the schools promoting masturbation. This happens because the schools rely on Dr. Alfred Kinsey's research on children in their sex-education programs. Since Dr. Kinsey interviewed sex offenders and pedophiles for his research, he failed to recognize how masturbation could become compulsive and the role it plays in perversions.

Today the schools teach masturbation as a safe outlet for draining off sexual energies. Some programs encourage masturbation as a way to avoid AIDS and other STDs. As the connection with perversions and compulsive masturbation shows, self-stimulation isn't necessarily a safe sexual outlet for draining off sexual energies. Without their parents teaching them otherwise, young boys and girls today don't understand the risks they run with self-stimulation. They are dangerously naïve (Jasper 1/19/1987).

The safer course for teenage boys and men seems to be to use God's built-in release mechanism — wet dreams. This is also a good outlet for single women — both young and older. Wet dreams are not sinful and do not involve outside stimulation that negatively influences the brain. For the Israelites, God's law of uncleanness controlled the young boy's sexual urges beginning with his first wet dream and did not allow him to degenerate into habits that could affect his future abilities to function as a man and a lover. God's law of uncleanness protected men and their wives in their ignorance about their bodies and sexual natures.

God's Wonderful Creation

God's design of wet dreams to push his people toward marriage and to help them choose a lifelong sexual partner shows his tremendous love for mankind. Sexual love originated within his mind. He designed it to bless his people and to help husbands and wives bond together at the deepest level of emotional and physical intimacy. For our good and to learn from, he's preserved the Song of Solomon and its recording of the Shulammite's two wet dreams.

A self-masturbator, whether male or female, limits the amount of intimacy he or she can enjoy with the mate. And the release of hormones through masturbation sends self-pleasurers down the road of intimacy anorexia as they create a fetish of self-love. Every person I know who lives with a masturbator also struggles to live with a spouse who withhold all 4 types of love and intimacy. They are always love starved.

We need to learn for ourselves and teach our children how self-masturbation is harmful when it is coupled with lust. God provides a safe outlet in wet dreams for lease of sexual tension. Solo sex destroys marriages and turns its participants into islands of loneliness. On the other hand, subtle wet dreams encourage husbands and wives to plan for romantic times together in each other's arms for *SPEAKING GOD'S BEAUTIFUL LANGUAGE OF LOVE.*

Orgasms of Love with Cervical Kisses

Dr. Helen Kaplan, a respected pioneer in studying the role of the brain in sex, states doctors can't find any differences either physically or functionally between the "desire centers" in the brains of men and women. The same hormones activate sexual response in both the male and the female brains and sexual organs. The main difference comes from what stimulates desire. The man responds first to physical stimulation while the woman reacts first to emotional stimulation (15).

Yet chapters on Proverbs 5 and 7 in my book *God's People Make the Best Lovers* show men and women respond to both physical and mental stimulations. Their emphasis is just different. They both require intellectual and emotional bonding before they can enjoy powerful orgasms.

The woman is the man's equal in the realm of desire and pleasure in God's wonderful creation of sexual love. God gave the husband and wife equal responsibility for satisfying their mate's sexual and emotional needs (1 Corinthians 7:3-5). Except for the man's ejaculation, a vaginal orgasm feels exactly like the man's orgasm. Following is a composite of an orgasm as experienced by both husbands and wives as described in several books and articles that recognize the role of the mind and emotions in sexual love.

Description of the Male and Female Orgasms

As excitement mounts, the vagina and the penis swell with blood and change in shape to prepare for a perfect fit with each other. In young couples this may take only a matter of seconds in both the husband and the wife if their minds are properly joined. In older couples it may take several minutes, but the response of the man and the woman remains equal. Their blood pressure, pulse, and breathing increase.

After penetration, their breathing becomes steadily faster and deeper and then changes to somewhat slower but with even deeper gasps for oxygen in response to the pelvic movements. Their temperatures rise slightly and they may feel hot to the touch. Muscles tense throughout their bodies. All these sensations increase to the point of orgasm. Throughout this time all other senses such as sight, smell, hearing, touch, and taste decrease while their bodies focus on the increasing pelvic sensations.

If the husband and wife have surrendered complete control of their soaring physical sensations to each other, then they go into a series of spasms that can shake their entire bodies. These are typical responses to an orgasm. Afterward their breathing, blood pressure, pulse, congestion of blood, and temperature all return to normal. Both the husband and wife are left with a feeling of deep relaxation and peace with each other and the world.

However, if the husband and the wife try to control their breathing and spasms rather than surrendering to the experience, they hamper the force of the orgasm. *A great orgasm requires both a mental and emotional union with the loved one and a total surrender of the body to the other.* Holding back even a little bit blocks the sensations.

This composite description was compiled from the following books and articles including the page numbers for your reference: Tim LaHaye and Beverly, *The Act of Marriage* (29); Herbert J. Miles, *Sexual Happiness in Marriage* (95); Marie N. Robinson, *The Power of Sexual Surrender* (23-7); Lorna Sarrel and Philip, "What Men Need from the Women Who Love Them" (115); and Bernie Zilbergeld, *Male Sexuality* (122-9).

The Role of the Clitoris in a Vaginal Orgasm

God designed the clitoris as a wonderful organ that increases the woman's pleasure as *it works with the vagina – not in place of the vagina.* Dr. David Rueben reveals in *Any Woman Can* that the clitoris' roots are filled with super sensitive nerve endings and reach deep into the walls of the vagina. The husband's movements and the woman's contractions all stimulate the clitoris and heighten the woman's pleasure (37-8).

The clitoris is connected to the labia minora, the small lips on either side of it. Respected medical writer Ronald M. Deutsch describes in *The Key to Feminine Response in Marriage* how during lovemaking the small lips engorge with blood and increase two to three times their normal thickness. At the same time the area in between the lips becomes engorged. This effectively adds one or more inches to the length of the vagina. The swollen lips help support and hold the penis during lovemaking (42-3).

In his book *Everything You Always Wanted to Know About Sex But Were Afraid to Ask,* Dr. Rueben explains that the clitoris is very sensitive to any tugging or pulling in this whole area which normally takes place during sexual intercourse. Instead of needing a certain position to stimulate the clitoris as the books promoting clitoral orgasms recommend, just the back and forth thrusts of the male member within the woman's vagina stimulate this whole region as the clitoral area is pulled toward the vagina (43).

The woman who discovers the secret of her thoughts over a vaginal orgasm finds that her clitoris becomes even more sensitive than before. Just her husband brushing against her pelvic region sends waves of desire through the vaginal area. She doesn't require manual stimulation.

However, if the woman is over-tired or out-of-sorts a brief touch to that region causes memories of past unions to flood her being. Even if she *wants to stay mad* at him for a while, because of these intense feelings her body and emotions yield to his caresses. This all takes place within a few moments for the woman who has learned to respond vaginally. Thus frequent lovemaking helps keep emotionally detrimental barriers at bay and impedes them from gaining a foothold in a marriage. (The description of the male and female orgasm and the role of the clitoris come from my book *God's People Make the Best Lovers* [184-5, 371].)

Go Deeper for a Cervical Kiss

When a woman experiences a vaginal orgasm, her vagina opens up and her husband can go deeper. David Deida describes the masculine experience in *The Enlightened Sex Manual: Sexual Skills for the Superior Lover:*

> Her cervix dipping inward, sucking at the tip of my penis like a delicate bird of thirst (92).

Most women have never experienced a cervical kiss because they are novices with vaginal orgasms. But once vaginal orgasms become common, they can easily move into enjoying earth-shaking cervical orgasms. It's the natural result of frequent lovemaking, sexual trust, and emotional bonding. Nothing compares to the exquisite, delightful sensations of deep intimate kissing.

If a woman has not learned the power of her thoughts over her body's responses, then touching her cervix may be painful. My advice is to forget about the cervical kiss. Instead, concentrate of layering your hormones with frequent lovemaking and turning vaginal orgasms into laughter. When the time is right, your vagina will open up, your husband will go deeper, and you will enjoy the most intimate of kisses.

Deida and many bloggers tell women it can take at least 15 minutes for them to start having vaginal orgasms and 45 minutes to begin enjoying cervical kisses. However, most of these writers don't promote marriage and monogamous relationships.

In a loving marriage, a woman who has learned the power of her attitudes toward herself, her husband, children, home, and work can frequently begin having vaginal orgasms within a few minutes of penetration. Some women respond just from the warm up activities. Such women can transition into cervical kisses very quickly.

Why a Woman Can't Fake a Vaginal Orgasm

A woman can't fake a vaginal orgasm because too much is going on inside her body that she can't control. She can only yield to it.

A husband knows when his wife enjoys an orgasm because her vagina opens up. This allows him to thrust deeper. Or he can back out to stroke her clitoris and vaginal opening with the head of his penis to start the process all over. Her vagina closes around his organ of love again to send her into another wave of spasms.

When a woman's insides are very sensitive to her man's presence, the head of his organ of love feels like hot, soft velvet tenderly stroking her. He's in control and can play her sensations like a fine musical instrument bringing her time and again to multiple vaginal orgasms until the ultra-climatic ones. Her pleasure is exquisite.

While her head tilts up toward God she whispers, "Thank you, Lord, for designing the way of a man with his maid!"

After the husband's orgasm and the wife has drunk her fill of his love she can enjoy several powerful grand finales. Instead of arching her back, her body pulls her head and shoulders forward into a strong compression of her abdomen. Her vagina squeezes and hugs her husband's penis in a powerful Kegel embrace of sensations for both that lasts for several seconds. This is somewhat similar to the birth process. When it's over, she may laugh and fall back in happy exhaustion.

Physical Limitations to a Vaginal Orgasm

Ronald M. Deutsch says in *The Key to Feminine Response in Marriage* that in about two out of three women the pubococcygeus muscle (PC muscle) tone is so weak that it causes incontinence, difficult childbirths, and limited sexual satisfaction within the vagina. When women have good muscle tone childbirth is easier, the birth canal is rarely damaged in delivery, and sexual responsiveness tends to be good.

This thick, strong muscle runs like a sling from "the bony prominence at the front of the pelvis, to the coccyx, the end of the spine" in both men and women. Athletes can have weak PC muscles as it isn't strengthened by general exercise. When the muscle is strengthened through frequent lovemaking or doing the Kegel exercises it supports the neck of the vagina in squeezing the husband's penis. This stimulates the nerve-rich area surrounding the vagina to give the wife wonderful sensations from her husband's penetrations. It also increases the husband's enjoyment (55-9).

Both the husband and wife benefit from exercising this muscle in dealing with incontinence and promoting greater sexual pleasure. Dr. Zilbergeld says in his book *Male Sexuality* that after he considered the physical similarities between the male and the female sexual organs he tried exercising his PC muscle and recommended it to all his patients. They reported that strengthening the muscle not only helped them with control, but it also increased their physical sensations and helped them enjoy stronger and more pleasurable orgasms. Several other male authors also recommend men exercise this muscle. Men perform the exercise the same way women do (129-30).

After the husband and wife climax the wife doesn't need to make her husband leave her warmth. She can deliberately exercise her PC muscle around his organ of love. This lets them practice deep caressing and begins to train their bodies how to respond. The husband can also exercise his PC muscle and add more sensations to the experience. I give instructions for exercising the PC muscle with Kegel exercises in *God's People Make the Best Lovers* and you can find them on the Internet.

Orgasms of Love Won't Cure a Sexless Marriage

When I began teaching marriage classes over 48 years ago I told my students, "If your husband has a strong sexual drive and is a hard worker hug his neck. You are so lucky. If you learn your role he'll respond." My observation still holds true.

Writers often tell men, "Loving starts with the way you treat your wife during the day. If you want more sex, satisfy her emotional needs during the day." The opposite is true for women, "The way you treat your husband in the bedroom affects how he treats you during the day. If you want more emotional love, be an active sexual partner." Now that we understand how hormones are released with hugs, kisses, and lovemaking, we know why both statements are true.

But if the husband or the wife is an intimacy anorexic, learning how to be a better lover won't cure a sexless marriage. The problem isn't a lack of lovemaking skills. A loving husband and wife learn how to be better lovers together. Anorexics are into manipulating and starving the spouse of their affection. They don't want to learn how to be a better lover *with the spouse.*

Being a Better Lover Can Trap You in an Unloving Marriage

Several wives learned how to enjoy a vaginal orgasm because their husband wasn't interested in sex with them and complained that they needed too much foreplay. Some of the wives read Dr. Robinson's book *The Power of Sexual Surrender* while others attended my classes or read my book *God's People Make the Best Lovers*. All the wives learned the secret of being mentally loving and receptive. Their enjoyment of sex increased as they responded quickly with vaginal orgasms.

Not even one of the husbands started initiating sex after the wives became ravishing lovers. The husbands simply began fussing about something else as an excuse to avoid lovemaking. The couples only had sex when the wife initiated. Most of the time when she tried to arouse her husband, he rejected her. Nearly every one of these marriages ended in divorce when the wife found evidence of her husband's long-term unfaithfulness. Accusing the wife of taking too long to arouse is a common excuse unloving men use to reject their wives sexually.

The same is true for men married to anorexics. Many husbands told me they bought books and searched the Internet on how to become better lovers. They hoped a different technique would transform their wives into passionate lovers. It never worked. The problem was not their lovemaking style, but their wives' unloving heart.

In some cases, the wives learning the secret of a vaginal orgasm made the problem worse because it trapped them in an unloving, sexless marriage. Since a vaginal orgasm is a barometer of the relationship, the wives worked hard to love their husbands at face value and to be content with their station in life. The husbands consented to just enough sex to keep the wives' sexual hormones stirred up to keep her loving him and living in denial of how unloving he really was. Likewise, anorexic wives often give their husbands only enough sex for their hormones to keep the men trapped and thinking someday it will be better.

One of the wives said, "I determined if my husband could perform, his hang-ups weren't going to be mine, and I would enjoy a vaginal orgasm. But decades later, I found evidence of multiple adulteries and emotional affairs throughout our marriage. I wish that early in the marriage I'd learned what God says about people without natural love for family and that Weiss had written his books. I would've insisted he change right along with me. It turns out his hang-ups really were mine after all and destroyed our marriage. The hormones released during my vaginal orgasms made me a sucker for his deceit and manipulations."

While learning how to be a better lover should be good, it wasn't the problem in these marriages. The problem came from one mate being without natural affection. My advice is to go through my free *Sexless Marriages Self-Assessment Survey* available at PatsyRaeDawson.com to learn more about the multiple 24/7 sins you're dealing with.

The class on fighting fair and facing anger in my *Challenges in Marriage: What to Do When Sin Inhibits Love* MP3s will help you develop communication skills so real progress can be made. The material teaches how to hold your mate accountable for his or her actions.

You can read Weiss's books to learn more about the sin you're dealing with from a secular view point. He offers genuine hope and tells how to know if your mate is making progress or is just pretending to get you to back off.

If you don't deal with your mate being unloving, sometimes learning how to enjoy a vaginal orgasm and be a better lover gives the anorexic free rein to continue withholding intimacy as usual.

Some Battles Are Worth Fighting

What's the answer if you're married to an anorexic? If you're emotionally loving, then you need to obey God regardless of what your spouse does. At the same time, God doesn't instruct you to blindly ignore the sins of an unloving spouse. Everyone in the family is harmed by one mate's refusal to love the other. The children are the biggest losers of all.

Unfortunately, all marriages can't be saved. Some intimacy anorexics don't want to give up their sin of being unloving. They use tricks to fool the mate into thinking they're trying to change, only to go back to their old ways when the pressure is off.

The greatest spiritual challenges often occur when sin enters the home—they don't come from persecution from the world. These sins in the home include withholding love, bitterness, assigning motives for either good or evil, drunkenness, financial abuse, adultery, deceit, verbal abuse, physical abuse, sexual neglect, incest, and homosexuality.

Covering up the mate's sins makes a person an accomplice or enabler. The resulting secrecy allows being without natural affection to flourish. Like spouse abuse, intimacy anorexia gets worse over the years if it isn't dealt with. A heart that's closed to love is open to hate.

When sin invades the home, a spiritual battle must be fought (2 Corinthians 10:3–6; Matthew 10:34–39). The best advice I can give is, "Get it out in the open and deal with it. Don't hide it. Don't make excuses for it." However, sometimes the unloving spouse objects to the mate seeking outside help as Paul advised in Galatians 6:1-2 with "bear one another's burdens."

Often the resistance comes because the person doesn't want anyone to know about his or her behavior. Jesus said, "For everyone who does evil hates the light, and does not come to the light, lest his deeds should be exposed" (John 3:20).

Sometimes the sexually-denied mate resists getting help because he or she is ashamed of being unloved. Thus the target or victim is also afraid of the light. By the unappreciated mate accepting the shame rather than bringing the problem out into the light, the rejected mate buys into the anorexic's need to blame others for everything.

Some battles in the home are worth fighting. Fighting for your children and yourself to be loved by an intimacy anorexic is one of those battles. The sooner you fight it, the better it is for your children. May God forgive us all for our past blindness to this hideous sin of being unloving that damages so many of our precious children.

God Doesn't Trap Anyone in an Unloving Marriage

God cares who we marry and who we remain married to. Some people think they must stay married to an unloving person for the sake of the children. To the contrary, God says getting away from such a person who refuses to grow up into love is all about protecting the children who were "unclean, but now they are holy" (1 Corinthians 7:14-15; Malachi 2:3).

If you have any doubts about how badly children are affected by growing up in an anorexic, sexless home please read *Beyond the Bedroom, Healing for Adult Children of Sex Addicts* by Weiss. This book doesn't deal just with sexual addicts. Weiss's work began with sexual addicts and expanded to include intimacy anorexics who withhold love from their mate in many ways. Regardless of how unloving spouses choose to take care of their own sexual needs, everyone in the family is harmed by the anorexic. The children suffer the most damage of all.

If you're married to an unloving person or grew up in an unloving home, I urge you to read this book. It'll show how you are hampered by trying to co-parent with an anorexic and the harm done to your children. It will help adult children of anorexic homes heal and learn how to love.

And if the mate refuses to work at learning how to love, read my article "Your Marriage Vows Imply the Biblical Right to Divorce a Sexless Spouse" and listen to my "Podcasts on Biblical Divorce in Sexless Marriages" at PatsyRaeDawson.com. I also recommend Barbara Roberts' book *Not Under Bondage, Biblical Divorce for Abuse, Adultery & Desertion.* In her very thorough book, Barbara gives word studies and shows how many Christians rip God's statement, "I hate divorce" out of context and ignore the meaning of the words.

5 Reasons I Emphasize Vaginal Orgasms

Here's the 5 main reasons I emphasize vaginal orgasms. The following points are ones I've covered many times throughout the Song of Solomon. Thus I only give a brief overview of them.

1. It's What the Shulammite's Mother Taught Her

The instructions the Shulammite's mother gave her are very similar to the ones Dr. Robinson gives women to teach them how to enjoy a vaginal orgasm in her book the *Power of Sexual Surrender*. Additionally, the Shulammite has the same healthy attitudes toward sex, herself, the Shepherd, and their future children that Dr. Robinson says prepare a woman to respond vaginally. She expects to enjoy her wedding night as much as her Shepherd will. As the Shulammite's wet dream illustrated, with hers and her Shepherd's healthy attitudes toward lovemaking she will respond with vaginal orgasms.

2. It's More Pleasurable for the Husband and Wife

This is a given for both husbands and wives who've experienced both clitoral and vaginal orgasms. *Glorious lovemaking requires some skill, but it's mostly an attitude.* It's worth the effort for a couple to take care of their attitudes so their bodies can enjoy the greatest thrills ever.

3. It's Best for the Children

Children thrive in a home where their parents obviously love each other and their affection spills over onto them. In the grand finale at the end of the Song of Solomon, the Shulammite addresses parents. God has preserved the Song of Solomon to teach parents how to create a loving environment in which to raise their children and grandchildren.

Clitoral orgasms don't require that a woman love her husband. In fact, a woman doesn't even have to know the man's name to experience a clitoral orgasm. But she can't enjoy a vaginal one if she doesn't love and adore him. This attitude and the hormones of love bless the fruit of their union—their children. Both the husband and wife become more emotionally and physically loving toward their children.

4. It's What the Purity and Hookup Cultures Need

I firmly believe the best way to deal with the rampant sexual extremes and confusion in our society is not to try to scare young people into being chaste. It's to teach them God has a much more enjoyable way when they learn how to truly love their mate. If we're going to impact the Hookup Culture, we first have to liberate the Purity Culture to enjoy God's proudest act of creation. Why would a hookup player ever want to be like any of the virginity pledgers who embrace a lifetime of sexual frustration and misery? The sad part is God doesn't want any of us to be like those who are trapped in the Purity Culture.

It's precisely because the Shulammite's mother taught her what she would give up if she married Solomon before they loved each other that she held out for true love and ecstatic vaginal orgasms. She wanted what she observed that her parents had. We need to have the same wisdom as her mother and teach our daughters and sons by example and words that a vaginal orgasm is definitely worth the wait. Consequently, they should be meticulous in choosing a mate and lover.

5. It's What Glorifies God

We've seen that lovemaking originated within the mind of God to bless husbands and wives. When a couple works at their relationship and fills their hearts with true love, their bodies respond with ecstatic orgasms. Their minds are flooded with beneficial hormones to bond them together in ever-increasing love and devotion.

When a wife's head is tilted back in response to her husband's powerful thrusts and the intense sensations he creates, she can look up to heaven to commune with her God. With strong vaginal orgasms she glorifies him and his design for *SPEAKING GOD'S BEAUTIFUL LANGUAGE OF LOVE* which transcends words.

Why Men Love Vaginal Orgasms and Women Should, Too

Three husbands tell how sharing vaginal orgasms with their wife brings joy to their wife and them.

1. Women Get More Enjoyment from Sex Than Men Do

"I've always thought sex is more for women than men because my wife has many orgasms while I can only have one. After I've come and we're still connected, she deliberately squeezes her PC muscle around me. She doesn't stop until she's had several more small orgasms. When she relaxes, we both laugh out loud."

2. The Husband Goes Deeper When His Wife Orgasms

"I hear men say, 'I can't tell if she's faking it.' I know they've never been with a woman having a vaginal orgasm because when my wife has hers, she opens up and I go deeper. We both enjoy a whole new range of sensations. You can't fake that."

3. The Husband's Greatest Joy Is His Wife's Pleasure

"It's very satisfying watching my wife orgasm multiple times and knowing I'm the cause of all that pleasure."

Nestled tenderly in each other's arms, with their bodies, souls, and minds they say, *Thank you, My Lord, for creating the way of a man with a maid. To You be the glory forever and ever for your profound love for men and women. Amen.*

The 4 Parts of One Flesh, Love, and Intimacy

After God made Adam and Eve, he declared that they would become one-flesh.

Genesis 2:23-24: "And the man said, 'This is now bone of my bones, and flesh of my flesh; she shall be called Woman, because she was taken out of Man.' For this cause a man shall leave his father and his mother, and shall cleave to his wife; and they shall become one flesh."

The *Theological Wordbook of the Old Testament* shows the significance of a husband and wife becoming "one flesh." It says, "*One* stresses unity while recognizing diversity within that oneness." God helps us understand what the definition of one flesh means by repeating the Genesis statement 4 times in the New Testament. Each passage reveals a different aspect of one flesh. When we combine the 4 diversified parts of one flesh, we create unity of purpose, function, love, and intimacy

We often assume one flesh refers strictly to sex. However, sex is only 1/4 of being one flesh. If we neglect the other 3/4, we doom ourselves to a make-do relationship. And the sex won't be all that great without the missing 3 parts. That's because all 4 parts of one flesh work together to create lasting, passionate intimacy that transforms lives and blesses children.

Deciphering the finer points of one flesh is important to our study because the 4 parts of love taught in the Song of Solomon reflect the 4 parts of one flesh. In other words, intellectual, emotional, sexual, and spiritual love correspond to the 4 parts of being one flesh. Notice the 4 New Testament passages that teach the 4 different aspects of the creation promise along with 4 snippets from the Song of Solomon to introduce the parallels. Review secrets 4 and 5 for more in-depth details.

1. Intellectual Love Recognizes Male and Female

Matthew 19:4-5: "And He answered and said, 'Have you not read, that He who created them from the beginning made them male and female, and said, "for this cause a man shall leave his father and mother, and shall cleave to his wife; and the two shall become one flesh."?'"

In this familiar passage, the Pharisees tested Jesus by trying to lead him into a squabble about divorce. To answer their question, Jesus quoted the creation account and said God "made them *male and female*." Then he added, *"for this cause."* What cause? Because they are *male and female* "a man shall leave his father and mother, and shall cleave to his wife; and the two shall become one flesh." Obviously, one-flesh love occurs between heterosexuals — not same-sex couples.

Intellectual love understands and values one's own gender while appreciating and valuing the opposite sex. We see this as the Shepherd begs the Maiden to end their separation and marry him:

> *Song of Solomon 4:8a:*
> *"Come with me from Lebanon, my bride,*
> *May you come with me from Lebanon."*

The Shepherd calls the Shulammite "my bride" 5 times in his proposal. He desires a permanent, committed relationship with her. As a helper designed by God for him, she will complete him and make him perfect. She is the answer to his problem of loneliness. His masculinity needs her femininity. He values and cherishes her for the person she is and what she will bring to the marriage. He begs her to accompany him wherever life leads.

2. Emotional Love Celebrates One in Mind

Ephesians 5:31-33: "For this cause a man shall leave his father and mother, and shall cleave to his wife; and the two shall become one flesh. This mystery is great; but I am speaking with reference to Christ and the church. Nevertheless let each individual among you also love his own wife even as himself; and let the wife see to it that she respect [reverence — KJV] her husband."

This passage emphasizes the mental union — the husband loving his wife as himself and the wife admiring her husband. Sadly, many couples overlook the emotional part of one flesh that makes them *one in mind —* the secret ingredient of one-flesh love.

For breathless sexual thrills, the coupling of the minds must take place before the bodies unite. It cannot take place on the spur of the moment in a several-minute foreplay ritual before sexual intercourse begins. This union of the minds comes from 24/7 emotional love that enables the bodies to speak God's beautiful language of love that transcends mere spoken words.

In his marriage proposal, the Shepherd references the emotional bond he and the Maiden share:

Song of Solomon 4:9a:
"You have made my heart beat faster, my sister, my bride."

He calls the Shulammite "my sister," referring to their emotional bond. Just as brothers and sisters share secrets, confidences, and look out for each other, the Shepherd and the Maiden totally trust each other emotionally. Three times the Maiden begs the Jerusalem Virgins to not force her and Solomon to marry until they've established the same kind of emotional intimacy that she enjoys with her Shepherd.

3. Sexual Love Honors One in Body

1 Corinthians 6:16: "Or do you not know that the one who joins himself to a harlot is one body with her? For He says, 'The two will become one flesh.' "

Thayer distinguishes between "body" and "flesh" claiming *they are not exactly the same.* He explains that the Greek word for "body," *soma,* used for the relationship with the harlot refers to a "skillful combination of related parts." *Sarka,* the word for "flesh," does not designate the same idea. Rather, it "signifies the entire nature of a man, sense and reason, without the Holy Spirit" (Thayer 567-571, 611).

God designed the "combination of the related parts" *so skillfully,* that the male and female organs can compensate for ignorance in either the man or the woman. For example, even if both of them yield to devastating Victorian inhibitions and fail to emotionally enjoy the sexual act, the man can still be sufficiently aroused to impregnate the woman. God requires neither the man nor the woman to enjoy sex to create another human life. But having sex is being only "one body," which amounts to only 1/4 of being one-flesh.

In his proposal, the Shepherd looks forward to joining his masculine body with the Shulammite's feminine one:

Song of Solomon 4:9b:
"You have made my heart beat faster with a single glance of your eyes,
With a single strand of your necklace."

Two of the times Solomon proposed to the Maiden, he rehearsed a polished speech he used on all of his wives. However, in two similar declarations of his love, the Shepherd accented different characteristics. For example, in his first speech he drew attention to her sweet voice; in his second, he spoke of a single glance of her eyes. First, he praised her lovely form; then he noticed a single strand of her necklace. He always describes her whole being instead of an assemblage of perfect individual pieces as Solomon did. His heart beats faster with desire as all the parts of one flesh come together in mature sexual love.

4. Spiritual Love Glorifies God Joining Them Together

Mark 10:6-9: "'But from the beginning of the creation, God made them male and female. For this cause a man shall leave his father and mother, and the two shall become one flesh; consequently they are no longer two, but one flesh. What therefore God has joined together, let no man separate.' "

"Joined," a fascinating word, parallels the meaning of "one" as in one-flesh. Joined conveys this same idea of turning *two* into *one*, for it means "to fasten to *one* yoke" (Thayer 394).

God takes a male and a female and fastens them to *one* yoke in marriage in a similar way to how a farmer fastens two oxen together with one yoke. When one ox tries to go one way to grind corn while the other tries to go in the opposite direction to plow a field, they pull against each other. Neither one does its work. Only by working together both physically and mentally can the two oxen turn the grinding stones or pull the plow.

God wondrously joins the intellect, emotions, and bodies of males and females together to create one-flesh love. We saw in the first chapter how God describes this—the way of a man with a maid—as his proudest creation. Thus, he blessed the marriage of the Shulammite with the Shepherd by telling them his 3-step secret for a lifetime of passion.

Song of Solomon 5:1-b:
"Eat, friends;
Drink and imbibe deeply, O lovers
[and drink, until you are drunk with love! – CJB]"

God told the young couple, "Get married and make passionate, frequent love until you're giggly and drunk in each other's arms. I created one-flesh love to bless you all the days of your life. And when you follow my instructions, you praise and worship me, the architect of lovemaking."

What a wonderful God we serve who created this amazing 4-part way for husbands and wives to love each other and to serve him with their whole being!

Sexual Words Used by Teenagers, College Students, and University Health Professionals

1. Abortion: Removal of unwanted tissue, sort of like a tonsillectomy.
2. Adolescents: Impressionable and confused; they are at a critical point in their development, questioning who they are and what they want. Many professionals are eager to teach their social agenda to them.
3. Alternative sexualities: Reassurance about homosexual thoughts, sadism, and masochism.
4. Androgynous culture: Where the differences between male and female are discounted or denied, and the bond-between them robbed of singularity.
5. Baby: Celebrated when born to a lesbian; suspect when born to a Christian.
6. Chest surgery: Proper term for mastectomy for transgendered person.
7. Dangerous behaviors: A personal choice; judgments are prohibited — they might offend.
8. Friend with benefits: No strings attached to sex. The girl usually prefers a real boyfriend, but tries to be realistic. This asserts women are just like men and denies the woman's depression and hating herself while the man is content. Is Zoloft the answer?
9. Gender-free partners: What difference does it make whether male or female?
10. Heterosexual: Never assume that a person is this or that sexual activity can lead to pregnancy.
11. High-risk behavior: Only concern, "Are you protected?" referring to condoms.
12. Hookups: Casual dating sex without getting to know the person or making a commitment.
13. In like: Falling "in like" as opposed to "falling in love" with a steady hookup.
14. Men and women as "opposites," as in "opposite sex": Avoid using this term to avoid polarization.
15. Motherhood: Can be delayed indefinitely.
16. Multiculturalism workshops: To confront sexism, racism, and homophobia. They are often mandatory for professionals working with students.

17. Organized religion: Major source of social injustice.
18. PDA: Public displays of affection.
19. Personal decision: On whether to be tested for AIDS after risky behavior. Avoids the question of whether his/her life will be cut short.
20. Political correctness: Muzzled society in the nineties. Before that time, a campus physician might advise a student, "It is love and lifelong fidelity that bring joy and liberated sensuality, and provide the best insurance against STDs." An unwanted pregnancy, an abortion—these were weighty issues. They understood that men and women are profoundly different and weren't afraid to say so. An STD was a serious event.
21. Polyamorous: Have open sexual or romantic relationships with more than one person at a time. It can be heterosexual, lesbian, gay, or bisexual, and relationships between polyamorous people can include combinations of people of different sexual orientations.
22. Preventing pregnancy: Only teaching in women's health centers as if motherhood can be delayed indefinitely just as males can become fathers much later in life.
23. Primary and casual sex partners: Tacit approval of promiscuity and experimentation by dividing partners into two groups; primary partner plus casual sexual contacts with others.
24. Rite of passage: Infection with one of the sexually transmitted viruses—first STD. It comes with the territory.
25. Ruben's girl: fleshy with a curvaceous body.
26. Safer sex: Do not teach that condoms are unreliable, only that they offer safer sex.
27. Shunning and intimidation: What happens to health professionals who speak out against the physical and psychological harm done to students by these activities and who don't cater to "political correctness."
28. Steady hookup: Turning casual hookup into a boyfriend. Maybe fall in love.
29. Traditional marriage: Just one option; there are other alternatives, all equally valid.
30. Transgendered person: While in transition, ask if they want to be addressed as a male or female.
31. Use latex: Use a condom.
32. Women's health: Focuses on contraception, not future families or the woman waiting too long to conceive.

(Adapted from *Unprotected: How Political Correctness Endangers Every Student* by Miriam Grossman and *Restless Virgins: Love, Sex, and Survival at a New England Prep School* by Abigail Jones and Marissa Miley.)

Works Cited

AARP. "Sexuality at Midlife and Beyond, 2004 Update of Attitudes and Behaviors." Conducted by TNS NFO Alanta. Washington, DC: AARP, May 2005. Web.

"AARP/Modern Maturity Sexuality Study." Prepared by NFO Research, Inc. Washington, DC: AARP, 1999. Web.

Allan, Bruce. "What the Bible Says About Sex & Foreplay." *The Bible,* 6/3/2014. HubPages. Web.

Amen, Daniel G. *The Brain in Love, 12 Lessons to Enhance Your Love Life.* New York, NY: Three Rivers Press, 2007.

Andersen, B. L., Cyranowski, J. M. "Women's Sexuality. Behaviours, Responses and Individual Differences." *J Consult Clinical Psychology,* 1995.

Anderson, Dianna E. *Damaged Goods: New Perspectives on Christian Purity.* New York, NY: Jericho Books, 2015.

---. "Taking the Lead in Developing New Sexual Ethics." Rachel Held Evans Blog, 2/4/2015. Web.

"Arrowleaf Balsamroot." *The Great Basin and Invasive Weeds.* United States Department of Agriculture Forest Service, 9/26/2006. Web.

Babbage, Stuart Barton. *Sex and Sanity, A Christian View of Sexual Morality.* Philadelphia: The Westminster Press, 1965. Quoting Workman, Herbert. *The Evolution of the Monastic Ideal.*

Barlow, D, H. "Causes of Sexual Dysfunction." *J Consult Clinical Psychology,* 1986.

Basson, Rosemary, Dr. "Rethinking Low Sexual Desire in Women." 12/2003. https://obgyn.onlinelibrary.wiley.com/doi/abs/10.1111/j.1471-0528.2002.01002.x.

---. "The Female Sexual Response: A Different Model," *Journal of Sex & Marital Therapy.* Britain: Routledge, 2000.

Beecham, Jahnna. "Writing for Teens." *Writer's Digest* (4/90).

Belliveau, Fred and Lin Richter. *Understanding Human Sexual Inadequacy.* Boston: Little, Brown and Company, 1970.

Bouchez, Colette. "A Woman's Walk Reveals Her Sex Life." *MedHeadlines,* 9/12/2008.

Brenton, Sir Lancelot C. L. "An Historical Account of the Septuagint Version." 1851. *The Common Man's Prospective,* 2010. Web.

Carey, Tanith. "Addicted to Viagra: They should be at their most virile, but a growing number of young men can't cope without those little blue pills." *Daily Mail Online,* 10/3/2012. Associated Newspapers Ltd. Web.

Carnes, Patrick J. *Out of the Shadows: Understanding Sexual Addiction.* Center City, MN: Hazelden Educational Materials, 1992.

---. *Sexual Anorexia: Overcoming Sexual Self-Hatred.* Center City, MN: Hazelden Educational Materials, 1997.

Carr, G. Lloyd. *The Song of Solomon, Tyndale Old Testament Commentaries*. Downers Grove, IL: Inter-Varsity Press, 1984.

Cass, Vivienne, PhD. *The Elusive Orgasm: A Woman's Guide to Why She Can't and How She Can Orgasm*. Cambridge, MA: Da Capo Press, 2007.

CDC, Centers for Disease Control and Prevention. "Youth Risk Behavior Surveillance — United States, 2013." Surveillance Summaries, 6/13/2014. MMWR 2014; 63(SS04).

Chesney-Lind, Meda. "Are Girls Closing the Gender Gap in Violence?" *Criminal Justice Magazine*, Volume 16, Issue 1, Spring 2001. Web.

"Chanel No 22 Raises Testosterone Levels in Men: Axe Has Same Effect on Women." Ergo-Log Blog, 8/15/2008. Web.

Chartham, Robert. *Mainly for Wives: The Art of Sex for Women*. New York: Signet Books, 1969.

Ciolino, Vincent. "Pollination Is a Fragile Process Easily Disrupted by Rain," *Montemaggiore Blog*, 12/15/2011. Web.

Cole, Michael. *Song of Songs*. Westarkchurchofchrist.org/library/songof songs.htm. Web.

Curtis, Kristen Lee. "Low Libido Affecting Your Lovemaking, Ladies? 33 Ways to Rev It Up Again." *Insiders Health*. Naples, FL: Insiders Health Group. Web.

Dart, John. "Porno Foe Has Unusual Ally in Killer Bundy." *Los Angeles Times*, 1/25/89.

Davis, Ellen F. *Proverbs, Ecclesiastes, and the Song of Songs*. Louisville, KY: Westminster John Knox Press, 2000.

Dawson, Patsy Rae. *Challenges in Marriage: What to Do When Sin Inhibits Love*. Amarillo, TX: Patsy Rae Dawson LLC, 2015.

---. *God's People Appreciate Marriage*. Amarillo, TX: Patsy Rae Dawson LLC, 2013.

---. *God's People Make the Best Lovers*. Amarillo, TX: Patsy Rae Dawson LLC, 2013.

Deida, David. *The Enlightened Sex Manual, Sexual Skills for the Superior Lover*. Boulder, CO: Sounds True, Inc., 2007.

Deutsch, Ronald M. *The Key to Feminine Response in Marriage*. New York, NY: Random House, 1968.

Dharmadhikari, Murli. "Apple Wine." *Iowa State University Extension and Outreach*. Web.

Dickey, Joshua. *The Complete Koine-English Reference Bible: New Testament, Septuagint and Strong's Concordance*. N.P. EBook edition, 2014.

Diefendorf, Sarah. "After the Wedding Night: Sexual Abstinence and Masculinities Over the Life Course." Unpublished doctorate paper at the University of Washington. Used by permission. Published *Gender & Society*, Vol. XX No. X, Month, IIII, 15 July 2015. Sociologists for Women in Society. Web.

Dillow, Joseph *Solomon on Sex*. Nashville: Thomas Nelson Publishers, 1977.

Dwyer, William M. *What Everyone Knew About Sex* *Explained in the Words of Olson Squire Fowler and Other Victorian Moralists*. New York: Bell Publishing Co., 1972.

Eddings, Bryce. "A few Thoughts About Apple Cider." *About Food*, About.com. Web.

Eichenlaub, John E., M.D. *The Marriage Art: A New Approach to Sexual Pleasure in Marriage*. Cabin John, MD: Wildside Press, LLC, 2011.

Falk, Marcia. *The Song of Songs: A New Translation and Interpretation.* San Francisco, CA: HarperSanFrancisco, 1990.

"FDA Approves First Treatment for Sexual Desire Disorder, Addyi Approved to Treat Premenopausal Women." FDA News Release 8/18/2015. Silver Spring, MD: U.S. Food and Drug Administration.

Freitas, Donna. *The End of Sex: How Hookup Culture Is Leaving a Generation Unhappy, Sexually Unfulfilled, and Confused About Intimacy.* New York, NY: Basic Books, 2013. Used by permission.

Gilder, George. *Men and Marriage.* Gretna, LO: Pelican Publishing Co. Inc., 1986.

Great People of the Bible and How They Lived. Pleasantville, NY: Reader's Digest Association, Inc, 1979.

Grossman, Miriam. *Unprotected: A Campus Psychiatrist Reveals How Political Correctness in Her Profession Endangers Every Student.* New York, NY: Penquin Books Ltd, 2006.

Grundy, Trevor. "Kissing Corpses Is Helping Spread Ebola, Expert Says." *Religious News Service.* Religious News LLC, 9/26/2014. Web.

Gye, Hugo. "Woman Driver Smashed Her Mini into the Back of a Van While Pleasuring Herself With a Sex Toy at the Wheel." *MailOnline.* Associated Newspapers Ltd, 7/13/2015. Web.

Harrell, Pat E. *Divorce and Remarriage in the Early Church.* Austin, TX: R. B. Sweet Co. Inc., 1967. Used by permission.

Hart, Archibald D. *The Sexual Man: Masculinity Without Guilt.* Dallas, TX: Word Publishing, 1994.

Henderson, Robert and Ian Gould. *Life in Bible Times.* Chicago: Rand McNally & Company, 1967.

Henslin, Earl. *This Is Your Brain in Love: Scientific Breakthroughs for a More Passionate and Emotionally Healthy Marriage.* Nashville, TN: Thomas Nelson, 2009.

Hess, Richard S. *Song of Songs, Baker Commentary on the Old Testament Wisdom and Psalms.* Grand Rapids, MI: Baker Academic, a division of Baker Publishing Group, 2005. Used by permission.

Hibbert, Christopher. *Queen Victoria: A Personal History.* London: HarperCollins, 2000. Quoted by *Wikipedia.* "Queen Victorian."

Home-Remedies-for-you.com. "Lily Flower." Everyday Health Network, 2015.

Hubbard, David. *Mastering the Old Testament, Ecclesiastes, Song of Solomon.* Dallas, TX: Word Publishing, 1991.

Instone-Brewer, David. *Divorce and Remarriage in the Bible, The Social and Literary Context.* Grand Rapids, MI: William B. Eerdmans Publishing Company, 2002.

Instone-Brewer, David. *The Jesus Scandals.* Grand Rapids, MI: Monarch Books, 2012.

ISBE, *International Standard Bible Encyclopedia.* Grand Rapids, MI: Wm. B. Eerdmans Publishing Co., 1939. InternationalStandardBible.com.

Jasper, William F. "Teaching the Perversions." *The New American,* 1/19/1987.

Jones, Abigail and Marissa Miley. *Restless Virgins, Love, Sex, and Survival at a New England Prep School.* New York, NY: HarperCollins Publishers, 2007.

Jung, Alyssa. "19 Aphrodisiac Foods Proven to Spark Romance." *Food,* Reader's Digest Association, Inc. Web.

Kaplan, Helen Singer. *Disorders of Sexual Desire.* New York, NY: Simon and

Schuster, 1979.

Keller, Philip. *A Shepherd Looks at Psalm 23*. Grand Rapids, MI: Zondervan, 1970.

LaHaye, Tim and Beverly LaHaye. *The Act of Marriage*. Grand Rapids, MI: The Zondervan Corporation, 1976. Used by permission.

---. *The Unhappy Gays: What Everyone Should Know about Homosexuality*. Wheaton, IL: Tyndale House, 1978.

Landers, Ann. "Column." *Los Angeles Times*. Chicago:IL: News America Syndicate, (7/13/88).

---. "Column." *Los Angeles Times*. Chicago, IL: News America Syndicate, (6/13/89). Used by permission.

Lecky, William. *History of European Morals from Augustus to Charlemagne, i.* London: Longmans, Green, and Co., 1890. EBook Edition.

LeSaint, William, translator and annotator. *Tertullian's Treatises on Marriage*. Westminister, MD: The Newman Press, 1951.

Leupold, H. C. *Exposition of Ecclesiastes*. Grand Rapids, MI: Baker Book House, 1952.

Lewinsohn, Richard. Alexander Mayce, translator. *A History of Sexual Customs*. New York, NY: Harper & Brothers, 1958.

Littauer, Fred and Florence. *Freeing Your Mind From Memories that Bind, How to Heal the Hurts of the Past*. Nashville, TN: Thomas Nelson Publishers, 1988.

Lockyear, Herbert. *The Women of the Bible*. Grand Rapids, MI: Zondervan Publishing House, 1967.

Lorenzi, Rossella. "King Tut's Chariots Marvels of Engineering." *Discovery News*. Discovery Communications, LLC, 8/3/2010. Web.

Martin, Gary. *The Song of Songs*. Kiel, West Germany: n.p., 1987.

McElroy, Molly. "Virginity Pledges for Men Can Lead to Sexual Confusion— Even After the Wedding Day," 8/16/2014. News and Information, *UWTODAY*. Seattle, WA: University of Washington, Web.

McGinniss, Mark. "The Song of Solomon and Hot Topics, bbc.edu/chapel/2013fall.asp, 10/29-31/2013. Web. Used by permission.

---. "The Song of Solomon and Hot Topics." *Outside My Door* Blog, 11/10/2013. Web. Used by permission.

McIlhaney, Joe E. Jr. and Freda McKissic Bush. "Meet the Brain," *Hooked, New Science on How Casual Sex Is Affecting Our Children*. Chicago: Northfield Publishing, 2008. Used by permission.

McKenna, K. "Central Nervous System Pathways Involved in the Control of Penile Erection." *Annual Review of Sex Research*, 1999.

McMillen, S. I. *None of These Diseases*. Old Tappen, NJ: Revell, 1967.

Miles, Herbert J. *Sexual Happiness in Marriage*. Grand Rapids, MI: Zondervan Publishing House, 1982 (Revised). Used by permission.

Miles, Oscar. "Youth Survey." Statistics used by permission.

Morgentaler, Abraham. *The Viagra Myth: The Surprising Impact on Love and Relationships*. San Francisco, CA: Jossey-Bass, Wiley Imprint, 2003.

Muller, Charla with Betsy Thorpe. *365 Nights, A Memoir of Intimacy*. New York, NY: Berkley Books, 2008. Used by permission.

Murphey, Cecil. *When a Man You Love Was Abused, A Woman's Guide to Helping Him Overcome Childhood Sexual Molestation*. Grand Rapids, MI: Kregel Publications, 2010.

Naftaly, Aryeh. *The Song of Songs, A Messiah's Confession, An Explanation, English Translation and Dramatic Adaptation of the World's Most Ancient Opera.* Moshav Mevo Modiim, Israel: Third Age Productions, 2015. TheSongOfSongs.net. Used by permission.

Nase, Joseph. "Proper transference makes wine taste better. So pour it out!" *New York Magazine,* 2014. Web.

"'Nones' on the Rise." *Religion & Public Life,* 10/9/2012. PewResearchCenter. Web.

O'Neil, Darcy. "Cocktails and Dairy Products." *Art of Drink,* 3/2011. Web.

Patton, William. *Bible Wines.* General Books LLC reproduction, 2009. *Bible Wines: The Laws of Fermentation and Wines of the Ancients.* New York, NY: National Temperance Society and Publication House, 1874.

Pettus, Robert L. Jr. *As I See Sex Through the Bible.* Madison, TN: Pettus, 1973.

Pfizer Labs. "Patient Information VIAGRA® (vi-AG-rah) (sildenafil citrate) Tablets." New York, NY: Pfizer Labs, 3/2015.

Popular and Critical Bible Encyclopedia and Scriptural Dictionary, II. Editor Samuel Fallows. Chicago, IL: The Howard-Severance Company, 1902.

"Premature Ejaculation, Causes." *Mayo Clinic.* Mayo Foundation for Medical Education and Research, n.d. MayoClinic.org. Web. 12/1/2014.

Reece, Tamekia. "10 Common Baby-making Mistakes." *American Baby Magazine.* Parents.com, n.d., Meredith Corporation. Web, 7/31/2015.

Réville, Albert. *The Song of Songs, Commonly Called the Song of Solomon, Or the Canticle.* Nabu Public Domain Reprint. Charleston, SC: Nabu Press, 2010.

Rhymes, Edward. "Woman as Aggressor: The Unspoken Truth of Domestic Violence." *MintPress News,* 9/19/2014. Web.

Roberts, Barbara. *Not Under Bondage, Biblical Divorce for Abuse, Adultery & Desertion.* Ballarat, Victoria, Australia: Maschil Press, 2008.

Robinson, Marie N. *The Power of Sexual Surrender.* New York: New American Library, 1959. Used by permission.

Ross, Phillip. "Ebola Death Toll 2014: How Many People Have Really Died From Virus?" *International Business Times.* IBT Media Inc., 10/23/2014. Web.

Rowan, Tiffany. "Myrrh—The Egyptians Choice for Sunscreen and Insect Repellent." TiffanyRowan.blogspot.com, 3/18/2010. Web.

Rueben, David. *Any Woman Can.* New York: David McKay Co., 1974. Quoted by LaHaye in *The Act of Marriage.* Grand Rapids, MI: The Zondervan Corporation, 1976. Used by permission.

---. *Everything You Always Wanted to Know About Sex But Were Afraid to Ask.* New York: Bantam Books, 1969.

Sabharwal, Neharika. "Pomegranate Juice: A Natural Aphrodisiac that Enhances Sex Drive." *TheMedGuru,* 2/18/2014. Themedguru.com. Web.

Sand, Avraham. *Mystical Aromatherapy, The Divine Gift of Fragrance.* Twin Lakes, WI: Lotus Press, 2012. Used by permission.

Sandford, John Loren. *Why Good People Mess Up.* Lake Mary, FL: Charisma House, 2007.

Sarrel, Lorna and Philip Sarrel. "What Men Need from the Women Who Love Them." *Redbook* (April 1977).

Schafer, John R. "Odd Facts About Kissing, A Kiss Is Not Just a Kiss." *Psychology Today.* Sussex Publishers, LLC, 28 Dec. 2012. Web.

Schauss, Hayyim. *The Lifetime of a Jew*. New York: Union of American Hebrew Congregations, 1950.

Smith, Jennifer. *The Unveiled Wife: Embracing Intimacy with God and Your Husband*. Carol Stream, IL: Tyndale Momentum, 2015.

Smith, William. *Dr. Smith's Dictionary of the Bible*. Boston, MA: Houghton, Mifflin and Company, 1888.

Snyder, Kimberly. "25 Foods that are Natural Aphrodisiacs." *Realize Yourself, Kimberly Snyder's Health & Beauty Detox*, 10/3/2011. Web.

Stanton, Elizabeth Cady and the Revising Committee. *The Woman's Bible*. New York: European Publishing Company, 1898. Edited by Jane T. Walker. Seattle, WA: Coalition Task Force on Women and Religion, 1974.

Stephens-Davidowitz, Seth. "Searching for Sex." *SundayReview, The New York Times*, 1/24/2015. Web.

Stepp, Laura Sessions. *Unhooked: How Young Women Pursue Sex, Delay Love and Lose at Both*. New York: Riverhead Books, 2007.

Stewart, David. *Healing Oils of the Bible*. Marble Hill, MO: Care Publications, 2012.

Strong, James. *Strong's Exhaustive Concordance, Hebrew and Chaldee Dictionary*. Grand Rapids, MI: Associated Publishers and Authors Inc., n.d.

Tannahill, Reay. *Sex in History*. Briarcliff Mannor, NY: Scarborough House, 1980.

Tavris, Carol. "40,000 Men Tell About Their Sexual Behavior, Their Fantasies, Their Ideal Women and Their Wives," Part I. *Redbook*, Feb. 1978.

---. "The Sex Lives of Happy Men," Part II. *Redbook,* March 1978.

Thayer, Joseph Henry, D.D. *Thayer's Greek-English Lexicon of the New Testament*. Grand Rapids, MI: Associated Publishers and Authors Inc., n.d.

"The Doctrine of the Goddess Ashtoreth." Kukis.org. Web. 7/30/2015.

Theological Wordbook of the Old Testament. Editors R. Laird Harris, Gleason L. Archer, Jr., Bruce K. Waltke. Chicago, IL: Moody Press, 1980.

Twitty, Conway. "I'd Love to Lay You Down." 8/23/2004.

U.S. Census Bureau. *Statistical Abstract of the United States: 2012*, "Table 75. Self-Described Religious Identification of Adult Population: 1990, 2001, and 2008." Web.

Waugh, Rob. "You Can Instantly Know a Woman's Sex History from Her Stride, Claims Study." *MailOnline*. Associated Newspapers, Ltd, 5/31/2012. Web.

WebMD. "Lily-of-the-Valley." WebMD LLC, 2005-2015.

Weiss, Douglas. *Beyond the Bedroom, Healing for Adult Children of Sex Addicts*. Deerfield Beach, FL: Health Communications, Inc., 2005.

---. *Intimacy Anorexia: Healing the Hidden Addiction in Your Marriage*. Colorado Springs, CO: Discovery Press, 2010.

---. *Married & Alone*. Colorado Springs, CO: Discovery Press, 2013.

---. *Sex, Men and God*. Lake Mary, FL: Siloam Press, 2002.

Wight, Fred H. *Manners and Customs of Bible Lands*. Chicago, IL: Moody Bible Institute, 1953.

Wikipedia. "Decanter." Released under the Creative Commons Attribution-Share-Alike License 3.0.

Workman, Herbert. *The Evolution of the Monastic Ideal*. Kansas City, KS: Beacon Hill Press, 1962. Quoted by Stuart Barton Babbage.

"World's Strangest Aphrodisiacs." *Travel+Leisure*, 2/2010, Time, Inc. Web.

Zilbergeld, Bernie. *Male Sexuality*. New York: Bantam, 1978.

Patsy Rae Dawson

Patsy Rae got her start studying and teaching about marriage as a young bride when an abusive husband baited her: "If a husband tells his wife to eat beans 7 days a week, don't you think she should eat beans 7 days a week?" She knew only a Bible answer would stop the man from trying to get her to say something he could use against his wife.

Believing the Bible didn't say much about being a woman and marriage, Patsy Rae was shocked to discover the Bible is full of marital wisdom. She has been studying, teaching, writing, and mentoring both women and men ever since — **for nearly half a century.** She's fascinated by the power of the scriptures to transform lives — hers and yours.

As an overcomer of a 46-year sexless marriage, Patsy Rae says:

I could not know the things I do if I had not lived the life I did. It gave me insights you can't find in any book or class. I thank God for what he has done for me and for allowing me to share his love and his marvelous sexual secrets with you. What a wonderful life of service he's given me!"

Sexless Marriages Self-Assessment Survey Administrator

Patsy Rae designed a comprehensive set of checklists of intensely personal questions. They help participants recognize the common 24/7 love sins in their sexless marriage so they can work on the real issues.

Sexuality & Personality Breakthrough Christian Coach

Certified as an Advanced Personality Trainer, Patsy Rae specializes in helping clients move out of childhood survival mode into their loving genetics. This skill helps her get quickly to the core issues of clients who have a variety of sexual problems.

Embarrass the Alligator Newsletter Editor and Author

Patsy Rae shares results from her checklists in her *Embarrass the Alligator Newsletter.* Due to participants asking for more information, she's working on books related to sexless marriages. She's the author of *God's People Appreciate Marriage, God's People Make the Best Lovers,* and the MP3 *Challenges in Marriage: What to Do When Sin Inhibits Love.*

You can contact her and learn more at PatsyRaeDawson.com.